Swords for Hire

Swords for Hire

THE SCOTTISH MERCENARY

James Miller

BIRLINN

Published in 2007 by
Birlinn Limited
West Newington House
10 Newington Road
Edinburgh EH9 1QS

www.birlinn.co.uk

ISBN13: 978 1 84158 446 1
ISBN10: 1 84158 446 0

British Library Cataloguing-in-Publication Data
A catalogue record for this book is available from the British Library

Typeset by Iolaire Typesetting, Newtonmore
Printed and bound by Antony Rowe Ltd, Chippenham

Contents

List of illustrations

The endpaper map and Figs 7, 8, 10, 11, 15, 17, 18, 19, 20, 21, 23 and 24 are taken from the multi-volume Theatrum Europaeum, a history of European affairs, by Johann Philip Abelin and others, published first in Frankfurt-am-Main in 1638 and on various dates thereafter. The artwork in the early volumes is by Matthaeus Merian (1593–1650).

Preface

I was in my teens when I first read in James Calder's history of Caithness about a party of Scots mercenaries who were massacred in the Norwegian mountains in 1612 while on their way to fight for the king of Sweden. The story had the dimensions of a legend and intrigued me, but it was not until a few years ago that I had the opportunity to put some flesh on the bones of Calder's account. I found that the massacre had really happened, although the assiduous Victorian historian had some of the details wrong. However, what was more surprising, it had been only one incident in a much longer, more complex story. My curiosity drove me on and the resulting search has been akin to exploring a weirdly designed mansion in which each door pushed open leads to other doors or sometimes to a dead end. In short, I came upon a phenomenon that was a common fact of Scottish life in the sixteenth and seventeenth centuries. Thousands of Scots went to Europe as soldiers and, looking at the records for the two centuries, it seems that at one time or another some served in the forces of almost every continental power and marched under every banner. Yet there was little in the popular arena about this, certainly nothing to compare with the library that has been written on the exploits of Scots in the British Empire. In histories of Scotland the mercenary soldier seldom rates a mention, let alone a footnote. Before new worlds lured us further afield, Europe was the ground on which we sought to fulfil our aspirations, and this we have largely forgotten.

It was not always so. The eccentric and prolix laird from Cromarty, Sir Thomas Urquhart, who died in 1660, wrote in inimitable style about the exploits of his fellow countrymen in Europe in a long panegyric called *The Jewel*. A few writers in the Victorian and Edwardian years brought out books for a wider public. One of the first was the prolific novelist and historian James Grant, who wrote *Memoirs and Adventures of Sir John Hepburn* (1851) and *The Scottish Soldiers of Fortune: Their Adventures and Achievements in the Armies of Europe* (1890). John Hill Burton's *The Scot Abroad* was published in 1864, and A. Francis Steuart's *Scottish Influences in Russian History* in 1913. The most important of this small group who surveyed Scottish activities in Europe was Th. A. Fischer, who produced three books of tremendous scope: *The Scots in Germany* (1902), *The Scots in Eastern and Western Prussia* (1903) and *The Scots in Sweden* (1907). All of these men wrote with pride of the Scots' achievements. James Grant typically allowed his enthusiasm to carry him away. 'In every army in Europe,' he states in his 1851 book, 'they have risen to eminence, and by their intrepid courage, persevering spirit, and inflexible integrity, though invidiously designated by some as adventurers, have attained the highest honours that can accrue to subjects.' It wasn't quite like that for most of them, but Grant lived in an age that was both imperial and incurably patriotic. Academic historians have always been aware of the Scots' involvement in Europe but the results of their research have usually remained within the covers of theses, journals and books aimed at a professional readership. The published work of several contemporary historians has been invaluable in the writing of this book, especially the volumes written or edited by Steve Murdoch, Alexia Grosjean, and David Worthington. Murdoch and Grosjean also edit a website dedicated to Scots who were active in northern Europe: www.st-andrews.ac.uk/history/ssne. Details of all the sources to which I have turned can be found in the notes and bibliography.

Within limits set by resources and time I have made an attempt to provide for the general reader a survey of the exploits and experiences of Scots who sought to earn a living as soldiers in Europe up until the late eighteenth century – that is, until roughly the time they found service under a British flag in an expanding empire. The focus of the story is on Scottish involvement in the Thirty Years War (1618–48) but I have also attempted to provide some indication of the Scottish presence in Europe before and after that monumental conflict. Much

more detail on certain individuals and incidents can be found in the
sources listed but I hope the text here is sufficient to show the extent
of our interactions with our immediate neighbours across the North
Sea in centuries gone by. It has been necessary to provide historical
background and context, and in the book the reader will come across
passages trying to explain the complicated political troubles and
manoeuvres of Europe's ruling dynasties. For reasons of space I
have had to simplify these accounts and, although professional
historians may baulk at some of the liberties I have taken, I have
tried to hold true to the main thrust of the historical record. In
summary, I found that Scots have a habit of popping up as protagonists in the most unlikely corners of Europe, many as miserable
foot soldiers far from home, but others as major players with the fates
of nations in their hands. Information about them probably exists in
almost every archive and museum where the documents on the
history of the continent lie. There has not been time to follow every
lead but I hope I have uncovered enough to show how closely
involved with past politics and conflicts in Europe we have been. This
book concentrates on military activity. It should not be forgotten that
there were thousands of Scots directly involved in more peaceful
pursuits – as merchants, traders, teachers and clerics – and their story
also begs to be re-explored. Tucked away in archives from the Atlantic
coast to the Urals are the details of the many parts we have played in
the history of Europe, with their implication that we have yet much
more to offer.

Acknowledgements

Many people have helped me during the research for this book. Here I can do no more than list their names and record my gratitude for their assistance, always cheerfully and generously given. *In Belgium*: the staff of the Bibliothèque Royale de Belgique in Brussels. *In Britain*: Inverness Public Library; Aberdeen University Library; Special Collections, Glasgow University Library; Elgin Public Library; the British Library; the National Library of Scotland; Alastair Macleod of the Inverness Public Library genealogy service; Catharine Niven and her colleagues in Inverness Museum and Art Gallery and Alastair Campbell of Airds, Unicorn Pursuivant of Arms. *In Germany*: Wolfgang and Gerda Rutsche in Augsburg; Dr Wilfried Sponsel of the Nördlingen Stadtarchiv; Dr Kramer-Fürtig and Alisa Neumann in the Augsburg Stadtarchiv; Frau Edith Findel in Rain Stadtarchiv; Frau Monika Rademacher in Hanau Stadtarchiv; the staff of the Kaiserburg Museum in Nürnberg, the Germanisches Nationalmuseum, Nürnberg, and the Stralsund Stadtarchiv. *In Norway*: Vidar and Dorothy Olsen, Oslo, and Jon Selfors of Vertshuset Sinclair in Kvam, Gudbrandsdalen. *In Poland*: Richard and Marie Jasinski, and Mariola Szeszycka in Szczecin; Anna Stasiewicz-Jakubik in Gdansk. *In Sweden*: Per Clason and his colleagues in Krigsarkivet, Stockholm. Particular thanks for help with illustrations go to Dr Joseph Marshall, National Library of Scotland; Sabine Jaucot, Bibliothèque Royale de Belgique; Bertil Olofsson, Krigsarkivet, Stockholm; Monica Lindström, Skoklosters Slott, Sweden; Shona Corner, National Galleries of Scotland; and Helen Trompeteler, National Portrait Gallery, London.

I am also deeply grateful to HI-Arts, Inverness, for their generous contribution towards the costs of travel and research; to Dr Steve Murdoch and his colleagues for help in accessing the Scotland, Scandinavian and Northern Europe, 1580–1707 (SSNE) website; and to Trevor Royle for reading the text and offering some valuable suggestions for its improvement. Aline Hill deployed her conscientious editing to clarify the text, and Jim Lewis his skill at creating proper maps from my crude tracings; I am grateful to both of them. Once again, I owe much to my agent, Duncan McAra, and to the staff of Birlinn for their never-ending courtesy and patience. And also I would like to thank all my friends who over the last two years or more have had to submit themselves to my enthusiasm for the Scotland–Europe connection. The errors in the book are my responsibility.

Note on text

Generally, dates have been adjusted to accord with the modern calendar. Spelling of Scots has been left unchanged except for some substitution of letters to clarify meaning.

Currencies

It is not easy to equate the various currencies in which mercenaries were paid, but the following information may offer some rough guidance.

Germany: the silver taler, thaler or reichsthaler, the source of the word 'dollar', became a standard throughout the Holy Roman Empire in the sixteenth century and something of an international currency.

1 reichsthaler = 24 groschen = 72 kreuzer = 288 pfennig.
During the Thirty Years War there was much counterfeiting, clipping and debasement of coinage. Coins such as gold riders and Rhenish gulden were also struck for the payment of troops.

Britain: the reichsthaler was roughly equivalent to the English crown (5 shillings sterling). In 1603 the Scottish crown was worth one twelfth of the English one. The Scots merk was equivalent to 13 shillings and 4 pence (two-thirds of the Scots pound).

Denmark: the rigsdaler became the basis of the Danish coinage from 1544.
1 rigsdaler = 3 marks; 1 mark = 16 skillings.

Sweden: the silver riksdaler became the basis of the coinage from the early 1500s.

1 riksdaler = 4 marks = 32 ore.

Holland: the basic coin of the States General was the rijksdaalder. It was divided into 40 stuivers (from 1583), 45 stuivers (from 1586), and 47 stuivers (from 1606). The gulden or guilder, initially equivalent to 28 stuivers, was struck from 1601. The patar or patard was a silver coin struck in some parts of the Low Countries from late fifteenth century.

France: The French livre, franc or pound was roughly equivalent in value to the Scots pound in the late 1600s. Further details on this and other currencies of the period can be found on the website http://pierre-marteau.com/currency.

Distance measures

Robert Monro makes consistent use of the Dutch mile in his memoirs of the war in Germany. The Dutch or German mile was equal to 7 kilometres or roughly 4.25 English miles.

Maps

Boundaries of states and provinces are indicated only approximately. More detail can be found in historical atlases and, for example, at www.euratlas.com.

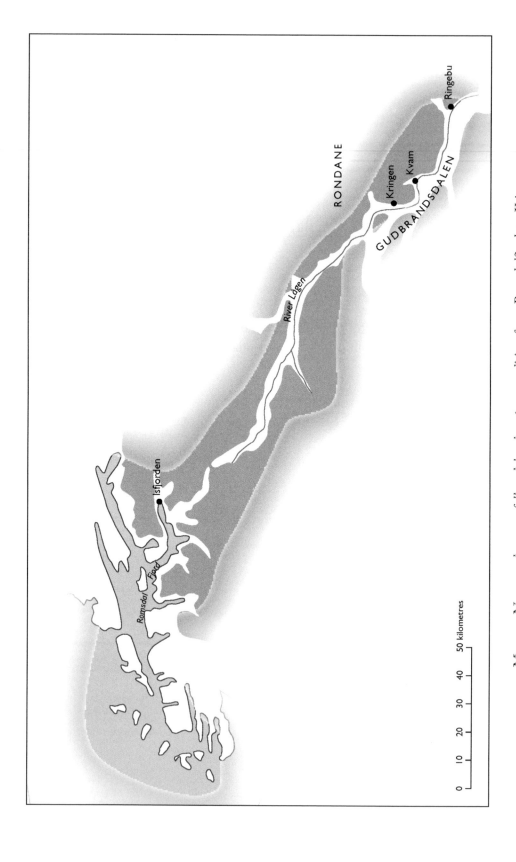

Ringebu

RONDANE

Kvam

Kringen

GUDBRANDSDALEN

River Lågen

Isfjorden

Romsdal Fjord

| 0 | 10 | 20 | 30 | 40 | 50 kilometres |

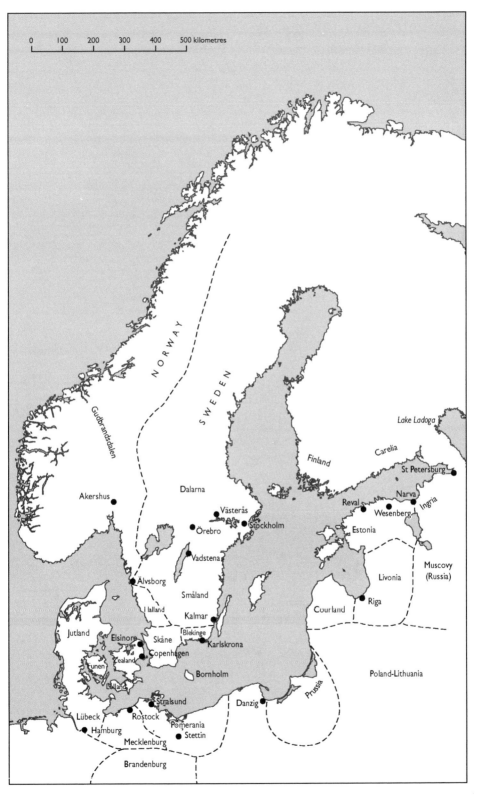

Map 2. *Scandinavia and the Baltic*

Map 3. *The Low Countries, or the Spanish Netherlands*

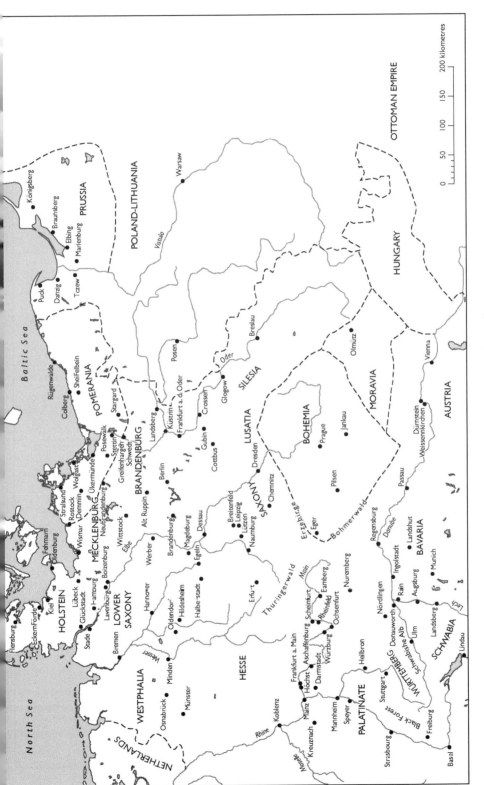

Map 4. *Central Europe in the 17th century*

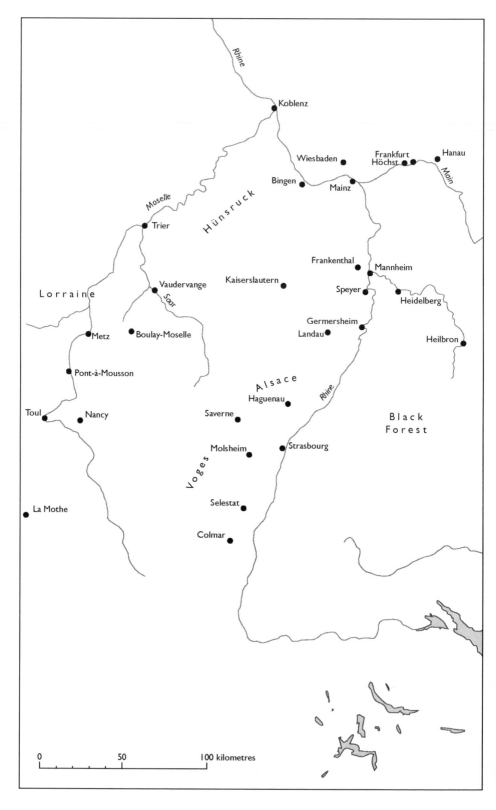

Map 5. *The Rhineland*

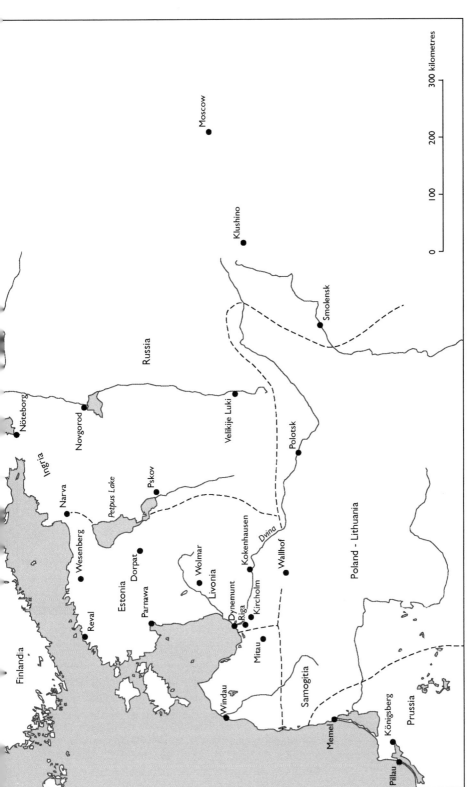

Map 6. *The Baltic states and western Russia*

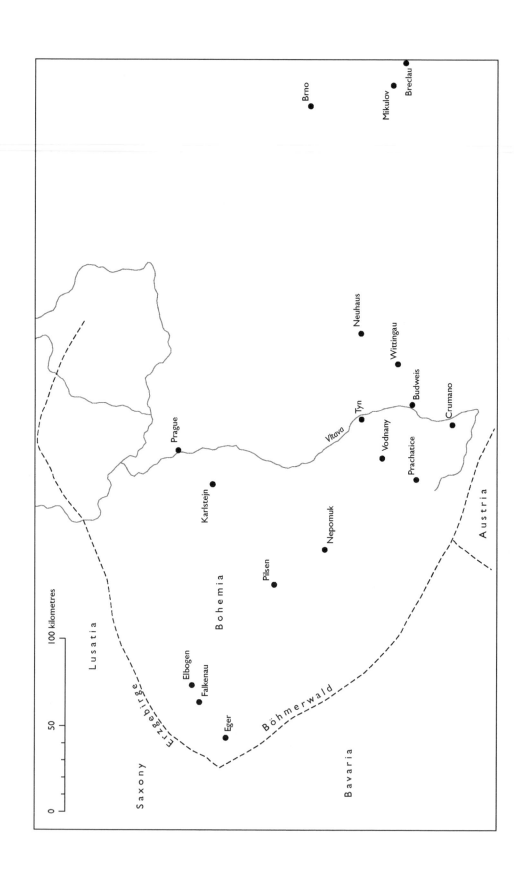

Family tree showing Leslies who sought armed service in Europe. Based on information in *Historical Records of the Family of Leslie*, Edinburgh, 1869.

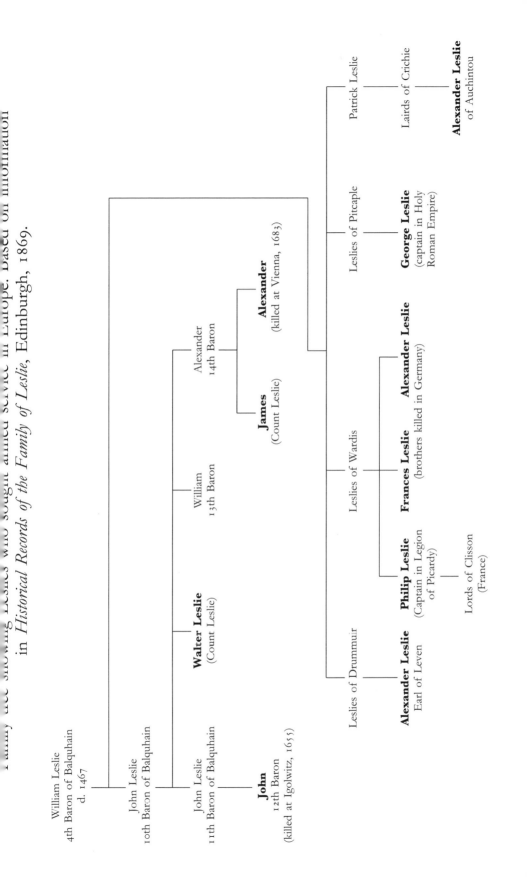

———◆◆×◆◆———

'God knoweth it greeved me much'
Norway, 1612

S IR ROBERT ANSTRUTHER had a problem on his hands in the summer of 1612. As ambassador from James Stuart, now the king of Britain, to Christian IV of Denmark, he was having to defend the honour and interests of his own monarch against the reprehensible actions of his fellow countrymen. Christian was James's brother-in-law, a factor working in Sir Robert's favour, but no king could be depended on to put personal relations above the good of his realm for long. 'Moreover Sir,' wrote Sir Robert in a despatch to London from Copenhagen on 18 June, 'they heire are much greeved against Scottis men'.[1] He went on to describe how the Danes were complaining not only because pirates from Orkney were attacking shipping on the coast of Norway, then part of the Danish kingdom, but because Scottish soldiers were fighting for Denmark's enemy, Gustavus Adolphus, the ambitious young ruler of Sweden.

The Swedish king was continuing to pursue the aggressive policy of his late father, Karl IX, aimed at making Sweden master of the trade routes from Russia across northern Scandinavia, a policy that had alarmed Denmark. In the spring of 1611 the long-brewing hostility between the northern kingdoms spilled into war and the Danes captured the fortress of Kalmar. Then Karl IX died. Gustavus Adolphus was only sixteen years old but, already experienced in warfare after leading attacks against the Danes, he took over the reins of power from the interim regency when he reached his seventeenth birthday. To bolster his weakened army, Gustavus Adolphus wrote from the castle of Nyköping in November 1611 to Sir James Spens, a

Fife merchant and the British ambassador to the Swedish court. In courtly Latin, the young king addressed his 'truly and dearly beloved Sir James Spens' to remind the Scot of a promise made to Karl IX to supply Sweden with 3,000 soldiers 'of proved faithfulness and bravery'. For this service, Sir James would have at his disposal in the city of Hamburg the sum of 20,000 imperials (reichsthaler) through the agents of Gustavus Adolphus's mother.

There was already a long history of Scots serving in the Swedish army but at this particular time it was a sensitive matter in the relations between Britain and the Scandinavian kingdoms. In the winter of 1611–12 a junior officer in the Swedish forces, an ensign called Pryngle, a Scot, was captured by the Danes. 'The King upone my most humble suit, and by meanes of the Chancellor, sett him at libertie, in regard that he was your Majestie's subject, as he hath done sindrie others,' wrote Sir Robert to London. Pryngle was required to swear an oath that he would never again take up arms against Denmark. Before long, however, Pryngle was captured a second time, on this occasion on a ship bound for Sweden. 'I am almost ashamed to speek any more in his behalfe,' wrote the exasperated Sir Robert, before he acknowledged ruefully: 'with such things I ame oft met heere.'

A more important figure than an ensign also fell into Danish hands. On 29 December 1611, three officials of Christian's government interrogated Andrew Ramsay and Robert Douglas, who had been captured some time earlier, before the death of Karl IX, while crossing from Sweden to Lübeck, and brought to Copenhagen. Ramsay and Douglas said they were cousins who had met by chance at a country house near Stockholm after the latter had returned from five years' service under an officer called Learmonth in Sweden's campaign against Russia in Livonia. They revealed that several foreign commanders and officers were still in Sweden, among them General Rutherford, his afore-mentioned lieutenant Learmonth, a Captain Wauchope, and a man called Greig, the commander of the artillery. Non-Scots included Johannes Mönnichhofen, a Flemish mercenary leader. Greig had been severely wounded at the siege of Kalmar when a cannonball had smashed his shin, and Ramsay seemed unsure whether or not he was still alive; indeed the only officer who had emerged unscathed from the siege had been Mönnichhofen because 'he surpassed the others in prudence and knew how to fight from a distance'. In his interview, Douglas said the Swedes were in trouble, panic-stricken, abandoned by their soldiers, hating their king, willing to sue for peace, and starving. He was exaggerating Swedish weakness, telling the Danes what he thought they might like to hear. His interrogators were clearly convinced that Douglas and Ramsay had been carrying letters dealing with recruitment of mercenaries; the Scots denied they had such documents, naturally omitting to mention that they had dumped them in the Baltic when their capture had been imminent.

The Danes were right, of course, to suspect Gustavus Adolphus's intention to strengthen his armed forces. At the same time as he had written to Sir James Spens, the Swedish king had asked Johannes Mönnichhofen to recruit a thousand men in Holland. The plan was that Sir James Spens's recruits would rendezvous with Mönnichhofen to combine forces at Älvsborg, the Swedish fortress at the mouth of the Göta River, the country's only access to the sea on the west coast.

Andrew Ramsay must have reached Scotland early in 1612 with Sir James Spens's instruction to recruit men to serve Gustavus Adolphus. In this task he enlisted the aid of his brother Alexander and three others: Robert Kerr, George Hay and George Sinclair. Hay, whose origins are obscure, and Sinclair, an illegitimate son of the laird of Stirkoke in Caithness, had already seen service against the Russians for Sweden in Samuel Cockburn's regiment for two years. Kerr was probably some kin to Sir Robert Kerr of Ancrum, who that year committed some men from his court to overseas service. Between them the four men probably recruited along most of the east of the country in defiance of the authorities.

The Privy Council in Edinburgh, governing Scotland for the Stuart king now resident in London, noted in August 1612 that men had been 'violentlie pressit and tane . . . aganis thair will', despite the king's refusal to allow recruitment for Sweden.[2] Ordinary people had grown so afraid of being seized by the recruiters that they did not dare go far from home on their lawful business without protection. Alexander Ramsay was ordered to present himself before the Privy Council, and other known military captains were asked to bind themselves not to leave the country or recruit for Sweden without a licence. Some were called on to deposit a substantial bail of 5,000 merks each to ensure they did not feel tempted to go back on their word. Three ships lying at Burntisland were searched by the authorities and the soldiers aboard them interviewed; those who said they had been pressed were released, and the ships were charged not to take soldiers to Sweden. A week later, the Privy Council issued a fresh instruction to discharge all the men levied for Sweden.

On 19 August 1612, James's secretary replied to Sir Robert Anstruther to say that the king had found out 'yesternight by meere accident' that the recruiting of mercenaries for service in Sweden had been taking place. He had forbidden it to continue and had ordered the discharge of men already embarked, and he wished his brother-in-law in Denmark to know through his ambassador that he had done so. James had brushed aside proffered excuses that the Scots were setting off to fight for Gustavus Adolphus against the Russians and therefore would not trouble Christian. The captains in Scotland, however, had no intention of complying with the royal command. Ramsay kept well away from the Privy Council and by the time he was denounced as a rebel in September he had managed to raise some men. The plan to rendezvous with Mönnichhofen had to be abandoned when, after the winter, Danish forces renewed their assault, captured Älvsborg, and threatened to sweep across country to descend on Stockholm itself. Mönnichhofen finally set sail from Amsterdam with four ships in July 1612 but, with the Kattegat under Danish control, he continued north along the Norwegian coast to land near Trondheim, an eventuality that would in time prove to have fateful consequences for the men now being recruited on the other side of the North Sea.

The Privy Council's attempts to prevent the mercenaries sailing had only partial success. Ramsay, Hay and Sinclair managed to get away with some of their recruits in two ships – one from Dundee and one from Caithness – that met off Shetland towards the end of August and turned their bows eastward. On the 30th they anchored in an inner arm of Romsdal Fjord a little to the west of the village of Isfjorden and began to disembark. There were only 300 men, far from the 3,000 Gustavus had called for. Neither were they the experienced fighters the Swedish king needed. Ramsay, Hay and Sinclair had scraped together by persuasion or coercion a party from different parts of the country that lacked cohesion, training and equipment. We don't know who they were but we can assume that their number included fugitives from Lothian jails and ploughboys and tenants from the Sinclair lands in Caithness, all tough enough in their way but not with the 'proved faithfulness and bravery' Gustavus had required. Only a handful of them would live more than a few days, let alone see their native shore again.

What Ramsay and his colleagues did not know when they landed was that Mönnichhofen had already aroused the anger of the Norwegians. The Dutch mercenary force had reached Stordalen in July and had seized two ships and plundered one district before compelling a local pilot to guide them to Trondheim. The Norwegians had failed to repel the landing – the mercenaries had successfully made their way east to Swedish territory – but they were now alert to the possibility of another incursion and probably determined to acquit themselves better.

On the day after they were safely ashore on the northern side of the fjord, Ramsay and his men set off for Sweden. Their march took them around the head of the fjord and up the valley of the Romsdal River. No one recorded what the Scots thought of the rugged, beautiful country with mountain peaks rising to over 1,800 metres through which they were now trudging, but the contrast with the rolling spaces they had come from may have pressed on their minds. With two guides from Romsdal, they climbed over the pass and descended into Gudbrandsdalen and the valley of the Lågen River. Their progress was now being closely watched. Lauritz Hage, the lensman (administrative official) in the parish of Vaage, called out the bonder (the farmers) in his area and in the neighbouring parish of Lassoe and kept ahead of the Scots, hoping for an opportunity to stop their incursion. Hage roused the bonder and peasantry in two more parishes, Froen and Ringebu, and, with over four hundred men now at his back, felt confident enough to consider action. Keeping two days' march in front of the Scots, he found his opportunity at Kringen, where the road squeezed between high rocks and the swiftly flowing Lågen.

Ramsay seems to have remained unaware of the trap into which he was leading his men. On the evening of 4 September, they halted at some farms and took stock of their progress. High above them to the

east soared the mountains of the Rondane; the wooded hills on the
west side of the river were lower but still a daunting climb. It seemed
best to push on down the valley and, after a few more days, turn east
in easier country towards the Swedish frontier. They set off again
through a fine, clear dawn.

Hage's men were now lying in wait for the Scots. In his official
report to the Danish chancellor on the incident, written at Akershus
(in present-day Oslo) on 27 September, the stadtholder (governor)
Envold Kruse summarised what happened next: 'Hage, having made
his arrangements and perceived his advantage, attacked, together with
another lensman, Peder Rankleff of Ringebu, and with all their men
together they fired upon the foreign troops and shot them to death
during an hour and a half.' Some of Ramsay's followers stumbled into
the river in search of escape from the hail of bullets and were
drowned; those few who splashed across the water were cut down
by the Norwegians waiting on the far bank. There is a tradition that
George Sinclair was the first to fall in the initial volley of shots, but
there are many traditions around the incident (see Chapter 18) and
Kruse's report makes no mention of the Caithness man. When the
ambush was over, 134 mercenaries were taken prisoner. The Norwegians, it is said, lost six dead and a dozen wounded.

No doubt traumatised by their experience, the surviving Scots were
shepherded down the valley for 15 kilometres to Klomstad near
Kvam. Here they were locked into a barn. Hage and the other leaders
wanted to send them all on to Akershus but the bonder and the
peasants had other ideas. Fired up by their stunning victory and
perhaps thirsting for revenge for a massacre of Norwegians perpetrated by mercenaries in Swedish pay in a church at Lødsøe, they
resolved to disobey Hage. In the morning, as the prisoners were
brought out one by one from the barn, they were shot or hacked to
death until the peasants' blood lust was satisfied. Only eighteen were
left. These included four officers: Ramsay himself, with Henry Bruce,
James Moneypenny and James Scott. Moneypenny, with previous
service in Denmark and Sweden, acted as interpreter and he was sent
with Ramsay, Scott and Bruce to Akershus. A few of the others
accepted offers to become servants locally, and some agreed to join
the Danish army and were sent to a regiment stationed at Älvsborg.

After interrogation by Kruse, Ramsay and his colleagues were sent on to Copenhagen.

Early in November, after being present at the examination of the captives, Sir Robert Anstruther wrote two letters about the incident: an official one to King James and a briefer, more succinct account to a friend in England, Sir Thomas Lach, one of James's secretaries. In the first Sir Robert emphasised that not one of them 'had any kynd off commission or warrant to shew, nather from the late King Charles [Karl of Sweden], nather from Gustavus, neither from Coronell Ramsay'. Christian IV was mightily displeased and Sir Robert seems to have been hard put to it to have the prisoners judged as simple, ignorant men deserving of clemency. This must have been especially difficult in the case of Moneypenny and of Bruce, who admitted he had already seen service under arms in Holland, Spain and Hungary. In his second letter to his friend, Sir Robert wrote: 'I dout not but you have hard the infortunat newis of these 300 Scottis men that went to Norroway; the bours of the country haue killed and murthered them all, except some few.' He explained how he had persuaded the Danes not to try Ramsay and the other three before a court martial but to send them home instead.

Back in Scotland, Ramsay was interrogated by the Duke of Lennox and Lord Viscount Fenton. Clearly, relations with Denmark were uppermost in the minds of the questioners, and Ramsay is recorded as having confirmed he had recruited his followers without informing anyone in the Scottish government of his actions and had never received any help from them. The hapless Ramsay was banished for life from British territory but relations with Denmark were secured. In January 1613, Sir Robert took up his pen to his friend Sir Thomas again: 'Concerning the proceedings with Mr Ramsay, his Majestie resteth weell contented: but I hope seeing the warres are ended, and a ferme peace maide that his Majestie will forget those particular querrels . . . Concerning them that were killed, and taken prisonners, God knoweth it greeved me much, both for the loss of the men, as also for the King Denmarkes cause.'

'bandis of men of weare'

Scotland, 1550–1650

SOME REPORTS OF the incident in Gudbrandsdalen may have filtered through to the ears of relatives or friends of the men who had gone to their deaths with George Sinclair and his colleagues, although it is equally possible that others went to their graves without ever finding out what had happened to a kinsman who had gone overseas in the illegal levy. Apart from the mention in James Calder's history of Caithness published in 1861, where incidentally the number of mercenaries is exaggerated to 900, and the fuller account in Michell's book in 1886, the story of the massacre has been largely forgotten in Scotland – though not in Norway, where it has acquired the trappings of an epic event in the national history, an aspect of the affair to which we shall return in Chapter 18.

The Scots were familiar enough with military service abroad, and the banished Alexander Ramsay probably found other employment in arms without much trouble. He may be the same Alexander Ramsay who turns up in the records of the Swedish army as a colonel in 1631. As a mercenary, his kind was, to our modern eyes, astonishingly common in seventeenth-century Europe. Except for keeping troops to maintain public order and to guard their persons, rulers avoided the expense of maintaining a large standing army and the political consequences of conscription in favour of recruiting fighters only when they were required. At the time of the Battle of Lützen in 1632, one of the turning points of the Thirty Years War, four fifths of the Swedish army were non-Swedish nationals;[1] and the opposing army of the Holy Roman Empire was equally cosmopolitan. The practice persisted into the eighteenth century: around 1750 the French army had over 50,000 foreigners, the Spanish army had 28 battalions of foreign troops, the Netherlands still had its Scots Brigade, and in the Prussian army only around one third of the troops were actually Prussian.[2] Men went to Europe as soldiers from all parts of the British Isles, though only the Irish were given the evocative name of the 'wild geese', a term first used for the thousands who left Ireland to join the French army in the 1690s. The Swiss were common as mercenaries and it has been calculated that in times of war one in every eight Swiss of military age was in arms somewhere in Europe. In the seventeenth century the Scots at times challenged and may have surpassed this figure.

Professional soldiers moved across borders like contract workers or economic migrants, and the Scot in military service could easily find himself fighting shoulder to shoulder with a man from almost any ethnic group in Europe, and against his own countrymen. Robert Monro noted how a Scot in the ranks of the Habsburg army attacking a detachment of Monro's Regiment in Holstein in July 1627 shouted 'Have with you Gentlemen, thinke not now you are on the streets of Edinburgh bravading' before he was impaled by a Scottish pike.[3] Monro and his colleagues were perfectly aware of their own identity as Scots but this did not prevent them fighting for a cause far from home, as long as their temporary loyalty did not bring them into conflict with that homeland. In April 1629 Monro noted that when the King of Denmark no longer had need of them 'we were ready to imbrace new conditions from a new Master'. In the writings of the time, the word 'nation' is used to mean ethnic or cultural identity rather than a political one; indeed, it has been argued that the emergence of the sovereign nation-state was an outcome of the Thirty Years War and, until then, Europeans most often saw themselves as belonging to a more local polity – a domain, a village or a city.

The Scots acquired a reputation for being courageous fighters and for maintaining a loyalty to the flag under which they were fighting, habits that naturally mattered a great deal to their commanders and paymasters. From time to time, Scots contingents mutinied in protest against lack of pay and miserable conditions but, from our perspective, they were willing to stick it out and showed at times astonishing endurance in the face of adversity. Their reputation as fighting men went before them. For example, in March 1632, the Swedish commander Axel Oxenstierna ordered his German mercenaries to beat the 'Scots March' as they went into attack against a Spanish stronghold on the Rhine, on the premise that the sound of the drum tattoo would 'affright the enemy'. On this occasion, the ruse failed as the Spanish held and the Germans 'made a base retreat till they were holden up againe by the valour of the Scots that were there',[4] but the message is clear: the Spanish were expected to recognise the drums and react accordingly. In 1573 the Habsburg emperor, Charles V, noted that the Scots, who at that time were flocking to the Low Countries to fight in the cause of the Dutch, were a poor but valiant lot who did not have much to lose, and that, therefore, it was better to treat them with care.[5] The dynamic Shah Abbas I of Persia, busily engaged on remodelling his army on European lines and seeking an alliance with Christian powers against the Ottomans, asked James VI for men in 1601.[6] As far as is known, none were sent.

No one knows exactly how many Scots sought service as mercenaries in Europe but the highest estimates place the total close to 50,000 over the duration of the Thirty Years War, between 1618 and 1648. Numbers before and after this period were lower but still significant. No figure exists for the population of Scotland before 1755 but it has been estimated to have lain between 1.1 and 1.2 million in the first half of the seventeenth century, its rise and fall reflecting the occurrence of famine and disease. If the figure of 50,000 is accurate for the number of mercenaries, and all the evidence points to it being not far off the mark, it means around one fifth of the adult male population of Scotland experienced military service in Europe, where they became especially prominent in the Swedish armies. It is worth making a comparison with the First World War when, it has been calculated, 688,416 Scots, or around 25 per cent of the adult male population, were in military service.[7]

Although the ordinary people in the villages and towns of Europe often came to fear and loathe mercenaries for very good reason, there seems to have been little general moral opprobrium attached to the practice of hiring oneself as a soldier. Most went with the blessing if not the active encouragement of their rulers, often as an instrument of foreign policy. The modern view of mercenaries as 'dogs of war', as men who fight purely for pay irrespective of the justice of the cause, no doubt applied to many in the seventeenth century but a majority would have protested they had more honourable motives. The terms 'mercenarian' and 'mercenary soldier' appear in English during Shakespeare's time, only becoming shortened to 'mercenary' later. In Scotland the government saw those subjects of the monarch who became, in a phrase current at the time, 'wageit men of weare'[8] as a problem only when their presence or their activities threatened national security or relations with other countries; the same government seldom hesitated to permit recruitment for service under a foreign flag if such should serve the interests of the dynasty. In June 1573 the Privy Council in Edinburgh noted that 'a gude nowmer . . . of this realme' were prepared to go abroad 'under pretens to serve in the wearis in foreyn countreis' without licence from the king, or, as James VI had still to celebrate his seventh birthday, without the leave of his regent, the Earl of Morton. There were fears that the mercenaries might rouse animosity towards the Stuart dynasty but there was also a real anxiety that recruiting for overseas service might be a cover for a plot to seize James himself. Only officers with licences were allowed to recruit; others risked capital punishment, a sanction also directed at skippers and shipowners if they were rash enough to convey men overseas without official permission. A considerable number of licences were issued in the 1570s for the recruitment of soldiers for service in the Low Countries, and the standard formula for these forbade the recruiting officer from poaching men already in the king's service and from assembling his men on the south side of the Forth or anywhere within 16 miles of Stirling Castle, where the boy king was being carefully educated by Protestant clerics. In September 1587, the Privy Council ordered that a proclamation be read at mercat crosses throughout the land forbidding anyone 'to rais ony bandis of men of weare, or to putt themselffis in armes, ather ressave wageis as men of weare, or inroll themselffis undir capitanes and commandaris, or to departe furth of the cuntrey . . . without his Hienes licence'.[9] Other laws were enacted to minimise the export of arms, prevent the recruits causing trouble before they left, and prohibit them from fighting other Scots or serving for a Catholic ruler against Protestants. As will become plain, these rules were often ignored.

Even when they happened to be fighting for you, mercenaries were liable to be trouble. In August 1605 the Privy Council learned that the roads leading from Scotland to the south of England were 'greatly filled' with men seeking to 'inbarque in these southren portes for the services of foreyne Princes' and making a nuisance of themselves. Two months later, on learning that 'grite nowmeris of personis of this kingdom . . . [passing] to seik thair fortounes in the service of the wearis' were committing robberies and generally bullying ordinary folk in England, the Council ordered all recruiters to embark their levies north of the border. When two companies of Irish mercenaries bound for Sweden were driven ashore in Peterhead by bad weather at the end of 1609 and trekked south to Fife and Edinburgh in search of food, the Privy Council, wanting rid of them quickly, issued 1,000 merks to supply them with victual, and enjoined them under pain of death to obey their captains and be ready to sail for Sweden as soon as possible; some of the Irish, pressed men, took the chance to desert and the Council warned west-coast seafarers not to give them passage home.

What led so many young Scots to risk soldiering abroad? Every man who took ship for Europe no doubt had his own reasons for doing so. Only a few of them have left us any indication of their thinking but some generalities can be safely ventured. For the sons of lairds and noblemen, being a soldier was in keeping with their social standing, 'the laudable profession of arms' as Robert Monro put it in 1637. Such men usually served as officers. There was a culture of armed service already present: as part of the system for national defence, able-bodied men took part in wappenschaws, decreed to be held four times yearly by a 1491 Act of Parliament and calling on all men to keep armour and weapons befitting their status. In January 1626 the court book of the Barony of Leys on Deeside recorded the names of men fined 10 shillings each for not attending a wappenschaw.

It was no coincidence that many mercenaries were either younger or illegitimate sons who stood little chance of inheriting any wealth if they stayed at home. For such men service abroad held out the promise of fame and fortune. A few fled to escape shame or justice. One of these may have been Sir James King, ennobled in 1642 as Lord Eythin, about whom an allegation was made in March 1619 that he had killed Alexander Seaton of Meldrum in a family feud before he had left to seek a new career in Europe.[10] The effects of peer pressure and friendship on the behaviour of lairds' sons, what Sir David Stewart of Garth in 1822 called 'the impulse of emulation', especially in a country as small as Scotland, should also not be discounted. Robert Monro happily served in Gustavus Adolphus's army in Germany under the command of Sir John Hepburn, a friend with whom he had shared adventures in their youth: 'we were oft Camerades of danger together; so being long acquainted, we were Camerades in love: first at Colledge, next in our travells in France, at Paris and Poitiers Anno 1615 till we met againe in Spruce [Prussia] at Elben in August 1630'.[11] Poverty drove many to seek service and also no doubt there was a basic thirst for adventure, and anywhere would do. Writing of his own experiences in the Thirty Years War, James Turner from Dalkeith said, in words that could probably stand for a widespread view, 'I had swallowed without chewing, in Germanie, a very dangerous maxime, which militarie men there too much follow; which was, that so we serve our master honnestlie, it is no matter what master we serve.'[12]

The example of a forebear or a sibling could also lead a man to look overseas, and in some extended kindreds there emerged what amounted almost to a tradition of service in Europe. This is especially noticeable among the Gordons and the Leslies, but was also true of other families, and it is perhaps significant that such a practice was common in the North-East, facing as it does across the North Sea. At least nine Leslies served in arms, and several more made careers for themselves in Europe as clerics or in other civilian professions. This achievement was surpassed by the Gordons; a historian of this family lists over two hundred men of this name in arms in Europe over the span of the seventeenth and eighteenth centuries.[13] There are many examples of brothers or cousins serving together: for example, Alexander Lord Spynie wrote to Alexander Innes of Cotts in Moray-shire in the 1620s – the letter is not precisely dated – to say 'Plese yow understand your soon George has offered his service to me . . . And seing the gentilmanis mynd was affectionat and bent to follow me, being my near cusing, I preferred him to ane coloris quhilk place will yeald him fourtie doloris a month upone conditione he sold list me threttie men upone my awin charges.'[14]

When we look at the rank and file, the ordinary recruits who made up the bulk of the numbers going overseas, we find that some were given little choice. In the case of the Innes family above, no doubt the thirty men young George had to recruit came from among his father's tenants. For others, the situation was more stark – it was either go, or stay and be hanged. On 22 February 1621, two brothers, Henrie and Andro Allirdessis, were plucked from the Edinburgh Tolbooth by Ensign James Vetche for service with Captain Edmond in the Low Countries. The brothers, who had been sentenced for the 'hoiching and goring' of horses and oxen, agreed they would never return to Scotland without the king's licence.[15] A month later the Privy Council accepted the request of another prisoner, William Cuming, in jail for stealing cloth, to be allowed to enlist for service abroad. Two penniless debtors in Edinburgh prison in December 1642 volunteered to join Alexander Lord Saltoun for service in France, rightly seeing it better to take their chances abroad than starve behind bars at home.[16] In March 1628 John Gowdie and his two sons were found guilty of the murder of a man in Smailholm and were handed over for service in Sweden; this case came to the notice of the Privy Council when the trio deserted and returned home.[17] Two Stirling men, John and Gilbert Water, 'convict of the stealing of seven sheep', were banished in January 1643 and delivered to Captain James McMath 'to be carried by him to the French wars'.[18] The courts in the Borders handed down sentences of banishment to some of the miscreants and reivers who came before them, and possibly at least some of these enlisted; others may have fled overseas before the law caught up with them. James VI noted to his Privy Council in 1612 that Sir Robert Kerr of Ancrum in the Borders had executed some malefactors but had sent others to Sweden; the king confessed himself at a loss to understand its being done without a licence.[19] We have seen how these men probably ended up being murdered by the Norwegian farmers in Gudbrandsdalen. In general, it is tempting to think that some of these unfortunates may have found in foreign fields the chance to make something of their lives, but the historical record is usually silent on their fates.

A few joined the colours to escape an awkward family problem or relationship. For such a reason Robert Monro, the Black Baron of Foulis in Easter Ross, went as a volunteer, although he seems to have found the campaigns in Germany to his liking and returned there later when he could possibly have stayed at home. A more common situation may have been the one described in the minutes of the Aberdeen Kirk Session in March 1621: 'Efter incalling of God, James Nauchtie . . . declarit he wald not marie Mariorie Hendersone, nochtwithstanding of thair contract and proclamatioun of thair bandis, because he hes conducit him selff to gang to Bohemia to play the sogeor'.[20] What Nauchtie probably experienced in Bohemia is explored in Chapter 8.

Other would-be soldiers sniffed an opportunity to chance their arm. Such a man might have been the Alexander Stewart, a former servant of the Duke of Lennox and Richmond, who wrote to his late master's widow in February 1626 to beg her to provide him with money to allow him to proceed with raising men for the Earl of Nithsdale: 'I have taken the boldnes humbly to entreat your Grace to put this last mark of your favor upone me in helping me with some money . . . without your Graces help I schall absolutely loose this occastione of my fortones'. It is not clear that the dowager duchess sent anything to Stewart but she admitted to her cousin that she had already done much for him, paying his debts and getting him out of prison, and although he clearly had not mended his rascally ways the duchess had a soft spot for him: 'I shall wish hee may prosper . . . indeede I thinke it is happie for him to bee gone out of England'.[21]

The economic predicament of the younger son or of one born outside of wedlock, with little or no chance of inheriting either money or social status, probably operated among the poor as among the better off. Stories of how a man 'from meane condition' could find honour and wealth could well have encouraged enlistment. The seeking of honour was no idle pursuit in the seventeenth century and affected every rank. Robert Monro admired the courage of a humble porter called Mac-Weattiche who had come with Mackay's Regiment from Foulis and who proved himself to be as adept with the sword as with the plough, 'fearing nothing but discredit, and the

down-looke or frowne of his Officers'.[22] A good name won on the
battlefield undoubtedly helped one pull oneself up a few notches on
the many-runged ladder of status that characterised European society
at the time and a few Scots were notably successful at acquiring one.
During the siege of Stralsund in 1628, Monro said 'we had no thought
of gathering of money, but of gaining credit'. Men were always careful
to establish their social position from the outset and some carried a
document called a birth-brieve with them, a testimonial to parentage
and ancestry, so that there could be no confusion or doubt when one
introduced oneself abroad as a 'gentleman'. One such birth-brieve
in the register of the burgh of Aberdeen, dated 25 October 1639,
assures the world that Captain George Gairdyne 'now residen in
Germanie' is the lawful and legitimate son of a Banchory man of
respectable pedigree. Another, in the same source, testifies that 'Johne
Sibbald . . . and David Sibbald, who (as is reporte) wes killed in the
German warres . . . being serving . . . under the croun of Sweden, ar
borne gentillmen and brother german lawfull sones to unquhill John
Sibbald of Keir, and Janet Strachan his spous.'[23]

Many would have insisted they were drawing their swords for
honourable reasons arising from political and religious allegiances,
these two being so inextricably intertwined in the seventeenth century
that they at times amounted to the same thing. How foreign troops
were referred to in Europe reflected this. The Scots were usually
regarded as allies by Protestant regimes: the Danes thought of British
soldiers in the 1620s as *hjaelptropper*, or helping troops, reserving the
term *lejetropper*, hired troops, for Germans; and the Swedish authorities
called them *värvade*, enlisted troops. The Dutch referred to the British
mercenaries as *huursoldaten* or hired soldiers. The conflicts that raged
across Europe from the mid seventeenth century had roots in the
struggle between the Catholic Church and the Reforming denomina-
tions and, as a nation that had officially adopted the Reformed Church
in 1560, many Scots were zealous in defending the rights of their
continental co-religionists. But Scotland had her Catholics as well, and
in 1622 Archibald Campbell, the seventh Earl of Argyll, busied
himself recruiting men to fight on the Spanish side in the Low
Countries, a bold and rash activity as popular feeling in the country
was firmly pro-Dutch. A Spanish galleon was attacked when it

anchored in Leith roads; this was also the time when the future
Charles I was wooing a Spanish Habsburg princess, and there was joy
in Edinburgh when that courtship failed. The North-East, Huntly's
territory, also had a significant number of Catholic sympathisers with
Spain and the Holy Roman Empire.

Dynastic politics, so often bound up with religion, were also crucial
in shaping motivation. Robert Monro thought it honourable to fight
for the 'liberty of our Kings daughter, the Queene of Bohemia and her
distressed Royall Issue, under the magnanimous King of Denmarke
our Master, who for her Majesties libertie did hazard not onely his life
but his crowne', the Queen of Bohemia here being James VI's
daughter. Many of the Scots officers were, therefore, fighting for
an entirely familiar cause, that of the Stuart dynasty. The presence of
the Stuarts among the various dynastic houses vying for power on the
European stage presented some Scots with a serious test of loyalty,
irrespective of their personal faith. Sir Henry Bruce, in the service of
the Holy Roman Empire in 1620 as governor of the town of
Nikolsburg (now Mikulov in the Czech Republic), felt compelled
to resign from this post to raise a regiment in support of Elizabeth
Stuart against his former employer. He may also have had purely
material reasons but it was clearly acceptable to put forward loyalty to
a dynasty as a motive for action.

A few mercenaries may have gone just for the money or to escape
crippling poverty and famine. In the Highlands, away from the more
fertile districts along the east coast, life was always hard. A Gaelic
proverb, probably dating from the time Lord Reay, the chief of the
Mackays, was recruiting heavily for service in the Swedish army,
summed up this situation: *Na h-uile fear a theid a dhollaidh gheibh a dolar
bho Mhac Aoidh* – any man who is down on his luck can get a dollar
from Mackay. Plundering was part and parcel of soldiering at the time
but, even if one found little in the way of loot, there was every
likelihood that in a regiment a man would at least be fed and clad. The
reality often turned out to be more harsh but any appreciation of the
fact that a soldier in the ranks was more likely to die from starvation
or plague than from wounds was shoved to the back of the mind.

Usually the Privy Council concerned itself with recruitment matters
at the behest of the monarch, levying men to serve overseas as

instruments of Stuart foreign policy. This was especially true during
the Thirty Years War. In April 1627 the Council strove to assist the
recruitment efforts of the Earl of Nithsdale, Alexander Lord Spynie
and James Sinclair of Murkle for Danish service by permitting the
arrest as potential recruits of 'all Egyptians [gypsies], strong and
sturdie beggars and vagabonds, ydle and maisterless men wanting
trades and competent meanes to live upon, and who in that respect ar
unprofitable burthenis to the countrie'. Murkle was given leave to seek
men in England but, even with the cooperation of the local authorities, he had trouble filling the ranks in Newcastle and Northumberland. The Privy Council had to step in again when rivalry developed
between recruiting officers. Captain Blair of Spynie's regiment and
Captain Ogilvie of Nithsdale's both sought men in their home
territory of Angus until the Council at Nithsdale's request allocated
areas in August 1627 for them to operate in. Broadly, Murkle was
assigned the north beyond the Cairngorms, Spynie a broad belt
running from Argyll to Buchan, and Nithsdale the rest of the country.

Some of the groups targeted by recruiters, which were believed to
contain deserters and fugitives who had changed their minds after
previous recruitment, formed themselves into 'societies and companies, armed with hacquebutts and pistolets and uther armour' to
resist.[24] Sheriffs and bailies were called upon to throw all likely
suspects into jail until their status could be ascertained, and at the
same time skippers were warned not to give passage to fugitives to
Ireland. The Privy Council also alerted the authorities to be aware of
recruited men pretending to be servants or apprentices bound to
masters, and thereby being set free. The Council declared that in
effect any man who had taken the recruiter's shilling was duty bound
to go and, should a master come forward to claim a servant, that
master should be obliged to give him up or agree to send him for
military service after the expiry of the civilian contract. On the other
hand, noting that recruiters 'hes tane diverse lawfull subjects out of
thair bedds, hes taine uthers from the pleugh, and some in thair
travelling athort the cuntrie', the Council issued in May 1627 a
proclamation against forced enlistment. This was not effective in
deterring all recruiters desperate to fill their quotas as, a month later,
Patrick Adamsoun, a burgess of St Andrews, protested that his son

had been taken by 'some of the sojouris lifted for the Germane or Swaden wearis . . . and violentlie hurlit aboard of ane of their shippis'. Adamsoun knew that there was an ever-present danger of young men being seized in this way, 'as ordinarlie hes beene done be people of that qualitie within this kingdome'. In the event, Adamsoun's son escaped when a mutiny took place aboard the ship; the Privy Council confirmed his right to be free. Occasionally a protest against forceful recruitment could be successful, as in June 1643 when a group of eleven men complained to the Privy Council that they had been 'tane by force and incarcerat within [Blackness Castle, a bleak stronghold by the Forth] wherein they ar yitt lying almost starving for want of maintenance, and their wyves and children ar begging through the countrie'. The Council sent men to investigate this case, with the result that five of the eleven were set free, the other six being judged to have freely volunteered.[25] A landowner might also appeal on behalf of a recruit: in September 1642 the Countess of Home obtained the freedom of a 'simple' collier and two saltpan workers from her Dunglas estates who had been, apparently easily, persuaded to join the colours. The levying of men for European service was beset with almost every aspect of recruitment that was to become more familiar in relation to the activities of press gangs for naval service at a later time. It is also clear that finding men to fill the ranks of mercenary regiments was not always an easy task, and that recruitment fell unequally upon the poor . In July 1627 the Privy Council was alarmed to receive complaints from the upper classes in Edinburgh society that the recruiting captains had been seducing boys from the college to join the ranks without parental consent: 'by thair alluring speeches [they] hes corrupted the boyes', read the minutes of the Council, 'whilk has bred suche a scandall upon the said Colledge and suche ane generall feare throughout the kingdome' that families were sending their sons to St Andrews, Glasgow or Aberdeen to continue their education.[26] A decade later, in 1637, as the Thirty Years War dragged on and as news filtered back of the often appalling conditions endured in it, the Privy Council was still issuing permission for the arrest of deserters from levies for Swedish service.

Recruiting officers must have been a common sight at markets throughout Scotland during the time of the Thirty Years War. They also made use of their social connections and were fully aware of the extended social networks based on kinship in the Highlands, where clan society maintained a ready ability to raise manpower for a campaign. James Fraser, minister of the parish of Wardlaw, west of Inverness, noted in 1633 that 'Now are young gentry again getting commissiones and providing recruits for the Swedish warrs, where many of our Scottish spirits have formerly gained honor; and there is here one Thomas Fraser, sone of the house of Belladrum, a commissionat oficer, gathering voluntyres up and down this country, and my Lord Lovat . . . was very helpfull to him, and in a court att Beuly got a list of severalls young men to be reased for that service'. In 1656, Frasers were again recruited: 'This yeare the Lord Cranstoun haveing gotten a Cornels Commission levyes a new regiment of voluntiers for the King of Poles service . . . The Collonel sent one Captain Montgomery north in June, and had very good luck, listing many . . . and himselfe followed after in August . . . sallied out to visit the Master of Lovat and in 3 dayes got 43 of the Frasers to take on.'[27] It should be noted, however, that social networks did not always furnish men: in September 1636 Captain Robert Innes, a laird's son from Mackay's Regiment, was angered enough to strike tenants of Gordon of Dunkinty near Elgin when they refused to allow their sons or servants to be recruited.[28]

In his account, published in 1851, of the life of the mercenary Sir John Hepburn, James Grant includes lines of a recruiting song, of which one verse (in modern spelling) goes:

> All brave lads that would hazard for honour,
> Hark how Bellona her trumpet doth blow;
> While Mars, with many a warlike banner
> Bravely displayed invites you to go!
> Germany, Sweden, Denmark, are smoking,
> With a crew of brave lads, others provoking;
> All in their armour bright,
> Dazzling great Caesar's sight,
> Summoning you to a fight! Tan-ta-ra-ra-ra!
> Oh Viva! Gustavus we cry!
> Here we shall either win honour or die!

Once recruited, the soldiers had to face the rigours of a voyage to the Continent. Tragedy could befall before the troop-carrying ships left these shores. On 3 October 1637, a very heavy storm of rain put the Dee into spate and four ships in the estuary were driven from their anchorages to be 'brockne against the bulwarke at the river's mouth . . . wherby a great number of souldiours, who wer levyed to be transported into Sweden, being that tyme on bord, wer drowned in the night tyme, and ther bodyes after ward cast out in severall places upon the coast'.[29] Usually the voyage was simply a few days, or at worst a week or two, of cold, wet, sea-sickness and hunger. In August 1627 James Galbreth, described as a quartermaster, wrote from Glückstadt to the Earl of Nithsdale after the arrival of a contingent of 216 men: 'The mariners and sojoures complaines that they war so bad providet that if the wind had anie wayes contraried they had been in great daunger of famishinge . . .'.[30]

Was it worth it? Were the rewards for the mercenary an adequate compensation for the abandonment of personal liberty and confrontation by discomfort, disease and a painful death? The question has to be considered in the context of the times. Personal liberty for most ordinary people was already circumscribed. Most of the men in the burghs were 'unfree', having no say in how their community was governed, relying on scraping a living from a trade, or semi-skilled or unskilled work to feed themselves and their families. The rural poor existed as tenant cottars or servants or, in the case of some industries, as virtual serfs, the 'property' of a master. Famine and plague were already familiar to all: there were four major outbreaks of plague in Scotland between 1568 and 1609, and four major periods of food shortage. In this environment, 'going for a soldier' was often a gamble worth taking. Recruits were generally provided with clothing and food by their employers and, although here again the system of supply often broke down, these offerings must have added to the attractions of being a soldier. Lord Ogilvie noted that his recruits at Burntisland in 1627 would not 'imbark with good will except they get thair clothes' and realised how important this was: 'it does mutch good, and incurages many, quhen they sie the soldieris weill used, and speciall quhen they sie them passe throch the cuntrey weill apperelled'.[31] As to food, they were generally happy to accept the beer, butter, cheese and bread they were accustomed to, although, if they suspected unfairness in the distribution of rations, they were not slow to complain. In Glückstadt in December 1628 the daily ration per man was one and a half pounds of bread, half a pound of cheese, two herrings and a can of beer. The diet could also include bacon, dried fish, salt beef or the other stock items of the day.

As we shall see, some Scots who rose to high rank in Europe died with titles, land and honours aplenty. Most would have had to rely on their wages or what plunder they could gather in the field. In the late sixteenth century in Scotland, a male farm servant could expect to earn between £1 6s 8d and £3 per year. The elite among the rural workforce, the ploughmen, could earn £6. Most lairds also had a fairly low standard of living, leaving in their wills only a few hundred or even tens of pounds. The Privy Council set the pay scale for men to be employed by the Earl of Angus to police the Borders as follows: captain of horse 100 merks per month (almost £70), his lieutenant £45, his cornet £35, a horseman £20; captain of foot £50, his lieutenant £30, his ensign £20, a sergeant £30, a drummer or piper £10, and a foot soldier £6.[32] Presumably the higher pay for horsemen reflected the need to spend more on mount and equipment. Although it is extremely difficult to equate wages in different currencies and countries, it is probably safe to assume that the amounts on offer to men in Europe were considered reasonable and possibly better. In the Low Countries in 1579, the sums paid to Scottish mercenaries ran from 12 livres per month for the drummer, at the bottom of the scale, to 90 livres for the captain in command. His lieutenant received 45 livres, his ensign 40, while the sergeant was paid 24. 'Livre' means 'pound' but it does not necessarily follow that these were pounds of equivalent value. The Dutch pay scale also provides 12⅓ livres per month for the surgeon, scarcely more valued than the drummer boy.[33] The records for the period show that in 1573/74 Captain Henry Balfour received £8,015, with similar though lower sums being handed out to other captains: these sums were for one year and included expenses for bringing men over from Britain. At the same time, under 'pay', Colonel Ormiston received £500, and this seems to have been the going annual rate for a man of this rank. In October 1575, the salary of Henry Balfour, by this time a colonel, was set at 800 guilders per year by the Dutch authorities. In 1577 the Dutch laid down that 'All captains [are] to pay their men 45 stivers each, half monthly, while the engagement remains at 1,100 guilders monthly for 100 men.' A worker's salary in the Low Countries at the time was around 200 guilders per year.[34] An attractive feature of service in the Low Countries in the Dutch cause was that the widows and children of soldiers killed in action were given state pensions. By the standards of the time, the Dutch were good at maintaining regular payment of salaries, although there were still occasions when the soldiers were stirred to complain over arrears or to resort to mutiny. The conscientious paymaster was always aware that the loyalty of a mercenary could be severely tested by a lack of pay, an eventuality that could easily occur when an army was in the field.

In his letter to Sir Donald Mackay of Strathnaver in June 1629, Gustavus Adolphus of Sweden set out the rates of pay for the regiment Mackay was to recruit. The colonel was promised 300 riksdaler Swedish per month, with the amounts for subordinates decreasing in accordance to their rank. A company captain received 100 riksdaler, a lieutenant and an ensign 50. Sergeants were paid 16 riksdaler, drummers and pipers 8, and the ordinary pikeman or musketeer 6. Scouts and reserves, on 5 riksdaler a month, were at the lowest rung on the pay ladder. Men were also fed and clothed. Clearly the Swedish king considered the terms of employ to be attractive. The letter also gives details of times of payment, deductions for damage to equipment and other terms of service. The rate of exchange at the time is revealed in the articles of an agreement drawn up between Sir James Spens and Alexander Hamilton in April 1629 for the raising of 1,200 men. Letters of exchange sent to Scotland would provide Hamilton with 'the somme of sixteene hundred nynetie six poundes lawfull English money, as the price of seavin thousand six hundred and fower score rex dollars'.[35] The rex dollar or riksdaler – the spelling varies considerably in documents – was the Swedish equivalent of the German reichsthaler, the international European currency of the time. In practice, especially when the soldiers were campaigning, the systems of victualling and payment often broke down, and arrears could climb to distressing heights. Even Gustavus Adolphus, generally a reliable payer, had to deal with

threats of mutiny from time to time, and what must have held many
men back from such a momentous step was perhaps the sense that it
was better to starve among one's mates than risk breaking the law or
deserting to try one's luck alone. Senior officers were much better
placed. In 1625 Sir John Hepburn was paid £380 per year as a colonel
of infantry. His captains received £128, his musketeers and pikemen
sixpence a day.[36] Rewards also came in material form or the owner-
ship of land. Patrick Ruthven received 4,358 riksdaler in pay in 1610
and, probably as donations in lieu of pay or reimbursement of
expenses, was awarded lands in Sweden from 1618. The highest
rewards were promotion to the ranks of the nobility and the
acquisition of hereditary titles, a path of advancement that a surprising
number of Scots successfully followed.

An often reproduced image of tartan-clad soldiers in Stettin in 1631
in the service of Gustavus Adolphus has been frequently labelled as
men of Mackay's Regiment. The picture is usually accompanied by a
text saying they are Irish but this has usually been explained by
mentioning the common practice of referring to Gaelic as Irish. There
are sharply divided views on who they really are – whether they are
indeed Irish, men from the Marquis of Hamilton's mixed levy that
arrived in Stettin in 1631, or Highlanders from Mackay's Regiment.[37]
Even if the figures were Irish, Highlanders may not have looked very
different, and some may indeed have stepped ashore in Europe clad in
tartan. The elements of Highland dress at the period were the linen
shirt, sometimes dyed saffron, with trews or the tartan plaid: 'a loose
Cloke of several Ells, striped and party coloured which they gird
breadth-wise with a leather Belt, so as it scarce covers the Knees', as
James Gordon has it in his contemporary *History of Scots Affairs*. On his
feet the Highlander wore raw-leather shoes. Lowlanders most likely
dressed themselves in the plain standard coats and breeches of
hodden grey or jackets with a simple checked pattern, with bonnets
possibly decorated with some sprig of plant, ribbon or feather, and
men from the Borders may have brought from home the steel helmets
and leather jackets worn by some of the reivers. Officers would have
been better dressed, befitting their status; Major General Sir David
Stewart of Garth noted that officers were in the habit of wearing rich
buttons or a gold chain about their neck, an insurance for securing

good treatment if taken prisoner or in need of nursing. Scots were laughed at in Denmark for their poor clothes and to keep up morale and develop esprit de corps recruiters often issued clothing, purchased in bulk at an economic rate. Nithsdale's quartermaster wrote of the men who landed at Glückstadt in August 1627 'The bleue clothes did grace this last compagnie vearie much.'[38] Troops in Swedish service were issued with woollen cloth, often dyed to match the name of the regiment although this was not always the case: for example a company newly arrived from Scotland in James Ramsay's regiment in 1629 was issued with 39 ells of red cloth, 42 ells of yellow, 351 ells of kersey, 113 ells of unspecified colour and 207 ells of 'anycoloured cloth'.[39] It seems that whatever clothing men wore when they arrived in Europe may have been soon replaced by standard-issue stuff. This is unfortunate for those who wish to imagine the Scots as appearing in full fig of plaid and bonnet. They can take some consolation from the fact that there were certainly musicians among the ranks – pipers are mentioned on the pay scale proposed by Gustavus Adolphus to Sir Donald Mackay in June 1629 as receiving the same as drummers.[40] The list of bowmen recruited in the Highlands in 1627 for service at La Rochelle includes two pipers and one harper – his name was Harie m'gra, suggesting he may have been Irish – and presumably other Highland contingents had musicians.[41]

The record of the Scottish Privy Council's decision in 1552 to send men to fight in France provides details of the weapons and clothing of those levies: 'all thai to be hagbutteris, weill furnist with pulder flask, morsing horne, and all uthair geir belangand thairto, gif it be possibill, and abilyeit [clothed] with new hoise and new dublett of canvas at the least'. Men without firearms [hagbuts] were to carry the pike – 'ane speir of sex ellis lang' – and were to be clothed in 'jak, steilbonet, swerd, buklair, splentis and slevis of plait or mailye'.[42] This is a summary of weapons commonly in use by rank-and-file troops by the mid sixteenth century, a suite of arms that would continue in use for many decades into the future.[43] Although bows were still to be seen at this time, they were rapidly giving way to firearms. The earliest reference to hand-held firearms in Britain may lie in the lines in Barbour's *The Bruce* in the poet's account of a clash between the Scots and English in 1327: 'But gynnys for crakys had he nane/ For in

Scotland yeit than but wene.'[44] These early firearms were all cannons
of some sort and it was not until the 1460s or '70s that matchlock
guns made their appearance, with the burning match or lunt, as it was
called in Scotland, to fire the powder. These were known as arque-
buses or, in German, *Hakenbüchse*, literally 'hook-gun', from which the
word 'hackbut' or 'hagbut' was derived. They had an effective range of
around 100 yards; the balls of lead used as bullets had enough force to
smash through armour and bone to make ugly, infected wounds, very
different to and much worse than arrow wounds. In the latter half of
the sixteenth century Spanish forces in the Low Countries began to
use a type of gun nicknamed *moschetto*, meaning sparrowhawk, from
which the word 'musket' is derived. The musket became the standard
firearm for infantry, although it was cumbersome, slow to reload and
prone to misfiring. The barrel – perhaps 4 feet long – necessitated the
use of a forked stick to support it during firing but it could kill a man
at 200 yards and puncture armour at more than half that distance. The
musketeer went into battle with his long gun, forked stick and ramrod,
and with prepared charges in wooden containers slung on a bandolier
around his shoulder, usually a dozen, whence the nickname 'the
Twelve Apostles'. After firing – often simply in the general direction
of the enemy, aiming 'no higher than the Girdle of a man', the
complicated process of reloading had to be accomplished before the
gun could be used again, and the lunt, blown on regularly to keep it
alive, could be again thrust into the firing pan. Musketeers operated in
ranks, replacing each other in sequence to fire and reload. In *Pallas
Armata*, his 1627 text on military practice, Sir Thomas Kellie listed a
sequence of thirty-three commands governing the actions of musketeers, a string of orders that in battle fell to only three: make ready,
present, fire.

Effective firepower in combat needed disciplined, well-trained men
with steady nerves and perhaps it was this, along with the deafening
reports and choking smoke associated with gunfire, that led Robert
Monro in 1637 to name the other main infantry weapon, the pike, as
his arm of choice. 'The most honourable of all weapons,' he wrote,
'and my choice in day of battell', perhaps consciously echoing the
Spanish claim that the pike was the queen of arms.[45] The pike was a
stout pole, often 15 feet in length though longer ones were also

common, with a iron spear tip. It had the virtue of simplicity but a body of pikemen also needed discipline and thorough training to be effective in combat. Sir Thomas Kellie detailed a set of sixteen commands for pikes, again a list liable to be cut in actual combat. The pike was very good in defending against cavalry, where horses shied away from the bristling points, but in infantry combat, when groups of pikemen fell to heaving and prodding against each other, to 'push of pike', success came down to determination and brute strength.

Musketeers and pikemen also carried sidearms in the form of knives or swords, although the latter were expensive and more common among officers. These were often made from blades imported from European centres of sword-making such as Solingen and Passau, where one pattern was known as *Grosse Schotten*, the type favoured in Scotland. Records from the late 1500s show that a sword could cost from 2 merks up to £10 Scots, depending on quality, and one document, dated 1605, gives the price of sword blades as 30s each. The levies for France in 1551 had to be equipped with funds raised from a special stent or tax.[46] Around the same period, a stand of armour for a horseman cost £50, and it was recognised that only a man with a considerable income could be expected to provide himself with such equipment. Officers were also the only men likely to carry pistols. Scots-made pistols date from the early 1500s, and are often elaborately decorated firearms with fishtail or lemon-shaped butts covered in scroll work, but these were generally expensive, prestigious weapons. An account book gives the price of a pair of pistols in Dundee in October 1597 as £12. The vast majority of the Scots who went overseas to fight had to be provided with arms and this was often done only when they reached their destination; in 1612 the men who were ambushed in the Norwegian mountains were probably mostly ill armed or even weaponless.

'these proude Scottes'

Prussia, France

*T*HE EMIGRATION OF fighting men from Scotland to continental Europe had been going on for a very long time before the political circumstances in the early seventeenth century offered a flowering of opportunity for the soldier. Early references to the phenomenon are scanty but intriguing. For example, we would like to know more about the William Douglas who, it is claimed, was sent to the assistance of the Lombards in northern Italy in the year 800, especially as this is supposed to have occurred around three hundred years before the surname Douglas appears in Scottish records.[1] A story from the early days of the Gordons claims it was one of that kindred, Bertram by name, who shot Richard the Lionheart at Chaluz in 1199.[2] A few Scottish knights answered the summons to join the contingents who set out for the Holy Land in the Crusades, and it was while conveying the heart of Robert Bruce to be buried in Jerusalem that Sir James Douglas perished in 1330 in a battle with the Moors in Spain. Sir Adam Gordon possibly died on his way to the Crusades in the thirteenth century. Safe-conducts were issued in 1363 and 1366 for four Scottish knights – William Ramsay, David Barclay, Walter Moigne and Laurence de Gelybrand – to pass through England to join a Crusade, but it is not certain they went. In the fifteenth century, Sir Colin Campbell of Glenorchy appears among the Knights of St John on Rhodes.[3]

The Crusades were a pan-European movement under the banner of all western Christendom. Out of them sprang the Teutonic Knights, a chivalric order like the Templars and the Hospitallers,

that had its foundations in a military religious brotherhood in the Holy
Land and was confirmed by bull by Pope Clement III in 1191 as the
Teutonic Order of Holy Mary in Jerusalem. The Teutonic Knights
soon turned their eyes away from the Levant to north-eastern Europe,
where their services were called on to protect the bounds of
Christendom against barbarian raids and where, in 1217, a crusade
was called against the pagan peoples of Prussia. This proved to be a
lucrative theatre of operations: members of the order acquired
fiefdoms and extensive trading rights and it became an institution
of political significance.[4] Although predominantly made up of men
from the German-speaking lands, the order attracted occasional
adherents from other parts of Europe, including from the British
Isles. Among them at one time was Henry, Duke of Lancaster, and in
his Prologue to *The Canterbury Tales*, composed in the late 1380s,
Chaucer describes his fictional knight as having fought in Lithuania
and Russia. One of the earliest references to Scots in this regard dates
to 1356, when the brothers Walther and Norman de Lesselyn, or
Leslie, obtained safe-conducts to travel to Prussia to join the Teutonic
Knights. The two brothers turn up in France in 1360 and in
Alexandria in 1365, and Norman may have been killed there. Sir
Walther was the sixth earl of Ross, and there is a record of his death in
the *Calendar of Fearn* as taking place on the last day of February 1382;
his exploits may have inspired a lost vernacular work *The Tail of Syr
Valtir the Bald Leslye*. In 1362 David de Berclay, probably from
Aberdeenshire, sought permission to take a dozen knights and horses
to Prussia; perhaps he did not go to the Baltic and is the same David
Barclay who obtained a safe-conduct through England shortly afterwards. Adam de Heburn sought a safe-conduct to Prussia with ten
knights in 1378. In 1390 or 1391, the Scots knight William Douglas of
Nithsdale was murdered by English knights either in Königsberg or in
Danzig, perhaps in a quarrel resulting from support for different sides
in the papal schism, although another reason may have been a pre-
existing feud with them. A contemporary chronicle noted a 'great
grief' amongst the lords after this deed, as Douglas was '*gar eyn truwer
man leibes guttes und ere*' – 'a staunch fellow in body, possessions and
honour'. One of the city gates of Danzig, the Hohe Tor, was once
known as the Douglas Gate and bore the Nithsdale coat of arms at

least until 1734, suggesting that Douglas may have played a leading role in defending the city.[5]

In the late Middle Ages, the most prominent foreign theatre for the Scottish soldier was France, linked with Scotland in the 'auld alliance' against the common English enemy. The relationship between the two countries weakened after the Reformation, but before Europe was split by this great doctrinal schism many Scots served in France, for example in the Hundred Years War. In most of the famous battles that we know as stirring episodes in English history there were Scots fighting on the other side.

Sir William Douglas escaped with his life from the field of Poitiers on 18 September 1356 when the English, led by the Black Prince, son of Edward III, won a notable victory. In the same battle, his brother Sir Archibald Douglas – both men were illegitimate sons of the second Earl of Douglas – was taken prisoner,[6] as was John of Islay, chief of the Clan Donald, present with a number of his clansmen.[7] John remained a prisoner in England until December 1357, when he was at last granted a safe-conduct to go home to arrange his own ransom. Scots who fell in the battle included Sir Andrew Stewart, Sir Robert Gordon, Sir Andrew Halyburton and Sir Andrew Vaux. As a prisoner of high status, Archibald Douglas would have been subject to a high ransom but, according to one story, a fellow prisoner, Sir William Ramsay of Colluthie, fooled the English into thinking Douglas was his servant.[8] One Scots knight, Sir John Assueton, fought in the English forces in the 1370s and an anecdote illustrating his foolhardy, if not mad, courage describes how one day he rode towards the French defences at Noyon in Picardy, alone except for his page, and challenged anyone to come out to fight him. When the French sensibly remained where they were, Sir John urged his horse over the barricades and fought everyone who approached him for close to an hour until the pleadings of his page to come away, as the English army was now out of sight, at last persuaded him that he had done enough, whereupon he fought his way out and rode off, unhurt.

Scots were present in larger numbers later in the Hundred Years War, opposing the invasions of France by Henry V, whose first campaign in 1415 resulted in the seizure of the port of Harfleur and the victory of Agincourt. Henry returned in 1417 and in the following two years made himself master of Normandy, exploiting a France disastrously split between the supporters of the Duke of Burgundy and those loyal to the dauphin, the heir to the French throne. The dauphin, his fortunes at a low ebb, disinherited by his unstable father Charles VI, sent a request to Scotland for assistance. In response, the estates governing the realm in the absence of the future James I, a captive in England, sent Sir John Stewart, Earl of Buchan, with, in the words of the chronicler Walter Bower, 'a vast crowd of nobles, knights and men-at-arms to the number of 7,000'. Later historians have tended to lower Bower's number, though not by a great deal. According to the sixteenth-century historian George Buchanan, it did not prove difficult to raise these volunteers but it represented an enormous investment by such a small nation; a large proportion would have hailed from the Douglas lands. The force landed at La Rochelle in 1419. Buchan had with him a number of prominent knights of the realm, among them his brother-in-law Archibald Douglas, son of the Earl of Douglas The hard-pressed dauphin welcomed them but the bulk of his people seem to have been less keen on this new army they had to feed. The fertility and riches of France, even a France wracked by war, must have delighted the Scots for they made the most of their opportunity and earned from the peasants the disapproving label of *sacs à vin et mangeurs de moutons* (winebags and mutton-eaters). Henry V brought his captive, James I, to France in an effort to dissuade the Scots from serving France but this had little success. Henry also proclaimed that all Britons who fought for the dauphin were rebels and were to be treated as such. When the town of Melun was captured by the English in November 1420 after a long siege, twenty Scots in the garrison were hanged.

The death of the regent, the Duke of Albany, in September 1420 brought Buchan and some of his fellow nobles back from France to see to their domestic affairs but they were soon recalled by the dauphin, landing at La Rochelle with another 5,000 men. Buchan moved with his small army into the region of Touraine, in the Loire valley next to Anjou, then occupied by Henry's brother, Thomas, Duke of Clarence. On Good Friday in March 1421, the Scots found themselves with French troops in the village of Baugé. It would have been customary to suspend hostilities during the religious holiday but

Clarence, when he learned of the proximity of the enemy, could not resist the temptation to strike a surprise blow. In his eagerness, he refused to wait for archers and relied on mounted troops. The attack might have succeeded but the sudden appearance of the English cavalry was spotted by French scouts. Buchan despatched thirty archers under Robert Stewart of Ralston to hold the only bridge across the River Couesnon on the approach to Baugé while the rest of the force scrambled for their arms. Hugh Kennedy, brother to the Laird of Dunure, and 100 men joined the archers. The English knights, with Clarence in the forefront, dismounted and charged the Scots, finally scattering them from the bridge. The delaying action, however, was sufficient to allow Buchan to come up with 200 horsemen to meet the remounted English as they assembled on the boggy riverbank. Wearing a coronet on his helmet, Clarence was easily picked out and became a target. According to Bower he was 'wounded in the face by the lance of the lord of Swinton and met his end after being struck to the ground by the earl of Buchan's mace'. The *Book of Pluscarden* credits Clarence's fall to an Alexander Maccalsland from Lennox. The battle, which had begun late in the afternoon, continued into the darkness and the confused, leaderless English were put to flight. The French chronicler Enguerrand de Monstrelet notes 'The Duke of Clarence . . . and, in general, the flower of the chivalry and esquiredom, were left dead on the field, with two or three thousand fighting men'.[9] Bower says 'On the side of the Scots no more than twelve fell', possibly another exaggeration from his patriotic pen. The victory greatly heartened the dauphin, who now mocked those who had been critical of the Scots by asking what they thought now of the wine-drinkers and mutton-eaters. Hearing of the battle, the Pope, in Rome, observed how the Scots were a true antidote to the English.

The dauphin awarded Buchan the baton of high constable of France, making the earl in effect the commander-in-chief of the dauphin's forces. As constable, Buchan led attacks on the towns of Gallardon, not far from Chartres, and Avranches on the Normandy border before returning to Scotland in the summer of 1423. The Scots who remained with the dauphin, who had now succeeded to the throne as Charles VII, suffered a serious defeat at the hands of the

Earl of Salisbury, allied with Burgundians, at the town of Cravant at the end of July. The Scots commander, Sir John Stewart of Darnley, was taken prisoner. In Scotland, Buchan persuaded the elder Archibald Douglas, the fourth Earl of Douglas, to come back with him to France, while the earl's son now stayed home to mind family affairs. They arrived in February 1424 with 6,500 troops and were reviewed by the French king on 24 April. Douglas was created Duke of Touraine and in May rode into his new provincial capital of Tours to a guarded welcome from a citizenry unhappy at the prospect of having to support a foreign army for an unspecified period.

In August Douglas led a thrust into Normandy and captured Verneuil. When the Duke of Bedford and Salisbury approached to retake the town, the French commanders gave in to the Scots' eagerness to stay and fight and formed up in two divisions to confront the enemy on open ground flanking the highway. For most of the day the two armies faced each other, and it was four in the afternoon before Bedford ordered the attack. After French cavalry chased the English archers from the field, the battle turned into a grinding slog between infantry and knights on foot until the French gave way and the Scots found themselves pinned between enemy formations. Douglas and Buchan had let the English know beforehand that any prisoners they took could expect no quarter and now their threat was flung back in their faces. Douglas, one of his sons and Buchan were killed along with a large number of men; in Bedford's words, 'The moste vengeance fell upon the proud Scottes, for thei went to Dog-wash the same day, mo than 1700 of cote Armoures of these proude Scottes.'[10] In his account of the battle, Bower recorded how it was said that 'it was the vain arrogance and reckless haste of the Scots which was the reason for their fall and ruin'. Buchan, Douglas and his son were laid to rest in the cathedral of Saint Gatien in Tours.[11] Scotland did not send another large contingent of troops to serve in the French cause but the survivors of the Buchan period stayed on, to fight, when the time came, behind Joan of Arc at the relief of Orleans and in other battles. In February 1429 Sir John Stewart of Darnley led an attack on a wagon convoy of lentils and herring, bound for Orleans as food for Lent, under the command of Sir John Fastolf, only to be beaten off with high losses; among the dead lay Darnley himself. As we have almost come to expect, Scots appear in unexpected places: the bishop in Orleans at this time was a Master John Kirkmichael.

Perhaps the most well-known body of Scots in French service made their appearance in this time. A small number of the Scots soldiers remaining in the country were chosen to form the French monarch's *Garde Ecossais*.[12] This elite corps of men-at-arms and archers was to remain in being until the revolution in 1789, although long before that fateful event its composition had changed and the Scottish connection had become no more than a proud memory. Throughout the fifteenth and sixteenth centuries, however, Scots emigrated to France to serve in the Garde. Among them was Patrick de Spens, who was sent to France in 1450 by James II. Documents surviving in French archives for the period from 1460 to 1488 provide us with the names of some of these men when they were granted *lettres de naturalité*; they include Jehan Chambre [John Chambers], Thomas Aigne, Jehan Nesbet, Guillaume Brun, Guillaume Tournebulle and Patris Mourra [Murray?].[13] In 1574, one of the Garde, Charles Crawfurde, visited Scotland and on his return through England the Privy Council gave an assurance that he would not carry any letters concerning Mary, Queen of Scots or any other person rebelling against James VI.[14] The Garde was a privileged body, with special access to the monarch's presence, and many of its members, all gentlemen, founded noble families.

Scots also continued to serve France in a more routine military capacity. This was such a common activity that in *Ane Satyre of the Thrie Estaitis*, written in 1552, Sir David Lindsay has the character of the parson say when he has to seek a new living:

> The Devill mak cair for this unhappie chance,
> For I am young, and thinks to pas to France
> And tak wages amang the men of weir,
> And win my living with my sword and speir.

There were some Scots at the Battle of Pavia in 1525, when the French army of Francis I was almost wiped out by the forces of the Habsburg emperor, Charles V, while besieging this small town 20 miles from Milan. In January 1558 a man called Gordon fought in the

Siege of Calais when the Duke of Guise finally ousted the English from that town. Gordon 'behaved himselff valiantly and was the cheiff instrument of winning the town, having lost one of his legs in that service', a sacrifice that earned him the governorship of the newly liberated port; the Gordon historians were keen to claim anyone with a likely name as one of their own but, as in the case of the archer who fatally wounded Richard at Chaluz, it is highly possible he was not a Scot.[15] Scotland raised forces in December 1552 to join the French army of Henri II, continuing his father's war against Charles V. The Privy Council extended the levy to include 400 horsemen from the Borders and the Lowlands, and men from Huntly territory in the North-East. Gilbert Kennedy, Earl of Cassilis, was appointed lieu-tenant-general, with Patrick Lord Ruthven as 'Coronet of the fut-men'.[16] In that year Henri made a treaty with German Protestant princes in return for France's possession of the bishoprics of Metz, Toul and Verdun. The battlelines that would split Europe and dominate its politics a generation later were being drawn. In a cruelly ironic development, Henri met his end in a tournament held as part of the wedding celebrations of his daughter to the King of Spain in 1559, when he was struck and mortally injured by the lance of the captain of his *Garde Ecossais*, Gabriel, Count de Montgomery.

'*mony zoung and valzeand men*'

Sweden, Estonia, 1573

*I*N 1523 UNION among the Nordic nations came to an end when the ambitious Gustav Vasa broke away to establish his own independent rule in Sweden. He turned his fractious realm into an autocratic state with himself as monarch at the helm, imposing a more efficient tax system, confiscating the properties of the Catholic Church, encouraging Lutheranism, killing or locking up any serious objectors and making himself the first member of a hereditary monarchy (he had been elected). He liked to compare himself to Moses, as a liberator and leader, and in his old age a long, forked beard and a drooping moustache gave his face the look of a Biblical prophet. Ten years after he split from Denmark, he supported Christian III in the latter's successful bid for the Danish throne, and in the process broke the power of the mercantile Hanseatic League that until then had held Baltic trade in its grip. The downfall of the league, with its headquarters in Lübeck, opened the Baltic to merchants from other countries. Gustav's son and heir, Erik XIV, turned his attention to trade with Russia and the territories on the eastern shore of the Baltic. The Estonian nobles accepted Swedish rule in 1561, a development that sent shock waves through Denmark, Poland and the rump of the Hanseatic League, as it promised prosperity and power to the Swedes, who now had greater access to trade in major commodities: grain, iron and copper, timber and furs.

War erupted between Sweden and her neighbours in 1563, the so-called Northern Seven Years War. A few Scots had already found their way into Danish military service in the first decades of the sixteenth century: for example, in a letter dated 9 January 1507, the Bishop of Linköping refers to the Danish king expecting 'a powerfully efficient force from Scotland'.[1] There were also foreign elements in the Swedish forces, mostly German but also Scots. The king of Denmark, Frederick II, whose daughter was to marry James VI, wrote to Mary, Queen of Scots at the beginning of September 1564 to ask for more Scots mercenaries, to the number of 2,000, for service in the Baltic, and to complain about Scots in Swedish service.[2] One of the Scots in Frederick's employ is mentioned by name in a letter to Mary in March 1567; the Danish king asks for Colonel John Clark, 'ministri et capitanei nostri', to be allowed to stay in his service. Also at around this time, Mary's estranged husband, the Earl of Bothwell, enters the picture. Early in 1567, Bothwell fled from Scotland via Orkney and Shetland, where he tried piracy for a spell, to Norway, and then ended up in Denmark. Some of Bothwell's friends enlisted John Clark in schemes to aid the fugitive earl, a conspiracy that resulted in Clark's imprisonment. In July 1570 the Scottish government asked Denmark to send Bothwell home and sought to clear Clark from suspicion. Bothwell was to die in exile in a Danish jail in 1578.

The Privy Council permitted a Captain David Moncur, with a company of men, to join the King of Denmark's army in September 1568.[3] Others went to serve Sweden and in August 1572 the Earl of Mar, then regent during James VI's minority, wrote to Frederick about four men who had been in Swedish service but were now prisoners of war in Denmark: Thomas Henryson, Joannes Strang, Jacobus Logan and Walterus Morisoune, as their names are given in the Latin used in diplomacy.[4] Captain David Moncur was in London in 1572. On 4 October that year, the Scottish Privy Council was threatening to outlaw a mercenary called Alexander Patersoun, who had returned from Denmark with other 'men of weir . . . quhair they had servit under wages'. Patersoun was accused of leaving Captain Moncur penniless and in prison in London after he, Patersoun, had promised to go to Dundee to fetch £100 of Moncur's own money to relieve the latter's debts and, apparently, had not kept his word.[5]

Most Scots on the Swedish side in the Northern Seven Years War went there in 1563 after Erik XIV sought to recruit 2,000 men, seamen as well as soldiers. Among them were a William Cahun or

Kahun and William Ruthven, whom we shall meet again. Cahun belonged to the Colquhoun family of Luss and, in 1565, with his brother Hugh, brought a troop of cavalry to Sweden, where they saw action at the Battle of Axtorna, a clash in which the Swedes were decisively beaten by German mercenaries in Danish service. Cahun's horsemen were obviously highly regarded; in 1568 they are recorded as being the most highly paid in the army. Ruthven's father, Patrick, had played a leading role in the murder of Mary's hapless Italian secretary Riccio and had fled beyond the Scottish border to die in Newcastle. William had also been involved in this plot, a strong incentive for him later to seek service abroad. In a harbinger of things to come, the Scots had difficulty in extracting pay from the Swedish treasury. Some of them signed a letter of complaint for Ruthven to carry to Erik in May 1566, lamenting they had had to borrow mounts because of 'the horses that were killed in the late battles and leaving us without our pay for the last three months'.[6] There were similar complaints about being paid in base coin, and about captains having to advance money to their men. The signatories on these documents have typical Scots surnames: Stuart, Wallace, Fullerton, Young, Greig and so on. In 1564 the Swedes captured the fortress of Varberg on the west coast. The Scottish troops in the garrison were taken prisoner and given the opportunity to switch sides to the service of Sweden. At last, in 1570, after seven years of fighting that had wrought havoc across the southern part of Sweden, peace was signed between the combatants at Stettin. The fighting and the swingeing terms of the treaty exhausted Sweden's treasury, and the people had also suffered from the depredations of the military. There was no longer any need to maintain foreign fighters and in December 1570 John III, who had deposed his brother Erik from the Swedish throne in 1568 on charges of madness, told Sir Andrew (Anders) Keith and other officers to pay off their men with two months' salary. An illegitimate son of the Abbot of Deer and a nephew of the fourth earl marischal, Keith had come to Sweden as captain of a troop of cavalry and, like William Cahun, was loyal to John; both had backed John and his younger brother Duke Karl in the coup against Erik and both, therefore, enjoyed respected positions in the Swedish court.

Sweden's expansion eastward into Estonia in 1561 brought her up against the territory of the Russian emperor, Ivan IV, more commonly known to us as Ivan the Terrible. The Russians had pushed their presence by 1558 as far west as Narva – still the frontier between Estonia and Russia today – making conflict between them and the Swedes inevitable, especially as Ivan, who had maintained friendly relations with Erik, and John III loathed each other. After the capture of Narva the Russians also acquired control over parts of Livonia, an advance that each of the Baltic powers – Sweden, Denmark and Poland – perceived as a threat to their interests. Ivan's troops made some probing forays into Estonia in 1571 before John decided on full-scale retaliation, with a campaign to capture Narva itself. For this, he needed troops but was unable to find them among his own subjects, exhausted and unwilling after the war with Denmark to contemplate any military adventure, and had to resort once again to the employment of mercenaries.

Meanwhile, William Ruthven had returned to Scotland and had set about restoring the family's fortunes, dashed low by the Riccio plot. In June 1571, now as the fourth Lord Ruthven, he was granted the post of lord treasurer of Scotland for life. Having ridden the wave of the Protestant Reformation back into prominence, the Ruthvens wasted little time in making the most of their opportunities. In September 1571, William's younger brother, Archibald, received an annual pension of 300 merks from the forfeited bishopric of Moray. In the following year he travelled to Sweden, armed with a letter of introduction to the king from his brother. At the end of the year, King John entertained Archibald in his castle at Vadstena on the shore of Lake Vättern and gave him a commission to recruit men to fight for Sweden.[7]

The Privy Council in Holyrood at the time was trying to regulate the flow of Scots going abroad to serve in foreign wars, fearing their activities would threaten international relations with Scotland, complicating the governance of the realm at a time when the young King James was still in his formative years. On the same day, 4 June 1573, as they warned of capital punishment for anyone who raised or carried abroad unlicensed mercenaries, they granted Archibald Ruthven leave to recruit 1,600 'wageit men of weare' for Sweden. Archibald agreed to recruit in stages, raising and shipping 200 at a time. He was also instructed not to take anyone already in the king's service or more than 500 'culveringis hagbuttis – or uther handgunnis morreonis nor corslettis', weapons and armour which he was told he had to bring back in the following year.

As his second in command Archibald had Gilbert Balfour, a member of another family that had managed to come through the intrigues of the time with its power intact. Balfour, who was some fifteen years older than Archibald and therefore more experienced in arms as well as in survival, had been a master of the queen's household and possibly an accomplice in the murder of the queen's husband Darnley. In 1566 he had been appointed sheriff of Orkney, a position in which he refused any help to Bothwell when he was on the run, and in January 1573 he and his brother had been granted a pardon for various misdeeds in return for a profession of faith and promise to protect the Protestant Reformation.

Archibald may have already recruited a number of men while waiting for the Privy Council to grant the licence, as he and Balfour had joined the forces that captured Edinburgh Castle from the supporters of Mary in May 1573, an assault that could have served as a useful training exercise. Most of the common soldiers taken prisoner from the castle are said to have enlisted in Dutch service but it is possible that Archibald Ruthven and Balfour snatched a few for Sweden. Possibly at William Ruthven's behest, the regent, the Earl of Morton, wrote on 10 June to John III to apologise for the delay in sending him men. The first consignment of mercenaries for Sweden sailed before the end of the month: 'In this mene tyme, mony zoung and valzeand men past of this realme to Swadene', noted the *Diurnal of Occurrents* on the 23rd.

King John's intention was for Ruthven's contingents to land at Älvsborg, Sweden's only toehold on the Kattegat, then march across his kingdom and embark again for Estonia on ships that would be waiting at Söderköping and Norrköping. The prospect of around one and a half thousand armed Scots tramping through the realm was enough to give any monarch pause and, to give him his due, John took some steps to control the situation. He urged his officials to keep the mercenaries on a tight rein, not to allow them into the west-coast fortresses and not to billet them on the peasantry, but he neglected one crucial factor – that of payment. John would have been alarmed to learn, also, that Archibald Ruthven had exceeded his commission and had brought with him not 1,600 men but possibly close to 3,500, including significant numbers of cavalry as well as foot sloggers. The royal treasury was still almost bare. The first skippers who brought the Scots to Älvsborg accepted quantities of butter in lieu of cash and the local governor of the fortress of Gullborg had to reimburse later shipmen from his own pocket. Seamen could always be expected to find a market somewhere to redeem dairy produce but mercenaries could not be paid off in this way. John hurriedly tried to scrape together funds from taxes and loans, and sent Anders Keith to greet and escort his fellow countrymen. Keith, William Moncrieff, heir to the Moncrieff lands back home, and William Cahun had meanwhile been busy raising troops of cavalry inside Sweden for the Estonian campaign, recruiting Scots already in the country. Keith was a good choice for the role of liaison officer in the present circumstances but he had to resort to unusual measures to cope with the lack of royal resources, for example, pawning a gold chain to pay off debts in Älvsborg.

In the wake of the contingents of Scots in their march across country came a stream of petitions and complaints, as the disgruntled, touchy mercenaries, unpaid and badly provisioned, helped themselves to corn, cattle, sheep, hens and geese. The surviving records for two dozen parishes in Uppland, north of Stockholm, tell how Scots also stole silver and clothing. To top off this catalogue of crime, the skippers who carried the Scots to Estonia would come back with lists of damaged and pilfered gear. King John urged his senior commander, the sixty-year-old French mercenary Pontus de la Gardie, to ship out his troublesome soldiery as fast as possible but, before this happened at the end of October, other problems had begun to brew, whose import was not to reveal itself until much later. De la Gardie suggested to Ruthven and some of his senior colleagues, perhaps as a means of avoiding conflict over conditions and pay, that they might find better service in Poland, but nothing came of this. Around 21 October Hugh Cahun, the younger brother of William Cahun, was arrested for accusing his fellow officers of conspiring against King John and, although there were doubts about his guilt, he was beheaded. Not only was there dissension within the Scottish camp but the Scots had also become implicated in the domestic intrigues of Sweden.

At last Ruthven's men arrived in Estonia, in the port and trading centre of Reval – now Tallinn – and joined the Swedish and German mercenary forces already there. The town, built on a hill beside the sea and with a population approaching five thousand, could boast that its church of St Olav had one of the tallest steeples in the world. The Swedish field commander, Klas Åkesson Tott, had been warned to keep an eye on the mercenaries and, for example, to ensure garrison duties were entrusted only to loyal Swedes. Balthasar Rüssow, the Lutheran pastor of the church of the Holy Spirit, noted that the Scots behaved themselves as long as they had money. Unfortunately cash was not always to be had – the demands of unpaid German cavalry were satisfied at one point by giving them possession of three castles.

John was keen for the campaign to capture Nöteborg, on the south-west corner of Lake Ladoga, and Narva to get underway. The first frosts and snows of winter would soon render the tracks and forests impassable, and the first ice would begin to seal off the sea routes. Narva lay around 125 miles to the east, a distance the Swedish army would take days to cover even if the weather stayed favourable.

At first the situation of the Scots showed some improvement. They had been issued with two months' pay before sailing from Sweden and provisions had come their way during November and December. Apart from Ruthven and a headquarters staff of forty, the Scots infantry contingent at this time comprised almost 2,500 men, divided into seven unequal *fanor* or companies under officers named Robertt Moray, David Spaldingh, Gilbert Wacop, Jören Michael, Hans Hansson (John Johnson?), Jacob Schrimpzen (Scrymgeour), and Hew Lauder. There were also a few Scots serving in the Finnish cavalry and, of course, several hundred in the cavalry troops led by Ruthven himself and Moncrieff. Another Scot with the forces was Jacob (James) Neff or Nevay (the surname is variously spelt), who probably came from Angus. The Lutheran priest Balthasar Rüssow was disturbed to find the Scots taking over a house for Calvinist worship but took comfort in the fact that the language barrier prevented many of his flock from understanding this dangerous doctrine. Presumably the soldiers were accommodated in some kind of barracks while the officers would have been quartered in private houses. Initially the men were provided with a varied diet of fish, grain and fresh and salted meat. It was later noted that the Scots soldiers did not like the unfamiliar black ryebread and exchanged or sold it for white or wheaten bread. Their officers received white bread in accordance with their higher status. Ruthven later accused the German mercenaries of preventing the Scots from using mills to process the raw grain issued to them, arguing that this led to the deaths of two hundred in the first two months, a charge that was strongly denied by the Swedish commanders. The deaths are more likely to have resulted from infectious disease. As winter tightened its grip on the encampments, supplies began to run low. The Scots turned to asking the inhabitants of Reval for food and, when that failed to be productive, to stealing. Foraging parties, roaming through the snowy countryside to lift cattle and grain from the peasants and local landholders, fell to attacking each other, and in the taverns drinking bouts led to quarrels and fights. Discipline and morale were breaking down rapidly, despite the efforts of the senior commanders to keep order.

Before control ebbed away, the decision was taken to begin action against the enemy, beginning with a march and assault on the fortress of Wesenberg (now Rakvere), halfway to Narva. The army departed from a relieved Reval at the beginning of January, the Scots reluctantly going along after initially refusing to budge until they were paid. After some ten days, the unhappy army reached Wesenberg, a large hilltop castle with pale grey walls, and began a siege. Two attempts to storm the walls before the end of the month failed, and the assault settled down into a kind of stalemate, another stasis likely to breed discontent. Pontus de la Gardie had special worries of his own. He had discovered that Gilbert Balfour and some other Scottish officers had been planning to desert because they feared losing control over their followers and not being able to lead into battle as many men as they had contracted for, in which case their honour would be besmirched. De la Gardie wrote to King John with this disturbing news, making it clear that he considered Ruthven to have had no part in the officers' plot, and locked up Balfour and his friends in the castle at Reval. Ruthven now revealed information about a further, much more serious plot in which Balfour had been at least dabbling, one to overthrow King John and bring his deposed brother Erik back to the throne. The prime mover in this conspiracy was said to be Carolus de Mornay, like de la Gardie a French adventurer who had risen to some prestige and wealth in Sweden, first in Erik's service and then in John's. Perhaps the execution of Hugh Cahun had been a canny move by de Mornay to divert attention from his own machinations.

A third, more considered plan to capture Wesenberg was implemented in February. The Swedish forces tried to dig under the walls
and deploy fire to weaken the defences before launching an all-out
assault to storm the fortress. It failed and the attackers reeled back
with heavy losses. Tott, the Swedish commander, blamed the failure
on the Scots, who, he claimed, were slow in pressing the attack, a
charge Ruthven denied with vehemence. De la Gardie was more
considered in his analysis of the reverse, ascribing it to a combination
of factors that included reluctance among the Swedes and Germans, a
shortage of powder and shot, superior enemy numbers and the winter
weather impeding the foot soldiers. To occupy his forces and combat
crumbling morale, the general led an expedition against a fortress at
Tolsburg on the coast, but this too was repulsed and the troops fell to
ravaging the surrounding district, in Rüssow's words, like Russians
and Tatars. Disaffection in the Swedish army was now widespread.
The Germans and Scots were deeply embittered, the former accusing
the latter of having received pay meant for them, although neither of
the contingents had received anything since the beginning of the year.
On 17 March a fight erupted between the mercenaries. Either an ale-
house brawl or the murder of a Scot by some Germans was the spark
but, whatever the cause, the conflagration spread disastrously. To the
peril of their own lives, Ruthven and other senior officers intervened
in vain to prevent the fighting; James Nevay is said to have rescued
the severely wounded Ruthven. The Scots turned artillery on the
Germans, who reacted to what may have been a dangerous bluff by
launching a cavalry charge that cut their former colleagues to pieces.
Handfuls of them – the best estimates point to 70 men – fled to
surrender to the Russian enemy in Wesenberg while their comrades
fell under the German blades and lances. The one-sided nature of the
clash leaps out from the reported casualties – 1,500 Scots and only 30
Germans. The campaign had now unravelled in bloody confusion
and, on 25 March, Tott ordered a withdrawal to Reval.

The news of the debacle angered John. He called for the mercenaries to be dismissed and Ruthven, Balfour and Moncrieff to be sent
to Stockholm under guard. The last mentioned reached Swedish soil
first, leading a troop of cavalry the long way home through Finland.
Moncrieff was not suspected of conspiracy but, in case his starving

followers caused trouble – they too had not been paid – they were confined to an island near the Swedish capital to lick their wounds and recuperate from their long ride.[8] Once they were back in Stockholm, Ruthven and Balfour were closely interrogated. They both denied any involvement in a plot to overthrow John but Balfour admitted that de Mornay had mentioned the existence of the conspiracy to him when they had met in Älvsborg at the start of the campaign. About de Mornay's own guilt there was no doubt, and he knelt before the axe in the market in Stockholm on 4 September. It was accepted that Ruthven was innocent of conspiracy but he was charged with failure to reveal what he knew and with being instrumental in the Wesenberg debacle. He countered the accusations by saying he had learned of the de Mornay conspiracy only after reaching Reval, when he had informed de la Gardie of what he knew, and by pinning blame for Wesenberg on the Germans and general mishandling of the campaign. The Swedes were uncertain how to deal with him and placed him under house arrest in Västerås Castle on the north shore of Lake Mälaren. Balfour, whose guilt was less obscure, was shut up in Stegeborg. In March 1576 he was accused of plotting to escape and he was eventually executed in Stockholm on 6 August.

The Swedes had to mend diplomatic fences with Scotland, who made appeals for the release of the prisoners, but Ruthven was never freed and eventually died in February 1578 in Västerås. Anders Keith continued his successful career in Sweden, becoming the commander of Vadstena Castle in 1574 and an envoy to Elizabeth of England in 1583. In 1584 James VI awarded him the title of Lord Dingwall – he had already been ennobled in Sweden – and later appointed him as an envoy to the Danish court, where one of his tasks concerned the marriage negotiations between James VI and Christian IV's sister. James Nevay also rose to a prominent position in Sweden and became a provincial governor. A few of the five hundred or so surviving Scots soldiers chose to stay in Sweden, in the hope of receiving some belated payment or finding a new service, and some were still in the country in 1575, after which a few more may have been sent home, with the remainder melting into Swedish society. The seventy or so who fled into the hands of the Russians at Wesenberg perhaps had a stranger fate, as we will see in Chapter 6.[9]

'university of war'

The Low Countries, 1572–1618

FAMINE WAS STALKING Scotland in 1572 and on 21 June in that gloomy summer the Privy Council conceded that with 'the present hunger, derth and scarcitie of viveris' any able-bodied man who wished could go to the Low Countries to join the struggle of the people there against Spanish rule.[1] In the low-lying provinces around the Zuider Zee there was a cause to be fought for, a cause that arose from the dynastic and religious politics of the period. The political map of Europe at the beginning of the seventeenth century was dominated by the sprawl of the Holy Roman Empire, a patchwork of territories varying greatly in size, wealth and importance. Since 1438 the title of emperor had been more or less continuously borne by a member of the Habsburg family. When King Charles I of Spain became the Emperor Charles V in 1519, this dynasty of Swiss origin – the name derives from Habichtsburg, the Fort of the Goshawk, the original stronghold of the family – had authority over lands from the Atlantic almost to the Russian steppe, and from the Alps north to the Baltic. In 1556 Charles abdicated the throne of the western Habsburg realms in Spain in favour of his son, who inherited the crown as Philip II, the ruler of the largest power in Europe, and two years later bequeathed the Holy Roman Empire to his brother, Ferdinand. Between Habsburg Spain and the Empire lay the rival state of France, ruled since 1589 by Henri IV, the founder of the Bourbon dynasty. For some time France had been expanding eastward at the expense of the Empire; the bishoprics of Metz, Toul and Verdun passed to France in 1558, but the present French territories of Alsace,

Franche-Comté, and Lorraine on the west bank of the Rhine were still within the Empire.

France's northern frontier abutted the Spanish Netherlands, the lands that now comprise the Netherlands and Belgium. Links between them and the east coast of Scotland were already well established through trade, and the Scottish merchants had their base, or staple, in the town of Veere on the island of Zeeland at the mouth of the Scheldt. It is here in 1570 that we come across Henry or Hary Balfour as an officer in charge of a hundred men.[2] His precise origins are unclear and he may have been a younger son of Bartholomew Balfour of Mackareston in Menteith or related to the Balfours of Pitcullo in Fife, the county that was home to a large proportion of the Scots involved in traffic with the Low Countries. One of his kinsmen may have been the Sir Henry de Balfour, 'a Scottish gentleman of prudence and experience in warfare', to whom on 18 June 1561 Prince William of Orange had issued a commission to arm a ship and raise a crew to attack William's enemies on the Iberian coast. The commission stipulated that subjects of the Protestant monarchs around the North Sea were not to be harmed, a typical indication of the religious divide of the times. Luther's reformation had found fertile soil in the northern provinces of the Low Countries and Calvinism had arrived in the 1550s. Over the next twenty years large numbers of the Dutch adopted this austere faith, thus strengthening the ties of religion with Scotland. Large areas of the southern part of the Spanish Netherlands remained loyal to the Church of Rome but Protestantism flourished to such an extent in the north that Philip II expressed fears that it might spread to overwhelm the Catholic Church in the south as well. To counteract the threat, he established new bishoprics, set up an inquisition and implemented the burning of both Lutheran literature and martyrs. The Low Countries were not only of obvious strategic importance to the Habsburgs in their wars with France; they were also rich and a valuable source of taxation. From the Dutch viewpoint, religious and fiscal grievances combined to fuel a growing impetus to revolt.

Habsburg rule in the Low Countries in the 1560s was implemented through Philip's regent, his half-sister Margaret of Parma. On 5 April 1566 some two hundred nobles forced their way into her presence with a petition to get rid of the inquisition and relax persecution of Protestants. Margaret felt forced to agree to their demands, a triumph that led to a burst of over-zealous iconoclasm among some Protestants. Churches across the land were sacked – in Antwerp no fewer than forty-two were robbed of their valuables and artworks – and Margaret had to call out her troops to restore order. Soon her soldiers were joined by the 10,000-strong army of Fernando Alvarez de Toledo, Duke of Alva. To this sixty-year-old veteran, Protestants were heretics and no accommodation with them was permissible. Alva pushed Margaret aside as ruler and set up his Council of Blood, inaugurating a reign of terror in which at least a thousand perceived enemies of the Church of Rome were arrested and executed while many thousands more sought safety in Germany and England.

As the duke's iron rule hardened the pro-independence feelings of the Dutch, the rebel movement found its leader in the person of William the Silent, Prince of Orange, stadholder, or governor, of the provinces of Holland, Zeeland and Utrecht. Alva had William's eldest son snatched from university and taken off to Spain to be raised as a good Catholic. In May 1568 an army of Protestant rebels under the command of Count Louis of Nassau, William's brother, won a victory at Heiligerlee in the north of the country but was defeated two months later by Alva's troops. On land William was able to do little more than annoy Alva but sea-going rebels, who had nicknamed themselves the Sea Beggars, had a greater impact and on 1 April 1572 seized the port of Brill (now Brielle). The larger harbour and town at Flushing (now Vlissingen) fell to them a few days later, encouraging fishermen in Veere to rise on their own account to take command of the town. The people in the then small village of Rotterdam tried to emulate them but were crushed by the Spanish. Rebels hurried from the German lands to capture the town of Zutphen and Count Louis led his army south to take the Habsburg fortress of Mons on the French border. As Alva went after Louis, town after town across the Low Countries fell into Protestant hands.

Alva's siege of Mons began on 3 June. Louis held out until the 19 September, by which time news of the St Bartholomew's Day massacre in Paris had eliminated any hope of aid from France and he surrendered the city to Spanish control. Alva then unleashed his soldiers on the town of Mechelen, where a large number of the inhabitants were slaughtered. Other towns began to surrender before the Spanish war machine and, as the Dutch revolt was snuffed out in centre after centre across the Low Countries, a despondent William retreated, first to Gelderland and then to Holland. The Spanish massacred people in Zutphen and at the beginning of December killed almost all the inhabitants of Naarden, only a few escaping to stagger across the snow with their terrible news. Across the North Sea the atrocities aroused outrage and, in response, into this violent, fluid situation, along with mercenaries from other lands, came the Scots; at some point, Henry Balfour was appointed to the command of some of them.

Alva turned his eyes on the city of Haarlem. One of the main towns in the province of Holland, Haarlem had a population of some 14,000 people; only Amsterdam was bigger. Its main industry centred on the brewing and shipping of beer, although by the late 1500s output had shrunk to one third of the level of forty years before. To the south stretched a great lake, the Haarlemmermeer, formed by centuries of peat cutting, and other bodies of water connected the city to the Zuider Zee to the east. The people decided to resist Alva: confident in their cause, they also knew from the examples of Mechelen, Zutphen and Naarden what they could expect if they surrendered.

'Upon the eleventh of December the Spanish armie came before Harlem,' wrote the English historian Edward Grimeston, 'being five and thirtie companies of Spaniards, two and twentie of Wallons . . . eighteene companies of high Dutches . . . and eight hundred horse, everie day more coming unto them with Ordnance.'[3] For the first week, while some of his patrols fought skirmishes with the defenders, the Spanish troops, under the command of Alva's son, laboured on trenchworks and brought up the big guns. The daytime bombardment threw cannonballs of 40 and 45 pounds' weight at the defences, smashing sections of the walls and ramparts, and during the hours of darkness the Haarlemers threw themselves into making good the breaches with bales of stone, earth and even wool. There were some Scots among the troops fighting to defend Haarlem but very little is known about them. One, John Cuningham by name, was in command of the defenders' artillery.

Meanwhile William had moved his forces to a village to the south, a base from which he sent in supplies and companies of reinforcements, 'both Wallons, French, English, and Scots . . . in all fifteene companies, besides foure Dutch . . .' In the bitter Dutch winter the ice of the Haarlemmermeer provided William with a route to the gates of the town. At the end of January, Henry Balfour led a force of Scots among 400 men who struggled across the frozen landscape, dragging sledges laden with munitions and food. This lifeline route enabled the defenders to continue to defy the Spanish and gave them the wherewithal and courage regularly to sally out to harass the attackers and maintain defending fire. John Cuningham plied his guns with skill and 'won great honour in the towne' for blasting down some Spanish works in half a day; 'The Spaniards would haue repaired it,' recorded Grimeston, 'and planted some ordnance thereupon, but Coningham still ruined it.' When the ice melted on the lakes and marshes in late February, boats could be launched on the Haarlemmermeer to continue the victualling of the city. In the middle of April, Balfour led a party in a night attack on the garrison of German mercenaries in the village of Russenburch. Driving the Germans out of a watermill, Balfour's men chased them until they reached the Spanish trenches, where they took advantage of the element of surprise to do some plundering before they returned to the Haarlem walls with their spoil.

The city finally fell to the enemy in June, after a stand that had dented Spain's reputation as Europe's strongest military power. Many, possibly most, of the foreign troops in the defence were put to death in the weeks that followed, the gentlemen being granted the dubious courtesy of despatch by sword while the rank and file were garrotted or drowned. This atrocity took the lives of around five hundred officers and two thousand men. On 11 August 'all the English and Scottish were beheaded. And to fill up this sea of bloud, all the wounded and sicke were beheaded before the hospitall doore.' Balfour, however, escaped this fate by agreeing to act in a plot to assassinate the Prince of Orange. It was an empty promise given under duress to save his life but later he was said to have been filled with remorse over it. He never attempted to threaten the prince but tried to expunge the guilt from his conscience by fighting bravely for the Protestant cause, and he eventually died in action.

We know of at least one other Scot who escaped death on this occasion. Bearing the unusual name of Cornellis (possibly he had been born in the Netherlands to a mixed marriage), he appears at the siege of Alkmaar, imposed by the Spanish soon after the fall of Haarlem. Described as having been an ensign bearer in the latter town, Cornellis distinguished himself in the fighting at Alkmaar: 'he slew above twenty with his owne hand, the which did free them from the jealousie which they had before of him', an unusual phrase whose exact meaning is unclear but which may refer to suspicions as to exactly how Cornellis had managed to survive the Haarlem massacres.[4]

The Dutch wars were tightly fought, complex struggles of manoeuvre, siege and skirmish in a relatively small arena. Each village, town or city was a strongpoint, rising like an island within its circling walls and ditches from a pastoral, partially flooded, flat landscape. Troops were usually dispersed as garrisons throughout the region, and strongpoints changed hands without always fitting a discernible strategic pattern. 'In Leyden was Monsieur de Lorges, son to that brave Earle of Montgomerie with a goodly French regiment, and other companies of Scots', noted Grimeston for August 1573, '. . . In Rotterdam were some companies of Scots . . . At Delft haven . . . sundrie bands both of French, Scottish, and of the countrey'. During 1573 several contingents of Scots sailed across the North Sea to join the struggle, after reports of what had befallen at Haarlem raised a howl for vengeance against the Spanish. The Privy Council gave permission to Captain Thomas Robesoun in June to raise 300 men for this 'defence of Goddis trew religioun', and in July to Captains John Adamson and the evocatively named Diones Pentland.[5] The latter was illiterate, and in the Privy Council minutes it is noted how he adopted the standard procedure in such an instance, 'with my hand at the pen led be the notar underwrittin at my command'. In August Captain Robert Montgomery came over with 1,000 cavalry and 2,000 foot soldiers, and another 1,600 men arrived in Holland and Zeeland in October. A spy noticed Scots disembarking at Flushing on 8 September and reported to his masters in Bruges that they numbered 500; another 300 had landed at Veere, not far away. This agent did not know the name of the mercenaries' leader but described him as '*ung homme de belle taille avec la barbe quelque peu rossette'*. It has been suggested that this figure was a Colonel Andrew Ormiston.[6] Ormiston, if he was the man of good height with a reddish beard, did not serve long in the Low Countries; in the following April he was killed by Henry Balfour in a duel, an act for which the hardy Balfour was pardoned and promoted to Ormiston's rank. The Scots were now in strong alliance with the Dutch and there were rumours that ties might be strengthened by the marriage of James VI, then a boy nine years old, to a daughter of the Prince of Orange. In the event, James was to find a wife elsewhere in Europe, a wedding that also had implications for Scottish mercenaries.

In October 1573 the Spanish began to besiege the city of Leiden with the intention of starving it into submission. The beleagured city was subjected to a two-phase ordeal. In the first six months Alva's forces threw up a ring of fortresses around the walls before unexpectedly withdrawing. It was a false dawn. The Leideners enjoyed only a short respite before the enemy returned and the siege once more tightened around them. As the autumn came on, food began to run out, plague and other diseases appeared in the city, and the burgers began to quarrel among themselves. 'In the richest houses horse-flesh was as delicate as a Partridge', noted one observer. Dogs and cats were roasted, all manner of weeds were added to the soup pot, a woman in childbirth was rationed to one pound of biscuit per day and starving men dropped dead on guard duty. Once again the peculiar nature of the Dutch landscape saved the day. The Prince of Orange ordered dykes to be opened to flood all the low country, a heavy decision that would put much fertile land out of use for a long time but one that broke the Spanish noose. Flat-bottomed boats were now able to sail with supplies to Leiden. Once again Henry Balfour with his companies of Scots played their part in harassing the Spanish: 'During the siege . . . certaine [Spanish] troops lodged about Bomell, Gorcom and Louestein, to make some attempt: but all places were so well fortified with good garrisons (and Colonell Balfour lying thereabouts with seven companies of Scots, to crosse their designes, by cutting off ditches, and other stratgems) as they could not effect anything.'[7]

The Scots suffered serious losses amounting to half their numbers in the late summer of 1575 when a Spanish campaign took in quick succession the towns of Oudewater and Schoonhoven and the island of Schouwen. In each place the resident garrisons were captured, killed or driven out, the capture of Oudewater in particular being attended *'avec tel massacre et effusion de sang que dédans ne resterent que vingt hommes en vie'* – with such massacre and spilling of blood that inside there remained no more than twenty men alive.[8] More reinforcements from Scotland and England landed at Brill in January 1576 and joined a long campaign to relieve the siege of Zierikzee. Later that year, in November, the Spanish forces attacked and 'desolated' Antwerp, only a few days before the provinces of the Low Countries signed the Pacification of Ghent, a diplomatic initiative to promote unity in the struggle for independence. One result was that the British mercenaries, formerly in the employ of the individual provinces of Zeeland or Holland, now were in the service of the States General, the unifying central governing body. The Spanish at first reluctantly accepted the settlement. For a few days it looked as if the war was over, and the Prince of Orange wrote to Regent Morton to thank him for the help received from the Scots and to pay tribute to Henry Balfour. It was not long, however, before both sides in the conflict began to break the terms of the pacification: Spanish troops moved back to provinces they had been asked to quit, and Calvinists tried to extend their influence in areas where Catholicism was predominant.

In January 1577, Henry Balfour was in command of Scots garrisoning the province of Limburg in the south-east when they encountered a troop of hostile Spanish near the River Meuse close to Jupil. The 1,500 Spanish horsemen, unaware of the strength of the Scottish force, attacked but were repulsed with considerable losses and forced to flee into Maastricht. Some deputies from Amsterdam, a city still loyal to Spain, fell into Scottish hands. On 11 May 1577 Henry Balfour was paid £6,000 Artois by the States General for his services and shortly afterwards sailed home to Scotland. Before long, however, as political tensions grew in the Low Countries, Balfour received a letter asking him to return. On 10 October he informed the Privy Council that he had been offered a commission appointing him 'as Colunnel ower certane cumpanyis of futemen of this natioun under his regiment'. The commission, dated in Brussels on 8 September, offered Balfour £500 with lesser amounts for his officers – £200 for his lieutenant, £100 for the sergeant-major, £40 for the quartermaster and so on down to £16 for each of the halberdiers. The Dutch also asked him to recruit men, and the Privy Council, in view of the good relations between the countries and the honourable way previous mercenaries had been treated, gave leave to 'stryke drummis, display handsenzeis [ensigns], and lift and collect the saidis cumpaneis of futemen'.[9] The council allowed Balfour and his captains each to recruit 'twa hundrieth wageit men of weir'. In all, fourteen companies were raised in Scotland that autumn and were shipped across to land in Zeeland at the end of November. Within a few days they were heading south-east towards action.

In January they were in the army of the States General at Namur with the prospect of a pitched battle with the Spanish. On the last day of January, as the army was withdrawing towards Gembloux, the Spanish commander Alessandro Farnese, Duke of Parma, spotted that his enemy was in a vulnerable, extended position passing through boggy ground and took the opportunity to send in his cavalry. The horsemen smashed into the rear of the States force and drove on into the main body, spreading panic forward through the ranks, shattering the withdrawal into a rout. The Scots put up a brave but futile resistance and suffered heavy losses, Balfour himself being wounded. One commentator noted: '*La plus grand tuerie se fit des Escossois et autres qui y estoient de la parti des Etats de Hollande et Zealande*' – the biggest killing happened to the Scots and others from Holland and Zeeland.[10] There is uncertainty over how the Spanish treated their prisoners: one report says most were thrown from the bridge at Namur to drown, another that they were hung and another that they were liberated. In the wake of this victory, a number of towns surrendered to the Spanish and one, Louvain, turned away its Scots garrison.

The States set about raising more forces and Scotland once again sent some recruits, including a Colonel William Stewart with a regiment of his countrymen who turned up from the Baltic. This Stewart had served Holland before and had since been in the service of Danzig against the King of Poland, but a commission from the

Prince of Orange to join 300 men 'of his own nation' had been an offer he had been unable to refuse. In July the armies faced each other again, this time at Rymenant near Mechelen. The States occupied a strong position with the English and Scots out in front under the command of an English colonel, John Norris. The Scots, under the command of William Stewart, had arrived only an hour before after a long march. Several observers also noted that during the long, hot day that was to follow many of the Scots and other soldiers undressed and fought in their shirts, which they tucked between their legs. As the Spanish attacked the van fell back, pausing to fire volleys between withdrawals. In this way they drew on the enemy, leading them against the entrenched main army of the States. Here the Spanish tried again and again to break through until, after eight hours, their commander, Don John of Austria, the illegitimate brother of the King of Spain, finally called the whole bloody affair off. The Spanish casualties numbered 1,000. A few days later the States rubbed salt into Don John's hurt when a combined Scots-French force, with Balfour sharing the command, captured the town of Aarschot only 2 miles from the Habsburg camp.

During December and January many of the provinces in the Low Countries reached an agreement at Utrecht in which they swore to uphold the struggle against Spanish rule. The first signatories were all from the northern part of the region and, although the cities of Antwerp, Breda, Ghent, Bruges and Ypres were later to join, the agreement, known as the Union of Utrecht, became in time the foundation of the new state of the United Provinces of the Netherlands, or the Dutch Republic. The southern provinces were to follow a diverging political course that, with some allowance for later boundary shifts, became the modern nation of Belgium. While this lull in fighting held, the States General allowed the pay of their foreign troops to fall into arrears. By March the aggrieved Scots and English mercenaries were resorting to thievery. The city of Bois-le-Duc (now 's-Hertogenbosch) refused to allow foreign soldiers through their gates, with the consequence that its defences suffered and the Spanish were able to regain it. The discontent among the soldiery must, however, have remained within bounds and, when Parma advanced on Antwerp on 2 March, the Scots and their colleagues showed no hesitation in attempting to hold up the Spanish at the village of Borgerhout. After two hours of skirmishing the defenders fell back behind the burning village to Antwerp's walls but their defiance had served its purpose and Parma, apparently reluctant to assault the city, switched his attention to the east to besiege Maastricht. The latter city, on the Meuse, had a garrison of 1,000 men – including French, Walloons and Scots – and, with the help of the burgesses and the peasantry, they held out for four months. Soon after the fall of Maastricht, many of the southern provinces, with the exception of parts of Brabant and Flanders, became reconciled to Spanish rule, further cementing the division created by the Union of Utrecht.

The struggle between the Habsburgs and the States for control of the Low Countries settled into a pattern of manoeuvre; towns were taken and lost as the campaigning forces shifted through the country-side. Henry Balfour was chosen to command an attack in October 1579 to seize the garrisoned village of Menen. The troops were guided by a disaffected brewer who had escaped from a Menen jail and had fled to Bruges with information on how his home town might be seized. In the darkness of the October night, the brewer guided Balfour up to the Menen ramparts. At the same time other troops approached the town from another direction in boats, and the resulting simultaneous assault scared the garrison into fleeing, abandoning to the attackers the spoil they had collected. Balfour fulfilled his pledge of loyalty to the Prince of Orange with his life in November 1580. While leading a company of cavalry from Bruges to attack the village of Wassenaar, he was killed in a skirmish with the enemy. 'He was much lamented, for the good services he had done in Flanders', noted Grimeston, who added, 'Neither died he poor'. In November 1575, in gratitude for his services, Holland had awarded Balfour a lifetime annual pension of 800 florins of 20 stivers a piece. He was given an honourable burial in Bruges, where his widow, Christian Cant, continued to stay and later married Captain John Balfour from Wester Pitcorthie.

Balfour had clearly been in a position to accrue some wealth but many of his countrymen were less fortunate. In March 1581 the discontented Scots garrisoning Vilvoorde, north-east of Brussels, mutinied for want of pay and drove out their commander, a Colonel

Stuart, before they were talked into accepting their lot. Similar trouble occurred elsewhere. Courtrai fell into Parma's hands again in February 1581. At the end of November, Tournai surrendered, despite a gallant drive by cavalrymen, under a Scots colonel called Preston, who cut their way through the siege lines into the town, taking thirty prisoners with them in the process but only adding to the mouths to be fed. This war of move and counter-move continued for several years more. Sometimes a town fell by subterfuge or treachery. For example, in August 1582, Captain William Semple and his brother allowed the enemy to gain the strongly defended town of Lier, a betrayal that has been ascribed to Semple's desire for revenge on the States General, possibly for arrears of pay. Semple's motives may, however, have been more complicated, and he may provide another example of a mercenary torn by conscience. A son, probably illegitimate, of the third Lord Semple of Lochwinnoch, he was a Catholic, and maintaining opposition to the Spanish cause must have troubled him, a conclusion reinforced by his later activities.[11] After the Reformation a few Catholic Scots had kept up links with Habsburg Europe – in the early sixteenth century Spain had looked on Scotland as a potential ally against England – and there were Scots on both sides in the Dutch conflict. Colonel David Boyd commanded twelve companies in Parma's army in 1584; John, the eighth Lord Forbes, also served under the duke.[12] In January 1584 Protestants in Bruges called on the Scots colonel of the garrison to assist them in the seizing of the Catholic nobleman the Prince of Chimay to pre-empt a Catholic move to gain control of the city; the colonel, whose name Grimeston gives as Boyde, probably the David Boyd mentioned above, betrayed the plan to Chimay, who had his enemies promptly arrested. Many Protestants left Bruges to find safer quarters in Sluys and Ostend, and Chimay was able in the following weeks to conclude an agreement with Parma. The Scottish garrison was presented with a choice: in the words of Grimeston, clearly loyal to the Protestant cause, 'to retyre, or to continue in the king of Spaine his service, of the which few remained: and although that colonel Boyde did soon find how little the Prince of Parma did esteeme him, yet he durst not trust the Estates.'

Gradually Flanders was falling into Parma's lap. Another blow was struck against the Dutch desire for independence when, on 10 July 1584, their leader, Prince William of Orange, was murdered by an

assassin. On the same day as William fell to a bullet, the Spanish
launched strong attacks against two forts on the Scheldt downstream
from Antwerp. One fell but the other, Lillo, held out. When the
attackers pushed up four pieces of artillery along the narrow crest of a
dyke, four companies of Scots under the command of Colonel
Barthold Balfour, the half-brother of the late Henry Balfour, fought
their way out from Lillo and seized them. Balfour's men also captured
the Spaniard's principal sapper, who revealed where the besiegers had
placed the mines intended to blow up the defences.

At this time Spain was watching closely the plight of Mary, Queen
of Scots, a prisoner of her cousin Elizabeth, which put pressure on
Philip II, the most powerful Catholic monarch in Europe, to act to
save her. Some senior Spanish commanders even entertained notions
of crossing the Channel to rescue Mary and restore the Catholic
Church in the British Isles. The fall of Antwerp to Parma's troops in
August 1585 alarmed Elizabeth and her advisers, and English troops
were sent to garrison the ports of Brill and Flushing to keep them out
of Spain's grasp. English mercenaries had been fighting on the Dutch
side for some time but now their presence was given greater state
recognition. Robert Dudley, Earl of Leicester, was appointed captain-
general of the English, a posting that angered the experienced English
mercenary leader, Sir John Norris, who left the Low Countries for
home. Leicester also annoyed his Dutch allies. Barthold Balfour and
the Scots also found the earl to be *odieux* and were glad when he went
back to England, returning command of the Dutch forces to Maurice
of Nassau, son of the assassinated Prince William.[13]

English Catholics, like many of their Scots counterparts, juggled
with their consciences, torn between loyalty to their monarch and
adherence to their religious beliefs. English Catholic troops, posted by
Leicester to defend Deventer and Zutphen, thought better of their
situation and opened the gates of these towns to the enemy. William
Semple was the centre of a group of Catholics working to further their
cause in Scotland – a group in which the sixth Earl of Huntly was
prominent. One of their aims was to secure arms and men to land in
Scotland to overthrow the Protestant regime – there was a plot to
smuggle in weapons hidden in shipments of grain – and Semple was
in Dundee in the spring of 1588; when the Armada was making its

attempt on England, he escaped and returned to the Spanish Netherlands. Parma may have had eight companies of Scots in the force assembled to invade England in 1588 as soon as the Armada gained control of the Channel and came to carry it across to Kent. These men possibly belonged to a Scots regiment, 'de Paton', in Parma's forces, whose commander was the same Colonel Aristotle Patton who, burning with anger over Leicester's threat to have him replaced, handed the Flemish town of Gueldres to the Spanish in July 1587. Once he had reached a secret agreement with the Spanish, Patton told the burgers he was supposed to defend that he had been instructed to keep his men ready to engage on a night-time foray, an enterprise in which horsemen were expected to join them. The townspeople suspected nothing until the mounted Spanish troops were already among them; they tried to defend themselves but to no purpose and had to pay a ransom. Patton received for his treachery 36,000 florins as well as payments from the richest burgers, and used his new-won wealth to impress a poor widow of noble birth, a suit he pressed successfully despite the rivalry of another nobleman and the fact that the widow's late husband had fought on the Dutch side. In the summer of 1587, in anticipation of the Armada's arrival, Parma moved to capture the coastal towns of Ostend and Sluys. A year later, however, the Armada, with the English fleet snapping at its heels, failed to keep the rendezvous. Deprived of the glory of invading England and faced with feeding his large army in a countryside already wasted by months of warfare, Parma unleashed his forces on Flanders again and in November 1588 laid siege to the town of Bergen-op-Zoom. Barthold Balfour, with 500 picked men, half of them Scots, attacked the besieging force in synchrony with a sortie from Bergen itself. Parma broke off the siege.

In January 1586 the States General appealed to Captain J. Balfour, presumably the John Balfour of Wester Pitcorthie who had married Cristian Cant after she had been widowed by the death of Henry Balfour, and others to have patience with regard to moneys owed to them. The prosecution of the war was understandably costing the Dutch authorities large sums and they continually looked for ways of spreading the burden. In September 1586 the Amsterdam authorities were asked to find payment for 150 newly arrived Scots: the amounts concerned varied from 1 florin for the captain down to 3 patars per day for the private soldiers. In December 1587 a colonel's salary was fixed at 400 guilders. Some at least of the Scottish captains had protested to the Scottish court over lack of pay because, in August 1588, at the time the Armada was lumbering northward through the North Sea on the long road back to Spain, James VI sent a herald to the States General to discuss debts owed to, among others, a Colonel Stuart. The outstanding amount was 500,000 guilders. Failure to settle, warned James, would give him no choice but to allow Colonel Stuart and his colleagues to take action to pay themselves, nothing less than a threat to plunder. The Dutch pointed out they were liable only for payments when the officers were in the service of their own particular provinces – obviously Stuart and the others had sold their services to more than just Holland and Zeeland – and protested that it was unusual for a prince to chase old debts in a time of war rather than wait for peace when everything could be settled. The States also called on Elizabeth of England to support their case and in the end James recalled the letters in which he had given the aggrieved Scottish officers leave to collect their pay by force. In the wake of this dispute, the States reviewed the methods for payment of troops, dismissing companies they could not afford, asking officers to promise not to pursue debts as long as the war continued, making soldiers swear to accept regular payment on the basis of a 48-day month – the officers were sweetened by being assigned a 32-day month – and farming out garrisons according to the different districts' ability to support them.

The war in the Low Countries dragged on for many years, with bursts of violence punctuated by periods of stasis, especially in the freezing winters. Gradually, however, the Dutch cleared the Spanish from a great arc of territory along what are now the present land frontiers of the Netherlands. For example, in the summer of 1591, Maurice of Nassau, in command of the Dutch forces, launched a new offensive against Parma. He made a feint towards Bois-le-Duc but changed direction by sailing up the Rhine to Arnhem and then down the Yssel. The towns of Zutphen and Deventer, important centres on the eastern fringe of the Low Countries, fell quickly into Dutch hands. Parma made a fruitless foray north from Brabant to curtail Maurice, and then had to abandon Nijmegen after further Dutch success. In the following year Barthold Balfour's regiment was sent with Dutch troops to assist the French king, Henri IV, but, in 1593, Balfour was back fighting in Maurice's renewed campaign, at the siege of Geer-truidenberg. In October that year he was wounded in the foot in a skirmish with troops retreating to Groningen, and not long after, perhaps as a consequence of the wound, he retired from command and his place was taken by Colonel Alexander Murray.

Scots feature frequently in the annals of the war. In March 1594 Brogh and Egger, two captains from the Scottish regiment, took part in an abortive operation to seize Maastricht by clandestine penetration of the defences in boats. Egger was killed two years later at the defence of Hulst. Colonel Murray met his end at the siege of Bommel on the Isle of Voorn when he was struck in the head during an artillery barrage: *'C'était un fort habile homme et qui avoit acquis beacoup d'honneur par ses services'*, noted one epitaph – he was a very capable man who had accrued much honour through his service.[14]

One of the more colourful Scots to put in an appearance in the Low Countries in the 1590s was Francis Stewart, Earl of Bothwell. The nephew of the Bothwell who had married Mary, Queen of Scots, and who had died in a Danish prison in 1578, Francis had been Mary's godson and was named after her first husband, the Dauphin of France. His life was every bit as fraught with intrigue as that of his more famous forebear. In April 1591, accused of consorting with witches in an effort to foretell the date of James VI's death, he was flung into Edinburgh Castle but escaped some two months later and hung about the capital, eluding any attempts to catch him and becoming involved in an abortive plot to seize the king. Finally, in 1594, after the failure of another scheme to grab James, he fled beyond the reach of the law, first to England and then to Orkney and Caithness. Two months after being excommunicated by the Church of Scotland, he slipped away to France. Here he outstayed his welcome by breaking the royal rule against duelling and carried on to Spain. At some point he converted to Catholicism and threw in his lot with Philip's forces, trying his luck as a soldier of fortune. In 1599 his attempt to persuade the Pope and Philip III to give him command of all the English and Scots in the Spanish army fell on deaf ears. In the same year he turned up at Brussels and conceived a plot to secure

Nijmegen for Spain. Strategically located at the head of the great delta of the Rhine, Nijmegen had been taken by the Dutch in 1591 and at the time of Bothwell's plot was garrisoned by four companies of Scots under the command of a Captain Masterton. Bothwell may have been over-confident, as Masterton had been a member of the Bothwell faction back in Scotland. Despite the past association, the captain remained loyal to his paymasters and had the two agents Bothwell sent along, with 3,000 crowns as a bribe, arrested. This vain ploy may have been Bothwell's only contribution to the Dutch wars as, not long after this, he ended up in Naples, where he managed barely to support himself by feats of arms and fortune-telling and died, suspected of necromancy, in 1612.

Taking advantage of the war between France and Spain to distract the latter's full attention, the Dutch secured in the 1590s all the territory north of the Rhine. In the summer of 1600, at the urging of the States General, Maurice of Nassau led his army into Flanders. At the end of June they passed Bruges. Although they let it be known that they would not spoil the country and tried to encourage the Flemish to rise with them against Spanish rule, they found that they were generally not welcomed. Peasants retired before their approach and left little for forage but, despite the resulting privation, Maurice forbade mistreatment of civilians. They laid siege to the fort of Albert, within cannon shot of the fishing and trading centre of Nieuwpoort, and planned how they might take two more strongholds at Ostend, a few miles to the east. The ultimate target was Dunkirk, home to pirates who menaced Dutch trade. Meanwhile the Spanish, under Archduke Albert of Austria, advanced quickly westward to retake towns that had fallen into Dutch hands and pin Maurice's forces against the sea. The Spanish dealt in bloody fashion with some Dutch garrisons. Some who escaped the slaughter brought the news of the enemy threat to Maurice who, when he learned of his predicament, was 'half a league' to the west of Nieuwpoort and in danger of being cut off.[15] So far in the war the Dutch had failed to win an outright pitched battle but now, on the beach and among the North Sea sand dunes, they had no choice but to confront what everyone at the time regarded as the most powerful land army in Europe. They had also been taken by surprise. For some time the morale and effectiveness of the Spanish army, which like the Dutch included many mercenary troops, had been undermined to the point of mutiny by grievances over pay and poor supplies, but the Dutch advance into Flanders had stirred them to remember their duty and now Archduke Albert was riding into battle before almost 10,000 men.

During a night-time conference with his senior staff, Maurice took the decision to despatch men under the command of his cousin, Ernest of Nassau, to hold the Leffinghe bridge east of the town and stop the enemy advance. One of the officers hurrying through the dawn on 2 July to halt the Spanish, with the sound of the North Sea within earshot, was William Edmond or Edmund, a Scot who had gone abroad like so many others early in his life to seek fortune. He had been in Dutch service for some years as a cavalry officer and had earned a reputation for courage and skill in a series of engagements, before being promoted to colonel. At the end of January 1599 he had led a force of horse and foot into Limbourg and Luxembourg, after these areas had defaulted on payments promised to the United Provinces government, and had come back with horses, booty and hostages. Now, Edmond was leading twelve companies of Scots, approximately half of Ernest's army, the rest of which comprised a Zeeland regiment, four companies of cavalry and two cannon. His aim was to prevent the Spanish crossing the only bridge leading to Nieuwpoort, giving Maurice time to move the rest of his men and to allow ships the opportunity to escape to sea. When the Dutch reached Leffinghe, they found the van of Albert's attackers already across the bridge in strength too great to be overcome. Ernest lost his two guns and had to make a rapid fighting withdrawal. Eight hundred men on the Dutch side fell, including almost all the Scots, the last of them dying in the North Sea surf. Anyone captured was murdered later in cold blood.[16] Seven Scots and three Zeeland officers were killed but among the few who managed to gain the safety of Fort Albert was Edmond. The action had, however, delayed the Spanish enough to allow Maurice time to form his army up for battle on the east side of the River Yser. On the left flank of the Dutch advance guard that day was a mixed force under the command of Sir Francis Vere that included two English regiments. For the rest of the day the archduke's forces tried to break through the lines of defenders strung between him and the town. The Dutch success was hailed as an astonishing feat of arms: the first time the mighty Spanish war machine had been brought to a standstill in a head-to-head contest. On the day after the struggle, the Scots murdered some forty prisoners in revenge for the slaughter of their fellows by the Spanish. There is a story that Edmond himself refused an offer of ten dozen crowns from a captured Spanish nobleman and instead ran him through.

The Dutch abandoned any effort to hold on to Niuewpoort but remained in Ostend, the low-lying fishing port that now became the focus of the struggle. Most of the 3,000 fishermen shifted to Veere and, when the siege began, early in July 1601, only around 250 households remained in the town. At low water the harbour almost dried out, but a channel recently cut to the east and named the Gullet provided an alternative haven for vessels; otherwise large ships could enter only at high tide. The sea provided the defenders with a ready supply route, as well as a highway for the evacuation of non-combatants. It also presented the besiegers with problems: during spring tides salt water could penetrate inland around Ostend for a considerable distance. The government of the United Provinces, had funded the building of walls around Ostend and twice in the 1580s the town had resisted capture.

Archduke Albert opened his attempt to reduce Ostend by deploying regiments of foot on the east side, a move greeted with cannon fire from the defenders. The latter were a very diverse bunch – men of many nationalities, prepared for a long fight – and from time to time their numbers were augmented by shiploads of reinforcements. One such in August brought in four companies of Scots. The siege lasted for an astonishing three years and eighty days, becoming a symbol of the Dutch struggle to overthrow Spanish rule. Its fame attracted tourists to view the fortifications and the proliferating siege works, and military men came to this 'university of war' to gain some insight into the latest developments in their profession.[17] One bulwark on the north side of the town was given the name Schottenberg, the Scottish Fortress; described as 'neere unto a Sand-hill', it boasted two cannon. The names of a few Scots appear in the records of the siege, among them William Edmond's, when he was sent to the town in January 1602, and a Captain Sinclair.[18] The Spanish gradually whittled away at the defences, most progress being made after September 1603 when Ambrosia Spinola assumed command. Winter storms also played their part in wrecking the fortifications. The long, bloody attrition forced the defenders into a smaller and smaller area, with even the bodies of the dead being used to restore ramparts. Ostend became less crucial to the Dutch after Maurice captured Sluys in August 1604 and, in the following month, the States General gave the exhausted Ostend garrison permission to yield. An accord was reached with the Spanish that enabled the surviving companies, with English and Scots forming the rearguard, to march out from the ruined shambles behind flags and drums, all honour intact.

While the eyes of the western world had watched with fascinated horror the struggle by the North Sea, actions had been fought elsewhere in the Low Countries. A detachment of 200 Scots under Count Louis of Nassau forayed 100 miles through hostile territory as far as the Ardennes in 1602, and Scots were also present at the capture of Grave in the same year. Recruiting continued in Scotland: in March 1602 the Privy Council granted permission for the levying of some 400 to 500 men for the Low Countries, with the proviso that it be done quietly, without drumming.[19] Some of Edmond's cavalry took part in the effort to resist the Spanish crossing of the Waal into Betuwe in July 1606. Later that summer Edmond was in action against Spinola's forces at the latter's attempt to besiege Rheinberg and it was here on 3 September that the Scottish officer received a fatal head wound. When the Rheinberg garrison surrendered on 12 October and marched out they carried Edmond's body with them.

At last, in 1609 the Spanish and the Dutch reached a truce that was to last for the next twelve years. Men from every part of western Europe had fought in the struggle that was now over. It is difficult to determine precisely how many Scots were involved but a review of the numbers mentioned in the various recruiting warrants issued by the Privy Council points to a total of around 5,000. The Dutch wars served as a bloody laboratory for innovation in warfare and the Scots who gained experience of the latest weapons and techniques among the flooded fields and villages of the Netherlands were soon to find plenty of opportunity for their use elsewhere on the continent.

SIX

---◆◆✕◆◆---

'a Company of pedeling knaves'
The Baltic, Russia, 1570–1618

*I*N THE SIXTEENTH century the destination of choice for
Scots emigrants was the south-eastern shore of the Baltic and its
hinterland, especially Prussia and Poland.[1] The Scots came as individuals and in families, as merchants and pedlars, perhaps as many
as 40,000, to the northern province of Prussia. Spreading out from the
Baltic ports of Stettin (now Szczecin) and Danzig (now Gdansk) they
became familiar figures in the Polish countryside and further afield,
welcomed for their goods but also disliked for their acumen; in
Bohemia and Moravia they were called *šoti*, and its derivative *šotek*
entered folklore as an imp or little devil. Over 120 Scots became
burgesses of Danzig between 1531 – when Thomas Gilzet from
Dundee enters the records – and 1710, when John Farquhar's name
appears. Scottish names are also common in the records of baptisms,
marriages and burials. Several were members of the Guild of Merchants in Königsberg (now Kaliningrad). They were ubiquitous
enough for someone to assert during a parliamentary debate in
Westminster in 1606 on the possibility of a union with Scotland that
'If we admit them . . . we shall be overrun with them . . . witness the
multiplicities of the Scots in Polonia.'[2] In 1610, Thomas Chamberlayne wrote that 'these Scotts for the most parte are height landers
men of noe credit, a Company of pedeling knaves', suggesting many
were Highlanders or at least from the north of Scotland.[3] Not all the
emigrants were favourably disposed to their fellow countrymen: Scots
at Danzig appealed to James VI in 1624 to curb the emigration as the
'exorbitant numberis of young boyis and maidis . . . transported hier

yierlie . . . ar burdenable to ws.[4] The emigrants were attracted to what was at the time one of the most powerful, prosperous regions of Europe. In July 1569 Poland and Lithuania forged from an existing union a commonwealth (Polish *rzeczpospolita* from the Latin *res publica*) under one king, Sigismund II Augustus, and one parliament, the bicameral Seym. The boundaries of this polity sprawled from the valley of the Oder in the west as far as Kiev on the Dnieper and from Vilnius south towards the Black Sea, and pushed against the Russian lands.

When Sigismund II Augustus died in 1572, the Poles elected Henri of Valois to be their king but two years later he went back to France from Cracow to become Henri III when his brother, Charles IX, died. In 1576 the Commonwealth gentry, comprising the lower house of the Sejm, elected Stefan Batory, Duke of Transylvania, to the throne. The senate, however, held out for another candidate, the Holy Roman Emperor Maximilien II, and Batory had to resort to arms to win his crown. The burgers of the port of Danzig also opposed Batory's election, refused to take the oath of allegiance to him and appealed for help from the King of Denmark. First, Batory tried to cow the Danzigers into submission by cutting off trade with them and declaring them rebels but, in return, they defied him by plundering and burning the Cistercian abbey of Oliwa to the west of the city. In the autumn of 1576, Batory's troops cut a swathe through the countryside around Danzig, isolating the rebels from their hinterland and leaving them surrounded. As was usual in European warfare, the winter brought a break in campaigning. The need to provide food for horses and men in the cold months, and the difficulty of travel through a frozen, snow-bound landscape, forced troops into winter quarters. The Polish forces, now under the command of Batory's chancellor, Hetman Jan Zborowski, set up their main base at Tczew on the west bank of the Vistula, 35 kilometres south of Danzig, with other bases in a loop from Marienburg (now Malbork) around to Puck on the coast.

Danzig at the time was the largest city in Poland. Situated on fertile ground by the Motlawa River to the west of the marshes and lagoons of the Vistula delta, it had grown fat on its trade. By the mid 1500s, its population had swelled to around 40,000, and flotillas of boats and

rafts brought to its granaries and wharves great cargoes from the
Vistula hinterland – mostly rye but also significant quantities of wheat
and barley, timber, potash, dyes, tar, hides and minerals. A thousand
ships came and went in a year, bringing grain and other raw materials
to western Europe and sailing home with salt, herring, wine, woollens,
paper, spices and glass. One of the city's suburbs was called Stary
Szkoty, 'Old Scotland'; it had 102 houses at the end of the sixteenth
century and contributed around 1,000 zlotys annually to the church.[5]
Also famed for its religious tolerance, Danzig was nicknamed the
granary of Europe and attracted artists, craftsmen and merchants,
who created streets lined with wonderful buildings. When confrontation with Stefan Batory looked likely to burst into open war, the city
had enough wealth to raise an army of 10,000, augmenting its own
volunteers with mercenaries. The Danzigers enlisted the services of a
German mercenary leader, Hans Wickelbruch Yon Koln, who, in
April, when the mud of the spring thaw permitted movement, went
on the offensive. At the head of a mixed force of Landsknechts –
German mercenary infantry – and town militia, with some artillery, he
struck south to cross the River Motlawa to attack Tzcew. At the same
time, he sent a small force up the Vistula in a fleet of boats. Although
outnumbered by a considerable margin, Zborowski skilfully deployed
his forces and took advantage of there being only two places where
troops could cross the swollen Motlawa. In the main battle, on 17
April, named after the nearby village of Lubieszow, the Polish cavalry
and infantry smashed Wickelbruch's forces, killing over 4,000 and
capturing most of the rest for the loss of only 58 dead on their own
side. Despite this success, Zborowski had too few men to mount a
fresh attack on Danzig and had to wait until Stefan Batory joined him
with fresh troops in the summer.[6]

Danzig used the lull to recruit more foreign soldiers. Among them
was Captain William Rentoun, who, in July 1577, was licensed by the
Privy Council in Edinburgh to raise 150 men for 'the service of the
citie and commoun wealth of Danskin'.[7] Rentoun and his men joined
Scots already there to make the contingent up to some seven hundred,
most of whom had come from the Low Countries under the
command of Colonel William Stewart, son of an Ayrshire laird.
The other officers were named as Robert Gourlay, William Moncrieff,

John Crawford, John Tomson, John Dollachy, and Alexander Morra (Murray). Both Murray and Moncrieff were moved to protest at the tardiness in payment of their wages. Moncrieff's letter reads, in translation from German, 'after offering you my very willing and humble services I beg to draw your attention to the fact that I have . . . brought all the men under my standard from the Netherlands at my own expense . . . I have thus laid out in food, conveyance and other expenses more than six hundred thaler, by which I was compelled to pawn my best clothes at [Elsinore]'.[8] The canny book-keepers of Danzig wanted all expenses to be itemised in writing, to which Moncrieff swore he kept no account books. Presumably the complainants were later satisfied. The Danzig authorities later paid tribute to the Scots: 'They have done so much noble service that they have got great fame for their country in these parts.' In one clash, Robert Gourlay was wounded but was unable in his armour to make a leap to safety in a boat and perished; his body was laid to rest in the city's Marienkirche with full military honours in the summer of 1577. A measure of the effectiveness of Batory's blockade was seen in the fact that only 150 ships sailed from Danzig that year, but, with strong support from Denmark, the city was able to launch a seaborne attack on Elblag, the town across the delta that Batory had begun to promote as a rival commercial centre. The citizens of Elblag repulsed their neighbours' assault. The conflict ground down into a stalemate, where neither side could achieve outright victory, and both were willing to settle a peace by the autumn. The experience at Danzig left the Polish king with an appreciation of the Scots' pugnacity. One of his officers noted how the Scots pedlars would abandon or sell their trading premises to pick up arms, adding: 'they are infantry of unusual quality, although they look shabby to us . . . 2,000 Scots are better than 6,000 of our own infantry'.[9] Batory thought them better soldiers than the Germans and brought some into his own army, now that he had another enemy to fight – Muscovy.

Ivan the Terrible was continuing his campaign to gain control of Livonia. The Swedes gave Batory some half-hearted assistance in his first attempt to turn back the Russians, but it was not until the summer of 1579 that the Polish king was able to mount the first of three successful campaigns to drive between Muscovy and the Baltic coast. By the end of August 1579, the town of Polotsk (now Polack in Belarus) was in Polish hands and, after a winter spent in Vilnius, Batory's army, now numbering 29,000, attacked again, penetrating east to Velikije Luki and Smolensk. Moscow now lay less than 250 miles away but a shortage of resources persuaded Batory to forego a thrust to the east and turn his attention instead to the fortified stronghold of Pskov. Scots were present at the siege and blockade that followed and, through the grim winter of 1581/82, suffered along with the rest of the Polish army. Batory's campaign convinced the ageing Ivan the Terrible to sue for peace. By the time a treaty was signed in 1582 the eastern frontier of Lithuania and the Commonwealth extended almost to Polotsk.

In Moscow in this period was an Englishman, Jerome Horsey, who worked for some years as a trusted servant of the Muscovy Company, a group of English adventurers who were trying to open up trade with the little-known country beyond the Baltic. In his account of his experiences, Horsey noted how Ivan's army 'ranged farr into the Swethians [Swedes] country, and did much spoil and rapine; brought many captives awaye to remote places in his land, Liefflanders, French, Scotts, Dutchmen and some English'.[10] Horsey did not supply his narrative with many dates, although we know he was in Russia from 1572 until 1585. In Moscow he saw the captives from Ivan's expeditions to the west; 'Piteous to behold', he wrote, 'among other nacions, there wear fower score and five pore Scots souldiers leaft of 700 sent from Stockhollme, and three Englishmen in their company, brought amonge other captives, in most miserable manner.' These were possibly the men who had fled into Russian hands to escape being slaughtered at Wesenberg in 1573, although they could have been captured elsewhere at various times. Horsey used all the authority he could muster to do something for the prisoners, probably putting himself to some risk, as Ivan was often in no mood to contemplate pleas for compassion. The young ruler, whom Horsey had described as 'comely in person, indued with great witt, excelent gifts and graces', had become in his old age suspicious, superstitious and cruel. Ivan did not hesitate to torture and kill Swedish prisoners. The enterprising merchant-cum-diplomat, however, managed to ex-plain to the unpredictable tsar that the Scots came from a different place and ought not to be treated as Swedes, indeed they might be of use alive. Horsey's argument, as he recorded it himself, made clear that 'They [the Scots] wear a nacion [of] strangers, remote, a venturous and warlicke people, readie to serve any Christian prince for maintenance and paye; as they would appear and prove, if it pleased his majestie to imploie and spare them such maintenance now owt of hart and cloths and arms, as they may shew themselves and valure against his mortall enemy the Cryme Tartor.'

The imprecations were successful. The Scots and English captives were allowed to settle outside Moscow and build their own church. Horsey provided some money and even a minister to tend to their spiritual needs, and soon their suspicious neighbours came to accept their presence. They were permitted to marry the reputably fair women of Livonia. At this time in western Europe the city on the Moscow River was mysterious and distant, seen as a place inhabited by an uncivilised race, many days' travel beyond forests and swamps and beset with cruelly cold winters; 'The whole countrie . . . lyeth under snow . . . The rivers and other waters are all frosen up a yarde or more thicke . . . from the beginning of November till towardes the ende of March . . . So that it would breede a frost in a man to looke abroad at that time', wrote Giles Fletcher, the English envoy, in 1588.[11] The heart of Ivan's realm was the fortress of the Kremlin, half-hidden behind red stone walls on its hills above the Moscow River. A second wall, this time white-washed, enclosed both the Kremlin and the neighbouring Kitaigorod, predominantly the merchants' quarter – a huddle of wooden buildings and narrow lanes – and beyond that were the beginnings of Belgorod, literally the white city, a ring of settlement with palaces and more elegant, spacious avenues. The ignorance of western Europeans about Moscow was matched by the Russians' own distrust of foreigners. Isolated by geography and by the Orthodox Church these feelings easily spilled into xenophobia, although, since the place had been captured by the khan of the Crimean Tatars in 1571, and would be attacked again by these warriors from the south in 1591, the Russian fear of foreigners was not altogether unjustified.

Horsey was not acting entirely from altruism, as he feared that if Ivan discovered the true identity of the three Englishmen among the prisoners he might use them to put pressure on the merchant company. The outcome was, however, the same. Those of the captives fit to serve in the Russian army were placed in a Scots contingent under command of one of their number, whose name Horsey records as Jeamy Lingett. 'Pore snakes afore, loke nowe chearfully', wrote Horsey. 'Twelve hundred of them did better service against the Tartor then 12 thowsand Russes, with their shortt bowe and arrowes.' At the time Ivan married his seventh wife in 1580, Horsey noted he had two armies; one, which was mostly Tatar, ranged against Poland and Sweden in the west, and the other 'consisting comonly of 100 thowsand horss, most of his naturall subjects, saving some few Pollaks, Swethians, Duch and Scotts emploied against his great enimye the Crim Tartor'.

Jeamy Lingett and his fellows were, however, not the only Scots to appear in arms in the Russian lands beyond the Baltic. One of the Carmichaels of Hyndford in the Borders had been in command of a force of 5,000 Russian troops in 1570 in the Northern War, and later became the governor of Pskov. A few years after he rescued the Moscow prisoners, Horsey learned of another Scot. This man's name was Gabriell Elphingsten and he had been captured after an expedition from England to explore the north-east passage to the Pacific had come to grief on the Siberian coast.[12] When Horsey met Elphingsten, he found that he was 'a valiant Scottish captaine, by the report of letters he brought to me from Coronell Steward, that served the King of Denmarke, in comendacion of him and six other Scotts, souldiers in his company'. On their arrival, after a long journey as prisoners through Siberia, the Scots were destitute. Horsey gave them 300 dollars, clothes, pistols and swords and through Elphingsten saw that they received further allowances. They 'Behaved themselves well for a tyme,' noted Horsey glumly, 'yet could not repaye nor recompence me to this day'.

Mercenaries from other parts of Europe also found their way to Moscow and by the end of the sixteenth century enough had settled there for a special district to be set aside for them on the fringe of the city. It acquired the name of Nemetskaya Sloboda, the 'dumb suburb', because none of the foreigners could speak Russian; *nemetskaya* came to mean foreigner and, in time, more specifically German.

Mercenaries were perceived as useful fighters against the Tatars but the Russians remained suspicious of their loyalty in service against European enemies. Giles Fletcher, Queen Elizabeth's ambassador to the tsar, observed the Russian army: 'Of mercenary souldiers that are strangers (whom they call nimschoy) they have at this time 4,300 of Polonians . . . of Doutches and Scots about 150: of Greekes, Turks, Danes and Sweadens, all in one band, an 100 or thereabouts.' Fletcher also noted that the regular infantry, called *streltsi*, numbered about 12,000 and all bore firearms; 5,000 were stationed in the Moscow area and the rest were spread in garrisons across the country. The soldier's salary was 7 roubles per year, with an allowance of rye and oats. 'The streltsey or footeman hath nothing but his piece in his hande, his striking hatchet at his backe, and his sworde by his side', wrote Fletcher, who did not think too highly of the soldiers' professional ability. 'The Russe trusteth rather to his number then to the value of his souldiers, or good ordering of his forces.' The ambassador acknowledged the skill of the mounted archers who, although they fought well against the Tatars, were ill-matched against the Poles, who were equipped with artillery. To such an army a corps of mercenaries brought welcome experience and needed skills.

Stefan Batory died suddenly in 1586 and plunged the Polish-Lithuanian Commonwealth once again into a contest over two candidates for the monarchy; this time the rivals were Sigismund Vasa and the Habsburg Archduke Maximilien of Austria. To force his suit, Maximilien led an army into southern Poland but he was first checked at Krakow in September 1587 and then, in January 1588, defeated in an outright battle at Byczyna by Commonwealth forces led by the chancellor, Jan Zamoyski. Maximilien had to endure the humiliation of being held prisoner in Poland until the Habsburgs abandoned their claim to the throne. Among the Scots in Zamoyski's army was a Thomas Buck, who was recommended by James VI to the Duke of Courland and also fought for Poland against Karl IX of Sweden. Buck lost an arm in the subsequent fighting but survived to return to Britain. In October 1614, Sigismund III of Poland received a letter from James VI in support of Buck's claim for payment: 'one who was prepared to pour out his life-blood in defence of your honour, after the great toils which he endured to an end, after the sufferings which he underwent, if he receives no gratitude, deserves at least from a liberal hand the pay which is actually his own', it reads.[13]

Sigismund Vasa's claim to the Polish throne stemmed from his mother, who came from the Polish Jagiellonian dynasty. As his name suggests, he was a member of the Swedish royal house, none other than the son of John III, who had launched the ill-fated campaign into Estonia in 1572 (Chapter 4). When John died in 1592, Sigismund as heir stood to unite the two nations of Sweden and Poland under one crown. Until he should return to his paternal home, Swedish government rested in the hands of his uncle, the regent, Duke Karl. One major obstacle stood in the way of Sigismund's ambition: he was a Catholic, a staunch one, and Sweden had embraced Lutheranism, a faith the new king gave no sign of tolerating. It is also likely that Karl had ambitions to hang on to power and used the religious division to further his own ends. When Sigismund landed at Stockholm with the fleet sent to bring him home, as the Swedes saw it, he seemed to give an offhand reply to Duke Karl's reminder to govern with a good conscience.[14] Sigismund resisted giving reassurances on religion until the eve of his coronation in 1594, a stubbornness the worried Swedes attributed to the malign influence of the papal legate and the Poles in the king's retinue. After his coronation Sigismund returned to the more congenial surroundings of Poland, leaving his uncle to govern a confused and uneasy country in his name. In 1598 Sigismund returned, landing at Kalmar with an army of 8,000 horse and foot. Interestingly Anders Keith and James Nevay, two of the Scots who had risen to prominence in Sweden, supported Sigismund as the rightful monarch; and among the latter's troops were several Scots, including an Abraham Young, the son of one of Queen Mary's courtiers who had settled in Danzig.

Confrontation between Karl and Sigismund was now inevitable. A clash between their forces at Stångebro gave victory to the duke. Finally, in July 1599, the Swedish parliament decided no longer to recognise Sigismund as king and the crown was offered to Karl. In time Karl's son, Gustavus Adolphus, would inherit the throne. Anders Keith was banished from Sweden and it is thought he went to Poland. James Nevay's fate was more tragic. His tenants in the province of Dalarna already hated him, probably for his harshness as a landlord, and an attempt on his life in 1596 had been thwarted only by the courageous intervention of a priest. Two years later, a mob of peasants threw him into a prison and murdered him.

Sigismund considered a second attempt to win Sweden and, in an effort to gain more support from the Commonwealth government, he granted to it in March 1600 the territory of Estonia. The Swedes were in no mood, of course, to tolerate such an illegal disposition of their territory and responded by invading Livonia. On this occasion the Sejm was prepared to back their king but it did not foresee that the conflict would last for the next nine years or, as some historians argue, with breaks, for the next sixty. At the beginning of the war the Polish general Jan Zamoyski had two Scottish company commanders, each in charge of 300 men: Alexander Ruthven and Abraham Young. Ruthven fell at the capture of Wolmar on 18 December 1601 but Young survived and was appointed leader of the Scots community in Poland in 1604. The first years of fighting saw the clearing of Swedish forces from most of Livonia but in 1605 the Swedes returned in strength. Duke Karl had now become Karl IX and his army of 12,000 included significant contingents of Dutch and Scots as well as large numbers of German mercenaries. Command of the Polish–Lithuanian forces, in size less than half the enemy, had now passed to Field Hetman Jan Karol Chodkiewicz, who had men enough only to form garrisons in important forts, with most stationed at Dorpat (now Tartu). On 12 August 4,000 mercenaries under Joachim Mansfeld, a German, landed at Dynemunt to begin a blockade of Riga. As the Germans manoeuvred their great guns towards Livonia's chief town, other Swedish forces came ashore against Reval, and on the last day of August Karl IX himself landed at Parnawa (now Pärnu) with 4,000 Swedes and Scots. Hampered by lack of men and resources, Chodkiewicz failed to prevent the three prongs of the Swedish attack from combining to begin a siege of Riga. He had, however, managed to gather some reinforcements and hurried west until, on 26 September, he reached the village of Kircholm (now Salaspils) about 10 miles south-east of Riga. The Swedish commanders decided to thwart the Polish attempt to relieve Riga by launching a surprise attack. Some 20,000 men toiled through the night and pouring rain to cover the distance to Kircholm but they failed to conceal their approach and, when daylight broke, the Swedes found Chodkowiecz's army ready and facing them from the other side of a shallow valley. Immediately to the south the church and houses of Kircholm crowned a small hill above the Dvina.

Karl deployed his troops in four lines, with seven blocks of infantry, or *tercios*, in the first rank, six in the third, and squadrons of cavalry forming the second and fourth ranks. The Polish forces comprised mostly their famous cavalry drawn up in three lines with two squadrons in reserve, and in the front rank stood the only infantry: two blocks with muskets. The Scots were most likely among this contingent. Neither side wanted to leave high ground to attack the other, and the stand-off lasted all morning until finally Chodkowiecz stretched Karl's patience too far. The Hetman ordered his arquebusiers to make an obvious and sudden withdrawal from the front line, a trick that convinced Karl the Poles were about to make a retreat and to which the Swedish king responded by ordering his infantry down the hill towards the enemy. The Poles opened fire when their attackers reached the bottom of the valley and then sent in their hussars at the gallop. The Swedish cavalry on the flanks of their foot were attacked at the same time by more Polish horsemen, a mixed force of hussars, reiters, Cossacks and Tatars. The Swedish wings collapsed in on their centre, adding to the confusion among the foot, and soon Karl's army abandoned the attack and sought to escape, chased back to Riga. They left some 6,000 of their comrades on the field, while Polish losses numbered only in the low hundreds.

Karl IX recaptured parts of Livonia during 1607 but in the spring of 1609 Chodkiwiecz began a campaign to strike at the enemy bridgeheads on the coast. An attempt to take Dynemunt at the mouth of the Dvina failed and he switched his attention to the port of Parnawa at the northern end of the Gulf of Riga, taking advantage of late-season frosts to ease movement through the swamps and forests. The defenders knew the enemy was at their door but remained unaware that the threat came from the main Polish–Lithuanian army and not bands of marauders. Chodkiwiecz ordered his men to the attack during the night of 16 March before Swedish reinforcements could arrive from Reval. In this battle Scots fought on both sides. On the Polish side were a company of Scottish mercenaries and 14 Scots sappers, while some 155 Scots under Captain John Clark were members of the Swedish garrison. Under fire the sappers, under the direction of two French engineers, managed to insert a bomb under the south gate of the town, which destroyed this section of the defences and allowed the Poles to burst in. The garrison retreated to the castle but after a short time surrendered. John Clark and his Scots then changed sides, a common practice during this period.

Chodkiwiecz's and Karl's armies marched and fought each other around the shores of the gulf during all 1609. Mansfeld, who had escaped from the catastrophe at Kircholm, returned to the fray at the head of an 8,000-strong army that included some Scots along with French, Swedish and Dutch. Riga and Parnawa endured sieges again as the combatants struggled for control of the lands around the gulf until, late in 1609, the Swedes were finally forced to surrender. By this time a former enemy of both sides had entered the contest: Russia.

A violent and confused struggle for power ensued in Russia after Ivan the Terrible's death in 1584, a struggle out of which Boris Godunov emerged as victor and tsar in 1598. Among the Scots in his service were two captains, Robert Dunbar and David Gilbert, both of whom entered Russia in 1600 or 1601. Of Dunbar we know little beyond his name and rank. One historian described Gilbert as 'an international scoundrel', a judgement that could just as easily be ascribed to many mercenaries of his ilk.[15] A challenge to Godunov's regime emerged from Poland in 1601 in the person of a defrocked priest who claimed to be the grandson of Ivan. This man, who is known to history as the first False Dmitri, launched a campaign in the direction of Moscow with the support of some Poles and disaffected Russians. Gudonov's army defeated Dmitri's force but Gudonov himself died in April 1605, giving Dmitri and the rebellious boyars a second chance to seize power. At this time David Gilbert was serving as a member of Dmitri's bodyguard, a unit made up entirely of foreign mercenaries, some three hundred English, French and Scots, deemed more trustworthy than native Russians. Moscow now entered a phase in its history remembered as the Time of Troubles. Dmitri himself was assassinated by boyars less than a year after his coronation, and the crown was awarded to Vasily Szujski. This new tsar was equally unable to bring order out of the Russian chaos and he too was challenged by rebels who gathered under the banner of another pretender, the second False Dmitri. Meanwhile Gilbert appears to have returned to Scotland, as in July 1607 the Privy Council granted a warrant to a man of his name as one 'being laitlie imployit be the king of Swadene to levey and tak up ane company of gentilmen to pas to Swadane'.[16] The company sailed from Leith that summer. Among them was a man called Robert Carr, a consummate horseman and possibly from the Borders. Back in Russia in 1608, possibly through a transfer of allegiance of the first Dmitri's bodyguard when his Polish widow, Marina Mniszek, married the second Dmitri, David Gilbert found himself in the retinue of the latter and, before long, charged with treason. Perhaps this had something to do with the Swedish connection in the Privy Council minute. Only the intercession of the Polish wife saved Gilbert from a judicial drowning in the River Oka to the south-east of Moscow. After this narrow brush with Russian justice, Gilbert clearly thought it was time to make himself scarce and switched his allegiance to Poland.

The Time of Troubles tempted Russia's neighbours to interfere in her affairs. Mercenaries also smelled an opportunity and several Scots officers in command of Germans passed east through Prussia, pillaging the country there. In February 1609 Vasily Szujski formed an alliance with Sweden, and in response the Polish king, Sigismund Vasa, sent his army into Russian territory to begin a siege of Smolensk in September. Surrounded by the pine forests from whose resin it takes its name, Smolensk marked the highest navigable point on the Dnieper River and the site of the portage to the Dvina and the Baltic. Strongly defended and well supplied, it held out over the winter, tying down the Commonwealth forces before its walls.

Vasily mobilised his army to relieve the city on the western fringes of his realm, and Karl IX lent him Swedish troops under the command of Jacob de la Gardie, the son of the commander with the first name of Pontus at Wesenberg. The combined Swedish–Russian army advanced towards Smolensk in the summer of 1610. Sigismund Vasa learned of the approaching enemy through a group of disaffected Russian boyars and, on 6 June, a section of the Commonwealth army was detached under the command of Hetman

Stanislaw Zolkiewski to intercept them. Although Zolkiewski's force was heavily outnumbered, he held the advantage of surprise and at dawn on 24 June his men swooped to entrap 8,000 Russians in the village of Carowa-Zajmiszcze. Leaving enough troops to convince the Russians they were still surrounded, he led most of his force on a two-day march through wet weather to meet the main body of Vasily's army. Zolkiewski now learned that there was dissension in the Russian camp between the native troops and the mercenaries and cleverly exploited this by letting the latter know through his network of agents that he was offering the foreign soldiers a bounty and a safe passage home for not fighting. De la Gardie discovered the subterfuge and quelled any mutiny but the seeds of temptation had been sown among the discontented mercenaries.

The two armies almost blundered past each other. Zolkiewski's troops moving through the forests in the night found themselves near the enemy but were not ready to give battle and were unable to take advantage of the surprise encounter. Vasily now deployed his army in entrenched positions on open ground near the village of Klushino, between the forest and a river. The Swedes and Russians, including the mercenaries under de la Gardie, numbered 35,000, the Commonwealth troops less than 7,000. Nevertheless, Zolkiewski attacked, sending in his waves of hussars with lances and flaming torches before dawn on 4 July. Time and again the Polish cavalry hurled themselves with pistol, carbine and lance against the Russians, who defended well until a Russian cavalry counterattack failed and melted into a confused retreat that spread panic among the other Russian ranks. Robert Carr was riding with the Swedish–Russian horse, but we do not know if he took part in this key moment in the struggle. A rout ensued, with the Polish cavalry chasing and cutting down the fleeing enemy. De la Gardie's mercenaries, deployed on the left of the Russian front line in strong redoubts, conducted themselves well, but they were weakened by dissension. One report, by Zolkiewski himself, states that the Scots and English among them chose not to fight and remained in their camp in the forest until they could surrender to the Commonwealth troops. These men agreed either to join the enemy or go home after pledging not to take up arms against the Commonwealth again. Carr returned to England in 1619

but it has been suggested he went back to Russia and founded a family
with the surname of Kar.[17]

In the wake of his defeat in the field, Vasily was overthrown. The
way was now open for the Poles to occupy Moscow and they stayed in
the Kremlin for the next two years. Smolensk also fell after a long
siege. The Polish occupation was brought to an end by the emergence
of a strong leader among the Russians; Mikhail Romanov was only
sixteen years old when he was elected tsar in 1613 but he proved
himself capable of regaining the lost territories. Gilbert campaigned
with the Polish army in Russian territory but unfortunately fell into
enemy hands and was taken back to Moscow, where he languished in
fetters for three years. Again he escaped capital punishment when Sir
John Merrick, ambassador to Tsar Mikhail from James VI, successfully interceded for his life. One may have forgiven Gilbert for
concluding he had seen enough of Russia but, in 1618, with one
of his sons, he returned and probably died there. Tsar Mikhail proved
to be as fond of employing mercenaries as his predecessors had been:
during his rule the number of foreign officers in Russian service rose
to over four hundred, presenting the Scots with more opportunities to
find service on the distant fringes of Europe.

SEVEN

'Your Majesty will need soldiers'

Poland, Sweden, 1582–1625

*I*N JULY 1 5 8 2, the Papal nuncio in Warsaw described in a letter to a colleague 'a youth who says he is a Scot . . . very honourably dressed, of a noble manner . . . fair of complexion with blonde hair and beard . . . and by appearance some thirty years of age. He knows several languages, namely Greek, Latin, Italian, French, Spanish and German. He claims to have left his home in his early years and to have served His Catholic Majesty . . . and to have been taken prisoner in Barbary; then, after his release, to have served Don John of Austria in Flanders.'[1] The youth's name was Robert Spens and the Nuncio's description of him conveys a distinct sense of having been impressed by the young man's attributes and appearance. Spens boldly offered 300 soldiers to the Polish king, Stefan Batory, a contingent the latter had to decline, as he had no need for them at that moment. We do not know the identity of the 300 men at Spens's beck and call but clearly he felt confident enough to be their leader and try to find employment for them as fighting men. Who Spens himself was also remains elusive but we can with some certainty assign him to the Fife family of that name, a family that liked to trace its origins back to the great Macduff who had fought with Malcom Canmore to defeat Macbeth in the twelfth century.[2] From the early fifteenth century the main stem of the Spens kindred held the lands of Lathallan in the East Neuk as vassals of the Scottish crown, and another important branch had the lairdship of Wormiston and provided the hereditary constables of Crail, placing them in an ideal situation to exploit trade links with Europe. A disastrous involvement in plots in support of Queen Mary deprived David Spens of Wormiston of his lands and his life in 1571, and it may have been this that set Robert Spens off on his adventures in Europe. Three years after David Spens's death at Stirling, however, his widow married into another influential Fife dynasty, the Anstruthers, and the Spens offspring could begin to restore their fortunes. James, who had been born around the time of his father's death, started on his rise in politics and diplomacy: he was one of the Fife gentlemen who backed the settling of a colony of Lowlanders in Lewis in 1598, a project that unravelled over the following ten years in a bitter clash with the islanders, resulting in riot and murder. Spens may have consoled himself over this failure by considering the more secure and lucrative outlet for his energies on the other side of the North Sea. With his younger brother, David, he was probably already trading to the Baltic.

In October 1605, having embarked on his war with Poland in Livonia, Karl IX of Sweden sought the Spenses' assistance in the recruitment of soldiers. The use of merchants as middlemen or agents in recruitment was an established practice – they had contacts, access to transport and, most importantly, financial resources at their disposal. Recruitment also took place through the agency of military officers. Both merchants and officers were expected to carry out the task at their own expense against later reimbursement and employment. The king had already employed a Colonel Thomas Uggleby (Ogilvie) in 1602 to secure Scottish troops and in January 1607 Robert Kinnaird was sent from Sweden to the North-East, to the Gordon country, to raise 200 horsemen.[3] Through Spens, Karl wanted 1,600 foot soldiers and 600 cavalry, a levy that had to be undertaken with the approval of the British monarch. James Spens's reward would be the sum of 1,600 thaler for every 300 men and the rank of colonel in command of his recruits. It was an enticing prospect but the recruitment of such a large number of men presented Spens with considerable difficulties; after two years and no sign of them, Karl obviously began to wonder what was going on and, a few days after despatching Robert Kinnaird in 1607, wrote to Spens to express the hope that he would arrive in the spring with the troops. When May came and there was still no sign of soldiers, Karl had to send another letter, following it later in the year with similar ones to Thomas Karr and William Stewart. The latter styled himself 'of Egilsay' and was the brother of the Earl of Orkney. A 1609 commission from him to Captain John Urry appoints the latter to be in command of a company of 200 infantry in Karl's service.[4]

It is difficult to pin down how much a recruiter might hope to gain personally through his activities in raising men; some profit could be expected but this could be conceived as reward in the form of status or war plunder rather than in cash. The Swedish government between 1620 and 1630 laid down a rate for recruitment of 8 riksdaler per man, a sum that fell to 6 in 1631 and dropped to 4 in the following few years.[5] As a riksdaler had an exchange value varying from 4 to 5 shillings sterling, the recruiter therefore could expect to have a sum of up to £2 per man to carry out what he had agreed to do. This sum included the provision of food and drink for recruits, probably some clothing too, and their transport costs across the North Sea, as well as a handout when a man signed on. In his study of recruitment for Sweden in the 1620s, J.A. Fallon calculated that it cost 6s 8d to ship a man from Scotland to the Elbe, and that two weeks' food and drink for a recruit cost 9s 4d. Fallon suggested that 4s would have been handed to the newly signed-on recruit – hence the 'dollar' in the saying about the chief of Mackay. These expenses add up to £1. Fallon suggested that a recruiting captain might typically expect a payment of £1 per recruit. It is possible that the difference between the captain's outlay and the overall sum afforded by the riksdaler–pound exchange rate went into the recruiting agent's coffers, as we must accept that there would always have been the temptation among agents to minimise expenses and redirect a little cash into their own pockets. They also faced a fine if the numbers they attracted fell short of the total they had promised to bring in.[6]

Spens was now running up against serious problems in fulfilling his side of the bargain with Karl IX, perhaps partly from difficulties with finance and shipping but also because James was loathe to allow so many men to go abroad to serve the Swedish flag, worried they might be deployed against his own brother-in-law, the King of Denmark. Karl IX sent a pair of falcons to James in August 1609 with a letter designed to allay the canny king's suspicions, a gift the latter reciprocated with a book. To further Karl's aims, Spens came over

from Sweden in December 1609 with what amounted to a delegation
of several Scottish officers that included Samuel Cockburn, who held
the rank of colonel and had been in Swedish service since 1598.[7]

The recruitment drive paid off at last but the numbers amounted to
only a fraction of what Karl had first sought. Three hundred arrived in
Sweden in January 1610, and further contingents were recruited in
Ireland and England. One shipload from the former was driven into
Peterhead by bad weather, provoking the Privy Council's measures to
deal with them already mentioned in Chapter 2. In March 1610 the
council noted a request from captains Johnne Borthuik and Andro
Rentoun, who had received no reimbursement from Stockholm for
the 4,000 merks and 300 riksdaler they had raised for the recruiting
and shipping of men for Swedish service and who were now seeking
the council to ask James to raise the matter with Karl on their behalf.[8]
The soldiers joined the Swedish forces in Russia, in time to be present
at the defeat at Klushino on 4 July 1610 and were among the men who
sat out the battle in response to the Polish commanders' promises
(Chapter 6). James Spens, although nominally the senior officer, was
not present in the field, and any blame, however slight, that may have
come his way after the levies deserted to the Polish side did not
prevent him from continuing a successful diplomatic career, not only
as ambassador from the Stuart monarch to Sweden but also, at various
times, to Denmark, the Dutch Republic, Danzig and Brandenburg.

Among the Scots who joined Karl IX's army around this time were
a few who would enter the gallery of notable soldiers of fortune. One
was Patrick Ruthven, second son of William Ruthven of Ballindean in
Perthshire. Born in the early 1570s and a distant relative of the
Archibald Ruthven involved in the Wesenberg incident, Patrick
Ruthven placed himself under Swedish colours in around 1608 and
must have impressed his colleagues enough to be included in the
delegation that accompanied James Spens and Samuel Cockburn. He
is noted as a captain of horse for a troop of Scottish cavalry in 1609.
He also acquired a reputation for an ability to consume large amounts
of alcohol, a trait that led the Germans later to play on his name and
dub him Pater Rotwein.

The path to Europe followed by James Ramsay was somewhat
different but had the cachet of individual royal approval. Born in

around 1589, as the eighth of nine children in the family of Ramsay of Wyliecleuch near Coldstream, James Ramsay followed some of his siblings into a post at the Stuart court and moved from Holyrood to London in 1603 in the retinue of his royal employer. He was later transferred to the Danish court and, in 1611, returned to Britain on a mission to raise men for Danish service in the Kalmar War. In 1614 he married Isobel, daughter of James Spens – family ties were important among the overseas Scots, as ever – and had switched his allegiance to the Swedish flag by 1615, when he appears as an ensign in the army of Gustavus Adolphus.

Another mercenary who enters the arena at this time and who was destined to be the most remembered of them all was Alexander Leslie, who was born in or shortly after the year 1580. His father, George Leslie, was an officer in the garrison of Blair Atholl Castle and it is generally believed that Alexander was illegitimate, the offspring of a long-term affair between his father and a woman whose name remains unknown. A contemporary writer, the Earl of Wemyss, who may have had his own axe to grind, describes her as a 'wench in Rannoch'. George Leslie may have married his lover after his first wife died, thus belatedly conferring legitimacy on a son who had by this time risen to prominence in the Swedish army. As Leslie became very famous at home and abroad, stories have accrued around his name. One credits him with being an illegitimate son of the Laird of Kininvie, a district near Dufftown. When his mother was pregnant with him, according to a traditional tale, she could eat nothing but wheaten bread and drink nothing but wine, although she was only a common servant, an indication that her child would grow up to be extraordinary. Nothing seems to be now known of Leslie's childhood and early life but it is possible he learned to read and write quite late in his adolescence or his early twenties, perhaps even after 1604 or 1605, when he went to the Netherlands to serve under Sir Horatio Vere. Leslie himself is credited with maintaining that in his schooling he had never passed the letter G in the alphabet; he was probably joking.[9] However truncated his formal education, he was clearly a shrewd and able man. In September 1639, when he was approaching sixty, he was described as an 'old little, crooked souldier' with great 'wisdome and authoritie'.[10] Illegitimacy may have produced in Leslie the drive to

succeed in life, and clearly he must have been a very confident
individual, albeit possessing enough tact and moderation to allow the
King of Sweden to trust him as a diplomat and governor. The
adjective 'crooked' refers to Leslie being lame, from a wound he
sustained in his foot. Sir James Turner, of whom more anon, found
Leslie to be avaricious and grasping and, although Turner may have
had private grounds for his dislike, it is abundantly clear that soldiering made Leslie rich.

In 1608, Leslie went to Sweden to begin a career under Karl IX.
Three years later, the king died and the throne passed to his son
Gustavus Adolphus, who was then aged sixteen but would over the
succeeding years be recognised by the Swedes as one of their greatest
monarchs and by the Protestants of Europe as their defender and
saviour from the Counter-Reformation. Schooled from birth to carry
on his father's work, exposed early to military command and political
negotiation, Gustavus Adolphus was a tall, energetic youth with
considerable charisma and great skill in all the main tongues of
western Europe. Many of his Scottish officers were to speak highly
of him in their later years, fondly remembering incidents that revealed
his impatient volatility and his quickness to forgive. He honoured his
father by continuing Karl's expansionist policies, but taking them
further than the old man might have dreamed of. The regent, Axel
Oxenstierna, headed the transitional government until Gustavus
Adolphus came of age, and continued to serve the young king ably
and well, administering the home country and freeing the master to
concentrate on campaigning abroad. Portraits of Gustavus Adolphus
abound, many of them copies of earlier representations. One, by
Merian the Elder in 1632, the year of Gustavus's death, shows the
heavy, thickset warrior king in his prime. In them all the artists try to
capture the long head and nose, the trimmed and pointed reddish
beard, the cropped hair and the staring, occasionally hooded eyes.
Those Scots such as Ruthven and Leslie who went to Sweden with
dreams of fortune in their minds were lucky to be hitching their fate
to that of the new king. In 1611, however, that lay in the future.

At this time the frontier between Sweden and Denmark ran across
the southern part of the former, and the present Swedish provinces
of Blekinge, Skåne and Halland were part of the Danish realm.

Norwegian territory also extended further south than it does now, making Sweden's only contact with the Kattegat a narrow corridor around Älvsborg at the mouth of the Göta River. Near here in March 1611 a band of Danes on an armed foray into Swedish territory captured the recently knighted Sir James Spens, travelling in his role as ambassador. The Danes killed one of his companions, held the rest of the party captive for a time and rifled through the diplomatic correspondence in Spens's pouches before they made away with letters and money. Perhaps Spens should not have been surprised that his missions attracted hostile attention but envoys had rights, and the outrage fuelled the growing tension between the Scandinavian kingdoms that erupted into the Kalmar War. Spens was back in London at the Stuart court later in the year when Karl IX wrote to him to ask him to levy a further 3,000 men. The diplomat demurred, well aware of James's unwillingness to allow his subjects to go to war against his brother-in-law on the Danish throne. Then Karl died and in November Gustavus Adolphus succeeded to the throne. Before long he reminded Spens of the request for 3,000 men, the outcome of which was the illicit raising of the 300 who mostly perished in the Norwegian hills, as we have seen in Chapter 1. Spens was sent by James VI in 1612 to mediate between Denmark and Sweden. The peacemaking efforts led to a settlement agreed in January 1613. Sweden had suffered badly in the brief period of hostilities but Denmark also found the conflict exhausting. In October 1613, Gustavus Adolphus offered Spens a permanent appointment as a diplomat and in December 1613 he was officially despatched as ambassador to the British court, where he remained until 1619.

With peace finally secured with Denmark, Gustavus Adolphus looked eastward and, in 1614, led an expedition against Muscovy, a polity internally riven and weakened by the domestic struggles of the Time of Troubles. The Swedish campaign pushed east to the shores of Lake Ladoga and secured the coasts of both sides of the Gulf of Finland, and at one time it looked as if Gustavus Adolphus's brother Karl Philip might be elected tsar. Swedish troops under Jacob de la Gardie, son of Pontus, had already captured the Russian trading centre of Novgorod in 1611 but the siege Gustvaus Adolphus laid against Pskov failed to achieve its aim. The campaigning in Estonia

and Livonia came to an end with the Peace of Stolbova in 1617
between Gustavus Adolphus and Tsar Michael Romanov, probably
none too soon for most of the troops, who had had to endure some
severe conditions in the field. During the early winter of 1615/16,
probably because they were suffering from lack of food, warmth and
pay, some Scots from Captain Cobson's company in Samuel Cockburn's regiment were driven to take matters into their own hands near
the town of Narva in Estonia.[11] In a letter that survives in the Swedish
archives they gave the reason for their rebellion and admitted they had
dragged the head of the army commissariat from his lodgings, before
begging the king to take pity on them and remember the hardships
they had had to put up with in a decade of service to the Swedish
crown. From the commissar, whom they did not harm, they tried to
learn whether or not their officers had received money and were
keeping it from them. Fear of what had happened at Wesenberg was
firmly in their minds as well as a sense of outrage that they were being
cheated of their rightful dues. 'Since [Your Majesty's] departure,' reads
part of their Latin letter, 'we have received now a couple of marks,
now half a dollar, nay sometimes only half a mark, and thus we have
led a miserable life, so much so that very many have on the very
streets exchanged death for life.' After a plea for payment or leave to
go, they ended with a prayer for Gustavus Adolphus's victory over all
his foes. To the Swedish king's credit, he forgave the mutineers after a
rebuke.[12]

   Swedish recruitment of Scots had been continuing for some time.
Some were modest initiatives, such as the one late in 1612 when
Robert Stewart, Earl of Orkney, brought over a company of his men.
Others, as we have seen, were on a larger scale. The enlistment of
Scottish officers in Swedish service rose from an average of three or
four per year between 1600 and 1608, to nine in 1608, eighteen in
1609, thirteen in 1610 and sixteen in 1611, before dropping to a lower
level for a few years until the outbreak of the Thirty Years War
brought about another, higher surge in numbers.[13] Jacob de la Gardie
told Axel Oxenstierna, the Swedish chancellor, in 1613 that the Scots
were the foreigners who got along best with the Swedes, and at least
five officers came to Britain in 1615–16 to levy for Sweden. Gustavus
Adolphus was a popular figure in Scotland, of the truth of which Sir

James Spens was to remind the king in 1629: 'Since Your Majesty will need soldiers, that their wishes may be met by Your Majesty's welcoming attitude I humbly ask for them to be tied by a closer bond of service to Your Majesty; liekwise I entreat you not to regard as worthless the esteem in which the British hold you . . . but if they [the soldiers] are not received in a kindly manner the same thing may happen to Your Majesty in these parts as befell the King of Denmark following unfavourable reports: even if his realm were in the greatest danger not even a dwarf from this kingdom would engage in his service.'[14]

The organisation of the Swedish army went through several changes during the lifetime of Gustavus Adolphus.[15] An infantry regiment, headed by a colonel or lieutenant-colonel, comprised a number of companies under the command of captains. From 1621, a regiment usually had eight companies, each of usually around 150 men with a lieutenant and ensign as junior officers, two or more sergeants, and several subordinate non-commissioned officers such as corporals and fouriers, along with miscellaneous drummers, clerks and muster-boys or servants. Alexander Leslie was promoted to lieutenant in 1611 and was made captain of his own company around a year later. Patrick Ruthven also enjoyed a fairly smooth rise in status: in 1614 he was a captain in Samuel Cockburn's regiment. In the following year Gustavus Adolphus commissioned him to raise a thousand men in Scotland and bring them to Narva, a task he seems to have discharged to the king's satisfaction as Ruthven soon filled a number of responsible posts, serving as a quartermaster general, a chief master of the watch and commandant or governor of Pskov, before, in 1617, being promoted to lieutenant-colonel for the Kalmar/Småland regiment. James Ramsay was appointed as an ensign in 1615 but nothing is known of his career during the next few years.

The Swedish army had been put on a new footing by Gustavus Adolphus's grandfather, who had introduced a system whereby each of the nation's nine provinces raised men for a regiment of infantry. Gustavus Adolphus increased the number of regiments and laid down new regulations governing the length and conditions of service. Conscription for all males over the age of fifteen was introduced in 1620, although only some 10 per cent were finally selected for service; conscription was naturally unpopular, occasionally provoking civil riots, and underlining the wisdom of using mercenaries. Throughout the 1620s Gustavus Adolphus and his administrator, Axel Oxenstierna, introduced innovations in almost every aspect of the army. Learning from the experience of the Dutch, he tried to ensure his men were always well clothed, fed, paid and equipped, and, by the standards of the time, he produced a professional standing army that was unusual, if not unique, among the armed forces in Europe in being closely identified with the population from which it was drawn and in being backed by a well-run administrative and supply system. He also showed care in his choice of mercenaries; the trust he placed in the Scots seems often to have been repaid by their loyalty, although the system did not bear every strain placed on it in the field. Robert Monro was unstinting in his praise of his commander-in-chief. Gustavus Adolphus, in Monro's opinion, had 'the right hand of the Lord for his assistance . . . for though he had bin no King, he was a brave warriorr, and which is more a good man, magnificent, wise, just, meeke, indued with learning, and the gift of tongues.'[16] This is conventional phraseology, what a loyal soldier might say of any monarch, but there is no reason to think Monro was not being sincere. The Easter Ross officer gave other examples of the king's temperament, describing how impatience could fire his temper and how 'no excuse, though true, would mitigate his passion' until he realised the circumstances and showed he was sorry. Discipline was encoded in Articles of War, which were read to the men at regular intervals to remind them of offences and punishments. Penalties for swearing, blasphemy, drunkenness and fornication – this was after all a Protestant army and it was not long after the Reformation – were seen as reasonably humane, and it was also accepted that more serious crimes such as pillage, rape and murder, as opposed to killing in battle, as well as serious dereliction of military duty would be met by the death penalty.[17]

Gustavus Adolphus looked to the Dutch wars for new approaches to military affairs and in general is credited with developing Dutch innovations and practices to new degrees of effectiveness. He noted how the flexible units under the command of Maurice of Nassau had fought well against the mighty formations of the Spanish army, for long seen as an unbeatable power. The Spanish generals marshalled their pikemen in great units or *tercios* of a thousand men or more, creating an irresistible juggernaut that could move across a battlefield trampling everything it encountered – until it came against a unit of pikemen determined and disciplined enough to resist, whereupon a battle could become a heaving, grunting scrum. Musketeers could make dents in the *tercios* with their firepower but this was of limited effect in an age when loading and firing took a long time. Gustavus Adolphus reorganised his foot soldiers into small, flexible units of pikemen flanked by and interspersed with companies of musketeers, all under the close supervision of NCOs and officers. His regiments could be combined into brigades of three or more to form larger tactical units. The pikes themselves were made less unwieldy and the men wore lighter armour – now they could actually mount something akin to a lumbering charge. Firepower was greatly enhanced and given a more prominent role, once better muskets, prepared cartridges and faster reloading allowed the salvo and the rolling barrage to be maintained. Gustavus Adolphus also reorganised the cavalry components of his army, forming the men into squadrons of riders and revising formations and tactics as the army gained more experience.

Sweden's senior artillery expert, Lennart Torstensson, studied the art in the Netherlands before being given command of this branch of the military in 1626 at the age of only twenty-seven. In the next few years the variety of guns in the Swedish army was whittled down to three types – called 'natures' at the time – throwing weights of 3 pounds, 12 pounds (the standard field gun) and 24 pounds. The 3-pounder was light enough to be moved on a single horse or by a couple of strong men, and it could be brought quickly into action where it was needed. Shot and powder were combined in cartridges, which facilitated reloading and increased rate of fire to a speed that at times exceeded what the musketeers could achieve. The standardisation of artillery saw off not only huge field pieces, such as the 48-pounder siege gun that needed to be drawn by a team of 39 horses, but also the light leather guns, made by binding a copper tube in rope and leather. One of the inventors of the latter was Robert Scott, but neither his model nor that of his German rival was adopted after their test firings in Stockholm in 1628. Scott wanted too large a payment for his invention, nothing less than 20,000 Swedish riksdaler, which Gustavus Adolphus refused to pay. The Danes were more generous, accepting Scott into their service with the rank of master general of artillery in 1628, but he stayed for less than a year before returning to Britain. He died in 1631 in London. His leather gun was adopted by British troops in the Covenanter wars, during which it was nicknamed 'Dear Sandy's Stoup' after General Alexander Hamilton.

Gustavus Adolphus's claim to the Swedish throne was still open to challenge from his cousin Sigismund III, ruler of the Polish–Lithuanian Commonwealth. The Polish monarch had of course Scottish mercenaries among his own forces, as well as Irish and a contingent of English led by the Astons, father and son. The eastern frontier of the Commonwealth stretched far out into the heart of the steppes, into the rolling, seemingly endless plains that were home to the free-spirited half-Russian, half-Asiatic peoples known as the Cossacks, who frequently served as cavalry units in the Common-wealth forces. The region was also prey to incursions by raiding Tatars and attacks by Turkish armies from the Ottoman Empire and, in September 1620, the latest of these resulted in a defeat for the Poles at Cecora on the River Prut. In January 1621 a Polish envoy, Jerzy Ossolinski, came to London to seek permission to recruit men to combat the infidel. Although the British parliament was impressed by Ossolinski's impassioned speech in Latin, it was also wary of sending men to fight for a Catholic monarch, men who might at some point be used against Poland's Protestant neighbours. King James's interest in eastern Europe was focused on the fortunes of his son-in-law Frederick, then defending his claim to the throne of Bohemia (Chapter 8) but Ossolinski could give no assurance that Sigismund would intervene on Frederick's behalf. Potential Scots recruits also baulked at serving a Catholic king under the English commander Aston and, as the parliament was also dragging its feet over funding, Ossolinski gave up and looked to Ireland as a more fruitful recruiting ground. In the end less than 2,000 Irish and English mercenaries set out for Poland. Misfortune still dogged Ossolinski – one ship sank on the voyage and the Danes delayed the passage of the others – and by the time the recruits reached their destination the latest clash with the Ottomans had already happened.

Ottoman sultan Osman II led an army of over 100,000 into Poland in the summer of 1621 and laid seige to the Polish forces sent to confront him early in September at Chocim (now Khotyn in Ukraine) a fortified town on bluffs above the Dniester River. Led by Jan Karol Chodkiewicz and Stanislaw Lubomirski, the Poles numbered 25,000 with a further 20,000 Zaporozhian Cossacks. A few Scots were present: for example between 10 and 20 served in Prince Wladyslaw's bodyguard, and Peter Learmonth had brought his regiment of 900 men, raised from among the Scots vagabonds and pedlars. Learmonth had seen a varied but not untypical career as a soldier: he possibly joined the Polish forces after he was captured while under Swedish colours in 1614–16, and then saw service against the Swedes and the Russians. He and another captain, William Keith, received documents in Warsaw in 1619 to levy their resident fellow countrymen. Their Scottish officers also included an Archibald Carmichael. The Commonwealth forces created a defensive barrier across the route of the invaders and held them back for over a month until the first snows of autumn and heavy losses induced the sultan to withdraw. Many had also been killed among the defenders, including Chodkiewicz, and, with honour thus bloodily satisfied, both sides agreed to peace.

Recruitment efforts for Poland continued in Britain. In June 1622, a Captain John Forbes was arrested in London on just such a mission when the French ambassador alleged he was recruiting to aid the Protestant fugitives in La Rochelle. Relations between the various European powers were now becoming increasingly complicated and sensitive as rulers sought to identify allies and potential rivals in the growing power struggle across the continent. Any British assistance to Poland was liable to upset Sweden. Gustavus Adolphus fired off a letter to the Privy Council in Edinburgh on 23 September 1623, protesting that a Scot called Robert Stewart who had been in his service was now offering to raise 8,000 Scots to fight for Poland in an invasion of Swedish dominions. Gustavus Adolphus reminded the Privy Council that Sweden was the one northern bulwark of the Evangelicals (Protestants) and that should the Papists prevail Evangelicals everywhere would be in peril.[18] Possibly Gustavus Adolphus had learned about Stewart's plan when Sir Arthur Aston, the English commander in Poland, showing that mercenaries could be just as

touchy as monarchs about their standing, had protested to Sir James
Spens that Stewart intended to command the levies himself. However,
James allowed Stewart, who was after all his own envoy, to proceed
with his recruitment, while extracting from Poland a promise that the
men would not be used against a Christian enemy. As a further
mollification James signed a warrant to allow James Spens, the son of
Sir James Spens, now a gentleman of the Swedish royal household, to
raise another 1,200 men for Gustavus Adolphus's service. As it
happened, Christian IV of Denmark refused to allow troops destined
for Poland to pass into the Baltic, and Stewart's efforts were in vain.

The Treaty of Stolbova, signed in 1617 with Tsar Michael, freed
Gustavus Adolphus to focus on his long-standing confrontation with
the Polish–Lithuanian Commonwealth and, in August 1621, he landed
at the mouth of the Dvina river with an army of 12,000, backed by 4,000
local troops. The first target in the campaign was the city and port of
Riga a short distance upstream of the sandbar-ridden estuary. Formerly
a Hanseatic town, the seat of the bishopric of Livonia and the capital for
the Teutonic Order and its successors, Riga lay on the right bank of the
river, protected by a wall with defensive towers and a moat. Stefan
Batory had incorporated it into the Polish Catholic kingdom but it was
still largely a Protestant, Germanic centre. Gustavus Adolphus called on
the defenders to surrender but, without the permission of Sigismund to
yield, they resolved to make the Swedes fight. Over the next few weeks,
Gustavus Adolphus's engineers and sappers ringed Riga with entrenchments, with breastworks for the artillery at suitable spots. One of these,
under the command of Alexander Seaton, was targeted by a defensive
sally but the attackers were beaten off. On 20 August, nine days after
their arrival, Seaton was able to open fire on the 'Jakobbastion' with
siege guns, throwing balls of up to 40 pounds' weight to crash down
on masonry and flesh alike. Grimly the defenders hung on, sending
messages upstream to Prince Radziwill, who tried to break through
the Swedish lines but found his forces too weak. As the noose of
trenches tightened, the prince decided to withdraw after sending in a
message of encouragement to the defenders. At the beginning of
September, the Swedish engineers discovered how to drain the moat.
It was now only a matter of time and on 15 September the city
surrendered.

The inland town of Mitau (now Jelgava) was occupied by the Swedes early in October, Wolmar (now Valmiera) fell in mid December and, although Samuel Cockburn's soldiers were held and defeated by the Poles in a skirmish on the approaches to Kokenhausen (now Koknese), Livonia and the neighbouring duchy of Courland fell under the invaders' control. During this period Prince Radziwill kept his army in the field but avoided battle. Winter struck and with the blizzards and frosts came hunger and disease. The garrisoning of the Livonian towns proved to be an ordeal for the soldiers, among them the troops under the command of Patrick Ruthven, and by the time the snows melted in the spring Gustavus Adolphus's army had shrunk to some 5,000 men. Among the lives claimed by the Livonian campaign was that of Gustavus Adolphus's younger brother Karl Philip, at one time a candidate to sit on the Russian throne. Holding on to Livonia was proving too costly and a truce was agreed with the Poles to run for three years. It was almost broken in July 1623 when a rumour that the Poles were about to send a fleet to invade mainland Sweden brought Gustavus Adolphus with twenty ships to Danzig in an attempt to force the independent-minded burgers to adhere to neutrality. During this alarm Ruthven was given shared command of Kalmar, with orders to torch the town if it could not be defended.

By this time, war was spreading across the heartland of Europe between the armies of the Holy Roman Empire and the German Protestant princes (Chapter 8) and, partly to distract Sigismund from allying with the Empire, Gustavus Adolphus renewed the assault on Livonia in 1625, regaining control of Windau (now Ventspils), Dorpat and Riga in three months. Polish forces fought back and delayed the Swedish movement south through Courland so that, by the end of November, Gustavus Adolphus was finding hunger, sickness and cold once again dogging the heels of his men. As if these were not enough, there seems to have been a breakdown in the supply of pay. A letter to 'Colonel Ramsay' (this was actually James Ramsay, now a lieutenant-colonel) dated 28 December 1625 records the shooting of Captain J. Craffert [Crawford], the wounding of Captain Seton, and the sickness of Captain Robert Lamb and Lieutenant Rutherfurd; neither Seton, Lamb nor Rutherfurd had received any pay during the previous year. Over Christmas 1625 Gustavus Adolphus resolved on a desperate

move before his army weakened to a useless state. With 1,000
musketeers, 2,000 cavalry and 6 guns he launched a fast march to
the south-east up the valley of the Dvina. In 36 hours he and his men
laboured through the winter forests and brought themselves to within
striking distance of the Polish army at Wallhof (now Walmojza). The
Polish commander Johan Sapieha mastered his astonishment at this
surprise advance and prepared his men for battle, confident that his
cavalry, generally held to be superior to their Swedish counterparts
and with a record of triumph stretching back to Kirchholm, would see
off the attackers. Gustavus Adolphus, however, caught the Poles off
guard by appearing from the forests with his troops in battle
formation, with the cavalry on the flanks and the musketeers ready
in the centre. Sapieha's forces were overcome and driven from the
field with heavy losses, while the Swedish casualties amounted to only
3 men wounded. This stunning victory was the Swedish monarch's
first in a set-piece battle, and it made him master of Livonia. It was a
forerunner of things to come.

———◆◆✕◆◆———

'sure men hardy and resolute'

Bohemia, the Rhineland, the Low Countries, 1618–1625

THE FIRST STIRRINGS of the conflict that would escalate into the bloody Thirty Years War took place in the kingdom of Bohemia, now the Czech Republic but then a part of the Holy Roman Empire, the conglomeration of electorates, duchies, principalities, counties, lordships, free cities and even free villages that sprawled across the heart of the continent. The power of the emperor was limited by a constitution first established in 1338. In the first place, he was an elected sovereign and in theory, if not always in practice, the title was not an hereditary one. Seven electors chose the emperor: three bishops – of Trier, Cologne and Mainz – along with the King of Bohemia, the Elector of the Rhineland Palatinate, the Elector of Saxony and the Margrave of Brandenburg. The emperor legislated through the Reichstag, whose members comprised three colleges, that of the Electoral Council (the seven electors mentioned above), the Council of Princes and the Council of the Imperial Cities.

This constitutional edifice, with its endless possibilities for intrigue and alliance, was further complicated by the Reformation, when many of the constituent states adopted Protestantism. By 1560, little over forty years after Martin Luther had nailed his call for religious reform to the door of a church in Wittenberg, Europe was split by a doctrinal divide. Spain, most of France, Italy and the Adriatic coast as far as the frontier with the Islamic Ottoman Empire, along with the Spanish Netherlands, the Tyrol and Bavaria, remained loyal to the Catholic Church, as did the Habsburg emperor himself. All of Scandinavia, the

Baltic lands, Prussia and the northern German-speaking territories adopted Lutheranism, before some veered again to adhere to the more extreme doctrines of Calvinism. The latter group included Scotland, which became officially Calvinist in 1560. It was not, however, a clean break. Parts of France had significant Calvinist minorities, and Poland, Lithuania, Hungary, Transylvania and various parts of Austria were split between all three sects. In Bohemia and Moravia a fourth denomination, the Hussites, also appeared. In some of the states of the Empire, rulers and ruled now attended different churches.

This was a matter of concern in an age dominated by dynastic politics, with powerful families vying for wealth, territory and power. Despite some features of government – such as elected rulers and parliaments of sorts – that could be seen as embryonic manifestations of the democratic systems of the modern age, Europe was governed essentially by a network of ruling families whose main aim was to nurture their own status and survival. In 1618 in Britain the Stuarts ruled, in France the Bourbons, in Sweden the Vasas, in Denmark the Oldenburgs, and slightly further down the social scale there were such dynasties as the Hohenzollerns in Prussia, the Wettins in the Saxon duchies and the Wittelsbachs in Bavaria and the Rhineland. The Habsburgs were the most powerful of all, ruling Spain and the Empire.[1] In this Europe of pernicious intrigue who married whom could be of the utmost importance.

In 1612 the Stuarts, James VI and I and his queen, Anne of Denmark, entertained in London the young Prince Frederick from the Rhineland Palatinate. The visit coincided with the fatal illness of the eldest Stuart prince, Henry, but arrangements for the marriage between Frederick and Elizabeth Stuart, James's eldest daughter, went ahead. The queen was initially averse to the match, thinking a Rhineland prince not of a status to merit her daughter's hand. Frederick was a catch in every other way. A handsome 22-year-old Wittelsbach with winning ways, he had turned his back on the drinking and hunting favoured by his forebears to establish a court in Heidelberg that was a showcase for the lavish styles in art and culture emanating from France. His capital had a theatre, a famous garden, library and university, and it was at the centre of the Lower

Palatinate, a spread of territories along the Rhine and the Neckar that were famed as the garden of Germany. The Palatinate lands also included a more rugged but still valuable stretch known as the Upper Palatinate, between Nuremberg, Pilsen and Regensburg, ruled on Frederick's behalf by Prince Christian von Anhalt-Bernburg. Frederick and Elizabeth married in Whitehall on 14 February 1613; it was a love-match that was to produce thirteen children and the couple would have had a peaceful, contented life, were it not that they allowed themselves to be drawn into events on the other side of the Empire.

On 23 May 1618 an incident in Prague brought to a head long-simmering discontent between the Protestants in Bohemia and their Catholic rulers. The incident is the famous defenestration: two city governors and their secretary were hurled through a window in Hradčany Palace by a mob of rebellious citizens.[2] Attempts to cool the over-heated confrontation and bring revolt to an end failed. As a candidate for the Bohemian throne and as a staunch Calvinist in his personal faith, Frederick supported the Protestant revolt. The Habsburg emperor, Matthias, in his capital of Vienna, sought to restore Catholic rights in this troubled corner of his domain and suppress the unrest, but the rebels, who had already expelled Jesuits and taken control of some towns, rejected the imperial olive branches. Two imperial armies were despatched into Bohemia, one from Flanders with Spanish backing and the second from Vienna. On 9 September they met and turned towards Prague.

The allies of the Protestants were also preparing for war and in September, with the help of the Duke of Savoy, who was no friend of the Habsburgs, Frederick sent an army to Bohemia under the command of Count Ernst von Mansfeld. Born in Luxembourg in 1580 as the illegitimate son of the governor of the Spanish fortress there, Mansfeld was a Catholic who had begun his military career in Habsburg service. 'Hee did so season his youth with imployment and discipline that hee was able to command his own infirmities and became a master over his owne passions', wrote one near contemporary of his.[3] Taken prisoner by the Dutch during the fighting with Spain, Mansfeld found his own way to freedom through impressing his captors with his honourable behaviour: he rode to Brussels, then under Spanish control, and, when he found his side had no ransom to pay for him, kept his word to the Prince of Orange and returned to captivity. His freedom was finally granted when he swore not to take up arms against the Dutch again, and he went off to join the service of the Duke of Savoy. He may have willingly joined Frederick's cause but, as a mercenary, he was using his military skills on behalf of his paymasters, the Protestant Union, an alliance of German Protestant interests. At thirty-eight years old, he was a veteran with a painful sense of the realities; he issued a warning to the Prague Protestants that the course they had embarked on could be wrecked by the unforeseen, no matter how firm their resolution. With 4,000 men, Mansfeld headed east and proceeded to capture a series of imperial garrison towns – 'nay, he was so powerfull and firtunate . . . that he cleered all the passages into Bohemia, and entred so resolutely into the verie bowells of the King-dome', in William Crosse's dramatic figure of speech – until the Empire retained control of only Pisek, Pilsen, Crumano (now Česky Krumlov) and Budweis (now České Budějovice). Mansfeld realised his guns were too weak to make much impression on Pilsen's walls but, in a foretaste of later difficulties, Prague dragged its feet in responding to his request for larger ordnance; he had to ride to the capital himself, only to return with two cannon reluctantly provided. They were enough, however, and on 29 November Pilsen fell once the walls were breached. By the end of the year only the towns of Budweis and Crumano remained in the emperor's hands.

The news of these events naturally was of great concern in the Stuart court in London, although James resorted to a policy of neutrality, refusing at first to send troops to assist his son-in-law but offering his services as a mediator between the rebels and the emperor. A belief in the divine right of kings bolstered strong doubts in James's mind about the wisdom of having elected monarchs but he still felt for his son-in-law, even when the latter showed an annoying propensity to ignore advice. The Stuart king also wished to remain on good terms with the Spanish Habsburgs, and was dreaming of an alliance with them through marriage, such were the priorities of dynastic politics. Meanwhile, the Duke of Savoy committed more forces to the Bohemian cause and, as expected, the Habsburg rulers of Spain declared for their Austrian cousins.

The Empire began to regain lost ground in February 1619. Soon, however, the Bohemians, under Count Matthias Thurn, struck into Moravia and thrust towards Vienna itself. The ageing Emperor Matthias died in March 1619, setting in motion the electoral machinery of the Empire to choose his successor. His cousin Ferdinand was his heir to Habsburg lands and, although there was no certainty the Imperial crown would also come to him, in August the electors chose him to succeed Matthias. Two days before, the Bohemian rebels had declared the same man no longer their king and had elected Frederick of the Palatinate in his place. Frederick accepted the offer of the Bohemian crown, a position that gave him two votes in the Imperial constitution – as king of Bohemia and as elector of the Palatinate – and thereby threatened the balance of powers in central Europe. Seemingly unfazed by his situation, on 31 October, at the head of a large and splendid retinue, he and Elizabeth completed the journey from Heidelberg with a triumphal entry into Prague. He resisted the attempts by other princes of the Empire to persuade him to relinquish his new crown, and finally Ferdinand issued an ultimatum: resign the Bohemian throne by 1 June 1620 or become a rebel against the Empire. The Bohemian armed forces were now facing difficulties: on 10 June, they had suffered a reverse when Mansfeld was defeated at Zablati, and now, late in 1619, Count Thurn's advance on Vienna ground to a halt.

There were some Scots in Habsburg service in the Empire, which was now poised to strike back at the rebels. For example, in 1619 Sir Henry Bruce, who had earlier served in the Low Countries and had joined Ferdinand's court in 1617, had been appointed captain of the garrison in the town of Nikolsburg (now Mikulov) on the Moravian–Austrian border. A Catholic, Bruce's shift in allegiance may have arisen from a sense of alienation from the resolutely Protestant Dutch, especially as in 1604 he had killed a Captain Hamilton in a duel and in 1607 had had to seek settlement of arrears.[4] He may have been the same Henry Bruce who survived the killing in Gudbrandsdalen in 1612 (see Chapter 1) but this cannot be established. The castle in Nikolsburg was threatened by rebel forces in December 1619 but Bruce managed to hold on for a time, though in the process he earned himself a bad name for his plundering of the nearby town of Breclav and his mistreatment of Jews and Anabaptists. Finally, in January 1620, he surrendered Nikolsburg to the rebels, left for Prague and then travelled to the Netherlands, where he tried to offer his military skills in the service of Elizabeth Stuart, an example of a Scot who was torn between loyalty to his faith and loyalty to a dynasty.[5] There were a considerable number of Irish soldiers in the Habsburg forces and some of them also found their allegiance tested in the same way. A letter from Colonel John Butler, an Irish officer, written over a decade later in 1631 says: 'I will let you understand whate a scruple I make of late to searve in these wars, for I protest before God, I did not heretofore understand as much as I doe now knowe, that the King of Sweedland is for the recovery of the Palatinate onely and we for the hindering of it, but for my parte I will sooner beg my bred than serve against my sacred King's sister.'[6]

A war resistant to all the diplomatic efforts to curtail it spread across central Europe during 1620 as the various nations took sides according to where they saw their interests lying, and as men of war turned their eyes towards this potential source of honour and wealth. Early in March a Scot called John Hume, then at Sedan, wrote to the minister of Libberton, near Edinburgh, to say that 'Thaire is a horse companie gone out of this toune to the King of Boheme.'[7] Four companies of musketeers under the command of Sir John Seton of Carchunoth (possibly Gargunnock near Stirling) left the Netherlands to make their way to Bohemia. They reached their destination early in May – Seton had to find 200 men to replace losses, probably mostly through desertion, on the way – and were assigned to watch the frontier with Saxony in the Meissen area. Meanwhile, Frederick had sent Sir Andrew Gray to London in February to raise men for his forces. Gray's background is obscure.[8] He had seen service in Sweden for some years in the regiments commanded by Patrick Ruthven and Sir James Spens before temporarily joining the escort of Elizabeth Stuart to Heidelberg in 1613. As a Catholic and having been imprisoned for alleged involvement in a murder in Sweden, he probably took the opportunity to remain in the service of Frederick and Elizabeth. In London Gray was at first commanded to recruit quietly so as not to alarm the Spanish ambassador – James was still pursuing friendly relations with Habsburg Spain – but this restriction was soon removed and recruitment proceeded apace. On 19 April, the Privy Council in Holyrood ordered criminals to be enlisted, adding on the twenty-eighth that beggars and vagabonds, 'maisterless men haveand no laughfull trade nor meanis of intertenyment' should join the colours on possible pain of a whipping or being burnt on the cheek for a first refusal, and hanging for a second.[9] The Privy Council also took the opportunity to rid the country of over a hundred mosstroopers from the reiving clans of the Borders. Some of the recruits soon deserted and were reported to be hiding in Edinburgh, Leith and Canongate. The Privy Council declared them to be 'feeble and unwor[thie] dastartis, voyde of curage and of all honest and vertuous d[ispo]sitioun' and gave them a period of grace in which to come back or risk hanging. Gray sailed with 1,500 men from Leith to Hamburg towards the end of May, and a further 1,000 English recruits took ship from the Thames estuary. One of them no doubt was James Nauchtie from Aberdeen, who preferred soldiering to marriage (see Chapter 2).

Among the officers who sailed from Leith was John Hepburn, the second son of the laird of Athelstaneford in East Lothian. Born in or around 1598, John may have studied at St Leonard's College in St Andrews, where his name appears in the records for 1615, the same year in which he travelled to France, visiting Paris and Poitiers with a classmate, Robert Monro from Easter Ross. Monro was also to make a name for himself in the European wars, as we shall see, and the coincidence of the two men being friends and then both becoming mercenary commanders suggests the fashion at the time for military pursuits. Unlike Monro, Hepburn came from an old Catholic family and when Sir Andrew Gray set up a recruitment campaign with a camp at Monkrig, not far from Athelstaneford, the fact that Gray was also a Catholic may have added to the allure of the colours.[10]

Gray's men disembarked on the banks of the Elbe and moved east, reaching Boizenburg on 10 June and Cottbus, close to the present German–Polish frontier, on the 16th, after following a northerly route across Germany to avoid contact with Saxony, whose loyalty to the Protestant cause was not yet clear. An anonymous commentator noted their arrival in July: 'Colonel Gray is (God be blessed) safely arrived in Lusatia with his Brittans: he hath mustred two thousand foure hundred brave men; they are mightily praysed for their modest behaviour in their passage.' After some more remarks on how well the soldiers had behaved en route, so much that one begins to suspect propaganda, the writer notes, 'They are all armed and the King's Maiestie [Frederick] hath given them leave to rest themselves three weekes and it may be, will let them lie there still upon the Frontiers.'[11] Gray's force, and probably also Seton's and that of Sir Horace Vere, were assigned to Mansfeld's corps, one of four comprising the Bohemian army. Some of the Scots and English troops from Gray's Regiment were despatched under the command of John Hepburn to guard Frederick in Prague.[12] In keeping his units together, Mansfeld had had to deal with discontent in the ranks. Pay had not been forthcoming, a perennial problem with mercenary armies, and one not helped when Frederick had hinted that officers were not treating their men fairly by possibly purloining the money sent for them. Mansfeld had to ride to Prague to confront the Bohemian government but came back with only a third of the amount he sought, and that grudgingly given. The commander spent it on treating the sick and wounded and settling debts, tried to get money out of the country landowners around him, and trusted to the good will his men showed to him.

The assembling defenders of Frederick and the Protestant cause were in action very soon in the south of Bohemia. In mid May Seton's men took Prachatice, and in June the forces of the Duke of Saxe-Weimar, which probably included Seton's contingent, and others fought off an Imperial attack on Vodnany. Early in July they recaptured Tyn on the Vltava River. After this, Mansfeld and Saxe-Weimar separated, with the former moving to Neuhaus (now Jindrichuv Hradec). Towards the end of July 1620, the army of the Catholic League, led by Duke Maximilian of Bavaria and his experienced general, Count Johannes Tserklaes of Tilly, crossed into Austria while Spanish Habsburg forces from Flanders spilled into the Lower Palatinate to occupy Frederick's home territory. Sections of the Bohemian army fell back before the advance, part of it reaching Neuhaus, at the time held by two companies under Seton, on 21 September. On the following day the combined Imperial forces reached Budweis. Mansfeld took his units, including Gray's, west to the area around Pilsen, between Prague and Bavaria. Then Pisek fell to the Imperialists and at Nepomuk a few days later Gray and his men came under severe pressure from the vanguard of the enemy. Mansfeld was effectively sidelined in Pilsen, tempted by a call to withdraw from the conflict under terms from Maximilian of Bavaria, a course of action that he finally took after reminding the hapless Frederick in person that his contract had expired and had not been renewed.[13]

The main part of the Bohemian army fell back on Prague. The final battle took place on 8 November on the slopes of the hill called, in Czech, Bila Hora, White Mountain, a few miles south of the capital. Thurn, still in command of the Bohemian forces, began the day with 15,000 men around him in a strong defensive position on the slopes but his troops, predominantly mercenaries, quickly crumbled before the Imperial attack, and a late cavalry charge failed to retrieve an advantage. The Bohemians broke, leaving 2,000 dead and wounded behind them, and the Imperial cause had triumphed. Frederick and Elizabeth fled along snowy back roads from Prague to Breslau (now Wroclaw). Here the heavily pregnant Elizabeth Stuart wrote a quick letter to her father that included a plea to James 'to protect the king and myself, by sending us succour'.[14] Long before the letter arrived in London she had given birth – to her fifth child, on 25 December – and was moving towards Wolfenbuttel in Brunswick to the safety of relatives. Shortly afterwards, she and Frederick set up a court in exile in the Hague, and became known thereafter as the Winter Queen and King. In 1623 Frederick was stripped of his rights as an elector of the Holy Roman Empire in favour of Maximilian of Bavaria.

At the time of the defeat on Bila Hora, Sir Andrew Gray was with an artillery detachment near the castle of Karlstejn, a towering stronghold on a high ridge some distance south-west of Prague, in the ring of defensive positions around the capital, while Seton's contingent was still in southern Bohemia. Some of Gray's officers were taken prisoner at Bila Hora and were later ransomed by him, and he withdrew to Pilsen.[15] On 16 November Mansfeld was formally released from his obligations in Bohemian service – the Bohemian estates promised to forward pay arrears to him. The old warrior rallied his remaining troops and led them west to the Palatinate, 'never desisting untill he came within the sight of Heydelbergh, where he was no sooner descried from the Watch-towers and his Drummes were heard to beate but immediately the whole Towne shouted for sudden joy.'[16] Gray withdrew slowly westward, occupying the town of Elbogen (now Loket) and then Falkenau (now Sokolov), where he resisted Imperial assault until a surrender in April, after which he and his surviving men – some three hundred in number – returned to the Rhineland and joined the garrison of the fortress of Frankenthal, now under threat from Imperial forces.

John Seton and his musketeers were still in Bohemia. After occupying the town of Prachatice and the country as far east as Neuhaus, they had been forced back by the advancing Imperial armies to Wittingau (now Trebon) and had been there since September. In July 1621 only two places held out against the Imperial forces: Wittingau and Tabor, where a Captain Remes Romanesco was in command. Seton kept his mixed force of locals, Scots and Germans on a tight rein, something for which he gained favour among the civil population, although in February 1621 he had threatened to pillage the burghers unless they provided him with some funds. That the ordinary inhabitants of Wittingau preferred such a soldier to the kind of marauder they might have found themselves stuck with is indicated by the fact that they warned him of an impending Imperial attack in time to allow him to mount a surprise ambush to thwart it. At the beginning of April he had replied in writing to one invitation to surrender:

> My dear sir, I have received from bugleman Antonia Banzio your estimable letter in which you inform me that Tabor has returned to obedience to His Imperial Majesty and request me to do the same. I am unhappy that a place such as Tabor, which so bravely defended itself against your forces, was obliged to surrender, and I may also say that the defenders conducted themselves with valour. It is my wish to conduct myself in a like manner, and since I have promised my king my loyalty unto death, my only course, if I do not wish to deserve the name of liar, is to declare that, as a testimony to my loyalty, I wager my life on the struggle. Awaiting whatever war may bring, I remain, etc.[17]

Seton's defence was brave but finally futile and at last, on 23 February 1622, he surrendered on terms: the defenders and the people of

Wittingau were granted a full pardon and confirmed in their lives and possessions. Seton later found service in the French army. His stand was not the last hurrah of the Bohemian cause: that honour belongs to the town of Kladsko, under the command of Franz Bernhard von Thurn, which resisted until October.

The Spanish army, under Ambrogio Spinola, gained control of almost all the Rhineland during the autumn of 1620, cutting off garrisons loyal to Frederick in Frankenthal, Mannheim and Heidelberg. English troops led by Sir Horace Vere, a thousand men who had crossed from Gravesend in May, formed the core of the defence in the former two fortresses, while a mixed Dutch–German contingent occupied Heidelberg. On 25 October Mansfeld relieved Frankenthal and then crossed the Rhine to winter his troops in Alsace. As was typical of the period, Mansfeld was content to allow his troops to live off the land, by plundering every village and settlement they came upon. Refugees streamed into Strasbourg to escape the pillaging soldiers, bringing with them typhus, which wreaked its own havoc on the displaced peasants. The Imperial forces, under Tilly, meanwhile wintered in the Upper Palatinate until campaigning resumed in the following year. Disturbed by the presence of Spanish troops in the Rhineland and sympathetic to their fellow-Calvinist Frederick, still in their eyes the king of Bohemia, the leaders of the German states of Brunswick and Baden-Durlach came out for his cause and put armies in the field. Frederick himself joined Mansfeld at Germersheim in April, just in time to witness a repulse of an Imperial advance at Mingolsheim. For the rest of the season the Spanish/Imperial forces and the Protestant armies played a game of manoeuvre in the Rhineland, shifting warily across the country, enjoying local victory and temporary advantage. The trend, however, was against success for Mansfeld. When the Baden-Durlach forces were cut off by the Imperialists at Wimpfen, the mercenary commander crossed the Neckar and moved north, trying to outrace Tilly to the Main. At Höchst, a few miles to the west of Frankfurt, the Brunswick army suffered a crushing defeat on 20 June. In September Frederick's capital, Heidelberg, fell to Tilly's army, and in November Sir Horace Vere abandoned Mannheim. Frankenthal held out until March 1623. The whole of the Rhineland now lay in Imperial hands.

The truce between the Netherlands and Spain had expired in 1621 and Spinola had renewed his offensive against the rebellious republic. At this time there were two Scottish foot regiments in the Dutch army, a senior one commanded by Sir William Brog and the other by Sir Robert Henderson. Spinola's first actions were to occupy the province of Jülich, on the Dutch–German frontier, and carry out a surprise attack on the Dutch camp at Emmerich on a Saturday morning, as a result of which Sir William Balfour was taken prisoner for a time and had to be ransomed.

A stir was created in Scotland when it was learned that Archibald Campbell, seventh Earl of Argyll, was recruiting for the Spanish cause – the Privy Council noted the 'disgust' of the people, who were decidedly pro-Dutch – and a Spanish galleon was attacked when it anchored in Leith Roads.[18] Argyll gave out that the destination of the twenty companies he sought to raise was Sicily, to fight the Turks, but, as he had been sticking his toe into Spanish affairs for some time, suspicions were not allayed. On a visit to Rome in 1597 he had become an ardent Catholic and had married the daughter of a prominent English Catholic family. In 1618 he expressed the wish to visit Spain, ostensibly for his health but really to gather Spanish gold for his debt-burdened estate. Spain was equally interested in the earl, as his lands in Argyll offered men and an invasion route into Britain. In February 1619 the burgesses of Edinburgh labelled Argyll a traitor. He took service in the Spanish army in the Low Countries, even visiting Madrid in the autumn of 1619, but he saw no fighting and finally changed tack and tried to restore himself to Stuart favour. Spain was also interested in the clan Donald, the traditional enemy of Argyll and his Campbells. A few Donald individuals, such as Sir James Macdonald of Dunnyveg and Ranald Og, a relation of the Keppoch bard Iain Lom, were in the Low Countries under a Spanish flag, and other Highlanders may have been among the contingents of Irish mercenaries, but there was no large-scale recruiting among the clans. Relatively few Scots in fact served in the Habsburg forces in the Low Countries. There were three captains in Brussels in 1619: James Maitland, Lord Lethington; William Carpenter and Robert Hamilton, both of whom had been with Semple at Lier.

The composition of Spinola's army, as estimated by the Dutch

government in August 1624, illustrates the cosmopolitan nature of the
forces now contesting across Europe. The Spanish commander had at
his disposal 12,000 High Dutch [Germans], 4,000 Spanish and
Portuguese, 5,600 Italians, 6,800 Walloons, 2,200 Bourguinions [Bur-
gundians] and 3,000 English, Scots and Irish (probably mostly the
latter).[19] With these motley thousands, Spinola initiated in 1622 a siege
of Bergen-op-Zoom, an important port and commercial town on the
North Brabant coast, where the garrison was under the command of
Sir Robert Henderson. The defending troops included English, Scots
and Dutch, and it was one of the former who noted: 'They [the
Dutch] mingle and blend the Scottish among them, which are like
Beans and Peas among Chaff. These [Scots] are sure men, hardy and
resolute, and their example holds up the Dutch.' Early in the siege,
Henderson fell while leading a large sally against the attackers. 'He
stood all the fight in as great danger as any common soldier, still
encouraging, directing, and acting with his Pike in his hand. At length
he was shot in the thigh.'[20] Henderson was carried to safety but he
died soon afterwards, impressing all who saw him with his bravery.
Command of his regiment was passed to his brother, Sir Francis.

As with the siege of Ostend some years before, the assault on
Bergen assumed the nature of 'a publique Academie and Schoole of
warre, not only for the Naturalls of the Countrie, but for the English,
Scots, French, and Alamines [Germans], who being greedie of
militarie honour, resoirted thither in great numbers'.[21] This notion
of honour seems to have led men into acts of great bravery, if not
foolhardiness. The near-contemporary English historian William
Crosse wrote of a typical incident: 'the English and Scottes being
jealous of their honours, and unwilling that any Nation should be
more active than themselves, resolved to assault the Spaniard works
which they had made . . . and to give them a Camisado the night
following. They effected this assault accordingly with their Musket
shot and fire-balles, by which they forced the Enemies to forsake their
Trenches, after they had lost many men in the fight.'

News of the siege came to Mansfeld and he set off westward to
Bergen's assistance. The mercenary commander's army was not in
very good shape by this time, suffering from hunger and ill-armed, but
he made good speed. 'When the Count departed from Manheim he

was sixteene or seventen thousand strong Horse and Foot of all Nations . . . and his Foot were all Musketiers, there being few or no Pikes among them.' The greater part of Mansfeld's force was mounted and this, combined with a lack of gear, enabled them to move fast, via Saverne and through 'the Straits and Fastnesses of Alsatia, the Wildes and Woldes of Loraine'.[22] Among them were the Scots under Sir Andrew Gray's command. They came through Sedan and crossed the Sambre at Marpont on 27 August and two days later reached the small village of Fleurus, six miles from Namur. The speed of the march had taken the Spanish completely by surprise but they recovered sufficiently to attempt to intercept Mansfeld here. The mercenary army battered its way through and continued towards Bergen, finally rendezvousing with Dutch forces. By now 'the Mansfelders were not above six thousand strong that could ride or stand under their Armes, and those wre for the most part Horse, all or the greatest part of their Foot being either slaine in the battell of Fleurie, or disbanded in their long march out of the Palatinate.'[23] But Spinola was also enduring heavy losses and the threat of a desperate relief force on its way was enough to make him call off the siege of Bergen.

While Mansfeld stayed with his troops, Sir Andrew Gray crossed to England to seek further assistance from the Stuart monarchy. He alarmed James when he was brought into the royal presence still wearing his customary weapons – sword, dagger and a pair of pistols – but he was appointed a colonel and prepared to lead a force of English mercenaries to rejoin his colleagues in Europe. Before this was to happen, however, Spinola laid siege in 1624 to the town of Breda, where towards the end of the year plague cut a swathe through the inhabitants, reducing the population by a third.

Mansfeld himself crossed the Channel in March 1624 to take command of the new English levies for the war, with the aim of recovering the Palatinate for Frederick and his Stuart spouse. Britain saw very high recruitment for the continent in the latter half of 1624 – including 6,000 for the Low Countries and 12,000 for Mansfeld. In November Alexander Hamilton was appointed as an infantry captain and ordered to lead his men to Dover by Christmas Eve,[24] and presumably other contingents were given similar instructions. Initially the plan was to land the men in France, through which country they would be allowed to pass to join the campaign to recover the Palatinate. At the last moment, however, fearing a counter-invasion of Spanish troops from the Low Countries, the French withdrew permission, and Mansfeld had no choice but to sail north to find a landing at Flushing. As the Dutch were equally unwilling to allow such a large body of undisciplined troops ashore under the control of Mansfeld, a commander they did not fully trust, the fleet of ships, almost one hundred in number, was left swinging at its anchor chains for two weeks at the end of February. The raw levies, described by William Crosse as 'the dregges of mankind . . . the verie lees of the baser multitude . . . the forlorne braune and skurfe of human societie', suffered dreadfully from cold, hunger and thirst and began to die in their hundreds. The Dutch provided some food but it was not enough. A few taken for dead and dumped overboard recovered in the cold sea and were able to swim ashore to start a new life. More commonly, corpses were washed up with all the consequent risk of disease. Mansfeld was caught in a terrible dilemma: he could not provide for his troops and equally he could not simply let men ashore for fear of desertion, although a few escaped anyway and joined the enemy. One of the infantry regiments was commanded by Sir Andrew Gray but, as the recruitment had taken place in the south of England, there were probably few Scots among the wretched rank and file, whose fate was as undeserved as it was typical of what could befall the common soldier. At last Mansfeld was able to land his men, but that was not the end of their woes.

The Dutch wanted to employ them in the relief of Breda but after this town fell to the Spanish at the end of May they had no further use for Mansfeld and simply wanted rid of him and his men as fast as possible. Mansfeld led them through Brabant to Cleves on the Dutch–German border, losing men daily through desertion. By this time, the unlucky mercenary commander had only about half of his original strength but he struggled on against tremendous odds, betrayed by those who had undertaken to supply him. Back in Scotland, the Privy Council issued a warrant to Sir James Leslie to travel about the country to levy another 300 foot soldiers to serve under Mansfeld. Leslie's recruits eventually rendezvoused with Mansfeld's main body in north-western Germany. At last, at the end of the

year, the survivors found some food and rest in the bishopric of
Münster, around the town of Dorsten. Before long, though, Mansfeld
had to lead them further north, through Lingen, Haselünne on the
River Hase, Cloppenburg and at last to Emden, extorting supplies as
he went, his men passing through each district like a swarm of locusts.
The prospect of having to feed mercenaries led the citizens of Emden
to open sluice gates and to flood land in an effort to deter them, but
this only angered Mansfeld, who had endured so much in the cause he
fought for, and he held the town to ransom for 130,000 reichsthaler,
until finally the King of Denmark stepped in to settle matters and
provide a degree of security for the bedraggled remnants of the army.

The fate of Sir Andrew Gray remains obscure but he seems to have
remained in the Netherlands before returning to Scotland and then, in
1630, going to France.[25] With a band of followers, John Hepburn
went north to offer his services to Gustavus Adolphus; he was
welcomed and made a colonel in command of a regiment. Hepburn
was to prove to Gustavus Adolphus that the royal judgement had not
been misplaced, and opened a new chapter in the story of the Scottish
soldiers in Europe.

'a rude and ignorant Souldier'

Denmark, the Baltic, 1626–1628

A s 1625 DREW TO A close and as competing armies sought shelter in winter quarters across Europe, the forces of the Holy Roman Empire seemed to be in the ascendant and victory close for the Imperial cause and the Counter-Reformation. Now, however, other combatants had begun to push into the arena to renew the conflict. In May Christian IV, King of Denmark but also Duke of Holstein and thereby having rights under the Imperial constitution, was elected leader of the Lower Saxon *Kreis* or circle, the subsidiary polity of the Empire that covered a significant part of north-western Germany. Christian was Protestant and was keen to take up arms against the Habsburgs, and in December he joined in alliance with the Dutch and Britain to that end. The Imperial commander Johannes Tserklaes, Count of Tilly, whose forces had overcome Protestant opposition in the Rhineland, had moved north to cross the frontier of the Weser River to winter in the bishopric of Hildesheim, more or less on Christian's doorstep.

Meanwhile the Empire had acquired the services of another commander, whose name rings through the annals of his time: Albrecht Weuzel Eusebius von Waldstein or, more commonly, Wallenstein. Born a Protestant in the village of Hermanice on the Bohemian frontier in 1581, Wallenstein belonged to a family not especially wealthy but with enough to provide him with a good education and launch him on a military career in the Imperial army. Marriage to a wealthy widow brought him rich estates in Moravia and this foundation, combined with courage, superb skill in administration and the ability to form useful relationships in court circles, enabled him in 1617 to lead out his own army against Venice in the Imperial cause. Two years later he distinguished himself in action against Mansfeld's mercenaries in Bohemia but, perhaps more importantly, he received in pledge for sums spent on arms extensive lands to the north-east of Prague that had belonged to the Bohemian rebels. The later acquisition of the lands of Friedland on the Silesian border gave him his title of Duke of Friedland. In further successful campaigning in the Imperial cause he cleared Moravia of rebels in 1621, and in June 1625, against the advice of some of his inner circle, Ferdinand appointed Wallenstein his overall army commander. In September Wallenstein led his army west from Bohemia to winter in the areas around Halberstadt and Magdeburg.

In the Baltic Gustavus Adolphus's conquest of Livonia was a severe setback to the Polish king, Sigismund, and the next move by the Swede knocked Sigismund futher offbalance and kept him from intervening in the wars in the German lands. It began with a landing at Pillau (now Baltijsk) on the East Prussian coast at the end of June in 1626. With the exception of Danzig, whose citizens clung stubbornly to their independence, all the coastal towns fell quickly to the Swedes, some indeed welcoming their arrival. Now well established on his career path in Swedish service after several years as a colonel, Alexander Leslie was appointed to command the port and fortress of Pillau, and set about strengthening it, building new fortifications and strong points, as well as ensuring the security of food supplies. As part of the latter, he oversaw the construction of a horse-driven mill; some trouble in persuading the Königsberg city authorities to supply timber for this was solved by a deal with a merchant but time was lost and the structure was not completed until January 1628. Nevertheless, Leslie's efforts to secure the base at Pillau, a deep-water port of strategic significance, impressed Gustavus Adolphus. John Hepburn was also among the Scots who served in Pillau under Leslie's command.

In Britain Charles I had succeeded to the throne after the death of his father in March 1625 and was continuing the policy to regain the Rhineland Palatinate for the ousted Frederick and his Stuart wife, now in exile in the Low Countries. As was related in the previous chapter, the instrument of this policy, Mansfeld's army, had been reduced to a battered remnant that had plundered its way to find some refuge under Christian IV. In the new year, the restless count set off again, south-eastward this time, up the Elbe into the heart of the continent. The Stuarts resolved on further levies to bolster their cause and in March 1626 the Privy Council in Edinburgh granted a commission to Sir Donald Mackay of Strathnaver to raise a regiment of 2,000 men 'in whatsomever pairt of this kingdome whair he may most commodiouslie haif thame'.[1] In King Charles's words, with these recruits Mansfeld would be 'the better enhabled for that warre whiche he doeth prosequute by our directioun'. Knighted in 1616, Mackay of Strathnaver was the head of a clan that occupied extensive lands in the far north-west of the Highlands. In their relations with their neighbours in Caithness, Sutherland and Ross, the Mackays had long shown a cheerful readiness to indulge in cattle-lifting and feuding. Tough, already used to discipline and field conditions, they seemed likely material for a military campaign. Sir Donald certainly thought so, for in his history of the clan, Angus Mackay suggests that Sir Donald was less motivated by religious principle than by military ambition. Perhaps he also wanted to upstage the Gordons who had, in his eyes, usurped by foul legal means the earldom of Sutherland: 'The ill gotten charter of regality by which Sir Robert Gordon governed the north so circumscribed Mackay's energies at home that he felt constrained to lure Dame Fortune in a wider field abroad by the offer of his sword.'[2] Charles I was willing enough to give the chief his head and Highland custom ensured that Sir Donald's offer of commissions to the leading young men in neighbouring clans was readily taken up. There may have been some reluctance on the part of ordinary recruits to come forward in the service of an unlucky, faraway queen, even though she was a Stuart, and perhaps news of what had happened in Norway in 1612 deterred a few, but recruitment proceeded apace among the Mackays and other north Highland clans during the summer of 1626. Mackay's cousin, Arthur, tenth Lord Forbes, lent a hand: 'of the two thousand men he [Mackay] caried over . . . the Lord forbes and his freends did furnish aucht hundreth'.[3] Lord Forbes also provided Mackay 'for above a thousand lib sterlin . . . wherof he was glaid to accept of half payment fuve years thereafter'. On the same day as it issued Mackay's commission, the Privy Council wrote to some Highland lairds to encourage them to support the recruitment drive – 'you haif a nomber of idle men in your boundis who lyis loitering at home and might be more profitablie employit bothe for the credite of the cintrey and thair awne weelis by trayning thame up in militarie discipline' – but this hint was un-necessary and in a little over two months 3,600 men had taken the proverbial shilling. The recruitment had gone so smoothly that the men were ready to sail before ships were able to take them. This is a marked contrast to what transpired in the following year, when the Earl of Nithsdale, Lord Spynie and James Sinclair of Murkle came up against severe problems in their efforts to recruit men for Swedish service.[4]

One of the officers who sailed from Cromarty with Mackay's Regiment, as it was known, was Robert Monro from Obsdale on the north shore of the Cromarty Firth. His age on joining the levy is unknown, and there is also uncertainty over the date of his death, which fell sometime between 1675 and 1680, but it is reasonable to assume that he was barely twenty years old when he embarked for the Continent. The second son of the Obsdale laird, he had served briefly in the French army before joining Mackay's. Many years later, on his return to Britain, he wrote an account of his experiences that was published in two parts in 1637 by William Jones, Red Cross Street, London with a long title that is usually abbreviated to *Monro's Expedition*. The book provides us with the only truly comprehensive eyewitness story of the Scottish soldiers who fought in the Thirty Years War under the Swedish flag. It was such an unusual theme for a book that Monro felt moved to explain why he undertook the task of writing it in his dedication of the work to the Elector Palatine and in his address to the reader: 'though a rude and ignorant Souldier, I was bold to set pen to paper . . . [to preserve the memory of] . . . those worthy Cavaliers . . . whereof some, from meane condition, have risen to supreme honour, wealth, and dignitie . . . If you ask; why I wrote these Observations? It was because I loved my Camerades. If why I published them, know it was for my friends, and not for the world, for which I care not, nor for any that is ungrate.'

With Monro went young men from prominent families across the north. Murdo Mackenzie went as regimental chaplain, and survived to become minister of Contin, then bishop of Moray in 1662 and finally bishop of Orkney, the last prelate to occupy the palace in Kirkwall.[5] One of the most colourful in the company was Monro's own cousin, also Robert Monro, the eighteenth chief of the Foulis Monros and known as the Black Baron or Robert Dubh because of his swarthy complexion.[6] While still only in his late teens, the Black Baron inherited the extensive family lands along the Cromarty Firth after the unexpectedly early death of his father. An impetuous and extravagant young man, he became involved in the various inter-clan feuds prevalent in the north and had to dispose of parcels of his inheritance to cover debts and obligations, especially to the powerful Frasers of Lovat. Simon Fraser actually took possession of Foulis Castle and the Privy Council had to intervene in the violent quarrel that followed. The Baron was equally unlucky and careless in his personal life: his first wife died during the birth of her first child and he left his pregnant second wife to go off with another woman, a scandal that resulted in another case before the Privy Council. Robert Monro in his account of Mackay's Regiment loyally ignored some of his cousin's more outrageous acts and said that he had merely been 'a litle prodigall' on a trip to France. The Baron joined the regiment as a volunteer, clearly seeing soldiering on the Continent as a handy way to escape from his troubles at home.

The regiment reached Glückstadt on the Elbe on 20 October 1626,[7] after an uneventful five-day voyage from Cromarty. Other contingents crossed from Aberdeen and Leith, as the regiment also had considerable proportions of North-East and Lowland men. Monro was impressed by the standard of living he observed 'in the fat and fertile soyle of Holsten', and no doubt it made a notable contrast to the state of things in Easter Ross. As mercenaries often found, the local people could be less than welcoming. They said, wrote Monro, that they had no need of foreign soldiers and were as perfectly capable of holding off the Imperial enemy as any province in Germany; before long, added Monro with some satisfaction, 'they felt the wrath of Heaven'. One can understand the reluctance on the part of ordinary people to show hospitality to alien soldiers foisted on them without their leave. Occasionally this ill feeling spilled into violence. When a Captain Boswell, following Mackay's Regiment, was caught alone and murdered by 'villanous Boores, ever enemies to souldiers' the Scots' response – to burn the perpetrators' village – would have done nothing to restore relations. Officers tried to impose a strong discipline on their men to prevent this kind of conflict with the peasantry; this was certainly Robert Monro's policy and, for example, he later approved of the hanging of three Scots in Zealand in Denmark for the gang rape of a farmer's daughter.

Sickness had prevented Sir Donald Mackay himself from travelling with the regiment, and command devolved upon Lieutenant-Colonel Arthur Forbes. He, however, died very soon after their arrival and his place was taken by Captain Sanders Seaton, a promotion that did not please all the officers. The Highlanders received their muster money, settled in and began to train. Some of the officers had a finely honed sense of honour, a trait fostered by the clan society they came from. They refused to wear or carry the Danish cross as they were unsure of the propriety of such an action, but none of them had the courage to risk the anger of Christian IV by trying to explain their feelings to him. In an attempt to clarify their position they sent Captain Robert Ennis [Innes] to England to ask what they should do; back came the word that they should obey who was paying them 'in a matter so indifferent'.

Monro found the winter on the Holstein plains 'tedious' but recognised the value of the time spent on exercises and establishing good order. One incident appalled him. A German captain, 'out of a mad humour' in Monro's opinion, cut a finger off a Highland soldier and refused to show any remorse. An outraged Highland sergeant assaulted the German and nearly killed him. Monro recalled: 'This duty begun with the shedding of Duch-bloud by one of my name and kindred. In the continuance of the storie, you shall hear much bloud shed, of all Nations in Europe, and of ours not the least. But of my freinds [sic] and myne, too much.'

Sir Donald Mackay finally joined his regiment at the end of March 1627 and preparations were made for the final inspection by their employer, Christian IV, at Itzehoe in a colourful ceremony. The senior officers kissed the monarch's hand and the Articles of War were read. The fact that Christian was the late King James's brother-in-law instilled among the Highlanders a feeling of loyalty to the Danish royal house, as Monro makes clear. On the day after the big parade marching orders came in. Sir Donald and Captain Seaton were commanded to cross the Elbe with seven companies, leave two to garrison the town of Stade and proceed with the rest to join General Sir Thomas Morgan's four English regiments of foot guarding the Weser river. The remaining four Highland companies, under Sergeant-Major Dunbar, were ordered to Lauenberg in case the enemy attempted to cross the Elbe in that vicinity. Mackay's men spent ten weeks with the English, a time of false alarms but no action; they were discontented to discover that Morgan's men were being paid weekly while they were supplied only with 'proviant bread, beere and bacon'. At last, on 20 July, the Highlanders left the Weser to march back north to Boizenburg. Here they stayed for five nights in the open.

The Imperial forces under General Tilly were now reported to be only 5 'miles' away to the south,[8] a serious threat and a worrying reminder of the battle in the previous August when Tilly had smashed the Danish army at Lutter am Bamberg. Leaving four companies under the command of Sergeant-Major Dunbar at Boizenburg, the bulk of the regiment was ordered to set off eastward in the direction of Alt Ruppin in Brandenburg, a march of six days under normal circumstances. Monro thought that Tilly now learned of the small force left at Boizenburg and moved to lay siege to the fort there. Dunbar led out a skirmishing party at night to harass the approaching enemy before retiring behind the fortified walls. Next day the Scots fought off the first assault, accounting for 500 of their opponents according to Monro, and then repelled a second, stronger attack. On the third assault, Dunbar's men ran out of powder and resorted to throwing sand in their enemies' faces and hitting them with their musket butts in what must have been a bitter, bloody struggle on the walls of the fort. The assailants withdrew to find an easier way across the Elbe. Dunbar was ordered to retire and save his cannon, and, after destroying the Boizenburg bridge, he moved down river the few miles to Lauenburg. Very soon after this, two companies of Scots under a Major Wilson failed to hold Lauenburg and had to submit, ignominiously losing their colours in the process, a faux pas that cost Wilson

his status and his command. The bravery of the defenders of
Boizenburg was reported in a letter from Glückstadt to the Earl
of Nithsdale in August 1627, where the writer adds: 'This peece of
service hath gotten our nation great honour by the Kinge in so much
that when Captaine Leslie's compagnie marched through Crimpe . . .
when some men did laugh at our men becaus they ware bad apparelled
he said it is no matter they have good heartes and clothes ar easier
helpit as of a cowardlie heart to make a courageous of.'[9]

The main body of Mackay's Regiment rested at Alt Ruppin for just
over a week in quarters distributed over various villages in the area.
Now it became apparent that the original aim of the expedition – to
reinforce Mansfeld in his campaign to recover the Palatinate – was a
lost cause, for by this time the veteran mercenary commander had
fought and lost his last battle. On 25 April 1626 Wallenstein caught
Mansfeld when the latter laid siege to the town of Dessau and gave
him a drubbing that reduced his already small strength by half. Close
to 3,000 men, half of Mansfeld's numbers, were taken prisoner. These
included Scots, and many of them switched sides to serve the victor,
possibly in the regiment of arquebusiers under the command of the
Scottish colonel Daniel Hepburn or Hebron. Originally in Polish
service, Hepburn had joined Wallenstein's army in 1625. Those who
escaped unscathed from Dessau regrouped in the Brandenburg area
and during the summer staggered on to reach Silesia, where Mansfeld
hoped to ally with the Hungarians against the Holy Roman Empire.
After a rendezvous with forces of the Duke of Saxe-Weimar, Mansfeld
pressed on up the Oder into Moravia. They reached a place called
Weissenkirchen (now Hranice), garrisoned by Imperial musketeers,
and attacked it. An English soldier called Sydnam Poyntz, who had
been recruited in Sir James Leslie's levy in 1625, was present and left a
description of what happened: 'where though wee were repulsed the
first tyme, yet the second tyme wee entred killing man, Woman and
child: the execution continued the space of two howers, the pillageing
two days.'[10] One officer leading this assault was a Sandilands from
Torphichen, possibly a son of James Sandilands, Lord Torphichen,
who was Stuart ambassador to Poland in 1609. Mansfeld's plan to join
with the Hungarians now fell through and finally, in the autumn of
1626, while on his way possibly to Venice, in the little town of Serato

in Bosnia the 46-year-old warrior, his surviving followers dispersed to the winds of fate, turned sick and died.[11] It seems that it was only now, some nine or ten months later, that the news of Mansfeld's demise reached Mackay's men. Sir Donald transferred his complete allegiance to Denmark but now was faced with the problem of being halfway after Mansfeld, far to the east of the Danish army and in danger of being cut off from it, as Tilly drove north into Holstein.

Tilly made good this threat in September, defeating the Danes at Grossenbrode. Mackay's only option was to head directly to the Baltic. A fast six-day march took the Scots to Perleberg and then, 'in great haste, night and day', Monro and his colleagues struggled on to reach the coast near the Hanseatic port of Wismar. A mile to the east of the town, they found a secure encampment on the isthmus of Poel and stayed there five weeks. Here they had plenty of meat but ran short of bread and salt; the bread ration was reduced to one pound per man every ten days, but they had so much beef and mutton that they grew sick of it, and to their great annoyance no assistance came from the burghers of Wismar. The 10,000-strong army was struck by disease, 'pestilence and flux' that Monro attributed to the unbalanced diet. Many men died and Monro was moved to record how well the survivors endured their hardships.

The Imperial armies of Tilly and Wallenstein had now united, but Mackay's retreat to the sea had done the needful in allowing the Highlanders to escape entrapment by evacuating. Sailing at last from the fetid camp on Poel, they disembarked to the west at the small port of Heiligenhafen and moved inland to Oldenburg to await the rest of the Danish army. Lying in the middle of a stubby peninsula thrusting towards the Danish islands, the road through Oldenburg provided the only route through low-lying wetlands strung with marsh, heath and small lakes. After reaching the village in the evening the Scots laboured to dig trenches to strengthen their position and had just completed these by noon next day when word of the approaching enemy reached them. Early in the afternoon the horse and foot of the Imperial army were in sight and before three o'clock the enemy batteries opened fire on what Monro calls their 'Leager', their fortified position.

No fighting took place during the hours of darkness, but it began in earnest at dawn. Sir Donald Mackay set off at the head of half the regiment to hold the road, leaving the other half under the command of Sanders Seaton in reserve, while Monro passed out ammunition and ensured the men were ready. As they marched up they met their commanding general, Duke Bernard of Saxe-Weimar. The duke asked if the soldiers 'went on with courage' and, says Monro, 'they, shouting for joy, cast up their hats, rejoycing in their march, seeming glad of the occasion'. The defenders took up position to endure the hail of musket and cannon shot hurtling down on them and tearing their flags to shreds. Lieutenant Hugh Ross was struck in the leg by a cannonball but he stayed conscious and yelled to his comrades to carry on, adding he wished he had a wooden leg. The same ball took the leg off another officer, David Ross, a son to Ross of Gannis (Geanies in Easter Ross). The incoming fire was now taking a toll. Monro himself was injured in the right knee when a ball shattered his partizan, a halberd he carried, and drove fragments into his leg. The German troops beside the Scots wilted under the Imperial onslaught and withdrew but, at the critical moment before the road was lost, Sir Donald Mackay rallied a platoon of his musketeers and, under their covering fire, the rest of the men pressed on, using a hedge for cover. Monro says the body of pikemen stood two hours 'under mercy of Cannon and musket' and suffered heavy losses. A barrel of powder accidentally blew up, wounding many soldiers and burning Mackay himself in the face. The enemy were now beginning to filter past the stubborn defenders but were stopped by Captain John Monro and a party of musketeers who set up sustained fire on a stretch of flat ground and forced them to retire. Seaton brought up his reserve to relieve the men in the front line and, when darkness began to fall after four o'clock, the fighting dwindled and ceased.

An odd incident, one of the freak occurrences that often seem to take place on a battlefield, happened in the evening. A barrel of beer was sent up from the camp to ease the thirst of the parched defenders and 'the Officers for haste caused to beate out the head of it, that every man might come unto it, with hat or head-peece, they flocking about the waggon whereon the Barrell lay'. A cannon shot hit the barrel and blew it into the air. No one was harmed but, says Monro, it was 'the nearest misse that I ever did see'.

As ammunition was now running low, the decision was taken to withdraw to the coast, a necessity for which Monro criticised Weimar's lack of attention to supply and fortification; if these matters had been attended to properly before the action, he thought, the position might have been held indefinitely. As it was, the Imperialists, fearing the approach of Protestant forces behind them, were also considering withdrawal, but of course this was unknown to the defenders. Aided by the moonlight, the regiment moved to the coast, reaching the shore at ten o'clock to find that the seamen on the waiting ships had been so scared by the sounds of gunfire they had been hearing all day that they were incapable of helping them embark. Monro seized a pier by force and began to bring ships in. At length, most of the men were aboard, except for a few who had wandered off in search of plunder. Horses and baggage were abandoned but Monro managed to bring off three boatloads of the sick and wounded before enemy cavalry took possession of the beach. The last Scots were fired on. An officer from the Western Isles, Alexander MacWorche, was mortally wounded in the head and arm by pistol balls but was able to swim to his comrades in the boats. The soldiers who had gone astray to plunder were taken prisoner and, as the ships slid away over the sea, Monro saw other units of the Danish army surrendering without a shot.

Mackay's men reached the town of Flensburg three days later. All of Holstein had now fallen into Imperial hands but the Danes still held their islands, and the regiment was ordered to proceed to Assens on the island of Fyn. When they reached the security of the island town, Monro records their numbers: 800 men, and 150 sick and wounded; their losses in the campaign had been 400. Mackay was invited to dine with Christian IV, who was very grateful for the gallant support of the Scots and had them assigned to decent quarters. As they moved through Danish territory, they found that their reputation was now going before them: 'After this service [the defence of Lauenberg],' wrote Monro, 'where ever we came, the Gentrie of the Country were ready meeting us, providing all necessaries for us.'

Unsurprisingly, Christian expressed a wish for more soldiers from Scotland and commissioned the Earl of Nithsdale to raise 3,000 men.[12] These, however, proved difficult to find. Throughout the summer of 1627 in Scotland, Nithsdale, Alexander Lord Spynie and James Sinclair of Murkle laboured to recruit 3,000 men each for Danish service, finally settling, it has been suggested, for little more than half the total of 9,000.[13] The Privy Council tried to assist them by instructing local authorities to apprehend gypsies, vagabonds, 'ydle and maisterlesse men wanting trades and competent meanes to live upoun' and deserters from Mackay's Regiment. That resistance to recruitment was growing is suggested by the report that some targeted groups were forming themselves into 'societies and companeis armed with hacquebutts and pistolets and uther armour'. To fill their quotas, recruitment officers turned towards easier targets, such as youngsters at the college in Edinburgh, with the result that outraged parents in the capital began to send their sons to St Andrews, Glasgow or Aberdeen to complete their education. By the end of July the Privy Council was starting to worry that the soldiers recruited by Nithsdale, Spynie and Sinclair would cause trouble while they waited for the ships. Another complication suddenly popped up in August to beggar the efforts of Nithsdale and his companions: Charles wanted 2,000 men for the Duke of Buckingham's expedition to La Rochelle,[14] and he asked the Privy Council to postpone the departure of levies to Denmark until October. Nithsdale finally published 10 October [Old Style] as the deadline by which all his personnel had to gather in Edinburgh to go to Germany, and on the same day the townspeople of Burntisland complained of 'manie great disordours' and the peace of the burgh 'verie farre disturbit' by the assembled levies.

While Mackay's Regiment was recuperating at Assens in the winter of 1627/28, news came through of their comrades' fate at Breitenburg Castle, near Glückstadt. Here Sergeant-Major Dunbar with four companies of the regiment and some German troops had been besieged by Tilly's forces. The castle was really a fortified house and, despite a moat, its defences were not strong, but Dunbar refused to surrender. For six days they held out behind the shot-torn walls and cost their attackers dear – Monro says a thousand men, which is scarcely credible. When Dunbar rejected further offers of parlay, the Imperialists retaliated with the customary warning that there would be no quarter. Dunbar was shot through the head soon after this but his stubborn pride had so influenced his fellow officers that none dared now to surrender. When the castle finally fell to the enemy, most of the males within were put to the sword. According to Monro, only some half dozen escaped by luck, and one of them was a young ensign who later told what had happened. Monro recorded: 'The service, thus begun Comedian-like, ends very Tragically, the whole Court and lodgings running with bloud, with which the walls and pavement are sprinkled with our Scottish bloud.' Three hundred of Mackay's Regiment perished in what was nothing more than a pointless defence. There were to be many more incidents like it as the Thirty Years War dragged its scarlet coat across Europe.

Monro was promoted to sergeant-major in Dunbar's place, in effect the third in command in the regiment, and he remained at Assens while most of the other officers returned to Scotland to recruit more men or enjoy some leave. Robert Monro, the Black Baron, clearly found his experiences as a volunteer to his liking and went off to raise his own regiment, beginning with a company of his own kin that he brought back to Denmark. Sir Donald Mackay found his second recruiting campaign to be slower than the first, and it took time to raise the numbers; a historian of the Mackays says he had 'practically drained Strathnaver of its able-bodied men'.[15] His efforts were appreciated where it mattered to him, though, and in June 1628 he was to be ennobled as Lord Reay, before he sailed back to Copenhagen with a thousand recruits behind him.

In their Danish quarters, some trouble erupted between the Scots and men from a German cavalry unit Monro calls Rhinegrave's Horse, resulting in bloodshed and a few deaths before order was restored. Later, the German regiment found respect for their fellows-in-arms and were to show this by coming to their aid at the battle at Wolgast. Early in 1628 Monro was ordered to take four companies to the fertile island of Lolland. Christian feared the Imperialists, who now had designs to gain control of the Baltic, might strike across the narrow strip of sea that here separated Danish territory from the German island of Fehmarn, particularly as Lolland was where the Danish queen mother had her residence, near the town of Nykøbing. Monro stationed two companies at Maribo in the centre of the island, one at Rødby on the coast and one near the royal house, and was delighted to find a local shipbuilder by the name of Sinclair, a man of probably Caithness ancestry, who could speak Scots.

At the beginning of April, the Highlanders rendezvoused with other troops at Rødby for a raid on Fehmarn. The men, a mixed bunch of Scots, English, Germans and French, boarded boats – Monro calls them open skouts – but an adverse wind prevented their sailing and they spent three days on the water, shivering in frost and snow, before the venture was abandoned. On 16 April they got away at last and, after a crossing that took two days, stormed ashore in squads of twenty and thirty, initially in the face of enemy fire until the defenders felt themselves outnumbered and retired to a fort. The Danes persuaded the garrison to surrender and, after saving them from the angry vengeance of the local farmers, packed them off on boats to the mainland. Christian now turned his eyes westward and on 21 April launched a raid on Eckernförde to the west of Kiel. Some of the Imperial garrison left the town but a captain and 250 infantry resolved to defend the skonce against the raiders. The Danes decided on a frontal attack, and the officers threw dice for the honour of leading the assault. Monro won. After the Scots chaplain William Forbesse had ministered to the soldiers, Monro detailed a company of musketeers to provide flanking fire on the skonce from a nearby house while he led the charge on the walls across an approach without cover. Some Scots fell to musket balls, and Captain Mackenzie, a brother to Lord Seaforth, was wounded lightly in the leg. A ball struck the hilt of Monro's sword. The Englishmen coming on in the second wave of the assault suffered more heavily from the defenders' fire but in the face of the determined attack the garrison quit the skonce for the town. The attackers soon broke down the town gate and chased the garrison through the streets until they barricaded themselves inside the church. The Highlanders forced their way in to find their opponents had taken refuge in a loft, but not before strewing trails of gunpowder in the body of the church as if, thought Monro, to booby-trap their pursuers. Remembering what had befallen their comrades under Dunbar at Breitenburg, the men of Mackay's Regiment blew up the church and very few of the Imperial garrison survived. Monro was burnt a little by the premature explosion of the gunpowder. In his account, he seems ambivalent about this incident, recognising that it was an atrocity but saying he was powerless to stop it. He excuses his own men's behaviour in assailing the church by stating the defenders had already 'made of the house of God a Denne of theeves and murderers' after their conduct at Breitenberg. 'Yet truly,' he wrote, 'my compassion was so much, that when I saw the house ordained for Gods service defiled with their bloud and ours, and the pavement of the church covered over with the dead bodies of men, truly my heart was moved unto the milde streames of pittie, and wept.' Monro was discovering, if he did not sense it already, the horror of war.

After plundering the town, the Danish force withdrew before the Imperial cavalry could come up and sailed along the coast eastward to Kiel. Here they ran into disaster; the attack on Eckernförde, says Monro, was 'like a pleasant Weathergall, the forerunner of a great storme', and noted that some of the men who had borne away booty did not live another forty-eight hours to enjoy it. At first, all went well. The little fleet – five ships and two galleys – made its way up the long, narrow firth that led to the town and stopped within a musket shot of the urban centre at six o'clock in the evening. The attackers perceived no threat but were unaware that the garrison commander had hidden musketeers in a deep trench along the shore with strict orders not to fire or show themselves. After a night afloat, Christian ordered a barrage of broadsides for an hour before commanding musketeers to land. This time the dice fell in favour of the German contingent. They suspected something was wrong and asked for a delay, precipitating a row among the senior officers. Christian settled the dispute by ruling that 'the partie should be commanded proportionally of all Nations alike, and to cast Lots who should send a Captaine to command them'. The dice rolled in favour of an English lieutenant whom Monro does not name.

The musketeers, 200 in number, piled into their boats and set off for the shore, but the hidden defenders opened fire as they approached, getting off two salvoes and killing or wounding most of the attackers before they could struggle to land. The English lieutenant gallantly urged his men on and the fight shifted to the shore where, after half an hour, the few German musketeers still alive were out of powder. Christian forbade another landing and brought off the survivors. The lieutenant came away last, with 3 bullet wounds, and died the next night. Monro praised the courage of the High-landers who had taken part: 'our Scottish High-land-men are prayse-worthy who for lacke of Boats made use of their vertue and courage in swimming the Seas, notwithstanding of their wounds, with their cloathes, shewing their Masters, they were not the first came off, but with the last.' He lost a Sergeant Mac-Clawde [Macleod] and 22 men.

Christian returned to Fehmarn, where he set up a strong fortified camp and sent 1,000 men across to Grossenbrode on the mainland to establish a strongpoint there. The Imperialists, only a short distance to the south, wasted little time before they attacked with a force of horsemen and dragoons. While part of the Danish force prepared to defend the route to the sea, Monro's men and the English contingent looked to the defence of Grossenbrode itself. Monro placed a party of musketeers behind a barricade of wagons a hundred paces from the houses and stationed the others in the village. The enemy cavalry tried to cut off their escape route but were held off by musket fire. A message now reached Monro from the king; if the Highlander thought it necessary, he was told, he could retire to the churchyard. Monro knew that this could lead to them being taken prisoner and sent back the riposte that he would rather fire the village in a fighting retreat. The Imperialists seem not to have pressed home their attack, and when darkness fell Monro took the chance to slip away to the ships, behind a screen of dragoons who fell back with them. At dawn the enemy attacked again but were held back by cannon fire from the ships. Once the fortifications on Fehmarn were complete – Christian had drafted in over four thousand peasants to labour on the entrenchments – the amphibious Danish force sailed for Lolland, leaving two German companies behind as a garrison.

While Mackay's Highlanders were serving under the Danish flag at the west end of the Baltic, other Scots were engaged with Gustavus Adolphus far to the east around Danzig, still blockaded by the Swedish fleet. Recovering from his initial shock at the Swedish landings and the swift occupation of the coast in the summer of 1626, Sigismund gathered his forces to combat the invaders. In 1626 he repeated a request for troops from Britain but this was rejected by

Charles I. There were, however, already a few Scots fighting for Sigismund, including William (Gilbert) Keith, Andrew Keith and Patrick Gordon. The English mercenary Arthur Aston, the son of a father with the same name, was also engaged on the Polish side, leading a company of 500 men.

Gustavus Adolphus's troops and those of the Polish king met in battle at Mewe (now Gniew), south-east of Danzig, on the west bank of the Vistula. Sigismund had invested the town with a strong army. The relieving Swedish force, under the command of Colonel Thurn and John Hepburn, reached the scene late in September to find the enemy entrenched on high ground. Though outnumbered – Hepburn had 3,000 Scots, and Thurn only 500 horsemen – the two men decided on a daring stratagem to oust the Poles. Hepburn led a flanking movement in the fading light to scale the hill up a steep, overgrown slope where his men had to scramble through the brush, struggling to keep their muskets and accoutrements from snagging, to follow him as he clambered before them with a white plume in his helmet as a marker. The Poles were taken by surprise but recovered and fought to drive off their attackers. Hepburn's pikemen held off several charges by the Polish cavalry and their Cossack allies before they were reinforced by men under the command of Welsh colonel Mostyn and a contingent of German arquebusiers. For two days they continued to hold the high ground while Gustavus Adolphus forced a way through to the town, compelling Sigismund to withdraw from the siege.

After the defeat at Mewe, Sigismund relinquished command in the field to Hetman Koniecpolski. The war turned into a dance of manoeuvre over the succeeding months. On one occasion, Alexander Leslie, now a lieutenant-general in the Swedish army, led a small contingent to reconnoitre the Polish positions around Danzig and found himself surrounded by enemy cavalry near the village of Girlinerwals. Leslie's pikemen had to break through the Polish horse twice before they successfully found an escape route, turning their withdrawal to their advantage by leading the Poles into the main Swedish army.

Over the winter of 1626/27 the Swedish army was sorely hit by outbreaks of disease, with some companies being reduced to only a

handful of men fit for duty. In April Koniecpolski regained control of
Puck to the west of Danzig but the war continued to be one of
manoeuvre and ultimately stalemate, with Gustavus Adolphus unable
to overcome a foe that could withdraw at any moment into the
immense Polish hinterland. In the skirmishes Gustavus Adolphus was
himself wounded. On 7–8 August, at Tczew, the Swedes defeated
Koniecpolski's army. Here Gustavus Adolphus suffered another
wound, a musket shot in the neck which resulted in lasting discomfort
that would prevent him wearing any chest armour again. Now Sir
James Spens comes back into the picture, arriving in September 1627
as ambassador from Charles I to the King of Sweden and bringing the
royal gift of the Order of the Garter. One of the witnesses of the
Garter ceremony was Robert Primrose, the son of the clerk to the
Privy Council; he wrote to tell his father what he saw: '. . . the King
ressaved the ordour of the Gartour with the whole robbes whilk after
he had ressaved he knightit Sir Peter Young and Sir Harie St George
and some Scottis colonellis, and then the whole ordounance bothe in
the towne and the liggar [camp] played with thrie or foure thousand
muskattis.'[16] The Scots colonels whom Primrose does not name
included Patrick Ruthven, now commanding the Kalmar Regiment
with an annual salary of 2,000 riksdaler, and Alexander Leslie. Spens's
mission had the more important aim of persuading Gustavus Adolphus to make peace with the Poles and direct his military resources
towards the war in support of the Protestant cause in Germany. As he
was still the overall commander of British mercenaries in Swedish
service, Spens was in effect playing on both sides in the diplomatic
game and was still fielding requests for more recruits from Scotland.

While Gustavus Adolphus was struggling to consolidate his hold on
Prussia, the Imperial armies under the command of Wallenstein and
Tilly established themselves in the Baltic areas of Germany, in
Holstein, Mecklenburg and Pomerania. A grateful emperor added
Duke of Mecklenburg and Admiral of the Baltic Seas to Wallenstein's
growing list of titles. Gustavus Adolphus and Christian of Denmark
were both concerned to keep the Habsburgs from the front door and
reached an agreement in January 1628 on the defence of the Baltic. An
unknown Scottish trader makes an appearance in the story here:

Wallenstein thought up a scheme whereby this man would receive a reward of 30,000 reichsthaler in return for the burning of the Swedish fleet. Presumably the Scot was expected to infiltrate the fleet to implement the arson but it seems he died suddenly and nothing ever came of the plan.[17] Central to the Habsburg ambition to become a Baltic power was the port of Stralsund. The Stralsunders, however, saw their future differently and rejected any opportunity to cement an Imperial alliance. Wallenstein despatched an army to take the city by force but, in June 1628, some five weeks after the Imperial siege began, the Stralsunders reached an agreement with Gustavus Adolphus, according to which the Swedish king promised to protect them. And, for once, the Danes laid aside their suspicion of their Swedish neighbours and also came to Stralsund's defence. Christian IV called off his raids on the Holstein coast, in which Robert Monro and his comrades had distinguished themselves, and instead issued orders to the Scots to prepare to sail east.

TEN

'new conditions from a new Master'

The Baltic, the Oder, 1628–1631

ROBERT MONRO WAS in Copenhagen early in May 1628
when he received the command to bring Mackay's Regiment
with all haste to Elsinore and learned that Christian IV had
chosen to send his Scots to the defence of Stralsund. Lieutenant-
Colonel Sanders Seaton, newly returned from Holland, set off with an
advance party of three companies, while Monro took ship with the
rest of the men for a destination several days' sailing to the east.

The port-city of Stralsund had been for long a member of the
Hanseatic League and had grown on its trade to fill what was now a
crowded island of squares, narrow streets, warehouses and red-brick,
spired churches. Lying on the mainland side of the narrow strait of
Strelasund between it and the island of Rügen, the city was almost
completely surrounded by water, and only narrow causeways bridged the
wide lagoons called the Knieperteich and the Frankenteich on the
landward side to link the urban centre to its hinterland. With these
natural obstacles supplemented by a massive stone wall with eleven
towers, it was not an easy place to capture. Wallenstein, however, wanted
this wealthy metropolis for the quartering of his army, but it was a wish
too much for the burgers, who refused to allow a single Imperial soldier
to enter their gates and called on help from Denmark and Sweden.

The Imperial army, under the command of the Saxon field marshal
Von Arnim, began its siege on 13 May. On 7 June the ships carrying
Mackay's Regiment lumbered into the Strelasund to a storm of shot from
the enemy batteries. The vessel carrying Monro went aground and was
struck by a cannonball, losing a mast, before it could be pulled off. While

one of the Highland companies was directed to garrison the tiny island of Dänholm, the others disembarked at the city wharves and swarmed up the curving, sloping street to the marketplace, where they paraded at four o'clock in the afternoon before being despatched to man the defences outside the walls at the Frankentor, the south-eastern extremity of the urban area. This was the weakest part of the defences and Monro says they were pressed by the enemy: 'And so *singulis noctibus per vices* [night on, night off], during six weekes time, that my cloathes came never off, except it had beene to change a suite or linnings [linen]', recalled the Highland commander. The entrenchments behind which the defenders sheltered at the Frankentor were 'scurvie outworkes, which were but slightly fortified with a dry Moate, the enemy lying strong before us' and threatening another assault at any time.

The burgers of Stralsund were 'wearied and toyled with watching, and also hurt by their enemies, whom they had beaten from their walles twice before our coming'. They should have been glad of the newly arrived Scots but they were slow to provide them with proper quarters. After bedding down in the street for four nights, some men from a Captain Monro's company decided to take matters into their own hands. Unknown to their officers, they sought out the burgermeister in his own home and told him that if he did not issue orders for proper accommodation he would find them staying with him. The flustered burgermeister sent them away with soft words and at once complained to Colonel Holck, the military governor. Holck formed a court martial and tried the soldiers for mutiny. They were of course found guilty and were told to draw lots to see which three of their number should be hanged. The unlucky trio was committed to prison to await the noose but Robert Monro's officers interceded with Holck and persuaded him that one execution would be enough to make an example. Monro does not give the details of their conversations but someone may have observed that in a siege they might need every man they had. As it happened, the trio condemned to death comprised two Scots and a Dane. They drew lots and the Dane was the unfortunate loser. This gave Monro some grim satisfaction: Holck had to hang one of his own countrymen but the lack of proper quarters had been his fault in the first place.

The defenders continued to strengthen the defences at the Fran-kentor and, at times, came so close to the trenches of the besieging army that they were able to exchange taunts with their opponents. Monro's men sallied out at night to disconcert the attackers and return with a prisoner or two and, during the day, the Imperial cannon and mortars continued to hurl destruction into the town. Monro recorded a macabre incident in which one cannonball decapitated an officer and thirteen soldiers at one stroke: 'who doubts of this, he may go and see the reliques of their braines to this day, sticking on the walles, under the port of Franckendore in Trailesund.'

This brutal stalemate promised to come to an end when, towards the end of June, Wallenstein himself arrived outside the city. Dissatisfied with the lack of progress of the siege under Field Marshal von Arnim, who had got nowhere in six weeks, Wallenstein swore he would take the city in three nights though it were hanging in iron chains from heaven. The spearhead of his assault would strike at the Frankentor, where the walls were no more than man-high. Probably from the prisoners they were snatching from the trenches, the defenders learned of Wallenstein's arrival and the likelihood that life would grow hotter. Monro increased the number of sentries and had a squad of eighty musketeers under Captain Hay 'sit by their Armes' ready to respond to attack. It came at last between ten and eleven o'clock a few nights later. Fifty musketeers under Ensign Johnston were caught outside the defensive works and some fell before they could retire to safety. The bitter struggle lasted for an hour and a half, Captain Mackenzie's section being very hard pressed. Monro had to send in Hay with his musketeers to a stretch where German soldiers had deserted. Monro 'being wearied and growne stiffe with my wounds, being helpt off, did meete a fresh reliefe coming to us, led by Lieutenant Andrew Stewart . . . brother to the noble Earle of Traquare'. Later, a mixed force of Swedes and Scots, led by a Colonel Frettz, a MacDougall and a Semple, with eighty musketeers, took their turn in the line. Frettz was killed, and MacDougall disappeared; six months later, Monro learned that he had been taken prisoner. The defenders held on. 'On the last storme, by the breake of day, the enemy was once entred our workes, and was beate back againe with great losse, with swords and pikes and butts of muskets.' When the fighting finally broke off, Monro reckoned that Wallenstein had lost around a thousand men, the defenders nearly two hundred.

Monro was taken to his quarters and confined to bed by a knee

. A close-up of George Sinclair's gravestone near Kvam in Gudbrandsdalen, Norway, showing
inscription recording his death on 26 August 1612 (5 September in the modern calendar).
 Larsen)

)VE LEFT. Scottish ensigns in Danzig in 1578, in the contingent of men under the command
Colonel William Stewart. The images were painted in the Low Countries shortly after the
ments returned there. *(Bibliotheque Royale de Belgique)*

)VE RIGHT. Sir Patrick Ruthven, one of the murals painted in Skokloster Castle near
:kholm. *(Skoklosters slott)*

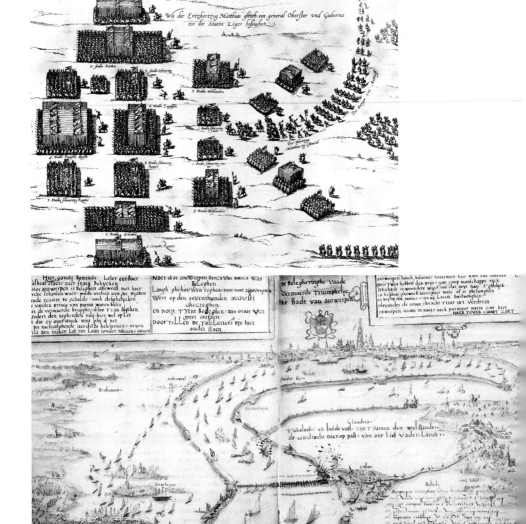

TOP. Forces with Archduke Matthias, appointed as governor general of the Spanish Netherlan[d] in January 1578. Two of the contingents of foot soldiers are identified as Scots. Some of these men, under the command of William Stewart, fought at the battle of Rymenant on 14 July 1578. *(Germanisches Nationalmuseum)*

ABOVE. Antwerp under attack in 1584. The River Scheldt curves south towards the city betwe[en] the dykes and flooded shores of Brabant (to the west) and Flanders. The fort of Lillo, defende[d] by Scots under the command of Colonel Barthold Balfour, is in the left foreground. *(Bibliotheque Royale de Belgique)*

LEFT. Sir Alexander Leslie, 1st Earl of Leven (*Attributed to George Jamesone, c.1580-1661, ~duced courtesy of the Scottish National Portrait Gallery*)

RIGHT. Frederick, the Elector of the Rhineland Palatinate and King of Bohemia. *~ional Library of Scotland*)

~VE LEFT. Count Ernest Mansfeld, mercenary commander. *(National Library of Scotland)*

~VE RIGHT. Sir James Ramsay. *(National Portrait Gallery, London.)*

Mansfeld's army engaging Spanish forces beside the village of Fleurus. *(National Library of Scotland)*

showing the old city surrounded by bodies of water. The Frankentor defended by Mackay's Regiment is in the upper centre of the image. *(National Library of Scotland)*

POMERANIÆ

DVCATUS

PARS

Verdröscken

Landt.

Landt.

STRALSVNDT.

Verdroncken

Moräst

Poppenhagen

MARIS BALTICI

Holm

PARS

Die Beldt.

Oost See

INSOLA RÜGEN

PARS

Ein Maß von 130. Ruthen.

Lucas Kilian. Augᵒ ad uiuum delineauit et sculpsit. 1627.

Vera Effigies
Jacobi Turner Equiti Aurati.

Printed for R. Chiswell at the Rose and Crowne in St Pauls Church Yard.

ROBERTVS DVGLASS. S.R.M.REGNORVM
SVECIÆ. PER GERMANIAM GENERALIS MILITI
PRÆFECTVS.

TOP LEFT. The Marquis of Hamilton (*Daniel Mytens, reproduced courtesy of the Scottish National Portrait Gallery*)

TOP RIGHT. Count Walter Leslie. (*National Portrait Gallery, London.*)

ABOVE LEFT. Sir James Turner. (*National Portrait Gallery, London.*)

ABOVE RIGHT. Field Marshal Robert Douglas. (*National Library of Scotland*)

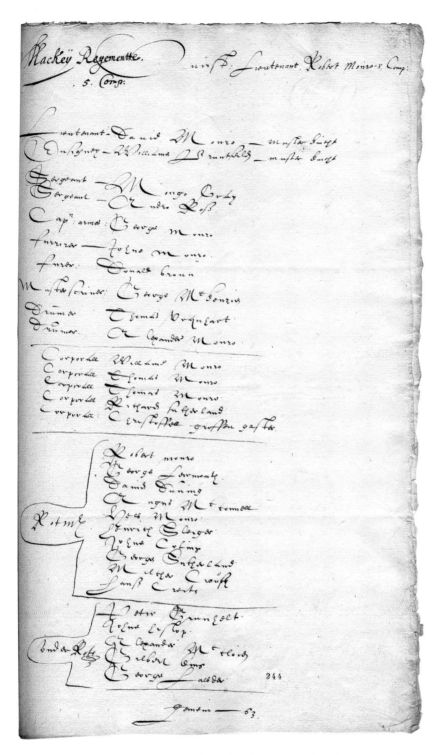

A page from a muster roll for Mackay's Regiment, showing the names of
Robert Monro and others. *(Krigsarkivet, Stockholm).*

The camp of the
Swedish army at
Werben on the Elbe.
The letter G in the
right foreground
indicates the forward
positions occupied
by Robert Monro's
musketeers to oppose
the advancing
Imperial army.
(*National Library of
Scotland*)

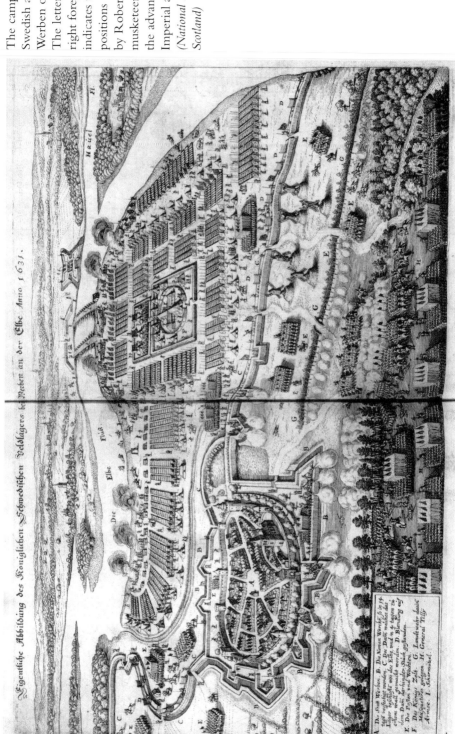

Eigentliche Abbildung des Königlichen Schwedischen Veldlagers bei Werben an der Elbe Anno 1631.

A. Die Stadt Werben. B. Das Neuen Werck, so 50 à 54
Lägst verfasset werden. C. Die Dam welche das
Lager beschütst wo die Elbe nach 4 à 5 tegen zu
einem weidt gemacht werden. D. Die Handlung auf
dem Dam daründer Stück gestanden.
E. Die Posten und Wachten.
F. Die Königs Zelt. G. Landwehr darin
Musqueten gelegen. H. General Tilly
Armee. I. Scharmükel.

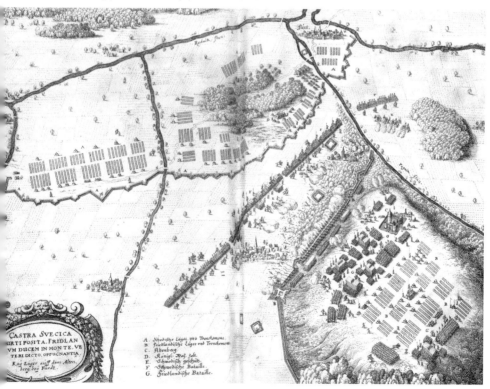

Images of tartan-clad soldiers in Stettin in 1631. The four figures may be Irish but they are claimed to be men from Mackay's Regiment. *(Germanisches Nationalmuseum)*

VE. Diagram of the Swedish attack on the Alte Feste, the hilltop stronghold of the Imperial near Nuremberg. Wallenstein, here identified by his title of Duke of Friedland, has his at lower right on the high ground while Gustavus Adolphus's men attack from the tion of their encampment on the plain. *(National Library of Scotland)*

A stylised image of the first battle of Breitenfeld, fought on 17 September 1631 between the Swedish forces of Gustavus Adolphus and the Imperial army under Count Tilly. The picture shows various phases of the conflict. The key indicates the following positions for Scottish troops: 82 – *vier Fahnen zu Fuss Obristen Hebrons* (four companies of Hepburn's Foot); 86 – four companies of Redwein's [Ruthven's] Foot; 68 – *vierhundert commandirte Mußquetirer Myn* (four hundred musketeers under Monro); 70 – *dreihundert und funffzig commandierte Mussquetir Ramsais* (350 musketeers under Ramsay). *(National Library of Scotland)*

ET SUBSECVTÆ
EXERCITUS CATHOLI-
CI STRAGIS FUGÆQUE AD
OMNEM POSTERITÄTEM
MEMORABILIS CUM INSTRUC-
TÆ ACIEITYPO DELINEATIO
QUAM
IUSSU ET AUSPICHS REGIS
SUPREM, CASTRORUM META-
TOR ET ARCHITECTVS
OLUF HANSON.
DELINEAVIT.

This contemporary series of pictures depicts the assassination of Wallenstein and his companions at Eger. *(National Library of Scotland)*

tail from a representation of the battle of Nördlingen. The battalions of pikemen labelled 5 in
 upper centre are identified as 'Die Schotten', the Scots under Gunn's command. The picture
 includes Field Marshal Gustav Horn (mounted figure Z), foot soldiers from Württemberg
, and Imperial units (30, 26 and E). *(Courtesy of Wolfgang Rutsche and Nördlingen Stadtarchiv,*
phische Sammlung.)

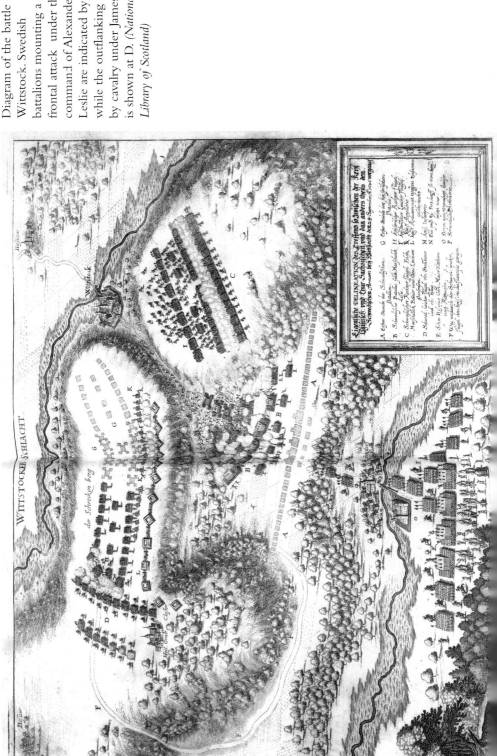

Diagram of the battle at Wittstock. Swedish battalions mounting a frontal attack under the command of Alexander Leslie are indicated by B, while the outflanking move by cavalry under James King is shown at D. *(National Library of Scotland)*

Hanau in 1636 at the time its defence was led by Sir James Ramsay. *(National Library of Scotland)*

RIGHT. Sir Samuel Grieg. *(National Portrait Gallery, London.)*

BELOW. This map shows the sea battle of Cesme between the Russian and Turkish fleets. *(British Library).*

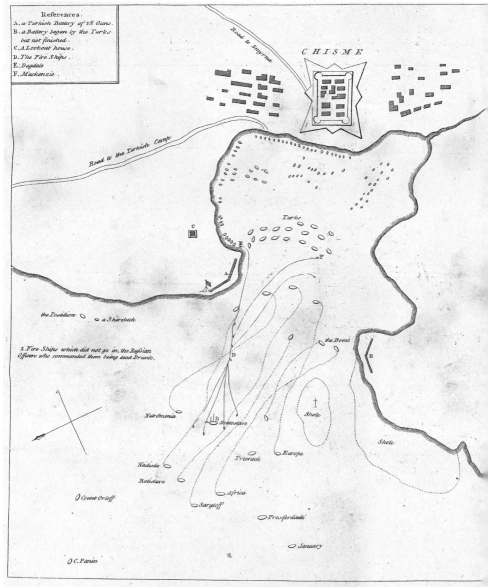

References.
A. a Turkish Battery of 28 Guns.
B. a Battery began by the Turks but not finished.
C A Lookout house.
D. The Fire Ships.
E. Dugdale.
F. Mackenzie.

Road to Smyrna

CHISME

Road to the Turkish Camp

Turks

the Postillion   a Sherebeck

2 Fire Ships which did not go in, the Russian Officers who commanded them being dead Drunk.

the Bomb

B

Shole

Shole

Nostromenia

Saratave

Europe

Nadieda
Raledave

Treeracle

January

Count Orloff

Africa
Saratoff

Froxforditelli

C. Panin

wound. Lieutenant-Colonel Seaton came to see him, to discuss how they might withstand the second attack, expected that night. During the day the Frankentor shook under a barrage of cannonballs, but the second attack failed to pierce the defences. Wallenstein's troops forced their way as far as the palisades and set to work to undermine the ravelin. In the morning, however, the defenders, 'with halfe pikes, Morgan sternes [a type of mace] and swords, being led with resolute Officers, they fall out, Pell mell amongst the enemies, and chase them quite out of the workes againe.' The vital ravelin stood.

Wallenstein now paused to consider another approach. A trumpeter came forward and initiated a discussion of terms for surrender. As the senior officer now present, Lieutenant-Colonel Seaton conducted the negotiation. He was probably glad of the opportunity to buy time until reinforcements might arrive from Denmark. A fortnight-long ceasefire ensued as Seaton discussed the articles of capitulation with Wallenstein. Monro does not describe in detail how these discussions were conducted and it seems that he was laid up in bed all the time. As Seaton hoped, Colonel Holck returned from Denmark in time, bringing with him another regiment of Scots under Alexander Lindsay, Lord Spynie, whose recruitment efforts in the previous summer had finally paid off. Even more fortunately for Stralsund, their arrival coincided with that of Sir Alexander Leslie, whom Monro hailed as 'an expert and a valorous Scots Commander'. Christian IV, having no wish to see an imperial Habsburg presence secure itself in the Baltic, had for once buried his differences with Gustavus Adolphus and had reached an agreement with him that Sweden should take over the defence of Stralsund. The Danish troops sailed for home and Swedes took their place, Leslie being appointed the governor of the city. The discussion of surrender terms was now abandoned. Monro took advantage of the lull to go to have his wound properly treated; no surgeon in Stralsund could guarantee to cut the bullet from his knee without leaving him lame and rather than risk disability he had chosen to endure the 'infinite paine' until he reached Copenhagen.

Leslie resolved to establish his presence by launching an attack on the enemy, using only his Scottish troops. Spynie's regiment was chosen, with Mackay's, under the command of Captain Mackenzie, as its support. The Scots attacked so vigorously that they drove the imperial

troops from their forward trenches and chased them as far as Wallenstein's gun batteries before they had to retire in the face of superior
strength. The imperial commander decided to waste no more time or
men on the city and withdrew his army on 24 July. Stralsund was now
safe and, thought Monro, the conflict changed the character of the
inhabitants: 'before this time being sluggish, dissolute, cowards, spend-
thrifts and voluptuous, [they] are now by this Discipline made active,
menagers, valiant, sparing and honest.' This is a harsh judgement on the
burgers and one wonders how the Ross-shire officer came to it. Monro
concluded they owed their improved, moral status to the Scots 'whose
bones lie in their ground, and to our Country-man [Leslie]'. The grateful
burgers awarded Leslie some rich gifts and a gold medal struck in
commemoration of their resistance to Wallenstein.

    Christian IV was now free to ship more infantry and cavalry to the
east, and chose to land troops at Wolgast, some 40 miles east of
Stralsund, to hold Pomerania against the Imperialists. Orders came to
Mackay's Regiment to march to the new base. By this time, Mackenzie
had only 400 men left, and no sooner did they join Christian's forces
than Wallenstein launched an attack. The battle at Wolgast on 2
September 1628 was the final blow to the Danish monarch's military
ambitions. With cannon shot falling about his camp and without
committing most of his forces, Christian thought better of his venture
and decided on a general withdrawal. Mackenzie's men and some of
Spynie's regiment with them were almost cut off, being saved only by
Rhinegrave's cavalry, who charged the enemy three times, halting the
onslaught long enough for the Scots to struggle to safety before
spurring out of danger themselves. Christian now ordered the Scots to
defend the gates of Wolgast until the rest of his army could get away,
and then to retire themselves, setting fire to the bridge behind them.
The Scots escaped from Wolgast with the rest of the defeated force.

    By the time Mackay's Regiment returned to Denmark, Robert
Monro reckoned that Mackenzie had barely a hundred men free from
wounds. Nearly five hundred had fallen in the defence of Stralsund.
Monro summed up his attitude to the loss of so many comrades: 'Let
none then, I say, bedew their eyes for them we left behinde us, seeing
the gaine is equall to the losse, if not more . . . those we lost, I
confesse, we loved, yet that love ought not to be so violent as to

undoe our selves with wanting of it.' By 'gaine' Monro meant the honour that had accrued to the men and the nation; he believed Heaven waited for those who died fighting in a just cause. The regiment recouped its losses during the winter. New officers came over from Scotland to replace some who had decided, for marriage or for other reasons, that they wanted no more of soldiering on the Continent. Robert Monro, the Black Baron, showed up with his newly levied company. Back to its full strength of over 1,400 men, the regiment was quartered in various parts of the Danish realm but a few officers, sensing that Christian had no more use for them, sought employment elsewhere: Captain Sanders Hay travelled to Sweden and became a major serving under Sir Patrick Ruthven in Prussia. When the peace negotiations between Denmark and the Empire were concluded, Christian thanked his Scots at a final parade and dismissed them. 'Free from our honourable Master his service,' wrote Monro, 'we were ready to imbrace new conditions from a new Master.'

The obvious place to seek a new master was Sweden, still involved in its war against Poland in the eastern Baltic. Gustavus Adolphus already had considerable numbers of Scots among his ranks and was welcoming more. In July 1628 Sir James Spens obtained authority through the Privy Council to raise 300 men to make good losses among the Scots in the Swedish king's service, a levy the Council requested to be done without tuck of drum or display of colours, perhaps because there had already in previous months been extensive recruiting for overseas service in Denmark and France and popular feeling was turning hostile.[1] Sweden also had Englishmen in her service, a notable example being George Fleetwood, from Bedfordshire, who raised a troop of horsemen for the Swedish flag in 1629 and became a major in Spens's regiment. Alexander Hamilton received a warrant to levy 1,200 men for Sweden in April 1629 and there were at least two other levies later that year for another 1,500 men.[2] From the time of the siege of Stralsund until the end of the Thirty Years War in 1648, some two thousand Scots served as officers in the Swedish forces.[3] The muster rolls that survive in the Swedish military archives testify to how common they were among the Swedish officer corps. For example, for the Swedish forces in Prussia in August–September 1629, roughly half of the infantry company captains bear obviously Scottish names.[4] The surnames for other ranks are more

mixed: for example, Captain Sanderson's company in Spens's regiment
has several Welsh and Irish names, and other companies have men who,
judging from their names, were probably English. As the leader of a
Protestant nation, Gustavus Adolphus retained a popular image
throughout Britain, making recruitment in his service relatively easy.
In general, the Swedish monarch was well pleased in turn with the
troops he received, especially from Scotland, even though they displayed a thrawn sensitivity to injustice, such as on the occasion in the
summer of 1628 when Scots in Livonia laid down their arms in protest at
the behaviour of an officer who had ordered one of their number hung;
the officer was later shot and the mutinous troops mollified.[5] In January
1628 some mercenaries, including Scots, who tried to desert from the
Swedes to the Poles were executed.

   Poland renewed her campaign against the occupying Swedes in
1629. The Swedish commander Herman Wrangel won a victory at
Gorzno on 12 February, but in June the Poles, reinforced with
Imperial troops, did well at the battle of Sztum (Trzciana). The
campaigns had, however, reached a stalemate, with neither side fully
able to achieve an overwhelming supremacy over the other, and on 26
September Gustavus Adolphus and the Polish Sejm agreed on a truce,
the Treaty of Altmark. Some coastal towns remained in Swedish
hands and Danzig, which had held out all along, had to hand over to
Gustavus Adolphus a percentage of its revenue.

   A few months before the truce with Poland, Robert Monro had
decided, with Sir Donald Mackay's approval, to seek a commission in
the Swedish army and money to bring Mackay's Regiment with him. A
man Monro calls David Martins, auditor, acted as go-between and
received a favourable response to Monro's enquiry. Six companies of
the regiment were despatched to Prussia, where they were garrisoned
in Braunsberg (now Braniewo) and another six were sent from
Holland to Sweden in November 1629. In February 1630 Robert
Monro and Sir Donald Mackay set off on horseback to join Gustavus
Adolphus. From Skåneland they rode north along the coast to
Göteborg before turning to cross the breadth of Sweden to Stock-
holm, breaking the journey to visit the arms factory run by Colonel
Alexander Hamilton at Örebro. They also stayed with a Captain
Sinclaire at his quarters, where they passed Easter Sunday. At last they

rode into Stockholm to kiss the hand of the king and swear allegiance to him. Gustavus Adolphus hosted a great feast in honour of having been awarded the Order of the Garter, and Monro noted proudly that thirteen cavaliers 'of our Nation', that is, Scots, sat at the table.

By this time Gustavus Adolphus had recruited large numbers of mercenaries into his army from many parts of Europe and had organised them into four regiments, each named after the background colour of their banners – Yellow, Blue, Red and Green, the last commanded by Colonel John Hepburn.[6] Further recruitment over the next two years enlarged the size of these regiments from eight to twelve or more companies, and four more colour regiments – Black, Orange, Brown and White – were added to the order of battle. By far the majority of the mercenaries were German but, as we have mentioned, a considerable number came from the British Isles, particularly Scotland, and Dutch, Flemish and French Huguenots also joined the Swedish ranks. At a review of the army, Monro noted with pride how the king praised the Scots in front of everyone, hoping that all his infantry were as well disciplined as Mackay's Regiment, before adding that he hoped one day to get good service from them for his money. Monro thought that abroad the English and the Scots generally rubbed along well with each other and were likely to offer mutual support: 'The English and our Nation are good seconds, one of another, being abroad, so commonly they take part with one another against any other Nation.' But relations were sometimes less cordial between mercenaries and home troops. Monro had noticed an instance of this in Danish service a few years earlier when Christian IV had equipped his own Danish soldiers with forty days' provisions of dry beef and bacon, and the Scots and the English in Danish service, disgruntled by their ration of dry biscuit and beer, had made their feelings clear by stealing Danish knapsacks and fighting with their allies.

The defeat at Wolgast had marked the end of Denmark's ambition to be a major power in the Baltic – the Peace of Lübeck was finally signed with the Empire on 7 July 1629 – and, with the triumph of Imperial forces across northern Europe, it could have meant the end of the whole war. The Habsburg emperor, however, showed an unwillingness to compromise with Protestant interests across the German-speaking lands, a stance that alarmed even some of his own electors.[7] There were also fears in the Habsburg camp that Wallenstein had grown too powerful and he was dismissed from his position, the command of the Imperial forces being given to Tilly in his stead. Gustavus Adolphus had also become alarmed by the advance of the Catholic and Habsburg forces, and resolved to intervene directly in the war, signalling this intention by landing his army on 6 July 1630 at Peenemünde on the island of Usedom on the Pomeranian coast.

Robert Monro did not sail with his comrades on that occasion but was given a commission to lead a 'free squadron' of the companies then in Prussia. He received final instructions from the Swedish chancellor, Axel Oxenstierna, and learned he was to muster his men, provide them with two months' pay and bring them by sea from Prussia to Germany in August to join the king. 'Our Ships being victualed, wee attended the winde', wrote Monro. Three vessels set out on 22 August 1630 from Pillau to convey the squadron to Wolgast: three companies on the *Lilly-Nichol*, and three on the *Hound*, with the horses and baggage in a smaller boat. On the third day of the voyage, the wind freshened into a gale and, as they drove before it, the three ships separated. Monro does not record the fate of the *Hound* or the boat with the horses. The *Lilly-Nichol* sprang a leak but was able to limp into shelter at the island of Bornholm, where they revictualled, waited for the wind to become favourable and sailed again for Wolgast. The leak grew worse and soldiers were put to the pumps in relays to keep the water from rising in the hold. The heavy ship could make little headway and had to turn before the wind to attempt to run to Danzig. In the darkness, however, they came too close to a strange coast and an hour before midnight struck the shore, the impact breaking the keel and leaving the *Lilly-Nichol* stranded and helpless. The company tied themselves to the breaking ship to avoid being washed overboard by the pounding seas. Monro found out later that the wife of one of the sergeants gave birth to a son in the midst of the mayhem. Two fellows, a Dane and a Scot called Murdo Piper, reckoned they were strong enough swimmers to attempt to make it to the shore – they both drowned. The crew launched two small boats but they were smashed. 'Under the mercy of the raging Seas and waves, going higher than the Mastes over the ship sides, wee patiently attended the Lords mercy with prayers', wrote Monro. In the middle of the next day, he and some of his men cobbled together a raft from spars, yards and planking and let it drift ashore on a tow with a few volunteers aboard. Some local peasants turned up and lent a hand, and slowly the entire company, including the sergeant's wife with her newborn infant, were brought to safety on rafts and tows. Some arms were rescued but all the ammunition and baggage had gone. Monro now found himself with his squadron in enemy territory without any means of defending themselves.

They had reached the Prussian coast near the town of Rügenwalde (now Darlowo).[8] From the locals, Monro learned that the captain in charge of the garrison in the castle there was sympathetic to the Protestant cause and opened negotiations with him, offering the help of the squadron to deal with the Imperialists and hold the area for Gustavus Adolphus, who was at that time further west in Stettin, a city he had occupied on 10 July. The garrison commander welcomed Monro's proposal and the shipwrecked companies moved into their new quarters. As the enemy was only some miles away at Colberg (now Kolobrzeg), Monro's men were still vulnerable and set about strengthening their position by making entrenchments and demolishing a bridge on an approach road. Monro despatched a peasant on horseback to inform Gustavus Adolphus of their situation, and back came the word to hold on and not to let the soldiers molest the country people. After a few days a Swedish ship arrived with 400 Germans of Colonel Fretz Rosse's regiment. Their commander, Lieutenant-Colonel Tisme Howsne, came ashore to ask permission to land his men, something Monro agreed to reluctantly. He suspected that Howsne might contest his command and, as the newcomer proved the Scot's suspicions to be well founded, Monro sent another messenger to seek the Swedish king's view. Gustavus Adolphus confirmed Monro in the senior post. Thereafter the Scots spent 9 weeks at Rügenwalde, fighting the occasional skirmish with the Imperialists, until Oxenstierna sent Sir John Hepburn to relieve them. The interlude had proved to be a pleasant one: 'Rugenwalde', wrote Monro, 'doth abound in Corne, Fruit and store, Cattell, Horses of good breed, Fishponds and Parkes for Deere . . . we were nobly entertained and kindly welcommed.'

After their relief, Monro and his men marched to the vicinity of Colberg to join Swedish forces under the command of Major-General

Dodo Knyphausen, who in the meantime had occupied that part of the country. This mercenary commander, who had fought under many banners, including Mansfeld's, had all the experience that thirty years in the military could provide. Monro quoted a saying of his that for a commander an ounce of luck was better than a pound of wit and thought junior officers could learn much from him, for all that he didn't care much for the Scots.

The force learned that Imperial troops intended to retake Colberg and were likely to approach via the small town and fortress of Scheifelbein (now Swidwin) on the River Rega. The task of occupying Scheifelbein was given to Monro's men but, when they arrived, they found it deserted by its inhabitants and 'layd almost waste with Pestilence'. Monro, daunted by his orders to hold the place to the last man, ordered peasants to come in from the surrounding districts to labour on the entrenchments he initiated. Two troops of horse were detailed to patrol in the vicinity to provide reconnaissance and, if necessary, harassment of the enemy. Luckily no Imperialists came for three days, giving the Scots the chance to strengthen the defences, but then a force of 8,000 horse and foot came by, intent on bypassing the tiny fortress and seemingly unaware it had been occupied. Monro signalled his presence with two cannon shots and immediately attracted an attack. He refused a call to surrender and retired to the castle. The burgers, who had in the meantime come back to their homes, opened the town gates to the enemy, who set up artillery in the marketplace and called on Monro once again to give up his defence; again he refused and thereby lost any chance of quarter. The attacking batteries advanced to within 40 paces of the castle walls before nightfall. Attempts by the defenders to set the houses near the walls on fire with grenades failed, and Monro resorted to a plan he had earlier devised. He had fixed to the roof of the nearest house what he terms a fireball, presumably a quantity of combustible material, perhaps straw doused in some oil, and now a soldier managed to set it alight. 'The whole street did burne right alongst betwixt us' wrote Monro. The blaze forced the enemy to retire and, at dawn, Monro sallied out with 80 musketeers, capturing 13 'Crabbats' (Croats) and dragging them back to the castle as prisoners.

The Imperialists broke off the attack and continued towards Colberg. The Swedish forces had been preparing to meet them and the noise of the ensuing gunfire reached the Scots in Scheifelbein before two horsemen came galloping up to the castle to report that the Swedes had been defeated. Monro refused to believe this and prepared for another assault. His instinct had been right. The withdrawing Imperialists passed by without doing much harm but now the defenders were struck by a more deadly enemy: the disease rampant in Scheifelbein. The Scots escaped more lightly than had the inhabitants, many of whom were presumably homeless and stressed by the warfare visited upon them, but an eighteen-year-old soldier called Andrew Monro died of the plague, and his cousin, John Monro, succumbed to fever. Robert Monro describes the latter as 'Kilternies grand-child', referring to Kiltearn on the Black Isle and providing a poignant indication of the close-knit, family nature of Mackay's and many other Scottish regiments. 'I made onely mention of their names', he added, 'because they lived vertuously, and dyed with farre more credit, then if they had dyed at home where their names had never bin recorded for their worth and vertues.'

Over the next few weeks, as winter tightened its grip on the Baltic lands, Monro and his regiment moved into winter quarters in a village called Prymhaussen, near the town of Stargard, a few miles from Stettin. 'The Pest raged so at Statin that divers brave Souldiers of the Regiment were buried there', wrote Monro. Sir Donald Mackay escaped the plague by leaving for Scotland, where he engaged Robert Monro's brother, Obsdale, to levy and bring to Stettin another regiment of foot. Mackay also commissioned an English mercenary commander, Sir Thomas Conway, to raise a similar force, but the ships bearing the latter across the North Sea were wrecked on the Danish coast and several hundred, including Conway himself, drowned; the survivors were eventually assigned by Gustavus Adolphus to another regiment. Monro says Sir James Lumsden of Innergellie also brought over a new Scottish regiment.

In January 1631, Gustavus Adolphus took the initiative from the forces of the Holy Roman Empire by launching a campaign that gave him control of Mecklenburg and Pomerania – almost all the Baltic coast. In snow and hard frost, the Swedish army marched on Neubrandenburg, horse, foot and artillery. They came within cannon shot of their destination late in the afternoon and deployed their superior force around the town in a noisy display calculated to intimidate the outnumbered defenders peering from the fortified walls. Monro's regiment was assigned the capture of a town port, and this was successfully accomplished. The Imperial garrison surrendered and was allowed to march away to Hagelberg. From Neubrandenburg, Gustavus Adolphus despatched troops to occupy other centres in the region. Altentreptow and Loitz soon fell, but Demmin proved a tougher nut to crack. The siege began in a time of freezing winds on 14 February. The castle held out for a night and a day, before seven companies in the garrison agreed to switch sides to join the Swedes. The town defied the besiegers more effectively, even making a strong sally that was only held and beaten back with considerable effort. Here the Scots distinguished themselves in the eyes of the Swedish monarch for not giving ground and for the rescue of a wounded captain from another regiment who had been left for dead. Honour satisfied, the town garrison at last decided to surrender, sending out an English mercenary, a Major Greeneland, to conduct the parlay.

The Swedes were now conscious that Tilly might be hot on their heels and Gustavus Adolphus did not linger at Demmin but dispersed his army into groups capable of lending each other mutual support. Johan Baner stayed at Demmin, Knyphausen with his own men and six companies of Mackay's shifted to Neubrandenburg, Major Sinclair took two companies to Altentreptow, Monro went with his squadron and other troops to Malchin, Field Marshal Gustav Horn garrisoned Friedland, and the king moved to Pasewalk, a strategic location on the route to the Oder river. Now Monro began a war of movement, staying a few days in one location before marching for two or three days to a new place – he lists Altentreptow, Malchin, Friedland, Anklam and Schwedt as the towns where they camped and, before the winter began to ease into spring, the Scots must have become tediously familiar with the woods, fields and gently rolling landscape of northern Germany.

Tilly did come, and he laid siege to Knyphausen in Neubrandenburg. The garrison included 6 companies of Mackay's Regiment under the command of a Lieutenant-Colonel Lindesey. Against them Tilly brought 22,000 horse and foot, and 26 pieces of ordnance, records

Monro. Tilly's wish may have been to draw Gustavus Adolphus into action but if so he was disappointed. The Swedish king left his force in Neubrandenburg to shift for itself while he devoted his attention to constructing a ship-bridge across the Oder and erecting skonces to defend it. The Imperial cannon breached the walls of Neubrandenburg. Knyphausen's offer to parlay was rejected as having been made too late. Clearly Tilly was in no mood to be benevolent towards his enemy. In the general storming of the fortress that followed, a large number of men, including Lieutenant-Colonel Lyndesey, fell or were cut down without quarter. The Scots Monro lists as having been taken prisoner include Captain Gunn, Captain Beaton and Captain Learmond. Captain Ennis and Lieutenant Lumsdell escaped by jumping from their position and creeping away through a marsh; they managed to make it to Friedland to rejoin their comrades. Monro blamed Knyphausen's rejection of an initial offer of surrender terms for the atrocities committed by Tilly's forces.

The Imperial forces moved on to attack Altentreptow but Major Sinclair threw his assailants off balance by surging out to attack them before they had deployed, cleverly directing his fifty musketeers to fire and move, to give the impression to the enemy of being a much larger force. Sinclair then retired to the town and held it for two nights until orders reached him from Gustav Horn at Friedland to retire. From Friedland, Horn retired to Anklam according to a pre-arranged plan. Tilly's troops found no one when they reached Friedland and, puzzled and worried that Gustavus Adolphus might be advancing to Magdeburg to the south-west, the Imperial commander moved away to Alt Ruppin. The officers in the Swedish army took advantage of the brief lull in the campaign to visit their relatives in Stettin. Monro saw his wife and family for what was to be the last time in three years.[9]

The Swedish army underwent another of its reorganisations in March 1631, with the formation of regiments into a new series of brigades. Sir John Hepburn commanded one of these, which came to be known as the Scots Brigade and included at this time Hepburn's, Lumsden's and Stargate's regiments, and Monro's squadron. On 3 April, Monro noted, they began to march on Frankfurt on the Oder, after Horn had been despatched on a diversionary move towards Landsberg (now Gorzow Wielkopolski) in the valley of the Warta 'to give the enemy somewhat to thinke on'. The Hanseatic city of Frankfurt had a garrison of 9,000 Imperial troops, a formidable foe for the 10,000 men in Gustavus Adolphus's forces. After five days, the army was close to the city, the Imperial defenders withdrawing before them as they approached. Gustavus Adolphus deployed his forces in their order of battle. According to Monro, he did this with John Hepburn's assistance, a remark that sounds suspiciously like patriotic exaggeration on the writer's part. In any case, the Easter Ross man found the scene stirring: 'The signe given for advancing, Trumpets sounding, Drummes beating, Colours displayed, advanced and flying, every Commander directed and appointed on his Command and Station; the magnifick and Royall King leads on', he wrote, 'This Royall Army marching in battell order for halfe a mile, as comely as one body cold doe, with one pace, and one measure, advancing, stopping, moving, and standing alike.' The defenders appear to have been daunted by this exhibition of martial power, and declined to give battle. Gustavus Adolphus decided to attack.

The defenders set fire to what Monro calls the 'fore-Towne', the buildings outside the walls, and Gustavus Adolphus took advantage of the cover afforded by the smoke to send a detachment of musketeers through the burning buildings to a position near a city gate. On a reconnaissance too close to the walls, the king came under musket fire and one of his companions was hit in the left arm. One of Monro's officers, Lieutenant David Monro, was shot in the leg by a musket ball. The defenders sallied out against the position of Major John Sinclair and his musketeers – they occupied a churchyard on an eminence close to the enemy entrenchments – and nearly over-ran it before they were beaten back. After further reconnaissance, Gustavus Adolphus ordered a general assault. Johan Baner and Hepburn led their men through the waist-high water and mud of the moat under the cover of smoke from cannon fire to assail a mud-built wall before the stone wall of the city. The defenders retired without much of a fight, giving the attackers the chance to climb over the strong palisade on the outer defences. Here Hepburn's men noticed their opponents retreating through a sally port and raced to follow them before the port could be shut, pressing their attack in the face of fire 'which made cruell and pittifull execution on our musketiers and pikemen'.

Charging at the head of his troops, Hepburn had got to within half a pike length of the port when he was shot above the knee and stumbled away in pain. His major fell dead, and the pikemen's rush faded. Lumsden and Monro reacted instinctively to the loss of momentum, called on their men to advance shoulder to shoulder and charged the port. The report of this moment in the *Swedish Intelligencer* has Lumsden 'with his drawne sword in his hand' crying '"Let's enter, my hearts", thrusting himselfe in amongst the thickest of them'.[10] To their amazement, they suddenly found themselves through the gate and unhurt, the defenders falling back in confusion. No one managed to close the portcullis, and the pikemen and musketeers crowded through the gap, formed up and advanced. The *Swedish Intelligencer* has it as follows: 'Lumsdell entring with his men makes a most pittifull slaughter: and when any Imperialist cryed Quarter; New Brandenburg cries the other and knocks him downe. One Scottish man protested he had kill'd 18 men with his owne hand. Here did Lumsdell take 18 colours . . . that the King after the battell bade him aske what he would, and he would give it him.'

Elsewhere in the battle, Major Sinclair and Lieutenant George Heatly, with a few musketeers, were the first to use ladders to surmount the ramparts of the city and had to make a stand with their backs to the walls until their musket fire won them a breathing space. The strongest defence – on the sector attacked by the Yellow and Blue brigades – was put up by a force of Irish mercenaries under Lieutenant-Colonel Walter Butler. Most were killed or wounded, and Butler himself was taken prisoner, a musket ball in his arm and a pike wound in his thigh. 'Had all the rest stood so well to it, as the Irish did,' thought Monro 'we had returned with great losse and without victory.'

As Frankfurt fell into the hands of its captors, discipline degenerated into rioting and plundering, an all-too-common feature of warfare, and some Imperial troops were murdered in vengeance for what Tilly's men had perpetrated at Neubrandenburg. Monro and Lumsden kept a group of 'honest Souldiers' together to defend their own colours from the rampage but could do nothing to stop atrocities. 'The whole streete being full of Coaches and rusty [rustic] waggons richly furnished withall sorts of riches, as Plate, Jewells,

Gold, Money, Clothes, Mulets and horses for saddle, coach and waggons, whereof all men that were careless of their dueties, were too carefull in making of booty, that I did never see Officers lesse obeyed', complained Monro. As fire, the frequent partner of a sacking, began to spread through the ransacked buildings, Gustavus Adolphus sent drummers through the streets to order all his soldiers, on pain of death, to remove themselves to the other side of the Oder, where Hepburn was now in charge of the outer defences. Even this did not command universal obedience. On the following day the king appointed Alexander Leslie the governor of the city. Instructions were issued to begin rebuilding the walls, and all the dead still unburied after six days were thrown into common graves in ditches.

On 15 April, Hepburn was sent at the head of some two thousand musketeers, with cavalry and artillery, to capture Landsberg on the Warta River. Monro went along as second-in-command. A skirmish with Croats delayed the advance but on the 18th Hepburn's men reached a well-fortified skonce, with cannon and a moat of running water, on the approach to the town. Monro oversaw a night spent digging siege works. A cannonade on the following day made little impression on the thick earth walls of the strongpoint. The impasse was broken by a Landsberg blacksmith, who had acted hitherto as a guide and now pointed out a way to bypass the skonce through the flooded fields on each side and isolate it. Monro with his musketeers, and other troops, followed the blacksmith, and their unexpected appearance so close to the gates of the town threw the defenders into a panic. The men in the bypassed skonce surrendered, the common soldiers being enlisted in the Swedish army and their officers made prisoners, but the forces inside the Landsberg walls recovered from their surprise and fought hard with musket and cannon, forcing Monro to order his Scots to start digging in. In half an hour he lost thirty men. The advance of Marshal Gustav Horn, however, made the defenders reconsider their position and they surrendered after a discussion of terms. Gustavus Adolphus rewarded the blacksmith with the post of burgermeister. With the capture of Landsberg, all of Pomerania and Brandenburg now lay before Gustavus Adolphus.

'betwixt the Devill and the deepe Sea'

Brandenburg, Saxony, Bavaria, the Rhineland, 1631

*A*FTER WINNING control of the Oder valley, Gustavus
Adolphus led the main body of his troops back to Berlin, then
a relatively small town and the capital of Brandenburg. In 1620 he had
married Maria Eleonora, the sister of George William, the Elector of
Brandenburg, in a political rather than a love-inspired match. Brandenburg and Saxony were the two most important Lutheran states in
the German-speaking world but, despite this religious affiliation and
the status of George William as his brother-in-law, Gustavus Adolphus was still unsure of the intentions of these putative allies. At the
end of April, George William entertained the victorious Swedish king
at his hunting lodge at Pankow, north-east of Berlin, while Swedish
troops moved into the castle of Spandau and set up open camps there
and at Potsdam on the western fringes of the city. John George, the
Elector of Saxony, the other potential ally, was holding back from an
alliance, and Gustavus Adolphus also became suspicious of George
William's loyalty. Both men were, naturally, disinclined to have a war
fought across their lands. To help George William make up his mind,
the Swedish troops camped in order of battle, ostensibly as a defence
measure but more as a thinly disguised threat. Monro describes
Gustavus as 'so incensed' by the elector's prevarication that he swore
to take Berlin and make the elector his prisoner. At last George
William recognised he had no room for manoeuvre and agreed to a
treaty. His wife and her mother, with a company of ladies, came out to
entertain the Swedish king and assured him that the elector would do
everything required of him. 'To which', says Monro, 'his Majesty

answered merrily that if the Duke [Elector] would not end with him friendly before night he would send the Dutchesse and all the Ladies prisoners to Sweden, and the Duke should follow.' George William had to agree to provide money and means to support the war effort, by quartering the Swedish army and paying a monthly contribution from his estates. 'There is no Oratory of such force to gaine both men and women, as a strong well-conducted Army', observed Monro wryly.

The consequences of an army's presence were visited more cruelly on the city of Magdeburg, which had allied itself with Gustavus Adolphus in the previous autumn. Occupying Mecklenburg, Tilly's Imperial army ran short of food, horses and supplies during the winter of 1630/31 and, as his men began to desert in search of pay and sustenance, the Imperial commander accepted the suggestion of his impetuous colleague, the Bavarian cavalryman Field Marshal Count Pappenheim, to lay siege to Magdeburg, whose capture promised plenty to replenish their stores. Magdeburg fell to the Imperial army early in May, before the Swedish king could whip his Protestant German allies into line and come to its aid. In an orgy of drunken plundering Tilly's troops sacked the city. A fire broke out, probably accidentally, and quickly spread, and by the time order was restored some twenty thousand civilians lay dead among the smoking embers of their homes. It was the worst atrocity of the war, and deeply shocking even by the standards of the time.

As the Imperial troops withdrew from the smouldering ruins of Magdeburg, Gustavus Adolphus prepared to move west. Early in July, Monro's men with Hepburn's regiment marched to the town of Brandenburg, to garrison duty, where Hepburn's knee wound would have a chance to heal. When they arrived after four days of relatively easy travel, they found a town ravaged by disease and had to camp in the surrounding fields. In one week over thirty of Monro's men succumbed to the plague, the fatalities including the ensign Robert Monro and Sergeant Robert Monro, 'Cull-crags sonne'. The main body of the Swedish army then carried on westward, crossing the Elbe near Tangermunde and occupying the small town of Werben. Here Gustavus Adolphus decided to construct a fortified camp in a meadow along the left bank of the river; protection on the landward side was afforded by an earth dyke that had originally been thrown up as a flood-prevention measure. The Swedes added stone facing and cannon to the dyke and laid a bridge of boats across the Elbe for easy access to the other side. They also garrisoned the nearby towns of Perleberg and Havelberg, where Monro, the Black Baron, was stationed. Foulis' men had distinguished themselves just before this by capturing the castle of Bloe.

Tilly learned of Gustavus Adolphus's action from post riders who came thundering after him and he turned back in an effort to surprise his enemy before the defences at Werben could be completed. Gustavus Adolphus encountered the Imperial vanguard at Tangermunde and drove it back in a sharp skirmish on 27 July. The king had bought time and it was four more days before Tilly's army came within firing distance of the Werben camp and began to cannonade the earthworks in a fairly ineffective barrage that ceased when night fell. During darkness, Gustavus Adolphus sent cavalry to patrol in no-man's land, and Monro with 500 musketeers was dispatched to lie hidden between the armies 'almost a Cannon-shot from our workes'. The Scots spent an uneasy night, straining to make sense of the noises of men and horses and seeing nothing. The Imperial cavalry did not attempt to attack before dawn and when they came the defenders were ready. As the Swedish horse fell back, Monro and his musketeers subjected the attackers to volleys of lead. The king himself came out to see how they were getting along, and he ordered more troops to join them for an assault. Gustavus Adolphus led a cavalry charge himself in a frontal attack after an artillery volley, smashed the opposing force of curassiers and made a fighting withdrawal to the Werben camp. Monro's men were still outside, hugging the ground as cannonballs whistled over their heads, 'as betwixt the Devill and the deepe Sea, for sometimes our owne Cannon would light short and grasc over us, and so did the enemies also'. The Scots stayed there until nightfall enabled them to be relieved. Before dawn the defenders of Werben heard trumpets and drums, as if the Imperialists were preparing another assault, but, under the cover of the mist, Tilly turned away and withdrew to the south, an occurrence not clear to Gustavus Adolphus until the weather cleared. The king lost no time in sending troops of cavalry to harass his retreating enemy but Tilly succeeded in breaking to the south, all the way to Halle, not far from Leipzig in Saxony.

Shortly after the repelling of the Imperial attack, Gustavus Adolphus received a visit from James, Marquis of Hamilton. This tall, handsome nobleman from the Stuart court had come on a special mission in the service of his king and friend, Charles I. A Swedish request to Charles for assistance had placed the British monarch in a dilemma; he could not be seen openly to be aiding Gustavus Adolphus as negotiations were underway with the Habsburg emperor over a peaceful restoration of the Palatinate to his sister and her husband, now in exile in the Netherlands. Yet there were strong reasons to aid the Protestant cause in central Europe. The problem was neatly finessed by allowing the marquis ostensibly on his own initiative to offer his services to Gustavus Adolphus, who was in turn pleased to reach an agreement. It was arranged that Hamilton would be general of a force of 6,000 men that he would raise at his own expense, in return for the revenues and emoluments from lands he would capture. For his part, Gustavus Adolphus would supply pikes and muskets, and iron for cannon shot, along with, if required, the means to purchase powder in the Low Countries. David Ramsay, described as a gentleman of the privy chamber, acted as courier during these negotiations and also oversaw the recruitment drive.[1] Ramsay approached several English and Scottish officers about service under Hamilton, and one who 'cordially' agreed to join was Sir Donald Mackay, in June 1628 ennobled as Lord Reay. The latter is reported to have said that, although he had already held regimental command under the Swedish king, he was 'so desirous to put life in his [Hamilton's] noble designs that he would serve him, were it but to carry a Pike in his Army'. The marquis himself wrote to the Earl of Sutherland to seek his help in the recruitment drive, pointing out that he would like the men to be at Leith at the beginning of July.

The Privy Council issued a warrant to Reay on 2 June 1631 to levy 2,000 men for Swedish service.[2] Captain John Maxwell was also employed by Hamilton to recruit and asked the Privy Council in the same month to order the town of Musselburgh to provide quarters for fifty men he had raised in the north. Recruitment proved slow and the indications are that men were now showing general reluctance to answer the call to arms. Some towns around Edinburgh were also refusing to quarter recruits waiting to sail. In the fall-out from the only partly successful levy started in company with Nithsdale and Spynie in 1627 for Danish service, Sir James Sinclair of Murkle had to be exonerated by King Charles for having spent £4,000 without result; the hapless laird even sought his king to plead his case before the Danish monarch as he felt he had been disgraced by his failure to attract recruits. Warrants to raise another 1,400 men for Swedish service were issued to a Colonel Lumsden and a Lieutenant-Colonel McDougall in 1632.

Reay's attempts to recruit proceeded slowly over the winter of 1630/31 and to cover the costs Charles advanced to the Marquis of Hamilton a lease of the customs on wine imports into Scotland. When this source of revenue did not prove to be enough, friends of the Marquis tried to persuade him to abandon the enterprise, a course he refused to take. In the spring of 1631 Hamilton sent Ramsay to the Low Countries in search of assistance and British officers who might consent to join him, and in hope of success wrote to Gustavus Adolphus to expect him with his army in mid summer. This gave rise to further complications: Gustavus Adolphus had agreed to send 3,000 foot and 1,000 horse to meet Hamilton's army and delegated this levy to a Lithuanian, a Colonel Farensback, who had switched to Swedish from Imperial service but who now changed sides back again in an effort to sabotage Hamilton's plan. Lord Reay also travelled to Denmark and the Netherlands in search of recruits. Hamilton was ready to leave the British Isles with a part-English, part-Scottish force, sailing from Yarmouth and Leith respectively. Reay and Ramsay returned from the continent with a few officers, including Sir Jacob Ashley, who had gained a reputation in Dutch service; the States government, however, had been reluctant to assist the recruitment as King Charles had not made a formal declaration of his intentions.

At last on the point of departure, Hamilton now ran into more trouble. He had enemies at court, among whom was a Lord Ochiltree, a Stewart whose family had long held a grudge against the Hamiltons. 'A man of a subtil spirit and good parts, had not these endowments of his mind been stain'd with some ill qualities' is how Gilbert Burnet, a royalist cleric and a supporter of Hamilton, described Ochiltree in 1673. What precisely happened and who said what to whom is unclear but Ochiltree claimed that Reay had relayed to him how David

Ramsay, known to be a man 'of an intemperate tongue', had told Reay
that Hamilton's real intention was to raise his army to stage a coup,
overthrow Charles I and seize the Scottish crown. Ochiltree also told
the government treasurer, Lord Weston, that Hamilton probably
intended to murder the king, a claim that Weston was duty-bound
to pass on to his sovereign. Charles dismissed the threat and, when
the unsuspecting Hamilton arrived at the court for his final instructions before his departure for Europe, welcomed him and told him
what had been going on. The horrified Hamilton begged to be put on
trial but the king reassured him he had his complete trust. Of the
other protagonists in this affair, Ochiltree continued to swear by what
he had said, Reay affirmed that Ramsay had told him what Hamilton
was up to and Ramsay denied he had ever said such a thing. Ochiltree
was sent to Scotland and ended up in Blackness Castle, a prisoner for
the next twenty years. Ramsay and Reay continued to contest each
other's statements, and even called to be allowed to settle the dispute
by combat. Ramsay was eager to fight for his honour and Reay,
although perhaps reluctant, was willing to meet him; a richly decorated stage was erected in Westminster to host the contest, but
Charles stepped in to prevent any duel from occurring, sending both
men to the Tower.[3]

Gustavus Adolphus wrote to Hamilton from Frankfurt-am-Oder in
April to tell him that he would send Sir Alexander Leslie to meet him
and share the command of the new force. Leslie left for Hamburg to
prepare for Hamilton's arrival and, if possible, raise 3 foot regiments
and 1,000 horse in that area, and in May he wrote to Hamilton to tell
him he would prepare for a landing at Bremen, although the presence
of the Imperial enemy across the country might interfere with the
plan. Leslie also warned that local hostility might make recruitment
difficult.[4] In the event, in case he should be prevented from marching
from the west to join Gustavus Adolphus, Hamilton chose to sail to
Pomerania. The fleet of 40 ships, with the 6,000 men aboard, departed
from Yarmouth roads on 26 July, stopped at Elsinore to pay respects
to the Danish king on 6 August, and finally reached their anchorage
on 12 August near Wolgast, where they lay 'about 3 weekes or a
Moneth for Arming and refreshing'.[5] Gustavus Adolphus's intention
was that Hamilton should lead his men south up the Oder valley into

Silesia. Rumour meanwhile exaggerated the size of the marquis's army to 20,000 men, enough to delight German Protestants and persuade the Elector of Saxony finally to agree to an alliance with Sweden, or at least Burnet in his pro-Hamilton account so claims. The influential Protestant princes, the Landgrave of Hesse and Duke Bernard of Saxe-Weimar, also offered their services to Gustavus Adolphus and, just as importantly, brought in convoys of supplies. On his part, Tilly had to take men from his field army to garrison the strongpoints Hamilton might threaten. The true situation was less sanguine for the Protestant cause, as Alexander Leslie realised when he met up with Hamilton's men at Ückermünde late in August: 'We . . . fond the soiours so weried, being unaqwainted with mairsching, I wes forced to ly still a day to repos them, and to prowyd for schipin to send the seik men be watter, which wer to the number of thrie hundreth.'[6] At this time the country of Pomerania and the lower Oder had not recovered from the destruction wrought by the war, and the newly arrived troops faced nothing but hunger and disease. Before two months had passed Hamilton lost a third of his numbers. Leslie did what he could to hurry them on to Stettin, a march on which they had to stagger along on a pound of bread each every four days; it was said later that a cry for food was the last word many of them uttered.

This baptism of famine was yet to come when Hamilton visited Gustavus Adolphus at Werben, turning up with four regiments armed and arrayed in glinting, untarnished mail. The marquis cut perhaps too splendid a dash among the battle-hardened troops in the camp, for Gustavus Adolphus felt moved to apologise for the humble state of their quarters and the impoverished countryside. He also pressed his visitor to seek more money and men from Charles I and asked him to occupy and hold the Oder valley, the essential Swedish withdrawal route from Germany if disaster threatened. Robert Monro probably watched Hamilton ride off from Werben to what the Easter Ross man dubbed 'the most ruined part within the Empire'.

The Marquis led his suffering forces up the Oder to Frankfurt, normally a pleasant landscape of woods and fields but now a waste-land: 'it was scarce possible for them to subsist. The Plague was also at Frankfurt, which broke in upon their Army so hotly that in a few days it swept away above a third part of them, and came so near the

Marquis himself that one of his Pages died of it.'[7] Fortunately the
troops showed great forbearance, remained loyal and did not mutiny;
but Hamilton must have been assailed by despondency, only slightly
dispelled when Gustavus Adolphus let him have only 200 horse and
300 infantry for the thrust into Silesia.

Now the Swedish king left Werben, marching south to reach
Wittenberg on the Elbe at the end of August. The assembled army
was joined here by a fresh company from Scotland under the
command of Lieutenant-Colonel John Monro, Robert Monro's elder
brother. With them came the son of the Monro laird of Kiltearn to see
his friends, says Monro, but he caught a fever and died. Field Marshal
Hans Georg von Arnim and the troops of the Elector of Saxony
rendezvoused with the Swedish forces, their new uniforms making a
brilliant display in contrast to the appearance of the men with
Gustavus Adolphus. Monro says his soldiers, who had slept out in
a ploughed field, looked like kitchen servants in their dirty, dusty,
ragged clothes, although under the garments and the grime 'were
hidden couragious hearts'. Among the Saxons was the Englishman
Sydnam Poyntz, who had escaped from the slavery he had fallen into
after Mansfeld's defeat and had arrived in Dresden in time to enlist in
the elector's army.

As the Saxons cemented their alliance with Gustavus Adolphus,
Tilly established his position in Leipzig, occupying the fortress of
Pleissenburg. The Protestant allies now hurried south towards him
and the opponents faced each other a few miles to the north of the
city on 17 September. 'As the Larke begunne to peepe' is the pastoral
phrase with which Monro begins his account of the ensuing battle.
Gustavus Adolphus deployed his troops in a series of lines, with his
own army on the right and the Saxons on the left. He implemented
one of the innovations for which he became famed: the brigades of
pikemen with attendant squads of musketeers stood in groups with
gaps between them wide enough to permit the passage of cavalry, and
artillery was placed before the lines. Three regiments of musketeers,
two of them Scots and one German, took up position ahead of the
main line; all three regiments had Scots colonels: Sir James Ramsay,
Sir John Hamilton of Traboun and Robert Monro of Foulis. Green
branches were issued to the soldiers as a distinguishing badge in the

expected melee, and the password for the day was the standard Protestant slogan '*Gott mit uns*' – God with us. At nine in the morning half a mile of countryside separated the front ranks of the two armies and Monro, from his position with Mackay's Regiment to the rear of the line in the reserve commanded by Sir John Hepburn, estimated the Imperialists arrayed before them on what he terms God's acre as numbering 44,000, against roughly the same number on their own side. The ground sloped up towards Tilly's lines but this slight advantage was less important than the fact that the Imperial troops had their backs to the sun and the wind, so that dust and smoke would tend to blind their opponents. Gustavus Adolphus made a speech that Monro does not report – perhaps he had trouble hearing it – and then the army moved forward before halting again.

It was close to noon and they were now within cannon range. Monro recalls the 'noise and roaring whistling and flying of Cannon-Bullets; where you may imagine the hurt was greate'. The artillery duel blasted on for two and a half hours, the balls ripping and bouncing through the assembled ranks, creating a mayhem the pikemen and musketeers on each side had simply to endure, closing up their ranks as their wounded comrades were dragged away to the surgeons. At last, at around half past three, the cannon eased and Tilly sent his troops forward towards each flank of the enemy. On the right, Gustavus Adolphus managed to repulse the attack and in turn launch his own Finnish cavalry in a counter charge that sent the enemy reeling back in disorder. On the left, however, the Imperial cavalry bested the untried Saxon troops and they began to flee in panic. Sydnam Poyntz explained how the Saxons were discouraged by the behaviour of their own leader: the elector, not a brave man, was stricken by fear at the sight of men falling about him and spurred his horse from the field, at which development his troops 'beeing young Cavalliers and Gallants and who had never seene a battaile fought, and seeing themselves drop, and the bullets fall so thicke . . . threw away their Arms and fled'. Poyntz says that he saved his own unit's colours, an act that kept him in favour with the elector and earned him promotion to captain of a horse troop.[8]

In the centre at the rear, Monro's men were blinded by smoke and dust for a while and, when it eventually cleared a little, they were surprised to find to their left not the Saxons but the enemy. Now Gustavus Adolphus's fresh approach to tactics proved its worth. Deployed in small groups, the men were able to wheel to the left or right in response to a flank attack, and this the reserve under Hepburn did. Their volleys of musket fire and then a mighty push with pikes drove back the Imperialists and they carried on their advance until they were able to seize some of Tilly's cannon. They could still see little – 'we were as in a darke cloude' – and Monro ordered a drummer to rattle out the Scots march until through the choking gloom the Scots could re-assemble in answer to the summons.

Elsewhere on the field, Gustavus Adolphus's men had also prevailed and in places Tilly's guns had been turned against him. The old Imperial commander was badly wounded and had to be escorted away, leaving the withdrawal of the rearguard in the hands of the cavalry commander, Pappenheim. A significant victory had gone to the Protestant allies. The Scots, full of pride after the Swedish king had singled them out for special praise, and their fellow soldiers camped that night on the field they had won: 'Our bone-fiers were made of the enemies Amunition waggons . . . and all this night our brave Camerades, the Saxons, were making use of their heeles in flying, thinking all was lost', wrote Monro, stooping to sarcasm as he remembered how strangers had fallen for the sake of Saxon freedom. The allies had lost 3,000 men, mostly in the initial bombardment, but the Imperial dead numbered nearly 8,000, thought Monro, and they had also lost cannon and supplies. The troops of Gustavus Adolphus had held public prayers that dawn and had gone forward confident that God was on their side. Monro ascribed the victory first to the Swedish king's zeal for the Protestant cause and was in no doubt that they had fought as instruments of the Lord, 'for to abate and lay down the pride of the house of Austria; and for to teare and strip naked that old proud and Ambitious General Tillie of his former glory and honour'. However, he continued with cold realism, 'a second helpe unto this glorious victory was the great execution made by his Majesties Cannon'. Named after one of the villages near which it was fought, the action is known today as the Battle of Breitenfeld. It seemed to mark a turning point in the fortunes of the Protestant cause; thanks to the 'Lion of the North', the King of Sweden, the northern German princes now felt free from fear of Habsburg-Catholic domination.

In the Oder valley, Sir Alexander Leslie and the Marquis of Hamilton were at last enjoying some success. With a force of 500 men, Leslie thwarted an attack on the little of town of Crossen (near modern Zielona Gora), where the garrison commander was short of munitions and likely to be taken by Imperial forces. A subsequent attack on Gubin on the Neisse River was a little more difficult. Intelligence that the garrison there had been reduced to only 500 men proved to be false but Leslie resorted to subterfuge, hiding his own men in the suburbs until, at sunset, the garrison let down the drawbridge. A sudden charge by cavalry took possession of the bridge. The infantry now proceeded to hack a hole through the heavy gate and gained entry. The resolute attack persuaded the garrison to surrender and, much cheered by their victory, Hamilton marched on to besiege Glogow, the second largest town in Silesia. The prospect of moving from ravaged country into Silesia, where supplies were still plentiful was, however, shattered when a letter arrived from Gustavus Adolphus with orders to hand over the occupation of Silesia to the Saxons and proceed to Lower Saxony on the other side of Germany to join Swedish forces there. The order annoyed Hamilton and seems to have planted in his mind a distrust of the Swedish king; disobedience, however, was out of the question, as Gustavus Adolphus could easily instruct his garrisons not to acknowledge the marquis. Leaving behind 1,000 men sick with plague and 1,000 as garrison troops, Hamilton marched with a mixed force of British and German foot soldiers, with 1,000 Swedish cavalry, back down the Oder to Küstrin (now Kostryzn), where he received fresh instructions to besiege Magdeburg, still in Imperial hands.

After the victory at Breitenfeld, John George of Saxony wanted Gustavus Adolphus to march on Vienna to deal a final blow to the Habsburg cause. The Swedish king was more cautious, partly because he could not trust the Saxon, and, leaving a garrison in Leipzig, he now continued his campaign south and west through the German heartlands. Three thousand prisoners taken at Breitenfeld changed sides and were distributed among the German regiments: Monro, searching for co-linguists among the prisoners, was disappointed to

find only three Irishmen whom he could recruit and pointed this out
to the king. In compensation, Gustavus Adolphus promised the Scots
they would have first choice at the earliest opportunity. They did not
have to wait long. After they captured the castle at Halle a few days
later, fifty old soldiers from the defeated garrison took service in
Mackay's Regiment. Gustavus Adolphus brought his chancellor, Axel
Oxenstierna, to Halle and installed him there as a legate and administrator before setting off again on the next leg of his march. The town
of Erfurt fell to the allies without bloodshed, providing the soldiers
with much needed quarters and supplies. Gustavus Adolphus's army
was now within the bishopric of Mentz, advancing into Catholic
Germany, the natural constituency of the Hapsburg Empire.
Although he ruthlessly exploited the Catholic Church for material
supplies and money, Monro says that Gustavus Adolphus was
scrupulous in allowing the people freedom of worship and conscience
as long as they adhered to an oath not to do anything to aid the
enemy. Leaving Monro of Foulis in charge of the garrison of Erfurt,
Gustavus Adolphus pushed on, his forces advancing in two columns
over the forested hills of the Thuringer Wald into Bavaria, sometimes
moving at night and lighting their way with candles and small lamps
hung in the trees.

An army on the march was like a moving, busy town. The long
straggling columns of foot soldiers were accompanied by bands of
women and children, pedlars, prostitutes, hucksters and hangers-on,
and mingled among the walkers were wagons, carts and livestock.
Officers such as Robert Monro left their families in relative comfort in
lodgings far from the action but the ordinary private soldiers brought
their women and children with them. These families tagged along as
an unofficial auxiliary corps offering various services as nurses, cooks,
menders, messengers, scavengers. Some of the train simply attached
themselves to an army as a more likely place to scrounge some food
and protection in the chaos of a war. The Privy Council had issued a
proclamation back in July 1581 in an attempt to curb this scandalous
behaviour among the Scots serving in the Low Countries: 'thair hes
cumit thairfurth of this realm many and divers trowpis and cumpanis
of licht women, uncumly and indecent in thair manners, countenance,
behaviour and array, not being mens wyffis or having ony necessar

knawin affaires or bissyness . . . to the tynsale [loss] of the great reputatioun quhilkis the said subjectis in the partis aforssaid [Low Countries] hes to thame acquirit sin thair cuming thairto.'[9] Shipmen were enjoined to take abroad only legitimate wives.[10] Even were this injunction strictly enforced it would not have taken long for an army to attract replacements.

Feeding an army on the move was a considerable operation. The basic rations of beer, bread and meat filled many wagons, lumbering on creaking wheels behind teams of oxen or horses through the mud and dust of the country roads. A full-strength cavalry regiment with over a thousand horses needed 50 to 60 tons of fodder per day for the mounts; the summer months comprised the campaigning season because horses could then find grazing. Artillery had to be dragged by oxen and horses, with accompanying wagons bearing the powder and shot. The giant, untidy cavalcade wound its way across the countryside at a speed little in excess of 10 miles a day and, as dusk began to fall, transformed itself into a mushrooming encampment with cooking fires. Monro advised officers to seek a meadow near water for a campsite in summer, and a wood to provide fire and shelter in winter. The following day the army might drag itself on again, leaving behind the detritus of 10,000 humans and several thousand beasts to soil the places it had passed.

Many a prayer must have been offered up in the hope that an army would keep well away. Anyone with some wealth was liable to be subjected to extortion. A party of English merchants who happened to pass the Swedish army in Pomerania had their goods seized; in this instance, Gustavus Adolphus offered the merchants their possessions back in exchange for a bond of 200,000 reichsthaler 'to give some contentment to his hungry Army', a bargain the merchants bravely refused and for which they might have lost everything, had not some Scots and English officers interceded on their behalf.[11] Relations with ordinary civilians met on the route could be nasty, especially where the passing army was seen as an invader and an enemy. Young soldiers, often brutalised by war, hungry, cold, and poorly clothed, had little patience to deal gently with complaining, unarmed peasants. Atrocities abounded. Good commanders tried to keep their men in line with a fierce discipline, hanging men for crimes committed against

civilians, but there were many bad commanders who turned a blind
eye to the excesses of their troops, and much happened beyond the
eyes and ears of authority. Whenever a soldier found himself a
survivor in defeat, he was likely to become a target for civilian
revenge. Monro gives an instance from his experience with the
Danish army when an Imperial garrison surrendered: 'at their coming
out, the Country Boores [peasants] remembering the hard usage of the
Souldiers to them in the Winter time, seeing them come forth
unarmed, ranne violently upon the souldiers . . . This insolency of
the Boores continued (in killing the poore Souldiers) till by his
Majesties charge I was commanded to put my Souldiers to Armes
to suppresse the Boores.' Soldiers who strayed too far from their
comrades easily fell victim to angry locals in a fever of revenge. Monro
describes how men from the Swedish army were murdered and
mutilated in this way during the 1632 campaign in Bavaria, actions
which in turn stoked up the soldiers for their own vengeance.

One of the Swedish columns, under the command of Lieutenant-
General Bawtish and Sir John Hepburn, went by way of Schmalk-
alden, Meiningen and Hammelburg towards the rendezvous with the
rest of the army at Würzburg on the banks of the Main river. In each
town on the way, money and supplies were garnered, and the burgers
were sworn to obey the Swedish monarch. There was opportunity
here for the unscrupulous and Monro, says Bawtish, pocketed over
50,000 reichsthaler – 'put all in his owne purse' – an act that provoked
the resentment of other senior officers. When the army was deployed
at the gates of Würzburg, Gustavus Adolphus called on the city to
surrender. To the curiosity of Monro and his fellows, the abbot who
came out to deliver the burgers' capitulation was a Scot, a Father
William Ogilvie. On an eminence on the west bank of the Main,
directly opposite the city, stood the Marienberg fortress, whose
garrison refused to yield and began to bombard the Swedish forces
with cannon. A bridge spanned the Main under the fortress walls but
the Imperial troops had broken down the central arch. Only a single
plank remained across the gap 'neere eight fathom' [16 metres] above
the flowing river, a daunting approach in the sights of the fort's
musketeers. Two Scots were shot in the early probing moves against
the fort, brothers called Bothwell, one of whom was a major in Sir

James Ramsay's regiment – they were both buried in Würzburg churchyard.

Gustavus Adolphus delegated the leadership of the assault on Marienberg to Ramsay and Sir John Hamilton. They declined to use the exposed plank and preferred to brave the enemy fire in a small-boat crossing of the river. Ramsay and Hamilton with a few followers managed to scrabble ashore on the other side and establish a tenuous foothold, skirmishing to hold on until they could be reinforced. Their success even inspired a few hardy souls to overcome their vertigo to dash over the plank and soon enough men had reached the other side to worry the defenders. As the Imperialists retired behind their walls, Ramsay was shot and his left arm disabled. Meanwhile Gustavus Adolphus had laid siege to the other sections of the fort. Night brought an end to the struggle but it was renewed at first light, and the defence of Marienberg finally crumbled when German and Swedish troops climbed the walls with siege ladders. Ramsay's wound put him out of the front line for a while but also brought him some wealth: Gustavus Adolphus granted him lands in the duchy of Mecklenburg.

Shortly after the capture of Würzburg, Robert Monro was eating his supper in his quarters one night when the footman alerted him to the presence downstairs of none other than Gustavus Adolphus himself. Monro says that the king rode alone to visit him 'in the remotest part' of the city, meaning perhaps Gustavus Adolphus brought no officers with him, as it is difficult to accept that the monarch would venture through the dark streets absolutely unattended. The king had acquired intelligence that Tilly, still within striking distance to the south, planned to fall on the small town of Ochsenfurt to gain a crossing of the Main. The garrison there comprised only 150 musketeers and it had to be reinforced quickly. Monro roused the 800 musketeers of the Scots Brigade and a little later, with Gustavus Adolphus in the lead with 80 horsemen, they set off for the vulnerable town, Hepburn commanding the brigade with Monro in charge of the rear of the column. At two in the morning they finally toiled into their destination and, as soon as daylight permitted, set about inspecting and strengthening the defences. Sounds of attack on the cavalry stationed half a mile away were heard and Monro was sent out with 50 musketeers to cover the withdrawal of the horsemen. However, Monro's unit itself was forced back by the Imperial forces until a reinforcement of musketeers turned the skirmish in their favour and the enemy retired out of sight over a hill. There remained the possibility that the assault on Ochsenfurt was a feint, with the main thrust likely to be directed at Würzburg, so Gustavus Adolphus hurried back to the city, leaving Hepburn's men to stand where they were. Preparations for a defence were made – buildings and walls that might provide cover for the attackers were pulled down, trees and hedges cut, scaffolding for parties of musketeers thrown up on the town walls – but it was not until late on the third night of their presence that the Scots heard a great cacophony of trumpets and drums – 'as though Heaven and earth were going together' – from the enemy outside. But the attack never materialised and dawn revealed the Imperialists to be melting away. Tilly was withdrawing towards Nuremberg to regroup.

Gustavus Adolphus set about consolidating his hold on the territories the Protestant allies had by now acquired, fully aware that he had come far from his base on the Baltic and was now occupying a country where not everyone was to be trusted. Garrisons were established in the towns and villages along the Main and a winter lager for the army was prepared in Würzburg. The strategic importance of feeding and sheltering troops during the cold season was a concern for all seventeenth-century commanders and extended military action was usually abandoned in favour of keeping men healthy until the spring came. In Monro's words, Gustavus Adolphus 'knew well twelve Souldiers with a good Officer to direct them were better . . . than a hundred naked and hungry Souldiers without'. This winter stasis did not necessarily rule out all activity. A floating force of artillery and 300 musketeers from Sir James Ramsay's regiment, under the command of Alexander Hanan, followed by troops marching up the riverbank, took all the forts that lay downstream as far as the castle of the bishop of Mainz at Aschaffenburg. Returning via Offenbach, which they reached on 27 November, they next struck west and captured Höchst on the 29th. Two hundred Scots from Colonel Ludovic Leslie's regiment garrisoned the fortress of Russelsheim, handed over to Gustavus Adolphus by the Landgrave of Darmstadt.

A ship-bridge was thrown across the Main and boats were sent downstream to blockade Mainz.

For Monro and his colleagues the winter of 1631/32 was easier than many they had endured as soldiers. They enjoyed good quarters and were excited by the relative prosperity of this part of the German lands. 'Francford is so pleasant for ayre, situation, buildings, traffique, commerce with all Nations, by water and by land, that it is and may be thought the Garden of Germany', enthused the man from Easter Ross. Frankfurt was also the site of a great trade fair where merchants from all over Europe met annually to cut deals and exchange money and goods, handling not only food and textiles but also books, maps and globes and the other products of the new sciences. Still, from time to time the Scots were called out to fight. Hepburn's brigade and the Blue Brigade under Colonel Winkel were tasked with capturing the fortified town of Oppenheim, a few miles upstream of Mainz on the Rhine. In tempestuous weather with snow and keen frosts, Monro's men slept under bushes by the river during the siege, trying to stay close to the campfires despite the danger of proximity to the flames that provided such an easy target for the gunners within the skonce. One night a 32-pound ball 'shot right out betwixt Colonell Hepburnes shoulder and mine, going through the Colonells Coach; the next shot kill'd a Sergeant of mine, by the fire', wrote Monro. That same night, they repulsed a sally with their pikes. Although they held a strong position and were well supplied, the 1,000-strong garrison of Italian troops realised their position was hopeless when they learned that Gustavus Adolphus had successfully crossed the Rhine and was approaching from the north-west. They chose to surrender to Hepburn but, before they had time to leave the fort, a forward party of Ramsay's musketeers, advancing with the king, stormed over the walls and, in the confusion, began to 'put all to the sword' before control was gained and the killing ceased. Some of the Italians joined Hepburn's regiment.

By early December the enemy troops, who were mostly Spanish, were withdrawing from all their stations in the area to their fortified base at Frankenthal to the south; only this and Heidelberg remained in Habsburg hands. Gustavus Adolphus laid siege to Mainz, opening the attack with a cannon bombardment that terrified the inhabitants enough to make them pledge 60,000 reichsthaler to the king to cease his destruction. The Bishop of Mainz had fled to Koblenz down the Rhine and on the third day of the attack the garrison of Spanish troops surrendered and were allowed to march, without their arms, in the wake of the prelate. Sir James Ramsay's regiment captured Bingen, Bacharach and the areas along the Rhine gorges. Gustavus Adolphus now had winter quarters for his men and, three days before Christmas, Monro and his Scots found comfortable lodgings.

They did not enjoy these undisturbed for, when news came in that the Spanish were advancing from the south, from Speyer, to attack the Rhinegrave's regiment in the vicinity of Bacharach, Monro and 500 musketeers were sent down the Rhine to reinforce the garrisons. After pausing at Bingen to pick up another 100 musketeers from Ramsay's regiment, they landed at Bacharach to a cool reception from the garrison commander, who refused to let them enter the town, forcing them to camp outside the walls. Monro and two officers, however, sneaked in via a lightly guarded water gate and cornered the commander in his own house until he agreed to provide his visitors with victuals and shelter. Monro repaid what he called this 'unthankfulnesse' by extorting protection money from the villagers in the vicinity. When he finally rendezvoused with the Rhinegrave, Monro received new orders to occupy a village near Koblenz while the Rhinegrave advanced to meet the Spanish thrust and force it back across the Moselle.

The Protestant allies, behind the banner of Gustavus Adolphus, were now in a very strong position, with armies controlling much of Germany – from the Baltic coast to its western frontiers – and over the winter a string of important visitors called on the Swedish monarch at Mainz. His queen arrived in January and delighted the assembled dignitaries when the royal couple met at Hanau by putting her arms around the king's neck and telling him he was now her prisoner. Frederick, still known as the king of Bohemia in Protestant circles, also came, once more on the doorstep of the Palatinate and once more in hope of regaining his patrimony. Gustavus Adolphus received him with courtesy but did little to reassure him that he would soon repossess the Palatinate.

The Swedish chancellor, Axel Oxenstierna, came to discuss strategy, and with him from Prussia rode Sir Patrick Ruthven. A string of ambassadors, legates and German Protestant leaders also flocked to the royal camp through the winter weather. There was much talk and much celebration, and Scots officers who had not seen each other for some time made the most of the opportunity. Colonel Alexander Ramsay was installed as the governor of Kreuznach, a man whom Monro described as loving 'nothing better than nobly and kindly to entertain his friends and strangers, being the common receptacle and refuge of all his Country-men.'

That winter the Marquis of Hamilton found himself in a less happy position. In the autumn he had quit his campaign in the Oder valley and had obeyed Gustavus Adolphus's instruction to join the Swedish forces under Johan Baner, laying siege to the city of Magdeburg and its imperial garrison. Also, onto the scene came a plump lawyer, Sir Henry Vane, as ambassador from Charles I to Gustavus Adolphus. Leaving his army under the command of Baner and Sir Alexander Leslie, Hamilton travelled with Vane to Frankfurt.[12] While Vane discussed the political situation with Gustav Horn, the Swedish representative of the king, Hamilton tried without success to extract more men from Gustavus Adolphus, only to have to return to Magdeburg 'loaded onely with hopes and fair words'. The country around the suffering city had little to offer the occupying troops except discomfort and hunger, but within its walls Magdeburg's garrison was also in sore straits. Hamilton felt Baner could attack and take it, but the cautious Swede and the impetuous Scot did not see eye to eye. It is unclear where Sir Alexander Leslie stood in this quarrel. The city was on the point of surrender on Christmas Eve when news came that Pappenheim was marching to its relief and negotiations were broken off. Baner, under orders to avoid battle, now decided to retire before Pappenheim's advance, a course of action that provoked Hamilton into disagreement, until the Swede reminded the Scot that he was the one whom Gustavus Adolphus had placed in overall command. Swallowing this blow to his status as ally rather than subordinate, the marquis pulled back from Magdeburg, clinging to the hope of the opportunity to engage Pappenheim that would follow the expected arrival of the Duke of Saxe-Weimar with 5,000 men. Baner withdrew to defensive positions at Kalbe on the other side of the Sala River and threatened to blow up the bridge and leave Hamilton to his fate. When Duke Bernard did not appear, Hamilton had no choice but to fall in after Baner and withdraw again.

The wily Pappenheim had implemented a successful campaign of disinformation. He had fewer than 5,000 men but, through the agents who had gone before his force to buy up supplies, had given the impression he had three times as many. The chance to face him was missed and he was able to make contact with the Magdeburg garrison and bring it out to safety. When Hamilton entered the abandoned city he found forty spiked cannon left behind, and stocks of ammunition and grain. He quartered his troops there until February 1632. The German mercenaries under his command were now demanding arrears of pay and once again Hamilton had to solicit aid from the Swedish king. Meanwhile Vane's attempts to persuade Gustavus Adolphus, who found the British ambassador an irksome nuisance, to give priority to the recovery of the Palatinate for Frederick were being stonewalled. As the Swedish king seemed to demand more and more from his allies, Hamilton felt that the pride of victory had gone to his head and that he was 'beginning to reckon on all Germany as his Conquest'.

'nothing els but fire and smoke'

Bavaria, 1632

T HE WINTER OF 1631/32 was the high point of the Swedish campaign. Robert Monro was proud of the contribution Scots made to Gustavus Adolphus's mastery of northern Europe from the eastern Baltic to the Rhine and listed the leaders among his countrymen, who, when they were together in numbers, must have made the Swedish mess halls ring to Scottish accents. As well as Colonel Alexander Ramsay at Kreuznach, Sir Patrick Ruthven was now governor of Ulm, Sir Alexander Leslie of the cities of the Mecklenburg coast, and Sir David Drummond of Stettin, while no fewer than twenty-one Scots were colonels of regiments. Three Scots colonels were in the king's service in his native Sweden, and three more in Prussia. Their triumph was, however, a fragile one. The Catholic League tried to blunt the success of the Swedish monarch by driving a wedge of suspicion between him and the French, putting forward the view that Gustavus Adolphus's real intentions were to overthrow the Church of Rome and assault France itself. For their part, the French, although delighted to see the Spanish armies and Habsburg power in disarray, nervously watched the Lion of the North, and they moved troops at one point up to the Moselle in case the Swedes should continue their advance beyond the Rhine. In charge of France's foreign policy, Cardinal Richelieu had a tricky situation on his hands, being both Catholic and anti-Habsburg; he tried to encourage Gustavus Adolphus to agree neutrality with the league. While envoys travelled to and fro between the interested parties, direct military action was also continuing: in January 1632, Tilly's forces took Bamberg from Gustav Horn but failed to retain it and, after Horn recaptured the city, they retired again to the west.

When the grip of winter began to slacken in the early days of March, Gustavus Adolphus prepared to renew his campaign against the Habsburgs. On the 16th the whole army paraded in the fields beside Aschaffenburg at the start of the march south-east towards the headwaters of the Danube and the frontiers of Bavaria. Skirmishes with Imperial units did nothing to delay the advance, and Gustavus Adolphus's main army, some twenty thousand men, passed day by day through the rolling wooded hills to Fürth and Schwabach. Protestant Nuremberg gave an ecstatic welcome to the Swedish monarch and Frederick of Bohemia, 'their eyes shedding teares of joy, being overjoyed with the sight of two Kings at once,' wrote Monro, 'as they thought, sent by the King of Kings for their reliefes . . . the whole City, Burgers and Souldiers were in their brightest Armes.' When he had become aware of the advance, Tilly had moved his forces towards Neumarkt in the Upper Palatinate, only a few miles south-east of Nuremberg and the Swedish van. Gustavus Adolphus headed for the town of Donauworth and its bridge across the Danube. He and Tilly were now in a race, the latter trying to get back across the river to join the Duke of Bavaria and the former to cross first to defeat the duke before Tilly could arrive. Meanwhile Maximilian of Bavaria garrisoned his frontier and tried to deprive the advancing Swedes of any victual and forage. The route to Donauworth took Gustavus Adolphus through the estates of Pappenheim, along the Altmühl river, and the king could not resist the temptation to sieze Mansfeld, the Imperial commander's castle, said to be the strongest in all Germany. Pappenheim's son was in command of the garrison and defied the Swedish threat to devastate his father's earldom should he refuse to surrender. Gustavus Adolphus gave up the attempt to overawe the young man into compliance and hurried on to Donauworth.

The city lay on the south bank of the Danube, here spanned by a single bridge. The garrison mounted a capable defence and one sally captured a battery of Swedish cannon, an incident after which the Scottish captain of the guns, a Semple by name, was arrested for fleeing with his men (he was later pardoned but was removed from command). The main part of the Swedish artillery, however, kept up a heavy, damaging fire on the city. As the day drew to an end, Sir John Hepburn was ordered to march a mile to the west, where another bridge allowed a crossing of the river and a second line of attack. Hepburn and his musketeers reached the walls of Donauworth from the south-west side a little before midnight. At dawn a firefight ensued between the opposing forces of musketeers. Then Hepburn sent in his pikemen. 'We came up with full squadrons of Pikes amongst them, and entred on the execution, till we made them thro downe their Armes, and cry for Quarters', wrote Monro. The two-pronged assault carried the day. A more objective commentator on the events, an anonymous contributor to the contemporary newsletter the *Swedish Intelligencer*, noted that 'Sir John Hepburne being thus gotten in and having first cut in pieces all resistance, his souldiours fall immediately to plundering, when many a gold chaine, with much other plate and treasure of the enemie, were made prize of.' Over five hundred defenders were killed and some three hundred Jesuits and monks who tried to escape the victorious Protestants were taken prisoner. Monro says a thousand men were forced to join the Swedish army but, as they were Bavarian Catholics on their home ground, they were able to melt away over the next few days 'as soone as they smelt the smell of their Fathers houses'. Gustavus Adolphus consolidated his victory by sending troops further south to capture Höchstädt.

Tilly had by this time reached the town of Rain near the confluence of the Lech River with the Danube and had fortified the country between there and Augsburg, while basing himself in the city of Ingolstadt. Gustavus Adolphus used a bridge of boats and planks to force a crossing of the Lech on 15 April, after subjecting Tilly's army on the opposite bank to a fearsome barrage of cannon fire; the Imperial troops were drawn up in thick woods and many men were hurt by branches and trees smashed down by the cannon balls. Tilly himself was struck in the knee – 'a cruell blow for an ould man', thought Monro in a moment of compassion for the 72-year-old enemy they nicknamed the old corporal – and was hurried off the field to die in pain in Ingolstadt before two weeks were out. With him gone, the Imperial troops lost heart and the Duke of Bavaria ordered the retreat. Rain surrendered to Gustavus Adolphus, as did the nearby town of Neuburg. A day's journey to the south, in Augsburg, the townspeople lived in fear or expectation, depending on their religious affiliation, as the streets filled up with troops, among them the black-armoured cavalry of Pappenheim, terrifying with their great mounts and closed helmets.[1] Two days after the successful crossing of the Lech the Swedish forces were camping in the village of Lechhausen close to the city. Maximilian ordered an evacuation of his forces to Ingolstadt and the Augsburgers were treated to a spectacular sight – the black-clad cavalry passing out through their gates at night with torches flickering in their helmets to guide them on their way. After a brief exchange of gunfire in an honour-saving exercise, the defenders accepted surrender terms that allowed the remaining garrison to march out to Ingolstadt. On 20 April the Swedish troops entered the city and established a camp in the Weinmarkt, where in the afternoon they listened to a sermon and sang psalms in full voice. Four days later Gustavus Adolphus made his ceremonial entry, attending a service of thanksgiving in the richly decorated surroundings of St Anne's Church. Like the good Presbyterian he was, Robert Monro noted the sermon was based on Psalm 12, verse 5: 'For the oppression of the poor, for the sighing of the needy, now will I arise, saith the Lord; I will set him in safety from him that puffeth at him.' To the Protestants of Augsburg Gustavus Adolphus had come as deliverer, as an instrument of their Lord, and a flurry of pamphlets hailed him as a new Gideon, a new Caesar, a second Constantine; but, in case his soldiers thought of plundering their houses, they painted the password *Gott mit uns* on their doors. All the Catholics on the city council were ousted and their places taken by Protestants, who promptly presented their deliverer with a table laden with corn, fish and wine.

As the governor of Ulm, Patrick Ruthven conducted his own campaign to seize all the towns between his new charge and Lindau at the east end of the Bodensee. He did not make himself popular among the people; despite his best efforts his troops inflicted atrocities and he was ruthless in extracting sums of money. Gustavus Adolphus had given him the post because, approaching the age of sixty, he was much older than other field officers. Clearly neither his age nor his love of wine had resulted in much diminution of his energy, and he was richly rewarded by the Swedish king, receiving the graveshaft or earldom of Kilchberg, a stretch of land close to Ulm that belonged to the rich Fugger family of bankers and was worth 10,000 reichsthaler a year.

Gustavus Adolphus wasted no time before making an advance

towards Ingolstadt on the Danube. The strongly fortified town put up a stiff resistance and their cannon fire almost claimed the crucial prize when a ball killed Gustavus Adolphus's horse under him, taking off one of the animal's legs. Monro's men also suffered and Monro himself was shaken by the pounding they had to withstand while they stood to arms all night in case the Imperial forces should launch an assault. 'At one shot I lost twelve men of my owne Companie, not knowing what became of them', he wrote, before adding, 'a Souldier . . . might passe prentice in our Calling in one night for resolution'. For once, Gustavus Adolphus was forced to pause. The capture of Ingolstadt would clearly be hard and very costly. News arrived that Regensburg had been taken by the Duke of Bavaria and, according to Monro, this persuaded Gustavus Adolphus to abandon the assault and make a fighting withdrawal to Moosburg on the Isar River. From this base, the Protestant army set about replenishing its coffers, extracting money from several communities, including the town of Landshut, and Catholic institutions, and Ruthven kept himself busy bringing in the contributions. Gustavus Adolphus had always shown a ruthless ability to make the Germans pay the costs of the war on their territory. Protestants had a vested interest in supporting him, however reluctantly they might do so, but the peasants of Bavaria simply saw it as robbery and reacted violently, attacking and killing soldiers who strayed from the main body of the army. Churchmen and towns-people paid up to avoid unpleasant consequences. The Bishop of Freising handed over 50,000 reichsthaler and the city fathers of Munich came to greet the king and promised him everything he desired if he spared their citizens from plundering.

Gustavus Adolphus and Frederick, still the king of Bohemia in many Protestant eyes, moved into the Munich Residenz, with Hepburn's Brigade to guard them. The soldiers were paid an extra 5 shillings to discourage them from looting the marvels they now saw around them. The Residenz was the principal home of the Wittelsbach rulers of Bavaria and much had been lavished on its decoration in the decades before the outbreak of the war. The Grottenhalle, with its elaborate sculptured fountain covered in shells, naked nymphs and monsters, and the Antiquarium, a vast chamber, said to be the largest of its sort north of the Alps, where the sound of the boots of the

soldiers echoed from the red and white marble tiles on the floor to the
arching, painted ceiling, must have made the Scots gape. The Marquis
of Hamilton remarked that the Duke of Bavaria's residence was the
finest house he had ever seen, a comment his fellows probably
endorsed, though a few hardened Calvinists may have condemned
the lot as vanity. Monro spent three weeks in this comfortable billet as
commander of the guard, while the two monarchs played tennis,
strolled in the pleasant gardens, admired the herds of deer that could
be driven into view for their delight and hunted hares in the
neighbourhood. Munich also yielded up valuable munitions, including
the cannon known as the Twelve Apostles that had been taken here
from the Palatinate. The sight of the guns that had been looted from
his own property early in the war made Frederick smile sadly, and not
just because a useful 30,000 gold ducats secreted within one of them
were found to be still there. Although he had ridden at the Swedish
king's tail all the way from Frankfurt, Frederick must have felt the
restoration of his own country to be no nearer. 'I do not anticipate . . .
any accelerated decision in my affairs', he had written to his wife
before reaching the Bavarian capital.[2]

Tilly's demise as the commander of Imperial forces opened the way
for the return of Wallenstein from the political wilderness. In August
1630 the commander's enemies at the Habsburg court had brought
about his resignation but towards the end of 1631, as Gustavus
Adolphus was taking all before him in his sweep through Germany, he
had at last responded to the imploring letters coming from the
emperor. Now Wallenstein was in the field again at the head of
his own troops. As Augsburg had been celebrating the triumph of
Gustavus Adolphus, Wallenstein had captured Prague and driven the
enemy from Bohemia. The news that the Imperial warrior was now
on the move with a strong army into the Upper Palatinate came to
Munich to interrupt the idyll in the Residenz.

Leaving Baner in occupation of Munich, Gustavus Adolphus made a
quick foray to Memmingen to suppress local unrest and returned via
Augsburg, taxing Munich a further 100,000 reichsthaler on his arrival.
At the end of May, the Swedish king decided to shift his main strength
north to Donauworth, taking with him hostages for the unpaid money
from the city. The Duke of Bavaria captured Weissenburg, only a few

miles to the north. There now ensued a game of manoeuvre as the enemies shifted like chess pieces to gain advantage and confuse the other. Gustavus Adolphus made a feint to the south-west but, leaving the Duke of Weimar and Ruthven with a detached force to confront the Spanish army in the region of the Bodensee, turned quickly back to Munich. Here he issued patents to Colonel Hugh Hamilton and Colonel John Forbesse to recruit two regiments of foot from the hill country on the Swiss border, wrote to the Swiss cantons to encourage them to interfere with the passage of Spanish troops, and moved north again, reaching Nuremberg on 17 June. By this time the Duke of Bavaria had met up with Wallenstein at Eger (now Cheb) on the western edge of Bohemia. Gustavus Adolphus struck east from Nuremberg, pushing back the Imperialists some 35 miles to Amberg. The country here had been devastated and could no longer support a foraging army, so the Swedes retired to Hersbruck, half way to Nuremberg, with Monro, Hepburn and 2,000 musketeers making up the rearguard. The weather turned wet and miserable: rain fell for two weeks, soaking alike the powder and the soldiers' clothing. The approaching threat of Wallenstein with the cream of the Imperial army did little to dispel the 'weake and discontented' mood among the Protestant forces, hungry and short of pay. Gustavus Adolphus took steps to restore morale. Monro wrote: 'To satisfie our hunger a little we did get of by-past lendings three paid us in hand, Bills of Exchange given us for one and twentie lendings more, which should have beene payed at Ausburg of the Munchen moneys; which we accepted of for payment, but were never paid.' Mollified by these offers the soldier retired to Nuremberg to lay out a fortified camp and await developments.

A free city within the Empire, Nuremberg had flourished for centuries as a commercial and cultural centre. The artist Albrecht Dürer lived here, Copernicus's revolutionary treatise on astronomy had been published here, and the city had been one of the first places to adopt the Lutheran Reformation. The urban area straddled the Pegnitz River, its streets rising steeply from the bank on the north side to the rocky eminence of the Kaiserburg with its fortress. At some point during the first days here, a quarrel erupted between Gustavus Adolphus and Sir John Hepburn. Robert Monro stays silent on this, for an unknown reason, and no evidence for the nature of the dispute seems to have survived. Possibly the spark came from a hasty remark by the king, who was known for his quick temper, a comment that may have dealt with Hepburn's Catholicism or his fondness for gaudy armour, or it may have been about some point of honour. It is also possible that Hepburn had given voice to a grievance over the treatment of another Scottish officer, Sir George Douglas, and this had roused the king's anger.

As a young lad, Douglas had come to England after James VI had moved to London, and had studied at Oxford. 'Thinking the Schooles an oversoft course of exercise, he left them and betook himselfe to Armes', wrote one contemporary historian.[3] Thus, Douglas had led a company of foot soldiers into Gustavus Adolphus's service in 1623 and after some years had risen to the rank of lieutenant-colonel of Sir James Ramsay's regiment. Ramsay's wound at the siege of Würzburg resulted in Douglas assuming command. He came to the attention of the king for his exemplary conduct in maintaining discipline during the capture of Kreuznach, after which Gustavus Adolphus had considered him for the post of governor of that town. For some reason Douglas had then been arrested and, although released on the king's order, had felt his honour so outraged that he had refused the commission as governor. Gustavus Adolphus had by now left on the march to Nuremberg and Douglas had had to deal with the chancellor, Axel Oxenstierna. All that the latter could do was give Douglas extended leave so that he could travel after the king to obtain the redress he desired, nothing less than a pass out of the army. For the journey to Nuremberg, Douglas attached himself to the retinue of Sir Henry Vane, who was also travelling to find Gustavus Adolphus. When they reached the city, it seems that the impetuous, fired-up Douglas sought out the king at once, interrupting a game of tennis he was playing with Frederick of Bohemia. Understandably, Gustavus Adolphus became angry and demanded Douglas tell him why he had left his post. Douglas replied to the effect he no longer had a post, whereupon the king ordered his arrest. Sir Henry Vane, whom the king didn't especially like in any case, was incensed over this complication. As the Imperial army approached, Vane prepared to leave and, in response to a question he put about Douglas, received a fiery earful from Gustavus Adolphus. In the event, Douglas and Vane left together, the former to return to England. Perhaps

Hepburn had tried to put a word in for Douglas and perhaps the king had heard enough of the matter and said so in no soft words. By 5 July, when skirmishes heralded the arrival of the combined Imperial forces of Wallenstein and Bavaria in the vicinity, a chasm had opened between Gustavus Adolphus and the soldier that neither could bring himself to cross.

Robert Monro estimated that the enemy now occupying the country around Nuremberg, effectively cutting off the city from reinforcement and supply, numbered 100,000 against 16,000 on their own side. Counting on the Swedish king to defend them and their religious liberties, the citizens of Nuremberg raised 24 companies of foot to fight alongside the Swedish forces and dug into their stores to find just enough to feed the 800,000 souls, including refugees, who had crowded inside their walls. Gustavus's men laboured to build fortifications around the city, adding outside the massive walls in ten days a system of skonces, redoubts, ditches, gun emplacements and stockades. Wallenstein set his own soldiers to lay out matching entrenchments and siege works and occupied an old ruined castle, the Alte Feste, on a hill nearly 2 miles to the north. The two armies settled down for a long wait, like 'two great new-founded Cities of short continuance, though it is certaine, many of them did get life-rent-leases of their new built houses'. An undeclared truce – 'a Stil-stand of Peace', Monro called it – emerged and lasted for two months, only broken when stray groups of foragers stumbled into each other's presence.

There may have been stasis at Nuremberg but a fluid war continued in other parts of the Continent. Far to the west, Spanish troops ventured across the Moselle but were beaten back to the Low Countries again. In Schwabia, around the town of Kempten and in other regions, the Swedes brutally and quickly snuffed out local risings. In Lower Saxony the Imperial cavalryman Pappenheim was pursuing his own successful campaign, capturing a few towns, such as Einbeck, and three colours from Obsdale Monro's regiment after a skirmish in which the inexperienced Swedish troops were surrounded. Captain Francis Sinclair was taken prisoner but was able to ransom himself free again, leaving other Scots with no resources to languish in captivity at Minden for another eighteen months. Pappenheim captured Stade but rather than risk being besieged there relinquished it to approaching Swedish forces and

headed for the Weser, where he received a call to assist the Spanish and
turned south towards Maastricht. In one of the many encounters in this
campaign Major-General James King was wounded and captured; he
recovered, ransomed himself and then recruited more soldiers to fight
for Sweden.

Gustavus Adolphus was determined not to let Nuremberg fall into
Imperial hands; the city fathers had presented him with a pair of globes,
one celestial and one terrestrial, and he had pledged himself to defend
the city against all mortals. Since the victory at Breitenfeld, which by
now must have seemed a long time ago, he had known that every eye in
Europe was watching to see if the great hope of the Protestant cause, the
Lion of the North, would prevail over the forces of reaction, as they saw
the Counter-Reformation. But all the king could do was fight a
defensive strategy and send out patrols and small forces to harass
the attackers. It was in the course of one of these probing skirmishes
that two Scots officers on the Imperial side, John Gordon and Walter
Leslie, were taken prisoner. Gustavus Adolphus promised the Scots
their freedom without ransom but they chose to stay for five weeks with
the Scottish officers in the Swedish army, 'with us their Country-men,'
recalled Monro, 'where we made merry as friends'. Such pleasant
interludes became rare as the summer wore on. 'In th'end,' wrote
Monro, 'our forrage grew so scarce that many did quit their horses for
want of entertainment.' There were moments of relief: at the end of July,
a strong party from the city seized a magazine and store at Furstat and
brought home provender and four hundred 'great and fat' oxen. But
even Nuremberg's well-plenished larders were beginning to turn bare.
Monro recalled that they were being taught by discipline 'heartily to
embrace povertie for their Mistresse'. Each side played a waiting game,
searching for signs of who seemed likely to crack first. One day a
foraging party lost a large number of their horses to the Imperialists,
leaving some of the Swedish cavalry with no option but to walk for a
while. Hunger gnawed at the Protestants but Wallenstein's men were
also facing supply problems, hauling their food by wagon over long
miles from as far as Bohemia.

Robert Monro was by August the oldest lieutenant-colonel in the
Swedish army and for the last three months had been acting
commander of Mackay's Regiment. Now Lord Reay let it be known

that he would not be returning to Germany and Monro was confirmed as colonel, a promotion he felt was long overdue, with Major
John Sinclair as lieutenant-colonel and Captain William Stewart as
major. Monro had hoped to take over another regiment but he had to
be content with the now 'very weake' unit that had left Cromarty six
years before. The stand-off in Nuremberg was now moving slowly
towards its climax. A Swedish relief force under the command of
Johan Baner and the Duke of Weimar fought their way from the west:
on 26 August it reached Bad Windsheim, on the 28th Aorach, and on
the 31st Fürth, where their appearance made an Imperial force swiftly
retreat to their own lager. Baner and the duke carried on to the village
of Grossreuth and Gustavus Adolphus led out his own troops to join
them beyond Schweinau. They deployed in battle lines beside Fürth
within half a mile of the Imperial camp but Wallenstein refused to
respond to the invitation to open battle, instead subjecting the
Protestant lines to a cannon bombardment that, according to Monro,
killed a few men but did little overall harm. All night the stand-off
persisted. Gustavus Adolphus brought up his own artillery but still
Wallenstein stayed in his camp before pulling back to the hill with the
ruined castle of Alte Feste on its summit at the end of the second day.
The Protestants manoeuvred around the hill during the night. At this
point Gustavus Adolphus was misled into thinking the Imperialists
had started to withdraw and ordered an attack to begin at seven in the
morning.

Wallenstein had lured his opponent into a rash move. The steep-
sided hill was protected on one side by woods above the Pegnitz and
where nature had not lent a hand the labour of the soldiers had built
up strong defences. Like waves breaking on a rock, the Protestants
fought to capture the enemy position. 'The Hill was nothing els but
fire and smoke', wrote Monro. In the furious fighting, Monro was
ordered to take the place of a dead officer, in command of 500
musketeers in the forward lines: 'I taking leave of my Camerades went
to the Poste, and finding the place warme at my coming, divers
Officers and Souldiers lying bloudy on the ground.' Monro re-
deployed his men to give them some measure of safety and ensnare
any parties that might sally out from the entrenchments. Then a sniper
hidden in a tree on the well-wooded hill scored a hit on the Scot 'right

above the Hanch-bone, on the left side, which lighted fortunatly for me on the Iron clicket of my hanger'. The musket ball that spent itself on the clasp of the officer's sword loop still pierced his flesh to a depth of almost two inches. Monro struggled on, despite the loss of blood, until he was relieved by Lieutenant-Colonel John Sinclair at nightfall.

After his quarrel with the king, Sir John Hepburn stuck to a vow not to fight but, unable to resist the opportunity to watch, he had come along in his full dress armour. Showing typical foolhardy courage, he stayed with the troops amid the plunging shot and, when the Duke of Weimar saw how success might be won and Gustavus Adolphus called for a senior officer to make a reconnaissance with the duke's idea in mind, Hepburn readily offered his services. 'Whilst Duke Bernard and Sir John Hepburn were at their view,' reported the *Swedish Intelligencer*, 'there was a Ritt-master shot dead hard by them: which showed that the place was not altogether so safe as was hoped.' Towards the end of the long, bloody day Hepburn responded again to a request from Gustavus Adolphus, this time to ride to direct some units to withdraw before they were cut off. In one history of the time, Hepburn is quoted as saying: 'Sire, this is the only service I cannot refuse your Majesty for it is a hazardous one.' After he had urged his horse through straggling units of Imperial cavalry and brought the men to safety he is credited with sheathing his sword and saying: 'And now, sire, never more shall this sword be drawn in your service. This is the last time I will ever serve so ungrateful a prince.'[4]

At the end of the day a thick mist turned into a miserably damp night. When dawn came, the king sought to know the status of Sinclair and his musketeers lying out in the rocks in the shadow of the hill. Once again Hepburn responded – apparently he had slept close by in his armour – and came back to report that his fellow Scots were all right, although half-buried in mud and water. He also claimed to have found a spot where four cannon could be sited to bear on the Alte Feste with advantage, but Gustavus Adolphus declined to try such a move. The king had decided to call off the attack. His error had taken the lives of 1,000 of his men, including many of his experienced officers, and left injured another 2,000. James Turner reported higher figures in his memoir, the numbers possibly exaggerated by distance and hearsay: 'for beaten he [Gustavus Adolphus] was with the losse of neere foure thousand killed . . . Neere six thousand wounded, so that all the hospitalls and lazarettos of Nuremberg were sufficientlie filld.'[5]

After some days, during which scarcity of food became a serious problem, Gustavus Adolphus began a withdrawal towards the west. Four regiments, one of them under the command of Monro of Foulis, were left in Nuremberg as a garrison. The guns were sent off under the cover of darkness and, at dawn, the remainder of the Swedish army paraded in line of battle before the Imperial camp, made a right wheel and marched away, a gesture saluting and acknowledging the Imperial efforts. The Protestant army halted at Neustadt an der Aisch while Gustavus Adolphus waited until the enemy movements became clear. Wallenstein made no attempt to pursue them but, after burning villages in the vicinity of Nuremberg, marched north through Forchheim and on to plunder Saxony and the upper reaches of the Elbe.

Back in April, the remnants of the Marquis of Hamilton's army, which had fought around Magdeburg had been reorganised into two regiments, one of English soldiers under Colonel Sir William Bellenden, and one of Scots under Colonel Sir Alexander Hamilton, commonly known as 'Dear Sandy', and assigned to the Duke of Weimar's army.[6] All summer the marquis had followed Gustavus Adolphus as a volunteer and all the while he had grown increasingly disenchanted with his position. Clearly the king was wary of giving the marquis any independent role to act in the interests of Charles I and the recovery of the Palatinate, and perhaps he hoped that the weary nobleman would give up and go away. At the beginning of August, King Charles wrote to Hamilton to reassure him and tell him he had to make up his mind: 'One of two you must chuse, either to stay or come away.' Charles thought Gustavus Adolphus might agree to allow the Marquis to proceed to the Palatinate to assist the French, now coming into the war against the Habsburgs, but if the Swedish king did not agree Hamilton had, in Charles's view, 'no more to doe but to seek a fair excuse to come home'. That the suggestion from the British king came via Sir Henry Vane did not help matters. The marquis tried to persuade Gustavus Adolphus to give him a new independent assignment, reminding the king that he had now been fifteen months in the field, incurring expenses for nothing, 'his Heart . . . to great to be a perpetual volunteer'. Gustavus Adolphus admitted that Hamilton had reason to be weary and that he was obliged to him and regarded him as a friend. It was all Vane's fault, he cried, before flying into one of his short-lived passions, snatching the marquis's hat from his hand, clapping it on his own head and stamping about the room. The nonplussed marquis could only wait for the royal temper to subside before making clear his wish to leave. On 18 September Gustavus Adolphus signed Hamilton's new commission to go home and come back with a new army.

The marquis and Sir John Hepburn left Neustadt together. Robert Monro and all the other Scottish officers 'most honourable conveyed' their compatriots from the camp for the first mile of the journey in a sentimental farewell, all the more deeply felt for the dangers the men had shared. Sir James Hamilton of Priestfield and Colonel Sir James Ramsay, 'called the Faire Colonell' to distinguish him from Sir James Ramsay 'the Black', also left. The debts incurred by Hamilton on his foray into the war turned out to have been well covered by his lease of the wine customs and, in a show of gratitude for his friend's efforts on his behalf, Charles I allowed the marquis to retain the lease. As for Hepburn, as we shall see, he found another outlet for his proud energy.

The Duke of Weimar led his troops on towards Kitzingen while the rest of the army, under Gustavus Adolphus, moved to Bad Windsheim. Lieutenant-Colonel Ludovick Leslie and his regiment went with Weimar's army, and the rest of the Scots stayed with Gustavus Adolphus. The effects of Monro's wound caught up with him and he lay for days with 'a burning Ague' before he received some treatment and rest in 'Dunkelspill', by which he seems to mean the town of Dinkelsbühl. Here he was left behind when the army hurried on to relieve Rain on the Lech, under siege by the Duke of Bavaria. In a thick mist on the morning of 10 October the Swedish forces opened fire on the town and, after two hours, regained control of it. After allowing the Bavarians to march away without arms or horses, Gustavus Adolphus showed his ruthless side by court-martialling and beheading the colonel who had allowed Rain to fall into enemy hands. Some troops, including the Green Brigade under Ruthven, now remained at Rain for a much needed period of recuperation and to keep an eye on Bavaria, while Gustavus Adolphus marched away again to the north, eventually to link up with Weimar's forces and carry on at a hard pace back through the Thuringer Wald to Arnstadt. Leaving his queen in relative safety and comfort at Erfurt, he carried on and almost fell on to the rear of Pappenheim's army on its way back to Leipzig from campaigning in the north-west. Gustavus Adolphus finally established a base at Naumberg on 8–10 November. Pappenheim and Wallenstein had met the day before on the flat country near Leipzig, and they had then moved their headquarters to Weissenfels. The two armies were now only a few miles apart.

On the 13th, Wallenstein decided to withdraw from Weissenfels and allowed Pappenheim to set off back to the west to counter Protestant successes in the Rhineland area. With winter coming on, and faced with the need to find shelter for his troops, Wallenstein was more intent on subduing Saxony than with facing Gustavus Adolphus in open battle but, despite Wallenstein's precautions, the king learned through his reconnaissance patrols what was happening and knew that this was the moment to attack. In the small hours of the 15th the Swedish army moved forward in battle order to pursue the Imperial forces withdrawing towards Leipzig. A large skirmish with the Imperial Croat rearguard at the crossing of a stream at the village of Rippach delayed the advance and it was not until dusk was falling that the main army straggled into the vicinity of the village of Lützen. When he learned of Gustavus Adolphus's pursuit, Wallenstein concluded that he had no option but to make a stand and, quickly dashing off a written order to Pappenheim to rejoin him at once, directed his own army into battle lines. Robert Monro must have learned of the details of the day later but he notes in his memoir how the capture at the Rippach of a Croat standard displaying fortune and eagle symbols was taken as a good omen. Within sight of the Imperial watch fires, Gustavus Adolphus prepared for an attack before dawn broke. Thick mist put paid to this intention and as the ranks waited for the sun to disperse the gloom the king offered prayers and addressed his troops, warning his Swedes and Finns to fight bravely, lest 'lest your bones shall never come in Sweden againe'.[7]

Much has been written about the great battle at Lützen on 16 November 1632 and here there is space only to give a summary of the action.[8] Most of the Scots who were present in the cosmopolitan

Protestant army were in Lieutenant-Colonel Ludovick Leslie's regiment in the front rank of the Duke of Weimar's formations on the left
flank. Leslie's men were in the Duke's Green Brigade, not to be
confused with the Swedish brigade of the same name mentioned
before. Ludovick was one of the Leslies of Lindores and it was
perhaps his father's association with James Spens in the disastrous
business venture in Lewis that led to the son's later enlistment as a
soldier through Spens. He had fought in Danish service and, like so
many of his compatriots, had switched to Swedish colours in 1628,
seeing action in the Prussian and German campaigns and reaching his
present rank. Not far from him in the battle lines that morning was
another Scot, Colonel John Henderson, commanding 180 musketeers
as a reserve behind the front line. This man's origins remain a mystery:
he may have served in the ranks in Danish and then Swedish service
from the mid 1620s or he may have come to the Continent in
Hamilton's army. Early in 1632 he had performed with distinction in
the army of Wilhelm of Saxe-Weimar in Lower Saxony and had been
promoted to colonel of dragoons, before being ordered to bring his
men to Naumberg, and thus found himself at Lützen, for lack of
horses leading his dragoons as a contingent of musketeers on foot.[9]

The mist drifted up from the flat boggy fields around Lützen to
reveal the two armies settling into battle array. Wallenstein stationed
musketeers behind the mud wall surrounding the village and in the
ditch running alongside the road that ran between the two armies. He
also had a strong fire position around windmills on a slight eminence
beside the road and just east of the village. Drainage channels running
through the open land delayed Gustavus Adolphus's men moving into
their final places and the artillery duel began before they were all in
position. In the last hour of the forenoon Gustavus Adolphus
launched his cavalry against the Imperial left wing with some success.
On the Imperial right Duke Bernhard's cavalry pushed between the
village, now deliberately set on fire by the defenders to deny it to the
enemy, and the windmills. The infantry had a harder struggle, failing
to dislodge the Imperial musketeers in the centre or from the village.
At around noon, having ridden for several hours after receiving
Wallenstein's summons, Pappenheim arrived with his cavalry and at
once engaged the Swedish cavalry, under Colonel Torsten Stålhandske,

which had swept around the Imperial left wing and was threatening to turn the flank. Very soon during his attack, Pappenheim was struck by a bullet and mortally wounded. Perhaps not more than half an hour later, Gustavus Adolphus himself, riding with the Småland cavalry, was wounded in the left arm. As he was being led to the rear by a few companions, a troop of Imperial cuirassiers emerged from the mist, recognised who was before them and killed the king before he could be rescued.

Early in the afternoon Wallenstein's regiments began to rally and beat back the assault in the centre, and the attack by Duke Bernhard's cavalry on the Imperial right was breaking down. Some Swedish troops, probably including Henderson's musketeers, captured artillery on the left of the Imperial line, unspiked the cannon and turned them with devastating effect on their former owners. Overall, however, the Swedish army was on the verge of defeat until Major-General Knyphausen pulled back and rallied the broken formations in the centre, during which a strange lull fell over the battlefield for some thirty minutes. The renewed assault captured at last the windmill position and the gardens around the village. By the time darkness dropped over the field and the fighting between the exhausted troops died away, the battle was still undecided but Wallenstein over-rode the angry protests of his senior officers to order a general withdrawal to Leipzig.

The struggle around the village had taken the lives of some 2,500 men, mostly on the Swedish side. Henderson lost 230 out of his initial complement of 600, and a similar proportion of Duke Bernhard's Green Brigade was killed. Some accounts of the battle give greatly exaggerated casualty lists, including Monro's, which states that 9,000 fell. We can, however, believe him when he says: 'of our Nation was hurt with the Cannon and musket twice Captain Henry Lindesey brother to Bainshow who for a time did lie almost dead in the field, divers Officers of Colonell Lodowicke Leslie his Regiment were also hurt, having behaved themselves well, being, for the most part, old expert Officers and old beaten blades of Souldiers.' Lützen would come to be remembered, however, not for the deaths of these men but for that of their leader. Gustavus Adolphus, the Lion of the North, was no more.

'that bloodie monster of warre'

Bavaria, Bohemia, northern Germany, 1633–1640

*T*HE BODY OF Gustavus Adolphus was removed from the battlefield to the church at Meuchen, but any admission of the king's death was at first kept from his army by his senior officers. The soldiers, who spent the night after the battle in their positions in the field and rose to find the enemy gone from the vicinity, speculated among themselves as to what truth there might be to the rumours of the king's fall as they assembled and withdrew to Weissenfels and Naumberg. Here, at last, the worst was confirmed. Across Europe, and even in the Habsburg camp, the news evoked expressions of profound grief. Alexander Leslie, who had not been at the battle and had last seen Gustavus Adolphus at Mainz earlier in the year, wrote to the Marquis of Hamilton to express his own reaction, in which he no doubt spoke for many: 'so ar we to our wnspeakable greife deprived of the best and most valorouse commander that evir any souldiours hade'.[1] Robert Monro recorded his tribute to the king in a long adulatory passage in his memoirs. In the manner of the times, both he and Leslie attributed the king's death to divine punishment for the sins of the army and the Protestant faithful. The man whose struggle to retain his throne in Prague had brought about the war in the first place survived his royal champion by only a few days. Frederick, the exiled king of Bohemia and erstwhile elector of the Palatinate, son-in-law to the late James VI, caught a fever, sank into a depression on hearing the terrible news from Lützen and died at Bacharach on the Rhine before the month of November had passed.

From the field at Lützen, Wallenstein withdrew to Bohemia, while the Swedish chancellor, Axel Oxenstierna, took over the helm of state and command of the main Swedish army devolved upon Duke Bernhard of Saxe-Weimar. In the autumn of 1632 in Alsace, the Swedish forces under the command of Gustav Horn had been enjoying success; by November they captured such key centres on the west bank of the Rhine as Selestat, Colmar, Haguenau and Molsheim. In Bavaria, Robert Monro joined Christian of Anhalt, commander of the Swedish forces in that province. They gained the town of Eichstätte and marched on to attack Landsberg on the Lech River. Crouching in their entrenchments, the Scottish officers devised a contest to see whose regiment should reach the walls first. The combined forces of Monro's and Spens's regiments won out over the neighbouring brigade of Patrick Ruthven. Cannon were manhandled into position to breach the wall twice before the defenders drummed a signal that they wished to negotiate, after which they agreed to surrender and march out. Ruthven's men occupied the town to seize all the supplies they could lay their hands on. The garrison was reinforced with four companies of Colonel Hugh Hamilton's regiment of new levies from Switzerland under the command of an Irish major, whom Monro does not name.

When Imperial forces attacked Rain, Christian responded by sending 200 musketeers under Captain James Lyell to take over the skonce there and defend the bridge over the Lech. Lyell arrived to find Swedish forces holding on in the face of the Imperial assault, and they retained possession until the rest of Christian's army could join them and launch an attack to drive out the enemy. News of Gustavus Adolphus's death reached the Imperial forces at this time, prompting them to fire salvoes in rejoicing, gunfire that puzzled the attackers, before they withdrew under cover of darkness, leaving the town to Christian. Patrick Ruthven wanted to chase the Imperialists but Christian restrained him, missing a great opportunity to inflict some serious harm on the enemy, in Monro's opinion. During the recapture of Rain, Monro had stayed in Webling attending to administrative matters, but he had to move north to Augsburg when an Imperial thrust regained Landsberg, an action in which Colonel Hugh Hamilton was taken prisoner.

Winter now set in. Monro and his colleagues lay in camp in

extremely cold weather for the next two months. During this period
Monro's horse fell on him and injured his leg so that for six weeks he
could ride but not walk far. Baner, still suffering from a wound he had
taken at Nuremberg, moved his army towards Ulm to join with
Gustav Horn's forces, including Sir James Ramsay's regiment, coming
from Alsace. Before they could meet, however, the Imperialists had
thrust further south-west to take Kempten and Memmingen. After
the rendezvous at Ulm, the Swedish forces crossed the Danube to
quarter in the district of Kilchberg, which had been granted to
Ruthven. This was only 6 miles from Memmingen and the Imperialists, and the army continued its advance in very cold weather to a
large village a mile from the enemy. A fire broke out during the
second night on the trail, destroying baggage and some horses but not
guns or ammunition, which Monro and his colleagues managed to
save, and they carried on to Memmingen. The Imperialists had
withdrawn in the hope of luring the foe into the town, in effect a
trap, but a trap the Swedes avoided by stopping outside in battle
formation. On the following day the Swedes came in pursuit of the
Imperialists and drove them all the way back through Kempten to the
far side of the Lech.

Now desperately short of food and forage, the soldiers could find
little to replenish their stocks in a countryside already stripped bare by
the passage of armies. After recuperating at Kaufbeuren for three
days, they moved west, crossing the low flow of the Iller on a bridge
made of planks laid across cannon. The Duke of Bavaria also moved
west, crossing the Iller, passing within a mile of Monro's camp in the
night. A race was now on, to get to the Danube and the bridge at a
place Monro calls Vertenberg. Horn reached the vital point in the nick
of time, learned the Imperialists were crossing a mile downstream and
ordered artillery and foot to hurry on through the night while a party
of dragoons stayed to destroy the bridge. No sooner were the timbers
ablaze, however, than Imperial troops attacked the dragoons and
drove them on. The enemy now fell on three regiments making up the
rear of Horn's column – three cavalry units, one of which was led by
Colonel Robert Monro, the Black Baron of Foulis. The regiments
charged the enemy in turn. During Monro's charge, he was hit by a
musket ball in the right foot. The desperate fight saved most of

Horn's baggage and gave the Swedes time to form a defensive position on a steep hilltop, where the artillery held off the Imperial attack until night gave Horn the chance to pull back and reach Vertenberg.

The Swedish army found good quarters and a breathing space at Donauworth for the next three months. As he jogged on his horse to Heilbron to visit Oxenstierna and obtain a settlement of his regiment's affairs – once again it appears their pay had fallen into arrears – perhaps Monro mulled over the fates of his companions. His elder brother John of Obsdale had been killed at Wetterau on the Rhine on 11 March and was buried at Bacharach; his regiment, reduced to two companies, had been amalgamated with Robert's own. Robert Monro, the Black Baron, had languished with his foot wound at Ulm for six weeks before he had died, most likely from infection; his spurs, standard and armour were hung in the Franciscan church to mark his burial place. Not long after this, in July 1633, Robert himself obtained permission to leave the regiment, handing over command to Lieutenant-Colonel John Sinclair, who before long was killed at Neumarkt in the Upper Palatinate. Monro went home to Britain. In 1634 he recruited more men for European service and in July that year approached the Privy Council in Edinburgh with a letter from the king, 'anent the erecting of ane hospitall for enterteaning of aged and lame souldiours'.[2] Monro's idea was that Scottish officers who had done well for themselves should contribute to easing the plight of their less fortunate comrades. The council granted him his warrant to pursue his plan but nothing came of it. Monro also sought the backing of the council in soliciting pensions from Sweden. Gustavus Adolphus, it seemed, had led recruits to believe that if they were wounded and had to return to civilian life, they would receive a pension and either stay in Sweden or go home to Scotland. The Swedish authorities had neglected to adhere to this pledge. Monro returned to the Continent and was in Hamburg early in November 1635, whence he wrote to Sir Robert Gordon of Gordonstoun about events in Germany, adding: 'My nephewe Mr George [Monro] haid a greatt mynd to have quatt his buick and to have followit warres, bot his friendis being against it, I have sent him to Leidene to pass his course in the lawes.'[3] In Stoltenow in April 1636 Leslie wrote a letter for him to carry back to Scotland, in which the general asked the Marquis of Hamilton to support Monro in his efforts to recruit more men: 'that he may have libertie to levie and bring forth men out of his native cuntrie'.[4]

The great battle at Lützen, with victory not going clearly to either side, could have opened the way to peace in the German lands. The German people wished it so, but among the political figures at work in Europe were influential individuals who wanted the conflict to go on. Axel Oxenstierna, taking over as regent after his king's death, was determined that Sweden fight on, and France, in the person of Cardinal Richelieu, and his opposite number in Spain, the Duke of Olivarez, were locked in a power struggle that neither could concede. Spain still had designs to recover her position in the Low Countries – the Prince of Orange had taken advantage of the European war to advance as far as Maastricht – and wanted the Austrian Habsburgs to stay in the fight. In March 1633 the leaders of the Protestant powers conferred at Heilbron, where the head of the British delegation was Sir Robert Anstruther, and formed a league to continue the war. France and Sweden renewed the anti-Habsburg alliance they had already sealed in the Treaty of Barwalde. Saxony refused to join the Heilbron League and tried to persuade Brandenburg, which still saw itself as the rightful owner of Swedish-occupied territory along the Baltic coast, to take the same course. In the summer of 1633 Wallenstein reached a truce with Saxony, but when this came to an end he advanced quickly into Silesia and forced the surrender of the Swedish forces in Steinau, following this at once with a lightning campaign that forced the Swedish occupation back to the north. The foremost detachments of Wallenstein's cavalry reached Berlin and he began to extend peace feelers to Brandenburg.

By this time, however, the Habsburgs in Vienna were nursing serious doubts about their commander. He had grown too powerful, said his detractors, among whom stood the all-important Archduke Ferdinand, son of the emperor himself, and he could turn his army loose on Bohemia or betray the Empire and desert to the Protestant cause. Duke Bernhard's army captured Regensburg on the Danube in November 1633 but Wallenstein refused to come to its aid, instead withdrawing his reconstituted army into winter quarters in Bohemia.

A man from relatively humble family, Wallenstein had always attracted more suspicion than admiration. His private army had performed sterling service for the Empire but fears that he might have designs on the Imperial crown itself had led to his dismissal in 1630. Only the death of Tilly had led to his recall. Perhaps his treatment by Vienna had left him with a grudge against the Habsburgs – after his career, he could have been excused a cynical view of them – and perhaps he was plotting something at the end of 1633. By then he had aged and turned sickly, suffering from gout. He had alienated much of the Imperial army through his public execution of some men for cowardice and treachery after Lützen, and he had grown irritable and cranky, demanding that no loud noises disturb him and closeting himself to study astrology – his chief astrologer was Kepler, more celebrated now for his astronomical discoveries. At the beginning of 1634 Wallenstein was in Pilsen with his soldiers around him. The emperor asked him to move his army to Bavaria. He refused and demanded that his officers swear an oath of loyalty to him, an order that suggests strongly he suspected his star might be in the descendant and was taking measures to defend himself. The Imperial decree of dismissal was signed on 24 January but the problem of how to neutralise the wily commander remained. At last, with desertions spreading among his men, Wallenstein sensed he was losing the initiative and, with a few loyal followers, quit Pilsen for the fortress of Eger on the Bohemian border, reaching its gates on the evening of 24 February.

The commander of the Eger garrison was Colonel John Gordon. From Milton of Noth near Rhynie, Gordon was a Protestant in Habsburg service. With his colleague Walter Leslie, one of the Leslies of Balquhain, he had been the man who at Freistadt near Nuremberg in August 1632 had been taken prisoner by the Swedes and then entertained by their compatriots in the enemy army, including Robert Monro. Major Walter Leslie was also at Eger, as Gordon's second-in-command, when Wallenstein arrived. On the way to Eger, the Imperial commander's party had been intercepted by a troop of dragoons led by an Irish officer, Walter Butler. Butler had been the military governor of Wallenstein's duchy of Sagan, where he had married a local countess, but in December 1633, probably already aware of the forces marshalling against his former commander, he had confirmed his loyalty to the emperor. The present encounter with Wallenstein was probably an accident – Butler was en route to Prague – but the Irishman, unable openly to disobey his former general, had fallen in with the fugitives. He managed to send away a message to the Imperial general, Ottavio Piccolomini, as to what had happened, and meanwhile bided his time by riding for some of the way with Wallenstein in his carriage and listening to the aged general expatiate on his misfortunes. At Eger Butler's troops camped outside the walls while he himself was assigned quarters inside the fortress along with Wallenstein's party.

There is some disagreement among historians over what exactly took place thereafter but the consensus seems to be that John Gordon recognised he had a duty as a loyal Imperial officer to take action to detain Wallenstein. Walter Leslie was firm in his support and Butler readily joined the conspiracy. The three probably worked out their plan of action while Wallenstein retired to his bed in the burgermeister's house beside the market square, his usual accommodation in Eger. Late that night a messenger arrived from Pilsen, bearing to Wallenstein the news that he was the subject of an imperial indictment. The general told Leslie that he planned to contact the duke of Weimar and the Elector of Saxony. The conspirators now knew that they did not have much time in which to act.

On the following day some of Butler's men were allowed into the town. Ilow, one of Wallenstein's loyal officers, appealed to Butler, Leslie and Gordon to take an oath of loyalty. In the evening, Gordon invited Ilow and three other senior officers from among Wallenstein's companions to a banquet in his quarters in the castle. As the diners neared the end of the meal, Leslie gave the signal for waiting Irish dragoons to burst in to overcome the guests. In the melee, Ilow gave a good account of himself, wounding Leslie before he fell dead along with his colleagues. Another Irishman, called Devereux, was sent with a party to deal with Wallenstein; finding him in his bedroom in his night clothes, the intruders stabbed him to death, and wrapped his corpse in his scarlet bed-hangings.

The three mercenaries were well rewarded for their unusual service to the Empire. Leslie received the sum of 120,000 florins to help him buy an estate at Neustadt (now Nové Mesto-nad-Metuji, near the town of Nachod, close to the Polish border) and was appointed an imperial chamberlain, the commander of two regiments and a count of the Holy Roman Empire in 1637. He later did some diplomatic work to further relations between the Stuarts and the Habsburgs, and he died in Vienna in 1667. Gordon received two awards of 120,000 florins, one of which he used to buy two estates at Smidar and Skrivany, and a golden chain. He died in 1648 in Danzig and was buried in the Nieuwe Kerk in Delft.[5] Butler had to pursue his reward with greater vigour than his fellow assassins but he too became a count of the Holy Roman Empire, as well as the owner of an estate at Hirschberg in north-west Bohemia, once Wallenstein's own property, although he did not enjoy these prizes for long as it seems he died of plague at the end of the year.[6]

In April 1632 the Privy Council issued a warrant to Colonel Sir James Lumsden, later of Innergellie, to raise 1,200 men.[7] One of those who joined the Lumsden contingent was an eighteen-year-old student from Dalkeith, James Turner. At the time, he was staying with his father and studying literature, history and religious philosophy but, he says in his memoirs, 'a restless desire enterd my mind, to be, if not an actor, at least a spectator of these warrs which at that time made so much noyse'. Turner signed up as an ensign under Captain Robert Lumsden, the colonel's younger brother, and a few months later found himself in a ship off Elsinore.[8] Another three days brought the Scots to Rostock, where they landed to march to Bremen. Turner promptly fell 'grievouslie sicke', a condition that in his view arose either from the change of air or diet, 'or by eating too much fruit whereof I saw that countrey abound more than my oune'. It took him six weeks to recover and join troops enforcing Swedish rule over northern Germany. He may have had regrets during the succeeding winter, when he had to endure the experience of the common soldier of hunger and constant shifting, but he stuck to his duty, noting the news that Gustavus Adolphus had met his death at Lützen.

Early in 1633 Lumsden's regiment and a regiment of English soldiers under Colonel Sir Arthur Aston were assigned to the Swedish army commanded by the Duke of Brunswick and Field Marshal

Knyphausen, which, after 'a lamentable cold, wet and rainie march', laid
siege to Hameln. The town later famous as the setting for the tale of
the Pied Piper resisted its attackers vigorously. On 28 June an Imperial
army advanced to its relief and a battle ensued. 'So much blood was
shed', recalled Turner, 'as was enough to flesh such novices as I was.
We gaind the victorie, which was a great one to be gaind with so little
losse on our side. Neere nine thousand of the Imperialists were killd
in the place, three thousand taken, with eighteene canon, and above
eightie standards and collors. The toune yeelded therafter on articles.'

The campaigning during the rest of the year inured Turner to this new
life: 'thogh at first I longd to be backe in Scotland . . . I fully resolved to
goe on'. The future grew considerably brighter for him in the spring of
1634 while his regiment was quartered near Oldendorf. He found
lodging with a widow who had a daughter, also widowed, and, although
the young woman's late husband had been an officer in the Imperial
army, this did not inhibit her relationship with the young Scot. 'She was
very handsome, wittie and discreet . . . thogh my former toyle might
have banished all love thoughts out of my mind, I became perfitlie
enamourd . . . she taught me the Hie Dutch, to reade and write it . . . I
learnd also the fashions and customes of the Germane officers.'

The two regiments were reduced to two companies, with Turner
surviving the re-organisation as an ensign; 'all the rest casheerd, and in
great necessitie and povertie'. Turner complained that the companies
were now ill used and badly paid, although by now he had grown
cunning and was able to find all he needed. At this point in his
memoir, he notes the news of the assassination of Wallenstein and
how the conspirators, especially Leslie, were well rewarded, information he must have learned later. After the assassination of Wallenstein
command of the Imperial forces fell to Ottavio Piccolomini and
Count Matthias Gallas, with the Habsburg Archduke Ferdinand, who
was also king of Hungary, in overall command. Uniting his army with
that led by his cousin, also called Ferdinand, the Cardinal Infante and
brother of the King of Spain, Archduke Ferdinand thrust west along
the Danube to regain the lands along the 'Spanish Road', the route
between northern Italy and the Low Countries. Regensburg fell to
them on 22 July 1634, Donauworth shortly afterwards, and the town
of Nördlingen came under siege on 19 August.

The Protestant forces mounted a campaign to save Nördlingen before the hard-pressed garrison was forced into surrender. Under the joint command of Gustav Horn and Duke Bernhard of Saxe-Weimar, the relieving army managed to seize possession on the night of 5 September of the hill of Hasselberg to the south-west of the city. With over 16,000 foot and 9,000 horse, Horn and Bernhard decided not to wait for a 6,000-strong force led by the Rhinegrave to join them and, next morning, launched an attack to capture the adjacent hill, called the Albuch. Horn's corps, in the front line of which was a Scots infantry brigade, had the right wing of the assault, directly facing the ranks of Imperial troops on the hilltop. The Swedish cavalry on the right were checked by the tercios but the foot soldiers in the centre, including Scots, made headway and drove the Imperial infantry from their positions before they were stopped by cavalry and pushed back.

The Scots units in Horn's army were under the command of Colonel William Gunn and Colonel Arvid 'Finn' Forbes. The latter was a Swede of Scots descent who had been born in Finland in 1598, where his father was a customs officer. Gunn, who had been born in West Garty near Helmsdale, was a Catholic but had been one of the earlier recruits to Lord Reay's regiment for Danish service and had since risen in rank in the army of Gustavus Adolphus. As a second son from hard-scrabble country on the Caithness-Sutherland border, military service was his way to success and he was good at it, gaining a reputation for able command in action and for having an unpleasant ruthless streak. After defeating an Imperialist force at Reutte on the Lech early in 1634, he had had all the captured horsemen put to the sword, and when he had commanded a garrison at Bugghorn on the Bodensee he had organised a fleet of boats to patrol the shores. His enterprise impressed his superiors and shortly before Nördlingen he had been placed in overall command of the musketeers in Baner's and Horn's armies. Gunn had led the attack to occupy the Hasselberg, a night assault that took seven hours to accomplish. Now he was instructed by Horn to repeat this success on Albuch, in daylight against strong defences. The infantry, with Gunn in the van, gained the summit of the Albuch, only to be once more beaten back by a counterattack. For some six hours the Swedish infantry threw themselves into the attempted capture of the high ground, but the repeated assaults were to no avail. Finally Horn had to order his remaining troops to retire to the river a quarter of a mile behind them. Now the full force of the Imperial cavalry was thrown against the Protestant positions. Duke Bernhard's troops on the left wing broke first, their flight inducing on the right among Horn's men a similar struggle to escape slaughter. Gunn added lustre to his reputation at this juncture in the conflict, leading his men away in good order in a fighting retreat.

Walter Leslie was present at the battle, occupying a mill on a stream near the town, and was almost killed when a cannon shot that took the life of one of his court officials struck close to him.[9] Sydnam Poyntz was also there and noted: 'wee tooke Prisoners Coronell Hew a Scottish man, Capn Christen and Capn Fiscots and Capn Ramsey a Scot, and many a brave sparke more'.[10] To interpret Poyntz's eccentric spelling, Hew was probably Lieutenant-Colonel Thomas Hume of Carrolside, serving in the Rhinegrave's horse, and Fiscots may have been Lindsay of Pitscottie. At the end of the day, the losses on the Protestant side amounted to around 8,000 men dead and another 4,000 taken prisoner, while all the artillery and 300 standards had been captured. Among the Scots who fell were a number of officers, including Captain Adam Gordon, a son of the Earl of Sutherland. The Imperialist side escaped with lower casualty figures: 1,500 dead and 2,000 wounded. The prisoners included Gustav Horn himself, but Duke Bernhard escaped from the field and began to rally his remaining troops.

James Turner was among the units hurrying to join Horn and Bernhard in the days before the battle. 'Sixe thousand or therby, whereof our two companies made up some part, were on our march to Nordling . . . and were within a few leagues of Frankford du Main when we heard of the rout, and so were countermanded to Westphalia. By this one blow the Sueds loosd more ground than they had gaind in a year before; and nixt yeare most of the Dutch [German] princes made their peace with the Emperor.' Just so – after the crushing victory at Nördlingen, and the capture of the town on the following day, the Imperial advance continued with little resistance The fortress of Philippsburg, to the south of Heidelberg, fell on 24 January 1635 and, by the end of February, the Imperialists occupied the whole east bank of the Rhine. At the same time, John George, the

Elector of Saxony, reached agreement with the Empire in the Peace of Prague, the culmination of some months of negotiation in which the elector had gone against the wishes of his wife and his leading commander in pursuing an escape from war for his benighted lands. To the cries of traitor from the Swedish camp, John George took his patrimony and his army out of the Protestant alliance and hitched it to the fate of the Habsburgs.

In the small town of Egeln, twenty kilometres south of Magdeburg, the commander of the garrison, Colonel Robert Douglas, decided that he could not go along with this reversal of fortune. Born a laird's son near Haddington in 1611, Douglas and his two brothers had joined Colonel James Ramsay's regiment in 1628. He served as a page to Gustavus Adolphus's brother-in-law and as an ensign at Stralsund, before joining the Green Regiment in 1631. After a spell recruiting for the Marquis of Hamilton in England, he had been promoted to a major of dragoons in 1632 and had become a colonel in 1633, still aged only twenty-four. Douglas was strongly loyal to the Protestant cause and was keenly aware that Egeln had been awarded to General Baner by the late king, two factors that would have made a surrender dishonourable in his eyes. Douglas decided the only thing he could do was to stay loyal to Sweden, and if necessary fight with all the men who wished to follow him. When he was obliged to hand over Egeln to Saxon control, Douglas and his men were allowed to march out without surrendering their colours or weapons, honour intact.

Shortly after the defeat at Nördlingen, Patrick Ruthven was appointed to the rank of lieutenant-general, second in command in Johan Baner's army, now the only Swedish force of significance remaining in Germany and now facing hostile Saxon and Brandenburg armies after the Peace of Prague. In October, Ruthven defeated Saxons at Dömitz and Lützen, and he fought in three more battles over the next few weeks as the Swedish forces were forced northward. Their fortunes were now at a low ebb and a serious mutiny broke out among Baner's forces, a rebellion it took the gruff field marshal most of the year to quell before he could consider field operations to compensate for the desertion of the Saxons. A truce between Sweden and Poland in September 1635 allowed the transfer of reliable Swedish troops from the east to stiffen Baner's army, and the mutiny subsided.

On 16 October Saxony declared war on Sweden but in a battle soon afterwards Baner and Ruthven defeated the Saxon cavalry under Wulff von Baudissin.

Sir Alexander Leslie remained in northern Germany during these years. He was at the recapture of Magdeburg in January 1632 and, a month later, he was wounded in the foot while commanding at the siege of Buxtehude, south of Hamburg, an injury that left him with a limp for the rest of his life. He continued to serve Sweden as the governor of several towns in the Baltic region. A brush near Stade with Pappenheim's forces, before the latter headed off to his fate at Lützen, resulted in Leslie's regiment coming off the worse, and the Scot suffered the indiginity of losing his own colours. He was in Stade at the end of November when he wrote to the Marquis of Hamilton with the news of Gustavus Adolphus's death. Axel Oxenstierna had resolved to strengthen the Swedish hold on the Baltic coast, with new armies on the Weser and Oder and in support of Baner. Alexander Leslie played a key role in this strategy, commanding forces in the north and, in April 1635, capturing Frankfurt on the Oder. After the death of Field Marshal Knyphausen, Leslie was promoted to that rank and given command of the army on the Weser, an area that included Westphalia. The other candidates whom Oxenstierna considered for the post were Patrick Ruthven, James King and Lennart Torstensson, a noteworthy shortlist in which three of the four names are Scots. James King was an Orcadian by birth and a descendant of James V through an illegitimate link on the maternal side. With his two brothers and a cousin, he had joined Swedish service in around 1609 and by 1619 was serving in the Småland regiment under Leslie. A steady rise in rank had ensued and he had been appointed governor of the town of Vlotho on the Weser at the end of 1632, an experience of the Westphalian area that no doubt was in Oxenstierna's mind when he appointed King lieutenant-general under Leslie in 1636. The chancellor wished Ruthven to stay with Baner, who was considered to be jealous of Leslie. Oxenstierna made further use of his Scots by placing Colonel David Drummond as major-general of the infantry in the army of the Oder under the command of Field Marshal Herman Wrangel. Born in 1593, Drummond had been in Swedish service since 1617 and was married to a daughter of Sir James Spens.

James Grant of Freuchie, at the age of nineteen in 1635, spent some time in Leslie's camp and described his experience in a letter to his father: 'The Failt Marciall Lesly hes entertained me werie kyndly, and hes promised to be my good friend. Sir, we have good days heir, and as for my self I can maik a fiftie dolours a mounth to bey boowts and shoun withall. But I feare our quarters shall be short heir, the enimie is couming doon heir werie strong one ws . . . As for your worship's cosing Colonel Ruthven I have resaved many words boot feu curtesies.' Clearly Grant found that his heart did not lie in soldiering, as he went back to Strathspey before long to become the seventh laird of Freuchie.[11]

Grant does not mention the location of the camp where he wrote his letter and neither does he provide a date but it may have been in May. On the nineteenth of that month, the field marshal was encamped at Herford, south-west of Minden, and wrote to the Marquis of Hamilton in England with news of the war.[12] Baner 'doeth carrie himself bravelie' said Leslie, describing how the Swede had retired from Magdeburg to Tangermund before an advancing Imperial force, adding: 'Felt Marschall Wrangle who commandit in Prussia is to have the leading of the army ordanit for Silesia; he is at this present in Hinder Pomer. As concerning this armie in Westphalia', he went on, '. . . our beginings, praisit be God, hes beine successful. The first rancounter we had with our enemie wes at a castle upon the Weser called Petershagen, whiche I unpatronized, and took of prisoners one Baroun Kotler, a colonel, with the compleit officiars of a regiment, and 185 souldiours.' A few days later Leslie won a field engagement and then relieved the siege of Osnabrück and installed a garrison in Minden. As a field marshal he had to bear in mind political as well as military matters and he reminded Hamilton that the Westphalia campaign would be the best way to recover the Palatinate, still an item on Charles I's foreign policy agenda.

James Turner had returned to Scotland towards the end of 1634, when his father had died, but by the summer of 1635 he was back in Bremen. He fell in with some officers who had hatched a harebrained scheme to go to Persia in a search for 'more gold than the philosophers stone can afford the alchymists'. And, as if that did not promise riches enough, they hoped to open up a trade route for silk;

in return the officers were to train Persian forces to match the Turks. The scheme never got beyond the dreaming stage and Turner went off to Osnabrück, where the governor was Sir James Lumsden, and arrived in time to be caught in the town when it was placed under siege by the Marquis of Grana and to be present at its relief by Leslie's forces.

Leslie joined forces with the Landgrave of Hesse to continue his campaign in the north-west. His immediate intention was to relieve the siege of a town where another Scot was governor. In May 1635 France had declared war on Spain, but in Germany the Imperial wave of success had continued. Augsburg had surrendered to Imperial forces after a long siege in which the citizens and the garrison had endured the horrors of privation, and instances of cannibalism had been recorded. Spanish troops had seized towns in the Rhineland, including Heidelberg, and in November Matthias Gallas had led his army into Lorraine. In one town – Hanau, near Frankfurt – the garrison had held out under the command of Sir James Ramsay.

Since his bad arm wound at the storming of the Marienberg fortress in Würzburg, Ramsay had been out of the main action, and four days after the defeat at Nördlingen the Duke of Weimar had appointed him as governor of Hanau, on the Main a few miles upstream from Frankfurt. Ramsay arrived in the town at the beginning of October 1634 with a German regiment, a company of Scots and two companies of Hessian cavalry, and they began at once to build up the defences and lay in stores of food. His expectation of an attack was soon realised but he fought back, leading out sallies to disrupt the enemy and capture more supplies. All the while he maintained a strict discipline. One commander, whom he judged to have offered poor resistance to the Imperialists, was court-martialled, found guilty of neglect of duty and shot in Hanau market place.[13] Imperial forces in greater strength appeared in September 1635 and threw a ring of entrenchments around the town. Despite the sickness that now afflicted the inhabitants, whose numbers had been swollen by refugees from the surrounding country, Ramsay earned the burgers' respect for his courage and his impartial fairness. It was a reputation widespread through Protestant Germany, for the citizens of Nuremberg had asked in vain for him to be made their governor in 1634.

Sydnam Poyntz includes in his own colourful memoir a tribute to Ramsay: 'old Coronell Ramsey a Scotch man having gotten notice of the Duke of Hessens coming to succour hym and at hand . . . sallyed out of the Towne, beat the Imperialists out of their Trenches . . . killed & drowned in the River of Mume [Main] as good as fower thjousand and levelled all their workes.'[14] The siege of Hanau dragged on for nine months until, in June 1636, Sir Alexander Leslie appeared with a Swedish-Hessian army to relieve the weary defenders. Ramsay remained as governor and repelled more assaults until Count Philipp Moritz, the lord of the town who had earlier fled, made his peace with the Habsburgs in November 1637 and returned to reclaim what was his. Negotiations failed to overcome the mistrust between the parties and to persuade Ramsay to give up Hanau, a place for which he had clearly developed great fondness. Rumours were put about that he was planning to sell the town to the French, perhaps a ploy to undermine his local following. In February 1638 Count Moritz sent in some troops. These occupied the old town under cover of darkness and then moved to corner Ramsay in his residence, *der Weisse Löwe*, the White Lion, where in the struggle he was wounded in the hip. Once this had healed enough to permit travel he was brought to the castle of Dillenburg as a prisoner. At first he was given comfortable quarters and treated with respect: he ate his meals with the owner, Count Ludwig Heinrich, and was allowed considerable freedom to go for rides and attend church. Unfortunately, the relationship soured and tighter confinement resulted. Ramsay finally fell sick and died in his prison in April 1639.

While Leslie was campaigning in Westphalia, Baner and Ruthven were marking time in Mecklenburg, in Leslie's words, 'stryving to wearie the Saxone by marching to and fro in a waist land where ther is nather intertainment for men nor hors, and thairefter he will tak his best advantage of them.'[15] With an army numbering barely 15,000 men, Baner was not strongly placed to meet in open battle the Saxons and their Imperial allies advancing down the Elbe, but after Leslie joined him in September he renewed the offensive. Only one third of the army was Swedish, with the balance being made up of Germans, Scots and English. John George of Saxony led his forces to intercept them and for over a week the opposing armies manoeuvred around each other in the rolling wooded landscape. At last, on 4 October, Baner's troops caught up with the enemy about 2 miles to the south of the small town of Wittstock, finding them waiting for battle on a range of sandy hills called the Scharfenberg. John George expected the Swedes to attack from woods to the south and laid down his artillery and threw up his ramparts accordingly. Commanding six companies of Imperial dragoons was Colonel Walter Leslie.

Baner had Lennart Torstennson in command of his right wing, with Alexander Leslie in the centre and Colonel James King on the left. Colonel John Nairn from Mukkersy had command of a cavalry troop in the right wing, among the units Baner sent into action first. Leslie then led his foot into attack. The focused fall on their left wing and flank rather than their centre took the Imperialists by surprise and they scrambled to carry out a hasty redeployment to meet the threat, largely abandoning the prepared defensive works. John George's numerically superior forces held off the Swedish attack, however, and looked about to repulse Baner's assault when James King and the cavalry, which had meantime skirted the field to the west, fell on the extreme right flank of the Imperialists. Taken completely unawares, the Imperial-Saxon army fell back. Leslie's troops, which had been taking heavy losses, now rallied. Although it was not yet apparent, the tide had turned before darkness put an end to the fighting for the day. The opposing armies camped for the night within sight of each other's cooking fires but the chilly dawn revealed to the Swedes that John George had ordered a total withdrawal, leaving all cannon behind. In the struggle, Walter Leslie's dragoons had taken heavy losses, with only some two hundred surviving. The way was now open for another Swedish advance into central Germany. Baner laid siege to Leipzig but failed to capture it and in January 1637 had to fall back to Torgau, the army ravaged by famine and disease, before continuing the withdrawal to Pomerania.

In 1637 James Turner served with Lieutenant General James King, recently promoted, in Hesse in an effort to drive out Imperial forces, 'who were makeing havocke of all among his [the Landgrave's] poore subjects'. The 'havocke' included the burning of 'three faire tounes . . . before our eyes', an Imperial campaign to persuade the Landgrave of Hesse to accept the Peace of Prague. 'A mournfull sight it was, to see the whole people folow us, and climbe the tuo hie rockes which flanked us', wrote Turner about the civilian refugees from these atrocities. 'Old and young left their houses, by the losse of them and their goods to save their lives. Aged men and women, many above fourscore, most lame or blind, supported by their sonnes, daughters and grandchildren, who themselves carried their little ones on their backes, was a ruthfull object of pitie to any tender hearted Christian and did show us with what dreadfull countenance that bloodie monster of warre can appear in the world.'

Alexander Leslie wrote to the Marquis of Hamilton again in September 1637, after he had returned to Stockholm to discuss affairs with Oxenstierna: 'I thought it my duetie to let your lordship know in brief the state of affaires in our armies and how matters are past since our retrait from Torgow: from whence wee being come to Pomerland [Pomerania], the ennemie did follow us and did lodge himself at Tangermund, Neustat and Sweth [Schwedt on the Oder].' Baner had to reinforce Field Marshal Wrangel at Anklam to repel several Imperial assaults but the outlook for Swedish forces, pushed back to the Baltic coast, was grim. Hope lay with Duke Bernhard campaigning in the Rhineland: if he could draw away the enemy, Leslie saw a chance to fight them 'as wee haue done heretofore'. When Leslie returned to Pomerania a few days after his letter was written he found that Baner had broken out and was advancing towards Bohemia.

Leslie was now beginning to feel his age. Nearing his sixtieth birthday, he could look back on some thirty years' service in Sweden's cause, and no doubt he was also beginning to yearn for his native braes. In 1635 he had returned to Scotland to tend to some land transactions and to receive the freedom of the burgh of Culross. He now asked to be released from Swedish service, citing ill health, and on 14 August 1638 Queen Kristina gave him leave to depart, awarding him an annual pension of 1,200 riksdaler. The news coming over the North Sea in the late 1630s told of a growing dispute between monarch and Church back home, and this too would have encouraged Leslie to look homeward. In October he took ship for Scotland, not to end his career but to begin a new chapter in it.

Baner ordered James King to combine his Westphalian troops with

forces under the command of Charles Lewis, the Elector of the
Palatinate and heir to Frederick, and his brother Rupert, but this
combined army suffered a defeat at Lemgo near Minden in October
1638. Rupert's dash and inexperience led to his capture by the enemy.
Although only the section of the army under King's command
escaped in an orderly manner from the conflict, Baner felt that
mistakes made by the Scot had contributed to this reverse and
quarrelled with him. This, and a sense that he could expect no futher
advancement in Swedish service, convinced King that it was time to
go. He told the Swedes that he did not wish to stay without Alexander
Leslie and he was granted permission to depart, with a pension for his
twenty-six years under the Swedish flag. Patrick Ruthven also felt the
tug of his native hearth and in June 1637 Queen Kristina sent him on
his way with a letter of commendation to King Charles. For him, as
for all the Scottish officers, there was plainly work to be done now at
home.

FOURTEEN

‘*vertews and valorous atchievements abrod*’

France, Germany, 1633–1648

S IR JOHN HEPBURN rode away from the camp of Gustavus Adolphus near Nuremberg in July 1632 to return to Britain. In London he was knighted by Charles I, although he had already been awarded this honour by the Swedish king, and gave information about events in Germany to the editor of the newsletter devoted to the wars, *The Swedish Intelligencer*.[1] He also seems to have paid a short visit to Athelstaneford and to have recruited more men for the Swedish service before offering himself to the French government and, on 26 January 1633, receiving a commission as colonel of a regiment. For some time Cardinal Richelieu, chief minister in the government of Louis XIII and the architect of Bourbon foreign policy, had been keeping a careful eye on the Habsburgs. Sooner rather than later, war between them seemed inevitable, now that Gustavus Adolphus was dead and the power of Sweden to keep the Empire in check was fading. Veterans such as Hepburn were therefore a welcome addition to the French army, and he was rapidly promoted to maréchal-de-camp, making him second-in-command to a lieutenant-general and charging him with organising the proper maintenance of camp and quartering, as well as commanding the left wing in action.

There were, of course, already several of his fellow countrymen in the French forces. The king’s Scots bodyguard, the Garde Ecossais, still flourished. The Duke of Lennox and his nephew George Gordon, the Marquis of Huntly, were appointed captain and lieute-nant respectively in this corps in February 1624 by the French ambassador to Britain, but when Lennox died suddenly two days later the marquis successfully applied for promotion to his place. In France he was called the Marquis de Gourdon. Andrew, the seventh Lord Gray, became lieutenant, in time turning out to be the last native-born Scot to hold this post. Gordon held his first muster at Leith in July 1625 before travelling to France. The short spell of hostilities in 1627 between France and Britain, the most significant event of which was the siege of La Rochelle, where Huguenots had found refuge,[2] interrupted the life of the corps but in 1629 it was re-organised. Gordon was summoned by the French king in 1632 and travelled across the Channel with his company. 'He listis a number of brave gentilmen to serve in the said gard weill armit and weil horsit . . . He had also with him his eldest sone Lord George and his second sone, James, Lord of Aboyne. He made ane brave muster in presens of the King of France, quhairat the King wes weill pleisit and receavit the Lord Gordon, his barnes and soldiouris gratiouslie', noted John Spalding.[3] In the early 1630s, James Campbell, a younger son of the seventh Earl of Argyll, also had command of a regiment of foot in France.

Cardinal Richelieu liked Hepburn and he, with his fondness for bright armour, probably enjoyed the showy manners of the French, a welcome contrast to the dour Lutherans of Sweden. It was common for officers to wear armour decorated with gold and silver, and to allow their hair to curl down over lace collars and gilded shoulders; the dandified appearance did not prevent them from fighting as well as the next man. After an audience with Louis XIII at Chantilly, Hepburn sailed back to Scotland in March 1633 to raise 2,000 men. In April he was granted a warrant by the Privy Council to raise 1,200 for a standing regiment in France.[4] By August he was back at Boulogne with 1,000 men of good quality, which was possibly some compensation for the shortfall in numbers, among them a pikeman called John Middleton who would later rise to prominence in his native land.

In the spring of 1634 French troops led by Marshal Jacques de la Force invaded Lorraine, to which Charles, the duke of that province, reacted by garrisoning his main towns and joining the Imperial cause. As well as the movement into Lorraine, Richelieu directed against the Habsburg threat thrusts northward towards the Spanish Netherlands and movements eastward into Milan and the Val Telline in the Alps, and towards the Rhine. Hepburn's regiment marched with the Lorraine contingent. After capturing the town and citadel of Bitche on the frontier of Alsace, the French advanced to La Mothe, another strongly fortified site, which proved much more difficult to seize. Hepburn and his colleagues laid siege on 5 March to the fortress perched on its high rock, surrounded with deep ditches and stone-faced ramparts. The attackers' cannon fire and attempts to dig mines through the hard rock failed to induce the commander of the garrison to surrender. De la Force took his army further into Lorraine, leaving Hepburn's regiment with two French regiments to continue the effort to reduce La Mothe. One of the French commanders was the young nobleman Henri de la Tour d'Auvergne, the Viscount of Turenne, who behaved with cool courage in action. Turenne and Hepburn were comrades in arms, though contrasts in other ways: only twenty-two years old at La Mothe, Turenne was a Protestant, while the Catholic Hepburn was already a veteran in his mid thirties. Direct assaults on La Mothe met with heavy losses, from gunfire and from the shrapnel effect of large rocks hurled from the ramparts above to shatter among the attackers, but a foothold was won in the outer fortifications. On 15 May Hepburn sent musketeers to a nearby hill to pour in flanking fire on the enemy but they were driven off by a sally. At last hunger began to achieve what force of arms could not and on 28 July, after nearly five months of endurance, La Mothe surrendered, a victory sought more for prestige than military necessity.

Hepburn now rejoined the main French army and in December led his men across the Rhine in an advance on Mannheim, before pushing on to Heidelberg through the Neckar valley. A series of skirmishes disposed of the Imperial troops in the area and on 23 December the Protestant garrison in Heidelberg welcomed in their comrades. Hepburn and de la Force decided now to advance to Landau, south-west of Mannheim, to link up with the army of Duke Bernhard of Saxe-Weimar, or rather the sorry remnants of the force he had led at Nördlingen. The duke's strength was reduced to 4,000 horsemen and 7,000 foot soldiers, many of them Scots, the survivors of the Green Brigade regiments of Ramsay, Robert Monro and Hepburn's former command. The reunion was an emotional one, with drummers beating the Scots March and the sole surviving piper from Mackay's Regiment blowing his heart out.[5]

All the Scots were incorporated into one new corps in French service, called le Régiment d'Hebron, numbering over 8,000 men at this time and fielding 48 companies of musketeers and pikemen, among them a few who had left home to be soldiers as long before as 1618. In the campaigns that followed in the Rhineland in 1635, a rivalry emerged between it and the Picardie Regiment over which of them was the senior member of the French order of battle and therefore entitled to honourable military privileges, a title Hepburn's regiment claimed on the arguable ground it covered the Garde Ecossais, in existence since the fifteenth century. The Picardie officers satirised this boasted antiquity by joking that Hepburn's Scots had been Pontius Pilate's guard, to which one Scot rejoined that if they had been in Pontius Pilate's service and on guard at the Holy Sepulchre, the body of Christ would never have got out of it. The French regiments, whatever their age, had need of their mettle to confront the Imperial forces, which were showing every likelihood of winning the struggle for mastery of the Rhineland. Spanish troops from Luxembourg gained possession of Trier, leading France at last officially to declare war on her Habsburg neighbour on 26 May. Kaisersleutern and then Heidelberg fell to Imperial forces led by Field Marshal Matthias Gallas, and Mainz came under siege and fell in December.

Under constant harrassment from Gallas's foraying cavalry, the French were unable to forage enough to replenish supplies and fell prey to hunger and sickness. The combined troops of Hepburn and the Viscount of Turenne were caught by a sudden attack by Duke Charles of Lorraine in a village called Fresche. Hepburn showed his experience and his cool head by leading a group of 200 musketeers to high ground on one flank and by sending a similar detachment to the other flank to entrap the enemy in a cross-fire. Without pausing to reload, Hepburn shouted to his French and Scots to charge downhill into the Lorraine ranks, using their muskets as clubs, an onslaught that won the day. The main French forces had to retreat; Duke Bernhard ordered his troops to burn their baggage, Hepburn's regiment did likewise, cannon were stripped down and buried in secret locations.

Moving swiftly through hill country to avoid Gallas, they reached the Rhine at Bingen and crossed on a bridge of boats. Hepburn's regiment fought off repeated attacks at the rear and one observer noted how they struggled for eight days without much rest 'leaving the ways by which they retreated more remarkable by the blood of their enemies than by their own'.[6] One story published in the *Gazette de France* on 6 October 1635 tells how Hepburn was caught at one point by Imperialists who were unaware of his identity; he issued orders in German with such assurance that they felt it an honour to let him go. Whatever luck remained with the hurrying army – reduced by sickness, wounds, fatigue, desertion and the marauding attentions of peasants – almost ran out in the hills between the Saar crossing at Vaudervange (now Waller Fangen) and Boulay-Moselle. Gallas, at the head of a powerful force of cavalry, had outflanked the French and was waiting for them in a narrow valley between wooded heights. Hepburn's musketeers, however, made skilful use of rocks on the steep slopes on either side to pour fire on the Imperial ranks and compel them to retire. The French army finally reached security at Pont-à-Mousson.

With many German Protestant princes now signing up for peace with the emperor, only Duke Bernhard of Saxe-Weimar remained to patch together an alliance with Richelieu, according to which he received French money to keep his army in the field and the promise of the more attractive prize of becoming prince of Alsace. In 1636 Spain attacked into Picardy and Franche-Comté, advancing to within 80 miles of Paris. In the east Gallas advanced to Dijon before he was stopped. By the spring of that year, however, Richelieu had raised more troops and could send his armies on the offensive. Hepburn's regiment now marched in conjunction with French troops led by the Cardinal de la Valette and the Germans of Duke Bernhard. In May 1636 they laid siege to the hill-top town of Saverne, garrisoned by Gallas's troops under the command of a Colonel Mulheim. After some days of cannonade, the town walls were breached and a fierce struggle developed as the defenders fought to throw back the waves of assaulting troops, clambering over the broken masonry through the smoke of the guns. This lasted for three hours and took hundreds of lives before fading light made the French retire. Two more attempts to storm the weak point were made in the following few days. Both were repulsed. On 8 July Hepburn rode forward for a closer look at the breach. It was a classic fateful moment. Perhaps a musketeer on the ramparts recognised him as an important officer from his armour, or perhaps it was a chance shot, but a musket ball struck the field-marshal in the neck at the joint of his gorget. He fell from his horse and was carried back to safety by his Scots, who had crept up with him. The Viscount of Turenne led a fourth assault, this time to victory, as Hepburn lay behind the lines, his life-blood draining away, murmuring his last words, said to have been regret at having to be buried so far from the kirkyard of Athelstaneford. When he learned the news of the Scot's death, Richelieu admitted he was deeply moved – 'Saverne has been paid for dearly, but we must bear in submission what God has sent.'[7] Hepburn's remains were laid to rest with great ceremony in Toul Cathedral, where a monument in the form of an effigy was later installed, with his helmet, sabre and gauntlets on display.[8]

The command of the Régiment d'Hebron passed to Sir John's cousin, Sir James Hepburn of Waughton, in September 1636, and, when the latter was killed in Lorraine in 1637, to Lord James Douglas. Douglas, who had been born around 1617, had gone to France at an early age as a page to Louis XIII. He was only twenty years old when the king appointed him to the command of the Hepburn regiment, upon which the name of the corps was changed – to the Régiment de Douglas. Hepburn's brothers, Lieutenant-Colonel James Hepburn and Andrew Hepburn, obtained permission through the Privy Council in Edinburgh to recover his possessions in France. The Privy Council letter reads like a summary of the achievement of Scots officers and like an epitaph : 'His said umquhile brother have by thair vertews and valorous atchievements abrod muche endeared themselffes to forraine princes, under whome and in whose service they preferred to charges of great trust and commandement, wherin they so worthily behaved thamselves as they did purchase thereby both credit and meanes. It hes pleased God now in end, when they were serving the French king in the warres, to call [him] to his mercie from this mortall lyffe.'[9]

Recruitment in Scotland for the French army was boosted by the open war against the Habsburgs, and as many as 11,000 Scots enrolled under French colours in the period after the declaration of war in March 1635. The Privy Council also sought to reinvigorate the provisions of the long-moribund alliance with France, something that was of little interest to Paris, although they allowed a few of the Scots privileges to continue until the end of the century. 'The Scots have always had a particular affection for [France] in which they have, at all times, been considered naturalised French subjects', wrote M. de Bellièvre, the departing ambassador in June 1646, in his notes to his successor in London.[10] For many Catholics service in France was preferable to enlisting in the Lutheran ranks of the northern powers – in 1638, 700 of the 1,200 Scots in Lord Gray's regiment were Catholic – but by no means were the recruits exclusively of the old faith. Captain Robert Hume was granted a licence to raise 1,000 men for Hepburn's regiment in March 1637 and, despite growing tensions and open conflict at home, a further six levies for French service took place between 1638 and 1643 for a total of 8,000 men.[11] The warrants for these were issued to Andrew, Lord Gray; Colonel Alexander Erskine, son of the Earl of Mar; James Campbell, son to the seventh Earl of Argyll and his second wife, and in 1642 created Earl of Irvine by Charles I; Colonel John Fullerton and Colonel Lord James Douglas. Recruitment of such a large number of men created difficulties: the Privy Council instructed sheriffs to impress idle persons for the Earl of Irvine in September 1642, several months after the original warrant had been granted to the earl in April, and there were numerous appeals to the council against illegal seizure of recruits. Colonel Alexander Fraser, Lord Saltoun, made good use of prisons on Irvine's behalf, recruiting 'poore miserable bodies unable to pay anie soumes, but ar like to sterve in waird and would willinglie goe with me to the French warres where they may be serviceable, whereas in this prisoun they can doe noe good to thamselves nor to anie others.'[12] There were complaints that Saltoun was deliberately committing men to jail in order to induce them to the colours. In the early 1640s, there thus came to be two Scots regiments in French service – the Régiment de Douglas and the Earl of Irvine's regiment, sometimes referred to confusingly as the Garde Ecossais but more properly named Régiment d'Infanterie Ecossais.

Charles I was still pursuing the restoration of the Palatinate to his nephew, Charles Louis, now the heir to the lands and dignities that had belonged to his father before the disastrous foray into Bohemian politics. To avoid unnecessary diplomatic entanglement during the time of the Imperial diet at Regensburg, where Charles hoped for progress on Charles Louis's behalf, parliament curbed recruitment for anti-Habsburg service: 'no leavies either of Armies Regiments Companies or recrues of Souldiors be licentiat or warranted to be sent out of this kingdome till ane resolute answer returne from . . . Rattisbone [Regensburg] . . . at leist quhill the first day of aprile nixt'.[13] Shipmasters and skippers were warned that their vessels were liable to search and that they would be fined £40 Scots for any soldier found aboard bound for a foreign country. Officers who had served abroad and were now in Scottish service were exempted from this restriction as long as they had a pass from their general. In November 1641, however, parliament approved the recruitment of 10,000 men for service in Germany for Charles Louis.[14]

After the death of Johan Baner in May 1641, the Swedish chancellor appointed the artillery officer Lennart Torstensson to the command of the Swedish army. In the spring of 1642 he launched another offensive into central Europe, defeated the Saxon army at Schweidnitz and advanced into Moravia, where he captured the capital, Olmutz (now Olomouc), in June. As the Imperial forces hurried to meet this threat, Torstensson turned to the west and laid siege to Leipzig. Here, on almost the same acres near Breitenfeld where Gustavus Adolphus had defeated Tilly in September 1631, the Imperial army caught up with Torstensson. What is known as the second battle of Breitenfeld was fought on 2 November 1642. John Nairn and Robert Douglas were present, and a cavalry attack under Douglas against the Imperial centre was a crucial feature of the conflict. The Imperial lines were broken before they could complete their assembly, and Swedish losses were less than half those inflicted on the enemy. Leipzig now fell into Swedish hands. However, any opportunity Torstensson might have had to build on his successes in Saxony was thrown away when he received in September 1643 orders to march north to deal with an old enemy – Denmark. Christian IV had been using the German war to advance his own position in the Baltic, raising tolls on shipping passing through Danish waters, much to the annoyance of the Swedes. The conflict between the northern neighbours ended in August 1644 but it granted to the Habsburgs and their allies a breathing space and a chance to regroup.

In the winter of 1641/42 Cardinal Richelieu appointed the young Duc d'Enghien to the command of forces defending France's northern frontier. Before the year was out Richelieu was dead, but his policies lingered on, implemented now by Cardinal Mazarin. During this time the French army underwent a minor revolution, becoming a better disciplined, more highly trained body – an improvement that was soon to be evident to the world. In the spring of 1643 Enghien directed his army in the defence of the flat country around the Meuse river and moved to relieve the fortress of Rocroi, three miles from the Flanders frontier and under siege by Spanish forces which had invaded France from the north. Among Enghien's army were the Scots of James Campbell's regiment and in the ensuing battle they fought in the centre of the French second line, positioned between two Swiss mercenary regiments. The Spanish recovered from initial surprise at Enghien's appearance on the afternoon of 18 May but the hard-fought contest, which began with the light of the following dawn, resulted in a victory for the French.

In 1644 the French moved once more into the Rhineland against the Bavarians, who had come west from the headwaters of the Danube to occupy Überlingen and Freiburg, and in the following year Torstensson and his Swedish army advanced again from the Baltic against Bohemia and Moravia. On 6 March he defeated Imperial forces at Jankau near Tabor, and by the end of April he had penetrated to within 30 miles of Vienna, precipitating a flight by the emperor's family, before turning away to Brno and running out of steam against the city's heroic defence. Turenne tried to cut through from the Rhine to join up with the Swedes but suffered a reverse at Marienthal from the Bavarians; these protagonist met again at Nördlingen in August and this time Turenne was victorious. The viscount's proposals to form a united front with the Swedes met with no welcome from Cardinal Mazarin but Turenne went off to join the Swedes anyway and the combined forces succeeded in 1647 in forcing Bavaria to make peace, if only for a few months. While these campaigns ran their course, tentative diplomatic initiatives to bring an end to the chaos engulfing the Continent were already being made, and these gradually acquired a momentum until at last, in October 1648, the signing of the Peace of Westphalia in Münster brought the war to a close.

The Thirty Years War, or the German Wars, as it was known at the time in Scotland, left much of central Europe in ruins. The fighting and campaigning had devastated swathes of country and disrupted social and economic life, and it has been estimated that the total population fell from around 16 million to only 10 million.[15] Some towns had shrunk to huddles of broken buildings sheltering struggling civilians, while others had lost substantial proportions of their inhabitants. Munich's population fell from 22,000 in 1620 to 17,000 in 1650, Augsburg's from 48,000 to 21,000, Chemnitz's from 1,000 to fewer than 200. On the other hand, a few centres, such as Hamburg, away from the main arenas of conflict, grew at the expense of their stricken rivals, and Dresden absorbed enough refugees to compensate for its losses, emerging from the war with roughly the same number of inhabitants.

By the end of the war many Scottish officers had returned to Britain to take part in the series of conflicts normally subsumed under the umbrella title of the 'Civil War'. With their experience they readily found employment. Most notable among them was Sir Alexander Leslie, whose arrival in 1638 was noted by John Spalding in Aberdeen: 'Thair cam out of Germany fra the warrs home to Scotland ane gentleman off bass birth . . . who had servit long and fortunatly in the Germane warris'. Of base birth Leslie may have been in the eyes of some contemporaries but he was undoubtedly richer than most of them, with estates in Scotland and Sweden; in 1640 someone noted with incredulity that he wore clothes worth £2,000 to attend the kirk.[16] He took command of the army of the Covenant and recruited many of his former colleagues on the Continent to stiffen its ranks. Leslie acted according to his principles but others chose sides by accident. Such a man was the irrepressible chancer James Turner. Holding the rank of captain in 1639 but unable to get along with his commanding officer, Turner left to go home, 'to look for some employment under the Prince Elector'; two weeks in Scotland convinced him of the 'verie great rumours of civile warrs', but nothing else and he sailed back to Germany. The pressure of developments at home, however, intensified as the summer of 1640 passed and Turner finally decided to go back for good. 'Without examination of the justice of the quarrell, or regard of my duetie to either prince or countrey,' he wrote, 'I resolved to goe with that ship I first rencounterd.' As it happened, the first ship he found a passage on brought him to Cove, near Aberdeen, whence he was able to ride to Edinburgh and then Newcastle to join Leslie's army; he narrowly missed boarding a vessel bound for Hull, a voyage that would have resulted in him joining the Royalists, as he recorded in his memoirs. This was perhaps an excuse for his behaviour, as when he was writing them the Stuarts had been restored to the throne and he may have felt vulnerable to persecution. The activities of the men from Europe during the wars at home are beyond the scope of this book but their numbers included Alexander Hamilton and Robert Monro on the Parliamentary side and, as Royalists, the Marquis of Hamilton, William Gunn, Sir Patrick Ruthven – old Pater Rotwein, ennobled as the Earl of Forth in March 1642 – and James King – made Lord Eythin at the same time. 'Word cam heir to Abirdene', wrote John Spalding, 'that generall King cam fra Denmark with about five hundreth thousand pundis striviling [sterling] to his Majestie, and thrie or four scoir brave commanderis. He was direct fra the king of Denmark and landit at Newscastell . . . and presentlie preferrit to be lieutenant generall to the erll of Newcastle's army.' The men from the Continent also presented examples of the classic civil-war trope of brother fighting brother: for example, Alexander and John Gordon, two sons of the Sheriff of Sutherland, went together to fight for Sweden, but the former fought as a Royalist and was killed at Edgehill in 1642, and the latter led a company in Covenanter service, although he later had a change of heart.[17] At first Lord Reay hovered between firm commitment to either king or covenant, although he plumped for the latter at least for a time before taking ship for Denmark in 1643 to stay with his son Angus, who had command of a regiment there; in 1644 he brought back money, ships and arms to Charles I and, with Ludovic Lindsay, sixteenth Earl of Crawford, defended Newcastle against his former comrade Sir Alexander Leslie. After various adventures, Reay decide⸢ Denmark was a safer place to be and returned there in 1648. He

in Copenhagen in the spring of 1649, and a grateful Danish king
charged a frigate to carry his remains home to be buried at Kirkiboll
beside the Kyle of Tongue.

The former mercenaries made good use of their European connections. On his return from Sweden in 1638, Alexander Leslie
brought 2 cannon, 10 field and regimental pieces and 2,000 muskets
with him. Further supplies of arms followed, such as those carried on
the 3 Dutch ships that docked at Leith in April 1640. According to
Spalding, Leslie 'caused send to Holland for ammunition, powder and
ball, muskets, carrabines, pistolls, pikes, swords, cannon, cartill, and all
other sort of necessar armes fitt for old and young souldiers, in great
abundance; he caused send to Germany, France, Holland, Denmark,
and other countries, for the most expert and valiant captains,
lieutenants and under officers who came in great numbers in hopes
of bloody warrs, thinking . . . to make their fortunes upon the ruine of
our kingdome.' The Marquis of Hamilton noted that the Covenanters
were sending for arms and ammunition 'not onlie from Hollen but
lykuys from Hamburg, Breme, Lubick, Dansick and Sued, that is none
part should faill they may be suppleud from ane other'; the links with
Sweden were tantamount to an unofficial alliance.[18] Among the
armaments were what at the time were known as Swedish feathers:
5-foot stakes with pike heads at either end that could be stuck into the
ground to fend off cavalry; the Covenanter forces imported these by
the thousand.[19]

Remarkably, recruitment for the Continent continued in Scotland
despite the unrest at home. The levies for France between 1638 and
1643 have already been noted. In 1644, the Swedes asked the envoy
Hugh Mowatt to seek 2,000–3,000 men in Scotland for their fight with
Denmark; Mowatt came ashore in London in December to seek
permission to raise 5,000 Scots troops and hire 24 warships. Some
Scots officers were also active in the Imperial cause. Ludovic Lindsay,
the future earl of Crawford, after fighting in Polish service against the
Turks for 4 years, collaborated with Adam Gordon and some other
Scots and Irish officers to levy 8 regiments in Silesia in July 1636 on
behalf of Spain. Lindsay's regiment spent the winter of 1636–37 in
Franche-Comté. In the following year Lindsay was complaining to
Philip IV of Spain that he had had to pay his men himself since they

had first been mustered and that this neglect had left them without shoes or adequate clothing. Almost three quarters appear to have deserted or died. Lindsay, who inherited the earldom of Crawford in 1639, received no redress from Madrid.[20]

Not all the Scottish officers resorted to their homeland when the Civil War began. One who stayed in Swedish service and rose to great eminence was Robert Douglas. He became general of the Swedish cavalry in 1643, married into a Swedish noble family, ruled as governor of Swabia from 1648 to 1650 (from a house in Ulm) and was ennobled as Baron Douglas of Skälby in 1651. A huge procession turned out for his funeral in Stockholm in June 1662, including four companies of horsemen with their pistol muzzles downward, drummers and trumpeters, five companies of foot carrying their muskets under their left arms and trailing their pikes, over a hundred ministers and the queen herself on foot.[21] Two other Scots in Swedish service were the brothers Thomas and Patrick Kinnemond. Thomas was first in Johan Baner's Ostergotland infantry in 1628. He became major of the city militia in Augsburg in 1633, and he held various other commands. Both he and Patrick were naturalised and ennobled in 1650.

Sir Alexander Leslie, created earl of Leven by Charles I in 1642, kept up his connections with Sweden, maintaining the informal alliance. In 1651 his military and political endeavours led to his arrest by Cromwell; he would have landed in the Tower of London had not his son-in-law pledged to keep him out of trouble at his house in Northumberland. Leslie let the Swedish court know of his predicament and both Queen Kristina and Karl X tried to have him released. Freed in 1654, Leslie travelled to Sweden as a Royalist envoy and helped his son-in-law William Cranstoun recruit men for Swedish service. In 1661 the old warrior breathed his last.

In 1647 Patrick Ruthven launched on a correspondence with Queen Kristina about pension arrears, and his will, bequeathing lands in Sweden, Mecklenburg and Selkirkshire to his widow and offspring, was complicated enough to keep his descendants in dispute for some years after his death in Dundee in 1651. James King, Lord Eythin, became a Swedish baron in 1645 and was commissioned to serve as lieutenant-general under the Marquis of Montrose in 1650 in the latter's futile bid to restore Charles II to the throne. In the event, Montrose landed in Orkney without King and was defeated at Carbisdale. King himself died in Stockholm in June 1652. One of the last to pass away was Robert Monro, who died in 1680 – in County Down, where he had earned a reputation in the 1640s for his ferocious campaigning in the Protestant cause.

Patrick Ruthven was not the only Scot who sought redress from his former employers. A group of 'divers distressed officers who have served under the crowne of Sweden' sought through the support of Charles II, probably in 1660 or 1661, to obtain 'present satisfaction or assurance in certane tyme to pay us what will justly be found to be due'.[22] Probably a considerable number of men who served in the ranks and survived the wars stayed on in Germany, too poor to make the journey home, and now likely with wives and children to support as best they could. Some may have been reduced to begging, others may have been able to continue as soldiers or ply a trade. Many of their stories have gone unnoticed or unrecorded, and even their names have disappeared into the cultures they adopted as their own, but the case of William Fraser from Beauly, who went to Sweden as an ensign in Lord Cranstoun's Regiment in 1656 and after his service stayed to become a merchant in Thorn (now Torun) in Poland, may not have been exceptional.[23]

'keen and fiery genius'

Russia, Poland, 1630–1699

*I*N THE 1650s Robert Gordon of Straloch summed up the people who lived in the high country around the valley of the Deveron in Banffshire in critical terms. 'The better classes, to their own great misfortune, disdain [trade] as unsuitable to their birth,' he wrote, 'and hence comes poverty, to alleviate which they address themselves to the profession of arms . . . [in which] with their keen and fiery genius . . . they make no little headway.'[1] The words could as easily have been applied to much more of the North-East. One of Gordon's 'better classes', an illegitimate son of the Laird of Crichie, lands not far from Fyvie, arrived in Moscow in January 1630 on a diplomatic-cum-military mission from Gustavus Adolphus to the tsar. The envoy bore the name Alexander Leslie, styled himself 'of Auchintoul' to distinguish himself from all the other Leslies, and was distant kin to the Sir Alexander Leslie who had already risen high in Swedish service – a factor that may have worked in his favour with the king he served. Another was the fact that he had been in Russia before, although in less propitious circumstances. As an eighteen-year-old officer in the Polish–Lithuanian army, he had been captured at the siege of Smolensk in 1618 and brought to Moscow a prisoner. Then foreign residents had vouched for him, securing his release on parole, and soon he had been on his way west again in an exchange of prisoners to resume his military career in the Swedish army. Leslie had proved himself capable of foreign missions in 1626 when he had gone to Britain to recruit more troops for Swedish service.

With a small retinue of servants and military men, including a

Dutchman familiar with the latest developments in the Low Countries, Leslie now reached Moscow to be received well by the tsar, Mikhail Romanov. Only sixteen years old when elected to the throne in 1613, the fourth tsar in eight years, Mikhail had brought a longed-for period of tranquillity to Russia. He had established a reasonably stable administration in the heartlands, a period during which he had wisely eschewed hostilities with powerful neighbours, even although large areas in the west and south were under the domination of Sweden and Poland. The Peace of Stolbova in 1617 had left the provinces of Ingria and Kexholm, the entire southern shore of the Gulf of Finland, as part of Gustavus Adolphus's realm. Now, the Lion of the North was offering through Leslie some tempting assistance in the reorganisation of the Russian army. The motive was far from altruistic: Gustavus Adolphus wanted Russia to make war on the Poles to keep them out of the conflict in central Europe. Leslie implemented his training mission in the summer of 1630, starting with two regiments, and reported his success to the Swedish king, who, once he was sure of the tsar's intention to attack the Poles, broke off his own efforts to re-negotiate a truce with them. Part of Leslie's package to seduce the Russians into making war on the Poles was a promise to provide further training and mercenaries to strengthen the Russian forces.

Tsar Mikhail's government initiated a period of reform in the Russian army in the early 1630s, with the formation of regular regiments. Prior to the appearance of these units, the country had relied mainly on a feudal levy, enacted in times of war under the administration of a series of military districts. Alexander Leslie was appointed as one of the foreign colonels charged with the training of the new regiments. At first the call for recruits evoked only a slow response, prolonging the need for mercenaries. The tsar sent a letter to Charles I in Britain in 1632 to explain his motives, ask for men and offer to buy weapons. On 25 May 1632 the Privy Council issued a warrant to Leslie and Lieutenant-Colonel Thomas Sanderson to recruit 2,000 men for the tsar's service. In the muster rolls that survive in the Russian state archives one can read such names as Leslie's own, Major James Wardlaw, Alexander Gordon (quartermaster), Primrose, Fleck, Crawford, Irving, Watson, Wallace, Mortimer, Anderson, David, Simpson, Brown – mostly, it would appear, men from the Lowlands or the North-east.[2] James Affleck was one of the lieutenants, who received 12.5 roubles per month, while the ensigns were paid 10. Holding the rank of lieutenant-colonel, William Keith's pay was 75 roubles. Two others who were in Russia at this time were Captain William Gordon and (in 1634) Lieutenant-Colonel Alexander Gordon, bearers of a name that would later ring more resoundingly through Russian military annals. Sir Thomas Urquhart also mentions a Thomas Garne, who was noted for his height and size, and was nicknamed the Sclavonian or the upright Gentile; in Russian service since the surrender of Scots mercenaries among the Polish garrison of Belaya in 1613, Garne turned down an offer of a transfer to the king of Bucharia's army because he had 'no stomack to be circumcised'.[3] Although the tsar was very willing to welcome recruits who could benefit his own forces, correct protocol could still be insisted on: Captain James Bannatine found himself turned down for tsarist service in October 1632 because his letter of recommendation from Charles I and the Prince of Orange bore the tsar's title in an incomplete form. Colonel George Douglas also had command of an 'English' regiment in Russia at this time. In the first half of 1633, the Privy Council permitted Captain James Forbes to raise two contingents, each of 200 men, for service in Russia under Leslie.[4]

When Sigismund III of Poland-Lithuania died in 1632, the tsar recognised this might be the moment to regain territories in the west and launched a campaign to retake Smolensk, the trading centre that had already changed hands several times. The old town, crowning a hill on the south bank of the River Dnieper, had been provided with extensive, thick walls some thirty years before and it was unlikely to fall easily into Russian hands. The tsar's polyglot army of 34,500 men, under the command of Mikhail Borisovich Shein, reached the city in October and initiated a siege that dragged on for a year, when a relieving Polish force arrived in September 1633 to tip the balance in the favour of the defenders. As could have been expected, there were large numbers of mercenaries on both sides. Among the Polish ranks, now serving Wladyslaw IV, the new king, were Scots called James Wallison, John Kirkpatrick and James Murray. In October 1633 Wladyslaw wrote from Cracow Castle to Murray, saying 'We . . . have been witnesses of your bravery under the walls of Smolensk during the whole time of the siege', before going on to order him to take command of 200 dragoons, recruit 800 men from among the foreigners and present himself at Smolensk by the beginning of June for service there.[5] Another Scot at Smolensk at this time, but serving on the Russian side, was George Learmonth; he had been in Polish service but had switched sides after the garrison at Belaya had surrendered in 1613 to become a captain of horse for the tsar. Learmonth was killed at Smolensk, but his three sons all followed his career path to serve in the Russian army. The Russian forces, of whom 12,000 remained, found themselves in danger of being entrapped at Smolensk by the Poles and asked for an armistice in January 1634. Wladyslaw agreed, stipulating among other conditions that the foreign element among the Russians should either join his forces or go home. The Russian surrender was signed at the end of February.

The disappointing performance of the Russian army was attributed in part to ill feeling between mercenaries from different countries and between the foreign troops and the native Russians. On at least one occasion they refused to take orders from a boyar, noted a Polish royal report on 24 Jan 1634. Leslie appears to have been deeply involved in a bitter dispute with English officers and on 3 December 1633 shot dead the Englishman Lieutenant-Colonel Thomas Sanderson, holding him guilty of treason. Leslie pistolled Sanderson at close range, 'so neere that hee fired his haire and hatt brims, so as he fell starke dead from his horse'.[6] Around this time perhaps, Leslie himself was wounded slightly by a French officer. The defeat exacerbated the bitterness among the touchy foreign officer corps and it must have been galling for Leslie and his colleagues to appear in humility on 1 March before Wladyslaw to kneel with their foreheads on the cold earth and lay their banners at the king's feet while the victorious Poles sang praises to the Lord. The English units carried Sanderson's corpse with them. 'Very awful to look at during this procedure was the fact that the defeated noblemen took with them their wives and children, the ill ones as well on sledges behind the regiments. Because of lack of horses the army had to pull the sledges, which was very shameful.'[7]

Perhaps Leslie took heart from the fact that the Smolensk campaign had worked out well for the Swedes by keeping the Polish army occupied to give them a freer hand in Germany, and possibly some Swedish influence was brought to bear to ensure the quarrelsome Scot did not suffer too much for the slaying of Sanderson. The English officer's relatives brought charges against him, throwing the expatriate British community in Moscow into some confusion. A trial for murder would probably have taken place but in April a fire broke out in Moscow, as ever vulnerable to such disasters, and no proceedings were held. The scandal was brought to an end by a writ, issued on 23 September 1634 in Charles I's name, declaring that Leslie had been insulted before the troops; the tsar also judged that his Scottish commander had acted in the right. Far from leaving Russia in the wake of the Sanderson affair, Leslie stayed and prospered, and it seems that he became the first man in the Russian army to be afforded the title of general. In December 1637, when he finally took his leave, he went with the good will of the tsar and a list of goods that included a gift of sable furs to the value of 150 roubles, 5 sleighs, servants, beef, 2 sheep, 2 geese, 2 hares, 10 chickens and several buckets of wine and beer, provisions that would have bolstered spirits considerably on the long journey across the frozen steppe. Soon after this, he wrote from Narva to the tsar to describe the Polish order of knights instituted in 1638 by Pope Urban VIII to combat the Orthodox breaking away from the Uniate adherence to Rome, and offered to raise an order of knights to oppose the Polish order.

A degree of stability was ushered into the Baltic arena by a series of treaties: between Russia and Poland in June 1634, between Sweden and Russia in September 1635, and between Sweden and Poland at Stuhmsdorf in the same year. Shortly after this, it seems that Alexander Leslie returned to Britain but after a few years he was back in Russia, offering his services, and was there in 1649 when the new tsar, Alexei Mikhailovich, expelled English merchants from Moscow in the wake of the execution of Charles I. The merchants moved north to Archangel. The ban did not apply to Leslie; on the contrary he did very well for himself, receiving an estate on the Volga in lieu of a salary as a foreign officer and living for a few years as a landed gentleman with his family and his own serfs.[8] There was some trouble when his wife was accused of overbearing behaviour, giving the peasant women too much work and offending against the precepts of Orthodoxy. She was accused of throwing an icon into an oven, an action that almost precipitated a bloody revolt among the serfs and allowed the patriarch of the Orthodox Church to press for sanctions against infidel foreigners and confiscation of their lands. Leslie settled the business by offering to convert to Orthodoxy and, after the required six weeks of instruction in a monastery, he and his family took the baptismal plunge. Now Leslie had a new name – Avram – but the peasants did not want him back and his estate was granted to another. Leslie had no option but to thole life on a monthly pension of 90 reichsthaler, a colonel's pay, from the tsar. His situation improved in 1654 when war broke out anew with Poland. Once again Smolensk was the target of Russian attack and this time Leslie succeeded in effecting its capture. He was appointed its governor and lived in comfort until his death in 1663.

In 1655 the newly crowned king of Sweden, Karl X Gustav, the nephew of the great Gustavus Adolphus, launched an invasion of Poland. James Turner, who was still travelling about Europe keeping the Stuart cause alive for Charles II, in exile from Cromwell's Britain, declined an invitation from some fellow Scots to join the Swedish army (Sweden had declared support for Cromwell). That summer Turner and his wife were in Bremen and among their guests appeared one man who would later become a bogey figure back home – Thomas Dalyell of the Binns. Dalyell was a Royalist and had left Scotland in disguise. After a few days with the Turners he went off to Amsterdam. 'Neither did I see him againe till his returne from Moscovia, which was not till ten yeares after,' wrote Turner. The Stuarts, anxious for allies on the Continent, sought assistance from Scottish expatriates in Poland, without much success, but as part of their attempt to woo them Charles raised regiments to aid the Poles: one of these was placed under the command of John Middleton, the son of the Laird of Caldhame in the Mearns who had first gone abroad as a pikeman under Sir John Hepburn and had since risen to command in the Covenanter forces. James Turner was enrolled under him as a captain. After a voyage that turned into an endurance test – the ship took one month to sail from Amsterdam to Elsinore, only to be trapped in ice at Copenhagen until the middle of January – Turner and his fellow officers at last reached Danzig only to find that the

Polish king had already left. Middleton refused an invitation to follow on unless he was paid; the hapless Turner, who had been dragooned into acting as Middleton's secretary, had to put his commander's refusal into diplomatic Latin and check the wording with two Polish senators in case it caused offence. Middleton had no funds left and once he had spent a loan, says Turner, 'we were forcd to disband our sojors and recommend them to a German Baron who was levieing for the King of Denmark.' The penniless pair had to leave their inn to rent a house 'where we keepd bot a very sorrie menage'. With their spare clothes in pawn and without credit, 'in that pitifull condition we breathd rather than livd three months'. Turner goes on to tell how some persons back at the exiled Stuart court had taken to blaming him for Middleton's misfortune and he finally had to confront his commander to get him to clear his name. By this time, the captain seems to have had enough. After telling Middleton he was useless in Danzig, he received permission to join the king of Denmark's service, borrowed 50 reichsthaler from Scots merchants and, with Middleton's fond good wishes and embraces, took ship for Elsinore.

On his arrival Turner found out from the local postmaster, who happened to be a Scot, that affairs in Denmark, where Frederick III had succeeded his father Christian IV as king in 1648, were in a pretty bad way. Sweden had given up its actions against Poland and was instead threatening Denmark's frontier in Holstein, after Frederick had launched a campaign to regain his country's losses to Sweden in the last war between the neighbours. Outnumbered and lacking confidence, the Danish army had retreated before the Swedish advance across northern Germany, to the scorn of the Swedes, who had resorted to hanging lanterns in the steeples of the villages they occupied to entice the Danes to fight. At the end of October 1657 Turner was placed in command of a squadron of dragoons in the Danish army and made adjutant general. 'Takeing some Scotch officers along with me, and arriveing at Christianstat (a skirvie litle toune, bot exceedinglie well fortified)', Turner dined with Henry Lindanaw, the Danish governor, and naturally fell to discussing the state of the nation. Lindanaw asked the Scot if he thought the country's leaders were 'all in their right wits', a question Turner declined to answer directly. If they knew what they were doing, confessed Lindanaw, who had been promoted to command the Danish army, they would never have made him a general, as he had never had a rank higher than ritmeister.

These gloomy pronouncements did not bode well for Denmark and Turner was unsurprised to find on his return to Copenhagen that Frederick and his counsellors, with 'bot little reason to trust the natives', had resolved to levy strangers to fight for them. Turner learned he was to be offered command of a foot regiment and was then commissioned to levy 1,000 men to form one of six new regiments. He was not at all sure he could bring this off, although he thought he could find 500 men in Danzig. The fee of 13 reichsthaler per soldier, to be paid out in Amsterdam, was allowed for the recruitment, and Frederick also gave Turner 150 ducats, an amount for which he was grateful but one he knew would not cover half his expenses. At the end of 1657 Turner reached an ice-bound Amsterdam, managed to extract half his levy money from the Danish ambassador and enlisted a major and three captains to undertake recruiting. Hardly had this effort got under way than events took a disastrous turn beside the Kattegat. Taking advantage of the extremely cold winter, in February Karl Gustav led his army over the ice from Jutland to the island of Funen, and then a week later he repeated the trick to cross to Zealand with guns and cavalry. It was a risk – the horses and men splashed through snow-water on ice that might break without warning – but it worked, and the unprecedented boldness of the Swedes left no one in doubt of the outcome of the war. English and Dutch envoys, anxious that Karl Gustav should not keep a stranglehold on the shipping route to the Baltic, mediated a peace settlement.[9] Turner, still in Amsterdam, had to cope with a Dutch government furious with Frederick for capitulating without their agreement: 'therfor they [the Dutch] discharge our leavies under paine of death, arrests our ships, sets our men ashoare and giveing each of them halfe a dollar bad them goe where they pleased'. Turner also felt aggrieved, sure that if he had been allowed to complete his recruitment he would have brought to Denmark men who would have given the Swedes pause. The war between Denmark and Sweden broke out again late in 1658 but by then Turner had given up on the Danes, complaining he had never received all his money and toying with the notion of taking the Danish ambassador to court, and he went to join his wife at the Hague.

In Danzig Middleton had at last managed to pay off most of his creditors and – with a Major Murray 'brother to Pomais' [Polmaise], and a servant – travelled overland through Brandenburg and Saxony to Brussels. His regiment had been given to the Viscount of Neuburg and was now in Flanders. Back together, Turner and Middleton involved themselves in various plans to aid Charles II and eventually returned to Britain at the Restoration. In 1661 a grateful monarch knighted the man who, in 1632 as a restless student in Dalkeith, had signed on to be a soldier.

In May 1656 Thomas Dalyell and William Drummond of Cromlix, another royalist fugitive, took ship from Amsterdam to Riga and entered Russia. Both achieved high rank in their adopted country in campaigns against the Turks and Tatars, Dalyell becoming a general and Drummond a lieutenant-general, before they received permission to leave when Charles II asked the tsar to release them from his service. Back home, as commander-in-chief of Scotland, Dalyell's ruthless attempts to suppress the Covenanter movement earned him the nickname of the 'Muscovia beast' and he was credited – falsely – with introducing thumb-screws to his native land. Legends accrued around his cruelty: he was accused of being under the care of Auld Nick so that in battle musket balls bounced off his coat and hat. As one historian of the Kirk put it, Dalyell's 'rude and fierce natural disposition hade been much confirmed by his breeding and service in Muscovia where he hade the command of a small army and saw nothing but tyrranie and slavery'.[10] The image of Dalyell in his mature years shows a stern man with watching, hawk-like eyes, a long white beard and white locks flowing from a bald pate, like a predatory Merlin. His death in Edinburgh in 1685 must have been quietly applauded across the country, yet for all the hatred heaped on him by Presbyterians he enjoyed with good humour the London children who ran after him in the street, attracted by his outlandish appearance. Drummond's later career brought him little opprobrium and consequently he has tended to be forgotten, although at one time he was governor of Smolensk and died as Viscount Strathallan in 1686.

After the end of the Thirty Years War there was an understandable

decline in the number of Scots who sought military service in Europe.
Some recruitment continued, for example in March 1656 both France
and Sweden looked for men in Scotland, and Lord Cranstoun took
2,500 Scots to Pillau for Swedish service at this time. Captain James
Fraser, son of Lord Lovat, joined Cranstoun with some of the Fraser
clansmen.[11] In August some of the soldiers, not long arrived in
Königsberg and still unfamiliar with their new environment, complained about being given black bread instead of oatmeal. There were
still enough enterprising and footloose young men in Scotland who
took ship as individuals to see what fortune would throw in their way.
The wanderlust struck many in the North-East, especially those not in
sympathy with the ardent Presbyterianism then to the fore, and one
such was Patrick Gordon, born on the last day of March in 1635 at
Easter Auchleuchries in the parish of Cruden, the second son in a
junior branch of the Gordon family of Haddo. Fortunately for us,
Patrick kept a diary, which survives in full in Russian archives and of
which only parts have been published in English. It is a remarkable
record of an adventurous life and only a flavour of it can be captured
here.[12]

    His schooling complete, Patrick concluded that his Catholicism
would not ensure a welcome at a Scots university and 'resolved . . . to
go to some foreigne countrey, not careing much on what pretence, or
to which country I should go'. With funds from an uncle, he bade
farewell to his parents and found a passage to Danzig aboard a ship
from Aberdeen on a calm, misty evening in June 1651: 'with many
sighes and teares, [we] bidd our native country farewell', he wrote.
Adverse winds lengthened the passage and it was not until late in July
that he reached his destination, where, at first, he lodged with a Scots
merchant John Donaldsone in Holy Ghost Street. The expatriate
network now proved to be invaluable, providing Patrick with lodgings
and companionship as he took the coach east to Braunsberg (now
Braniewo) to enrol in a Jesuit college run by a priest called Alexander
Menezes. Within two years, however, any ambition he had entertained
to take religious orders had withered – 'yet could not my humor
endure such a still and strict way of liveing' – and he set off with his
meagre possessions to make his way on foot to Danzig. His spirits fell
to a low level, isolated as he now found himself, with church Latin,

little German and no Polish at his disposal, not even able to trust all the Scots he met. Finally he ended up in Chelmno, where he found lodging for the winter with John Dick, a merchant's apprentice. Patrick expressed some wish to be a soldier, to which Dick rejoined that he should travel on into Poland to find a place with the Scots company in the service of Duke Jan Radziwill. This option came to nothing and he wandered about Poland for most of 1654 until, at last, he found a situation in the retinue of a noble of the Opalinski family.

In 1655 Patrick travelled to Hamburg with his benefactor and there parted company with him. The young Scot fell in somehow with a cornet and a quartermaster who were drumming up recruits for the Swedish army. He resisted their blandishments and their flattering remarks about how desirable Scots were as soldiers until he heard from them about a ritmeister called Gardin whom he, homesick perhaps, took to be one of his own name. When Patrick met Gardin, he turned out not to be a Scot but by now the youth was depressed, short of money and possibly vulnerable. When he was told he couldn't go home because he would be laughed at, he caved in, joined the colours and accompanied Gardin as far as Lübeck, where he fell ill. He passed part of the onward journey to Stettin lying in a wagon.

'On the fourteenth of July I rode out of Stetin,' he wrote, 'and the next morning came to the army, when they were drawing up in a large meadow . . . It was a most delightfull and brave show, the ruiters being very well mounted, and the foot well cloathed and armed, and above all, the officers in extraordinary good equippage.' Apparently cheered by this sight, Patrick settled as a soldier in the army of the new Swedish king, Karl Gustav, eager, in Patrick's opinion, to make a name for himself on the fields of glory by invading Poland. Two days after Patrick's first view of them, the army marched from Stettin to camp near Poznan. At the end of August they moved on, behind giant drums mounted on wagons whose beating resounded across the countryside, and thrust further south-east. Patrick's experiences now take on a breathless character more usually found in a picaresque or romantic novel. First he was shot in the ribs in a skirmish when his unit in the Swedish rearguard was surprised by some Polish cavalry and, as the army neared the northern suburbs of Cracow, already set on fire to deny succour to the invaders, he saw action again, this time having his horse shot from under him and taking a wound in the leg. His commanding officer at this point was General Robert Douglas, now at the height of his career in the Swedish military. Cracow surrendered on 17 October. Patrick now received a discharge from Ritmeister Gardin but, as the troops were moving into winter quarters and as he probably had nothing else to do, he re-engaged as a volunteer, this time under a Scottish officer called Duncan.

One day in January 1656, when he was riding in haste to catch up with his regiment after it had moved on while he was absent on a reconnaissance, he was captured by some Poles and bundled off to a nobleman's house. Here he was divested of his money before being sent on to Sandets south of Cracow, where he was kept under close arrest for seventeen weeks. The ubiquity of Scots throughout Poland now saved him: a Franciscan monk called Innes persuaded his captors to let him go on condition he joined the Polish army. Thus he became a dragoon under the command of Constantine Lubomirski, starost or governor of Sandets, and found himself the very next day riding off to tackle the Swedes who, meanwhile, had occupied Warsaw. As a combined Lithuanian-Polish force laid siege to the Swedes in their capital, Patrick was given the duty of protecting a village that belonged to Lubomirski's brother. Evidently the young Scot had made a favourable impression to be granted this duty. There now followed what seems to have been a fairly idyllic time. Patrick learned Polish from the daughter of the house in which he was quartered, while resisting her attempts to win his love (or so he says) and showed his entrepreneurial streak by accepting payment to protect peasant refugees and to recover stolen cattle. The pendulum of his fortunes was soon, however, to swing the other way. A month after the surrender of Warsaw, the Swedes won a victory over the Poles and once again Patrick found himself a prisoner, this time in the hands of a German unit in the Swedish army. Hauled before General Douglas, he managed to convince him that he had been coerced into joining the enemy and showed his willingness to re-join his erstwhile comrades, finding a comfortable billet for the next three years in an officers' training unit composed of picked Scots. During his time there Patrick recruited two dozen more Scots from among the expatriates in Warsaw.

In 1657 he was captured again, this time by Polish peasants when he was riding alone, and dragged into Danzig. He managed to conceal 14 dollars from the prying hands of his captors, refused to exchange his new English boots for a pair of theirs and, adopting a high tone, threatened to report them to the commandant of city, before he was put in a cell under the guard of a corporal who kept his Latin edition of Thomas à Kempis. Patrick resisted pleas to join Polish service and was soon set free in an exchange of prisoners that included a few other Scots — Lieutenant-Colonel Drummond, Major Fullerton and Lieutenant Scott among them. One of the Polish officers who had tried to tempt Patrick to switch sides again was a man of the same name and possibly a relation — Patrick Gordon 'with the Steel Hand'. This colourful individual of obscure origins — apparently he lost his hand in his youth — was a Royalist and a violent anti-Covenanter who had fled from Aberdeen by seizing a merchant ship in the harbour with some companions. He became a captain of cavalry in the service of Poland; he had also been excommunicated for a time, but not much is known of his career in Europe after 1660.[13]

Shortly after his release Patrick fell ill with a fever. While he was being nursed, the village where he lay was suddenly attacked and overrun by the enemy but the woman of the house pretended he was her sick husband, while his attendant Alexander Keith hid in a barn, and they became the only two of their party to escape death or capture. Later that year, in a skirmish with troops of the Holy Roman Empire, Patrick's horse was shot under him and he was wounded in two places before being taken prisoner again. One of the captains of the Imperial forces was none other than James Leslie, nephew and heir to Walter Count Leslie, who had assassinated Wallenstein in 1632. James Leslie had arrived in Austria as a young man in 1655 in answer to his childless uncle's summons to complete his education and join the Imperial colours. Patrick recorded that the lad from Balquhain showed no interest in his Scots prisoners. Patrick resisted attempts to persuade him to join the Imperial army and, after some six weeks during which he recovered from his wounds, he managed to escape and make his way back to the Swedish lines.

Now Patrick showed some mettle and enterprise. Arguing that because he had received no pay during his period of captivity and had

found his own way to freedom he was now free from any obligation
to the Swedish army, he received a letter of discharge and a
recommendation to join Karl Gustav's bodyguard as an ensign. He
was, however, in no hurry to assume this new duty and, with
Lieutenant Hugh Montgomery and sixteen other Scots, set off on
a private marauding expedition, capturing Imperialists for ransom but
keeping their horses. Patrick fell in with James Leslie again, this time
in November 1658 when he was again captured by the enemy,
although that word defined a concept clearly accepted loosely by
someone of Patrick's ilk. For all his unscrupulousness Patrick was
clearly valued by the Swedes as they now made an offer of exchange
for him but the Poles, also desirous of his service, refused to let him
go. In his memoirs he rather charmingly notes here how, although he
had no objection to serving Poland, he felt he ought to show some
reluctance to change sides. He refused the proffered command of a
dragoon company, feeling that would be a dead end to his career, but
finally accepted early in 1659 a post as quartermaster, adding by way
of justification in his memoir that in the Swedish army he had been in
danger of being starved to death.

The Polish Commonwealth also had to contend with Russia over
her eastern borders. After the Polish defeat of Russia at Chudnovo
(Czudno) in 1660, some Scots left to join the tsar's forces while others
stayed on in Polish service. For his part, Patrick considered joining the
army of the Holy Roman Empire in 1661 but then received an offer of
employment in the tsar's army from the Russian ambassador and a
Scot, Colonel Daniel Crawfurd, who at the time was governor of
Smolensk (he died as governor of Moscow in 1674). Patrick accepted
reluctantly, despite the belief that Russian pay was reputed to be
reliable and the chance of advancement high, and travelled eastward,
arriving in early September in Moscow and two days later being
admitted to the tsar's presence to pledge allegiance and kiss the
royal hand. Other Scots had joined Patrick while he was en route
through Riga, among them Paul Menzies, son of Sir Gilbert Menzies
of Pitfodels, who married a Russian and served the tsar as envoy
and soldier until his death in November 1694 with the rank of
lieutenant-general. Before long Patrick realised the truth behind
the reputation of the Russian army – that their money was unreliable,

that mercenaries were looked on as an evil necessity and that any move to leave without permission brought the risk of banishment to Siberia. He seems to have resigned himself to his situation, which probably improved after he was promoted to lieutenant-colonel in the following year.

In 1665 he married Katherine von Bockhoven, aged thirteen, daughter of a German officer and a Welsh mother, and took his place in the colony of Scots expatriates in Moscow, a group that included physicians and artisans as well as soldiers. Prominent among them were the Hamilton sisters, married to Russians, who had a reputation for hospitality and welcomed Tsar Aleksei as their guest from time to time after he was widowed in 1669. Three years later the tsar married one of the Hamilton daughters, Nathalia Narishkina, who thus became the mother of Peter the Great.

In the year of his wedding the news had reached Patrick that his elder brother had died. The tsar had not allowed him to go home but, mindful of the request, when the need arose in the following year to send an envoy to the British court he chose the Scot. After the earlier refusal the command to leave came abruptly: 'I should make myself ready in three or four dayes to be gone', wrote Patrick, feeling aggrieved because he had been underpaid. On the morning of 29 June 1666, he took his leave of his friends in Moscow and directed his party down the road towards Tver. On 20 July he reached Riga and found passage on a ship to Lübeck where, on 5 August, after a tedious voyage, 'about fyve a clock in the morning, came to anker just under the towne'. On the following day he travelled on to Hamburg but because Britain was then at war with the Dutch he resolved to continue by land, via Hannover, Minden, Nijmegen, Flushing – where he was kept awake in miserable lodgings by 'some Scotsmen gott into the next roome, who passed the whole night carowsing, swearing and blaspheming' – and Bruges. At last he managed to hire a boat to convey him to Dover, where he landed on 1 October.

Patrick returned to Moscow two years later, bearing a request for the privileges of the banished English merchants to be restored, but fell foul of the Russian authorities. For reasons now unknown, he was ordered to stay within the confines of the foreigners' quarter until it was realised his services might be valuable elsewhere and he was sent with his regiment to the Ukraine in 1670 to subdue a rising among the Cossacks, a duty he apparently carried out with courage and despatch. A recall from the Ukraine was not forthcoming, however, for another seven years, a period he spent in study and military administration. After successfully defending himself in Moscow in 1677 against complaints from some soldiers, he was ordered back to the Ukraine, where his services were now needed in combating another incursion by the Turks and Tatars. He led the defence of Tschigirin and succeeded in ousting the invaders from the Ukraine. The death of Tsar Alexei gave Patrick hope that his wish to leave Russia might now be granted but the new tsar, Fyodor, was equally appreciative and desirous of his officer's abilities. He was told to stay where he was.

On 8 July 1678, a great Turkish army, some 50,000 in number, accompanied by an almost equally large force of Tatars hove into view of Tschigirin. There were fewer than 12,000 in the garrison, among whom was Patrick with a regiment of dragoons and another of foot soldiers, but, in his capacity as engineer, he had had time to strengthen and extend the defences. For a month, the great guns of the attackers hurled ball and shell into the fortress and the town, and it was only by labouring at night on breaches in the fortifications that the Russians were able to hold out. After a bomb-burst on 8 August claimed the life of the governor, Patrick's fellow officers begged him to take over command. A massive assault three days later might have succeeded if he had not rallied the fearful defenders, but this success won only a breathing space. His repeated requests to the relieving Russian army for reinforcements met with no response until at last he was ordered to evacuate the fortress, a command he refused to contemplate until he received it in writing. One of the last to leave and unable to swim, Patrick rushed in the darkness on foot across the bridge that was the only route to safety, through Turkish troops bent on slaughtering their foe, and made it without a scratch. Behind him the magazine he had set on fire blew to pieces with a terrible explosion. For these exploits he was promoted to the rank of major-general and appointed to command in Kiev, and he was promoted again to lieutenant-general in 1683.

The death of Tsar Fyodor in 1682 rekindled hopes of a restoration to Moscow in the Scot and he travelled to the capital to see what he could win from the new ruler. This was the regent, the tsarevna, Sophia, the older sister of the half-brothers Ivan and Peter. The boys had been crowned as joint tsars but, as Ivan had severe mental deficiencies and as Peter was only ten, both were unfit to reign. Patrick had no luck with his request to go home and was told to stay in Kiev, but a second attempt, in 1686, obtained for him a six-month leave of absence, although his wife and family had to remain in Russia to ensure his return. In the spring of 1687 he was back in action, at the head of his troops, marching across the steppe in the valley of the Dnieper against the Tatars. Further promotion followed and at last he was permitted to reside in Moscow, where he formed a close relationship with the young Tsar Peter, a friendship with signal consequences in a society where foreigners were still viewed with suspicion.

Peter was now seventeen years old, married, in his early manhood and at odds with his ruling half-sister. On 6 August 1689, Patrick noted in his diary 'rumours unsafe to be uttered' and on the following day Peter had to flee from Moscow under threat from Sophia, to find sanctuary at the monastery of Troitzka. The young tsar wrote to his foreign officers to tell them of a conspiracy against his life. Patrick faced a dilemma but within hours decided to throw in his lot with Peter, influencing his fellows to do likewise. Peter was eating his midday meal at Troitzka when the loyal regiments arrived and Patrick was at once ushered into his presence to stay with him. A triumphant entry into Moscow followed four days later.

The last decade of Patrick's life saw the consummation of a remarkable career. He cemented a relationship with Tsar Peter, they dined together, with Patrick sometimes mentioning in his diary that he suffered a hangover, and clearly the Russian ruler found him to be a valuable and loyal military advisor. Occasionally, in his letters to Scotland, Patrick showed a yearning to see his native heath once more and in one letter to the Duke of Gordon on 12 January 1692 complained, 'I am still in a cumbersome court lyfe.' In two campaigns, in 1695 and 1696, he fought against the Turks. In the first, in which the Russian forces failed to storm the city of Azov, Patrick protested about his advice being ignored and noted the 'angry looks and sad countenances' among the senior officers. In the following year, the

tsar was more willing to listen and Patrick's plan, of throwing up a
rolling rampart of earth, was adopted. It meant thousands of men
plying spade and shovel for days on end, the opposite of martial glory,
but it worked. The sloping mountain of soil filled the defensive fosse
and allowed the attackers to overtop the town ramparts and oblige the
overawed defenders to surrender. This time the Russians lost only 300
men; these included a Scottish colonel by the name of Stevenson.
Patrick was well rewarded – with a medal, a gold cup, a sable robe and
an estate with 90 serfs. In 1697 Peter set off on his famous journey
through western Europe. In his absence Patrick was placed in
command of the army quartered in the Moscow suburbs and, in
April 1698, had to suppress a mutiny. When Peter heard the news – he
was in Vienna at the time – he hurried home. At the end of that year
the tough old soldier from Cruden, at the age of sixty-four, 'felt a
sensible decrease of health and strength'. His health continued to
deteriorate during the following summer – the tsar came several times
to visit him – until he breathed his last on 29 November 1699. Joseph
Robertson, the editor of the Spalding Club edition of his diary put
it well: 'the eyes of him who had left Scotland a poor unfriended
wanderer were closed by the hands of an Emperor'.

------◆-◆▶◀◆-◆------

'where I might again begin my fortune'
Russia, the Netherlands, Prussia, 1700–1758

*P*ATRICK GORDON fathered three sons and two daughters.
Of the lads, the eldest succeeded to the lands of Auchleuchries
but the other two followed their father's path into the Russian army.
His eldest daughter, Katherine, married a German officer but was
widowed in 1692 when her husband lost his life in an accident
with fireworks. In 1700 she married again, this time to a kinsman
of her father, Alexander Gordon. The latter came to Russia in 1696
after a spell in the French army, no doubt enticed by the success
and status of Patrick, and stayed on to rise to the rank of major-
general.

After securing his position on the throne of Russia, Peter the Great
embarked on a drive to make his backward nation a powerful and
significant force in Europe. At the start of his reign Russia's only
direct access to the open sea was through the cold, distant port of
Archangel, and the temptation for Peter was to establish outlets on
the Black Sea and the Baltic. It was an ambition, however, that
brought him into conflict with the Ottoman Empire and Sweden. In
1697 Karl XII had succeeded to the throne of the Vasas and almost at
once had to contend with troublesome neighbours: as well as Russia,
Poland and Denmark were itching to recover lost territories. In 1698,
all three formed an alliance to combat Sweden. Karl got his blow in
first, capturing Copenhagen in 1700 and forcing a surrender on
Denmark, before switching his attention to the east, defeating the
Russians at Narva and Riga, and occupying Courland. In 1701 the
Swedes moved into Poland and then on into Saxony. Karl, however,

was stretching his resources dangerously thin, and it could only be a matter of time before he would meet a reverse. It came at the siege of the fortress of Poltava in Ukraine in July 1710: in the battle the Swedes lost almost 16,000 men as casualties or prisoners and, although Karl himself escaped with a handful of followers, it marked the end of Sweden's dominance of the Baltic. Among the prisoners taken by the Swedes at Narva was Alexander Gordon. Back in Russian service, he defeated his former captors at Kysmark and went on to defeat the Poles at Podkamian. He died at Auchintoul in 1751.

The Gordons – Patrick and Alexander – stand out as examples of Scots in the service of Peter the Great, but there were several more of their kinsmen and their countrymen in prominent military positions. For example, take George Ogilvy. A grandson of James Ogilvy of Airlie and son of an Ogilvy who became governor of Spielberg in Moravia, George was born in 1648 and rose to the rank of major-general in the service of the Habsburgs before Peter the Great spotted him in Vienna in 1698 and invited him to join the Russian army. His work in training and modernising Peter's forces brought him to the rank of field marshal. He later switched to the service of Poland and died in Danzig in October 1710. Then there were the brothers James and Robert Bruce, whose father, William, had been a colonel in Russian service. James followed an interest in the natural sciences, including chemistry, and Tsar Peter put him in command of artillery. He also apparently showed a talent for shady financial dealing but this did not prevent him playing an important role in the Peace of Nystadt in 1721 when Russia finally acquired Estonia, Livonia and the lands around the head of the Gulf of Finland from Sweden. James was rewarded with an estate, where he died in 1735; he was buried in the Simonoff Monastery in Moscow. His titles were inherited by his nephew Alexander, who also achieved the rank of major-general and fought against the Turks.

Among the many Scots who distinguished themselves under the different flags of Europe it is worth noting a few who are remembered for exploits on their home soil but who had their first taste of armed conflict abroad. John Graham of Claverhouse, Bonnie Dundee himself, travelled to France after he graduated from St Andrews in 1668 to be a volunteer in the service of Louis XIV. He moved four years later to the Low Countries to a commission as a cornet in one of the Prince of Orange's troops of horse guards. His arrival coincided with the outbreak of war between the Netherlands and France, when William of Orange was able to form an alliance with, among others, the Habsburgs. On 11 August 1674, a joint Spanish–Dutch force under William's command was attacked by a strong French army at Seneffe near Mons and forced into retreat. During the desperate confusion, William might have been captured when his horse foundered in a marsh had not John Graham dismounted to give his commander his saddle, an act for which he was promoted to captain. Perhaps Graham presumed too much on the prince's good will for he was passed over when he later applied for promotion to lieutenant-colonel of one of the Scots regiments in Dutch service and was aggrieved enough to quit the Low Countries, returning to Scotland at the end of 1676.[1]

Graham of Claverhouse's life ended in the battle on the braes of Killiecrankie in July 1689, falling in his moment of greatest triumph. It is perhaps typical of the twists of Scottish history that his opposing commander that day, Major General Hugh Mackay, had been a colleague in arms at Seneffe fifteen years before. Hugh Mackay was born in Scourie in the west of Sutherland in around 1640; an uncle had been killed fighting for Gustavus Adolphus at Lützen and his father had been a Royalist officer in the Civil War, and it was entirely natural that he also should pursue a military career. In 1660 he became an ensign in Dumbarton's Regiment and went to France with it. In 1669, he was among a number of officers who volunteered to fight for Venice in an attempt to drive the Turks from Candia (now Iraklion), the capital of Crete, an ultimately unsuccessful campaign in which he nevertheless distinguished himself. Now a captain, in 1672 he served in France's invasion of the Netherlands, where the horrors of the war struck him with such impact that he seriously thought of resigning to go home to his native braes. Fate, however, took a strange and happy turn. In Guelderland he was quartered in a widow's house and so impressed his hostess, Madame de Bie, with his grave manner that she decided she could safely bring her daughters back from the refuge whither they had been consigned to keep them from the eyes and hands of rapacious foreign officers. Mackay became as one of the family, playing chess and reading with the widow and her daughters, and it was perhaps inevitable that the serious young officer should feel attracted to the eldest, Clara. She turned down his first proposal of marriage but changed her mind when Mackay made it clear that, like many Scots before and since, he liked the Dutch and was willing to leave French service to find employment under their flag. The transfer was completed, Hugh and Clara married, and Hugh now became a captain in the Scots Brigade.

He fought at Seneffe, where Graham of Claverhouse brought himself to princely attention, and at the siege of Grave in October 1674, and it was Hugh Mackay who was chosen to fill the post of lieutenant-colonel in preference to Graham. By 1680 Mackay was a colonel and not long after a brigadier. Implementing the terms of a 1678 treaty between Britain and the Netherlands, under which the British monarch could call on the three Scottish and three English regiments in Dutch service, James II summoned the help of the Scots Brigade to combat the rebelling Duke of Monmouth in 1685 and, although it saw no action before it returned to the Netherlands a year later, the king was so impressed by its appearance that Mackay was promoted to major-general. As James II's power unravelled and relations with the Dutch deteriorated over the next two years, the brigade and the three English regiments in Dutch service were faced with the threat of divided loyalty. The Dutch government refused to allow the ordinary soldiers to respond to James's call for them to be sent back to Britain but officers were permitted to choose the course to follow. Only a quarter of them opted to offer their swords to the British monarch. Mackay stayed with the majority in Dutch service, and he commanded a division of English and Scots troops in the subsequent landing in Britain by William of Orange and the successful ousting of James. Mackay was appointed as commander in chief in Scotland in 1689 and was set on the course that would lead to the confrontation with Graham of Claverhouse, once his companion in arms.

John Leslie succeeded his father as the twelfth baron of Balquhain in 1638 only to inherit a patrimony much burdened with debt and reduced to a castle and a farm.[2] To support himself and possibly regain some wealth and honour, John took to soldiering under his

kinsman Alexander Leslie during the Civil War and in 1647 left
Scotland, as so many of his forebears had done, to see what fortune
held for him in Europe. He ended up in Russia, where he became a
colonel of cavalry but was killed at the storming of Igolwitz on 30
August 1655 when Russia invaded Poland. His cousin James Leslie
had better success in the service of the Holy Roman Empire, where he
inherited the title and lands of their uncle, Count Walter Leslie, the
assassin of Wallenstein, when the latter died childless in 1667. James
was in Habsburg service in 1683 when the Turks launched a major
assault from the east, driving into southern Poland and up the Danube
to lay siege to Vienna itself. In the fighting to recover the city, James
Leslie played a conspicuous and gallant part, at one point managing to
break through the enemy lines to reinforce and replenish the besieged
citizens. He went on to command in further campaigns against the
Ottomans in Hungary in 1684 and 1685 until ill-health forced him into
retirement. James's younger brother Alexander followed his sibling
into Habsburg service and reached the rank of lieutenant-colonel,
before being mortally wounded during a sally against the Turks.

The overthrow of James II and the subsequent attempts of the
exiled Jacobites to restore the Stuart dynasty led to many Scots
seeking refuge on the Continent. Several of these 'attainted' political
exiles found a living through military service, and a prime example of
the breed was James Keith.[3] Born in June 1696 at Inverugie Castle
near Peterhead, Keith came from a privileged and honourable background. For centuries the Keiths had been the hereditary earls
marischal of Scotland, and James's elder brother George was the
tenth to bear the title. George served in the British army under
Marlborough but on the death of Queen Anne he stayed loyal to the
Stuarts and joined the Jacobites. The brothers were both present in
1715 at the shambolic defeat of the Earl of Mar's rising at Sheriffmuir
and both had to flee the country. In May 1716 they stepped ashore at
Paul de Leon in Brittany. James went to Paris to seek service with the
exiled king, the would-be James III, but, as he was just seventeen years
old, he was told by the king's mother to stay in Paris to complete his
education, for which the exiled royal household would pay. Unfortunately, nothing came forth from the treasury for some time and James
Keith, too proud to borrow from friends, had to get by through

selling 'horse furniture . . . and other things of that nature which an officer commonly carries with him'. At last, however, the Stuart promise was fulfilled and James began his studies. A plot in 1717 for the king of Sweden to invade Scotland on behalf of the Jacobites brought James a commission as a colonel of horse before the scheme was abandoned. In June 1717 Peter the Great visited Paris and James tried in vain to secure a post in his service: 'I thought it high time (being about 20 years old) to quitte the Academy, and endeavour to establish myself somewhere, where I might again begin my fortune.'

Some friends advised James in 1718 to offer his services to Spain, said to be about to invade Sicily in a war with the Holy Roman Empire, but now he had a reason to be reluctant. 'But I was then too much in love to think of quitting Paris, and tho shame and my friends forced me to take some steps towards it, yet I managed it so slowly that I set out only in the end of that year, and had not my mistress and I quarrel'd, and that other affairs came to concern me more than the conquest of Sicily did, it's probable I had lost many years of my time to very little purpose, so much was I taken up with my passion.' Early in 1719 George and James Keith took a ship from Marseilles to Palamos on the Catalan coast, only to be arrested by the local commandant on suspicion of being agents of the French enemy. The confusion was sorted out with the help of the Duke of Liria, none other than a fellow Jacobite, James Fitzjames, an illegitimate grandson of James II. The Keith brothers now became intimately involved in the planning for a Jacobite invasion of Britain via the Highlands, the enterprise we know as the 1719 Rising, and James sailed with the invasion force. The mixed force of Spaniards and Scots reached Loch Duich in mid April 1719 and set up their headquarters in Eilean Donan Castle. For the Jacobites the campaign came to an inglorious end after a skirmish in Glen Shiel, on the back of which the Spanish surrendered and the others had to look to their own safety. 'As I was then sick of a feavour,' wrote Keith, 'I was forced to lurck some months in the mountains, and in the beginning of September having got a ship I embarcked at Peterhead, and after 4 days landed in Holland.' A perilous journey through France, then at war with Spain, followed for the Keith brothers before they reached safety in Madrid.

There now ensued a string of unsatisfactory years for the younger

Keith, when he found that a bureaucratic mix-up seemed to have deprived him off his commission in Spain and he had to kick his heels and rely on the sympathy of friends. He thought of going home but was advised it would be unsafe to return to Britain. Instead he went to Paris and stayed for two years, pretending to be still receiving treatment for a tumour he had had removed from his shoulder, making half-hearted attempts to join French service, and, it seems, having another love affair. When hostilities erupted in 1726 between Britain and Spain, his offer to join any invasion force was turned down; but he did take part in the siege of Gibraltar in 1727 before he concluded that no further advancement in Spanish service was possible for a Protestant. Hoping for promotion to the command of a regiment of Irish mercenaries, Keith 'received the answer I expected: that His Majesty assured me that howsoon [as soon as] he knew I was Roman Catholick, I shou'd not only have what I asked, but that he would take care of my fortune'. The Duke of Liria, newly appointed as the Spanish ambassador to the Russian court, agreed to help him and successfully obtained for the young Scot an offer of a post from Tsar Peter II. At the beginning of 1728, Keith set off across Europe to a bright new future.

Reaching Moscow in October, he 'received orders from the Felt Marechall Prince Ivan Dolgorusky to take command of two regiments of foot belonging to his division, but being as yet entirely ignorant both of the language and manner of service, which I already saw was very different from that of other countries, I desired a delay of three months in which I might inform myself both of the one and the other, which he readily granted me.' The Russian court was as full of intrigue as it had ever been but, as a newcomer, Keith stayed clear of close involvement with the cabals and cliques, a wise stance in view of the constitutional upsets that took place soon after his arrival. Peter II, the grandson of Peter the Great, fell ill and died, probably of smallpox, in 1730, at the young age of fifteen, and was succeeded by Anna, the Duchess of Courland. The powerful Dolgorusky family hoped to retain the power behind the throne but underestimated the mettle of the new tsarina. Anna won over the loyalty of her troops, and the leading Dolgoruskys were banished to Siberia. Not long after these changes, Keith was surprised to receive a letter one evening informing

him that Count Levenwolde, the adjutant general of the army, wanted
to see him. 'I reaved all night what cou'd be the meaning of such a
message . . . I concluded I might have some enemy at court.' The
interview, in fact, was to offer Keith the rank of lieutenant-colonel in
a new guards regiment, a post he accepted 'in an instant'. 'All Mosco
was as surprised as I was myself', recalled Keith, 'I received hundreds
of visits from people I had never seen nor heard of . . . who imagined
that certainly I must be in great favour at Court, in which they were
prodigiously deceived.'

Early in 1732 he received further promotion, being appointed as
one of three inspectors of the army under an inspector-general.
Assigned the frontier districts along the Volga and the Don and part
of the Polish frontier at Smolensk, he set out on a long journey,
travelling more than '1,500 leagues' to visit around thirty-two regiments. He arrived in St Petersburg at the New Year to find everything
'in mouvement' because the king of Poland had died and the
supporters of the claimants for the elected monarchy were competing
for Russian support. The candidates were Augustus, the Elector of
Saxony and son of the late king, and Stanislaus Leczczynski, the
father-in-law of Louis XV of France; the majority of the Poles
favoured the latter but the Russians preferred Augustus and mobilised
the army to ensure his ascendancy to the throne. Keith was ordered to
lead 6,000 foot soldiers to Ukraine to be ready to cross the frontier. In
August, with the election likely to go against Russian desires, troops
under the command of the Limerick-born soldier Count Peter Lacy
headed for Warsaw. Stanislaus departed from the capital for Danzig,
where Lacy hemmed him in. Keith moved to combat pro-Stanislaus
forces in the province of Volinia, now the west-central region of
Ukraine. In mid December he led his troops, which now included
4,000 Cossacks, across the frozen Dnieper and spent ten fruitless days
in search of the enemy before the Cossacks captured a troop of
cavalry on Christmas Eve. Rumours that the Volinian force was
increasing in strength prompted the transfer of command to Lieutenant-General Prince Schahofski, who had orders to disrupt the
province. Keith found dishonourable the prince's instruction to ruin
the enemy's estates and tried in vain to avoid such action. 'In my
march I assembled some thousands of cattel, and some hundreds of

miserable bad horses, which I sent immediately to the army, and at the same time reported to him [the prince], that the whole inhabitants were abandoning their villages, and most of them retiring into Moldavia; that if he continued to ravage the country it wou'd very soon become a desert, and our own troops wou'd be in hazard of dying of hunger.'

At the end of January the army advanced to Vinnitz on the Bug river. Keith was lodged in the village of Litin when word came in that the enemy was in camp about 12 miles away and preparing to confront the Russians when their westward march brought them through the forest near a place called Latitchef. According to Keith, Prince Schahofski dismissed this warning brought by a spy and refused to countenance a change in the order of the march to meet the threat. In the event, the Poles sprang the ambush too soon, attacking a quartermaster's party moving ahead of the main army. This allowed Keith to lead some Cossacks and dragoons to the attack and, finding the enemy numbers much lower than feared, routed them for the loss of only twenty on their own side. Prince Schahofski was now recalled to the Ukraine to attend to internal business and command reverted to Keith.

Advancing to Medziboz, Keith was invited to enter the castle where, he was assured by the governor who had met him outside the town, everything had been prepared for his arrival. Leaving his army to make camp and with only twenty-four dragoons as an escort, Keith accepted the invitation. The castle garrison was on parade with drums beating and colours flying. 'I soon perceived the folly I had committed,' wrote Keith, 'but it was too late to retreat, and my only way was to put a good face on the matter.' He sent his adjutant to bring in his equipage in all haste and to mix grenadiers among the wagons, and then waited fretfully until they came. Ironically, as he had only light artillery, he could not have taken the castle if the garrison had shut the gates in his face, but now he was able to turn the tables on the foe and order the protesting governor to march his garrison out.

Keith's memoir goes on to describe a series of manoeuvres and small battles across the plains and woods of Ukraine until the text peters out at the end of 1734, with the army going into winter quarters. The War of the Polish Succession came to an end in 1736 and by then Keith's reputation had grown in stature, bringing a promotion to lieutenant-general. Russia now embarked on another war with the Turks. Keith had a narrow brush with death or at least disability; wounded in the knee at the siege of Ochakov on the Black Sea on 2 July 1737, he was saved from undergoing amputation of the shattered limb only by the intervention of his brother George, who hurried to his aid and brought him away for better treatment than army surgeons could provide. This was good news for the Tsarina Anna, who is reputed to have said she would rather lose 10,000 of her best soldiers than Keith.[4] A two-year convalescence gave the Scot the opportunity to visit Paris and London where, to his surprise, he was acclaimed a hero and received by George II, his Jacobite youth clearly forgiven if not forgotten. He returned to Russia to be the governor of Ukraine.

During peace negotiations with the Turks in 1739 there occurred an incident that has acquired some legendary status in the annals of the Scots who fought in Europe. At the end of a session of talks conducted through interpreters, the Turkish vizier bowed and, taking the astonished Keith by the hand, said in a broad Scots accent that it made him 'unco happy' to meet a fellow countryman so far from home. The vizier was the son of a bellringer in Kirkcaldy.[5]

The death of Anna in October 1740 let loose the usual intrigues and attempts to establish power until Elizabeth, the youngest daughter of Peter the Great, emerged the winner in November 1741. Keith at once declared his loyalty to her. By now he was once more in the field, commanding in the war that had broken out against Sweden. At the siege of Willmanstrand he came across an orphan prisoner called Eva Merthens. It was an odd way in which to meet a lover but Keith's mistress is who Eva became, and to her and their children he left what little wealth he managed to accrue. She died in 1811. Once hostilities with Sweden ended, Keith was appointed to head a military-diplomatic mission to the former foe. Honours now came his way in dizzying fashion: ceremonial swords from Sweden and Russia, the Order of Saint Andrew and an estate in Livonia among them. The former Jacobite ignored the 1745 Rising back home.

By this time, however, dissatisfaction was beginning to cloud the mind of the general. Once again there was an animus against foreigners in the Russian government. George Keith, still seen as a Jacobite, was refused permission to enter the country to visit him and James's letters to his brother seem to have been intercepted. He should not have been surprised that his position at Elizabeth's court invited jealousy and resentment – the tsarina paid him a great courtesy when she reviewed the troops at Narva in 1746 – but he felt aggrieved when he sensed he was being passed over and was falling out of royal favour. There was a rumour that the plump, attractive monarch had amorous desires for her general, a delicate problem for Keith, for if he refused her advances he might find himself travelling to Siberia. At last, in 1747, he obtained permission to leave Russian service.

His fame had preceded him and he was at once welcomed into the service of the ruler whom Elizabeth viewed with most suspicion: Frederick II of Prussia. Left broken and wasted at the end of the Thirty Years War, the economy, prestige and administration of Prussia had been restored by the energetic Hohenzollern ruler Frederick William to such an extent that it had become a major power in northern Europe. In 1675 the Prussian army, trained under French officers, had even defeated the more powerful Swedes at Fehrbellin. Frederick William's skilful foreign policy had extended his rule over East Prussia, and his son Frederick I consolidated the advance by making Prussia a kingdom in 1701, encompassing most of northern Germany and extending east beyond Königsberg, much to the concern of the Holy Roman Emperor. Frederick II showed every inclination to build on the achievements of his father and grandfather to extend Prussia's reach. In 1740 he ordered an invasion of Silesia, then part of the weakened Habsburg Empire. Other European leaders took their cues and their sides, and the result, the War of the Austrian Succession, lasted on and off for eight years. It was thoroughly natural that the bellicose Frederick should wish to draw James Keith into his circle of advisors. With the newly conferred rank of field marshal, and comfortable with a monarch he found affable and polite, James wrote to his brother George, then in Venice, to join him in Berlin, where both began to participate in the cultural and social life of the Prussian capital. In 1749 James became governor of Berlin; he is also credited with the invention of the *Kriegsschachspiel*, or war-game, as an exercise.

The war with Austria came to an end. Silesia remained in Prussian hands and Austria, fearing Frederick would now descend on Saxony,

sought an alliance with France. Prussia formed an alliance with
Britain. The flurry of diplomatic shadowboxing and alliances resulted
in the Seven Years War, which broke out in 1756 with Prussia's
expected attack on Saxony. Frederick was in a precarious position,
with France, Austria, Russia and Sweden ranged against him, but he
had, as well as senior officers of Keith's calibre, an extremely well-
drilled, fiercely disciplined army, practised, for example, in a manoeuvre labelled oblique order that allowed the troops to march across
the enemy's front, wheel and exert increasing pressure on the enemy
flank. The Prussian fusiliers could fire between three and seven
rounds per minute, and the cavalry could sustain a charge over a
great distance. These attributes enabled the Prussians to overcome the
Saxons in the autumn of 1756 and invade to Bohemia to lay siege to
Prague in the following spring. The Austrian army, equipped with new
artillery, held them at Kolin in central Bohemia in June 1757 and a few
weeks later near Königsberg the Russians overcame the Prussians and
swept west along the Baltic coast. Frederick showed that he still had to
be reckoned with when his army defeated the advancing French at
Rossbach in November 1757, wheeled about and dealt a blow to the
Austrians a month later at Leuthen, 250 miles to the east near
Wroclaw. In the following year the Russians were checked at Zorn-
dorf on the Oder.

At the beginning of October 1758 Frederick had his army positioned in an elongated formation stretching over 4 miles of countryside in eastern Saxony, facing the Austrians. The central command
post lay at the village of Rodewitz. The end of his right flank, 2 miles
to the south, under the command of Keith, rested in the village of
Hochkirch, a small place huddled on a hilltop around its church.
Densely wooded hills, now taking on the colours of autumn, stretched
away to the south. 'The Austrians deserve to be hanged if they don't
attack us here', Keith is reported to have said.[6] Frederick recognised
his vulnerability and intended to move to stronger ground as soon as
possible. This proved to be the coming Saturday, the fourteenth. On
the night of the thirteenth, however, the Austrians launched a bold
and effective move.[7] Cutting a route through the woods during the
dark hours, they managed to insert infantry around Hochkirch, ready
to attack before five in the morning. The Prussians were caught

unawares but they responded quickly and a firefight ensued in thick mist and semi-darkness. The struggle swirled around the churchyard in Hochkirch. In the confusion Keith had mounted his horse, shouting desperately for his aides to assist him to regain control of their predicament, when shots hit him in the right side. Then, as a cannonball knocked him from the saddle, a final fatal bullet struck his heart and he fell into the arms of his servant, an English cavalryman called John Tebay. By 7.30 the Austrians had Hochkirch and Frederick was pulling back. Keith was buried on the following day in the village churchyard with full military honours. Some months later Frederick had the remains brought to Berlin to lie in the crypt of the garrison church, but a memorial urn was placed in the village church in 1776 by the general's kinsman, Robert Keith, who was British ambassador to Vienna at the time. If one had to summarise the character of all the Scots who sought their fortunes as soldiers in Europe, then perhaps James Keith or Sir Alexander Leslie would emerge as the embodiments of the best.

SEVENTEEN

'We bore down upon them with all the sail we could croud'

The Mediterranenan and the Baltic

*I*N 1644 CAPTAIN GEORGE SCOT had a ship built in Inverness that, according to one eyewitness, was 'of a prodigious bignes, for bulk and burden, non such ever seen in our north seas'.[1] As an expert on nautical matters, the witness, the Rev. James Fraser of the parish of Wardlaw, may have been wanting but there is no mistaking his sense of wonder. Fraser goes on to say that the ship sailed for the south on the day before the battle of Auldearn (9 May 1645) and that Captain Scot fitted her out as a frigate and took her to the Mediterranean, bringing with him on the voyage his brother William. William Scot became a colonel in Venice and George became a vice-admiral in the Venetian fleet 'and the onely bane and terror of Mahumetan navigators'. According to Fraser, George Scot's name and the reports of his victories, as he hunted along the creeks and bays of the eastern Mediterranean, struck terror into the Ottoman empire: 'Many of their mariners turnd land souldiers for fear of Scot; and of their maritim officers many tooke charge of caravans to escape his hand . . . he was cried up for another Don John of Austria.' Scot died of a fever at Candia (now Iraklion) on Crete in January 1652,[2] and a statue was erected in his memory on the Rialto. Fraser saw it on a visit in 1659, when he also met George's son John.

Most Scots who sought martial fame in Europe did so on land but a considerable number also made a name for themselves at sea. This should come as no surprise for, in common with all the nations around the North Sea, the Scots have always been seafarers. Neither should it come as a surprise to learn that many were active as pirates or privateers, and it is a short step from piracy in one's own interest to applying the same skills in the pay of a foreign monarch. In 1534 a Scots captain whose name remains unknown to us offered his services to Gustav Vasa of Sweden in conflict with the city of Lübeck over trade in the Baltic.[3] In the War of the Three Crowns – between Lübeck, Denmark and Sweden – the four great ships of the Hanse city, the *Angel*, the *Joshua*, the *Marian* and the *Eagle of Lübeck*, the largest warship of the day, it is said, were defeated in a sea battle off Gotland in 1566.

Gustav Vasa was determined to build up his navy as well as his army, and he sought foreign assistance not only to man his ships but also to design and build them; Scotland was one of the places he looked to for this help. By the time the king died in 1560 he had some nineteen warships in his fleet. Erik XIV continued this naval development, with the principal aim of confronting the power of Denmark, and indeed the Swedish navy, under the command of the sea-going general Klas Horn, defeated the Danes as well as the Lübeckers in 1565–66. Frederick II of Denmark wrote to Mary, Queen of Scots, in April 1566 to protest about a ship being made ready in Leith to join the Swedish fleet.[4] Among the Swedish ships in 1566 was one called *Skotska Pinckan*, taken from the Danes but recaptured again; the name suggests a Scottish origin. Another, in the early 1600s, was bought from Scotland and bore the name *Skotska Lejonen* – Scottish Lion. Karl IX established the main naval base at Karlskrona in order to benefit for as much of the year as possible from ice-free water.

Despite these developments, by the time Gustavus Adolphus came to the throne the Swedish ships were still outgunned by the Danes. The ability to project military might overseas was essential to Gustavus Adolphus's foreign policy in the Baltic; as navies have always done, his had to convey troops safely to foreign shores, maintain supply lines, defend trade and also impress outsiders as symbols of prestige and authority. A new threat to Sweden appeared in the late 1620s when, by the capture of north German ports, Wallenstein created the spectre of a Habsburg navy afloat in the Baltic. As we have seen (Chapter 9) it was a threat real enough to persuade Gustavus Adolphus and Christian IV to overlook their rivalry and cooperate to keep Stralsund from the Imperial grasp. The Swedish king was in need of experienced sea captains and, as with his army, he found some of them from across the North Sea.

In June 1612, Sir Robert Anstruther wrote from Copenhagen to James VI to report how 'much greeved' were the Danes about some Scots ships that had 'done great hurt' on the Norwegian coast, adding the important information that one of the ships belonged to the Earl of Orkney and that 'one Stewart is Captane of herre'.[5] The Stewart in question was Simon Stewart, although no relation to Earl Patrick Stewart of Orkney. The latter, whose father was an illegitimate son of James V, is remembered to this day in Orkney for his avaricious, oppressive rule, and he certainly was not averse to pursuing ill-gotten gain at sea. His motive may have been simple piracy but suspicion remains that it may have been tied in with the mercenary expedition already described in Chapter 1. Be that as it may, there were three Scots ships active off the Norwegian coast that summer; the second also had a skipper called Stewart and the third was captained by a Dutchman. Simon Stewart hailed from Ayrshire and at a young age had found his way to Orkney, possibly as an 'enforcer' in the service of the earl. His piracy brought his name to the attention of both the British and Danish kings, and it was probably to escape the law that he decamped to Sweden, where he turned up in June 1616 in Gustavus Adolphus's navy and found employment in reconnaissance and transport missions in the eastern Baltic.

Already sailing under the Swedish flag were Alexander and Hans (John) Forrat. Their surname suggests they may have originated from Fife, and Hans was a Dundee burgess. Alexander appears as a captain in Swedish records in January 1611 and later that year he was in command of a ship called *Lejoninnan*. He was clearly held to be a responsible man, as he was charged with carrying some important passengers on various occasions in the following years – an envoy to Lübeck in 1616 and Gustavus Adolphus himself in 1618 and 1620. Hans became a captain possibly as early as 1604, and in 1610 and 1611 he led attacks on Danish ships. In 1620 he was captain of the vice-admiral's flagship *Svärdet*, a vessel on which Simon Stewart served as an ensign.

Another prominent Scottish officer in the Swedish navy was

Richard or James Clerck. He seems to have gone first to Norway, where a man of his name was accused of illegal shipbuilding in 1605–06; soon after this incident a master shipwright called Jakob Clerck appears in Sweden. By 1610 he had become a captain and, only some months later, an admiral in charge of a small fleet in the Riga area. He carried out several sea-going missions in the following decade and also served as *holmadmiral* or admiral of the Stockholm shipyard.

In April 1622 occurred an incident that gives some insight into the character and way of life of these hard-bitten men of the sea, as well as of the tensions that could brew in a close-knit expatriate community. Clerck, Alexander Forrat, Simon Stewart, another captain called James Muir and an ensign by the name of James Logan, who was related to Muir and who had recently been appointed in the navy, visited the house of Hans Clerck, Richard Clerck's brother, to drink some beer. Logan came late, and Forrat asked him if he could now pay money he owed, seeing he had been appointed as an ensign. Clearly Logan was not abashed by the seniority of his companions, or the teasing may have struck a sore point of honour, for, after going to another house where more beer was drunk, ill-feeling boiled over into violence. Forrat either hit Logan with his drinking cup or punched him; Logan retaliated, threw Forrat down and held a knife to his throat and the others piled into the fray. Clerck may have tried to separate the combatants but was wounded for his pains, while Muir took a sword and ran Logan through the body, possibly accidentally, but he soon died in any case. Logan's widow brought Forrat and Muir to court. The trial imposed a fine and the liability of further royal punishment on Forrat for starting the quarrel and a death sentence on Muir for the murder of his relative, although there is doubt over whether or not it was carried out.

Gustavus Adolphus clearly considered Alexander Forrat to be a valuable officer for in the following year he was commanding a vessel called the *Engel* in spying missions to Danzig and, after two years in charge of the Göteborg shipyard, was again patrolling off the Danzig coast. Here, in November 1627, Forrat achieved lasting fame for a selfless act of courage that is recorded in a letter James Spens wrote to England. Spens, who was as active in securing men for the Swedish navy as he was for the army, said that Gustavus Adolphus had reduced his blockade of Danzig 'for winter storms of frost and snow often lead to loss of ships in the narrow rocky waters'.[6] As six Swedish ships set sail with the offshore wind to return to their home ports, the Poles sallied out in ten vessels to engage them. The three Swedes in the van were unable to beat back against the wind to the assistance of their companions. In the subsequent action, which spread over two days, the Swedish flagship, *Solen*, was boarded after a brief exchange of fire with the Polish *Meerman*. Rather than let the vessel fall into enemy hands, Alexander Forrat set fire to the magazine and blew up his ship in a desperate, suicidal act of defiance.

Apart from Forrat, and possibly Muir, the Scots officers survived their campaigns in the Swedish navy and most reached high rank. Simon Stewart was a lieutenant admiral in 1644, and before his death in 1646 he may have reflected that he had not done so badly since starting out as a pirate for the rascally Earl of Orkney. The Clerck and Forrat families provided Sweden with several officers, ashore and afloat. In early 1628 around nine Scottish-born captains graced Swedish decks, some two thirds of the total in regular service, and more followed. Some English captains also joined the Swedish navy but they did not number as highly as the Scots, except for a brief time in 1658–60 when Cromwell's Parliamentary navy was in formal alliance with Sweden. Scots also held significant posts in shore establishments and administrative departments.

Two captains, Alexander Muir and Michael Kloch, who are also described as pirates, are known to have been in the Polish navy in 1622 when Colonel James Murray was working to improve it as a fighting force. Murray first appears in Poland in 1601 or 1603 at the court of Sigismund, and by 1609 he was employed as an envoy from the Stuart court. Murray oversaw the construction of ships for the Polish fleet, after Sigismund appointed him as senior naval architect in 1620. The first, a two-masted, fourteen-gun pink, was launched in 1622; some of his ships later took part in the battle off Oliwa in which Alexander Forrat was killed. Murray himself was absent from this clash, as he had taken umbrage at being passed over to be admiral. He was versatile enough, however, to command troops in the field, seeing action at Smolensk, and to be an administrator, as mayor of the town of Puck near Danzig.

Peter the Great recruited officers and shipbuilders from Britain, the Low Countries and Denmark to help fulfil his ambitions for a Russian navy. For example, shipwrights went to Russia from Davenport. In the early 1700s Peter ousted the Swedes to acquire control over the head of the Gulf of Finland and embarked on the building of the great capital city named after him. The island of Kotlina was fortified to become the naval base of Kronstadt and the growth of the Russian fleet in the Baltic began. By 1713, the year of the indecisive naval battle with Sweden at Högland, Peter had a fleet that included fourteen ships of the line and several frigates. One of his captains was Andrew Simpson, who, in command of the 52-gun *St Michael*, took part in several brushes with the Swedes in 1714. Other Scots were Thomas Gordon, William Hay and Adam Urquhart. In the autumn of 1718 Gordon was promoted to rear-admiral of the Red (the Russian navy adopted colour names for its squadrons, as did the Royal Navy) and became involved in the disputes that seem often to have broken out among the members of an officer corps drawn from different nations. Probably emboldened by booze, Gordon complained to Peter in 1721 about preference being given to Danish and Dutch officers, to the detriment of the British and their ships. The Russian general-admiral, Feodor Apraxin, let his emperor know that 'he looked upon Gordon and his associates as men of turbulent dispositions and malevolent principles; that having set their native country in a flame . . . some of them were forced to fly from justice and were now caballing to foment divisions in Russia'.[7] This was a reference to the fact that some of the British were Jacobites. Despite these opinions, Peter, sensing Gordon's talents, appealed to his officers to live in peace with each other. In the summer of 1722 Lord Duffus arrived in St Petersburg to become superintendent of the shipyard and magazine at an annual salary of 1,000 roubles (around £500). For general officers the pay Peter offered was slightly less than that they received in the Royal Navy (£20 per month against £21 per month) but seamen and warrant officers obtained a higher remuneration from the Russians. Andrew Simpson was dismissed from the service in 1714 for unknown reasons. Adam Urquhart was killed accidentally in the service in 1719 while cutting masts free after his ship, the *Portsmouth*, had run aground in bad weather on a sandbank 5 leagues from Kronstadt. More Jacobites went over to Russian service in the 1760s.[8]

Two Scots in particular stand out in the annals: John Elphinstone and Samuel Greig. John Elphinston may have been born at Lopness on the island of Sanday, a low, windswept finger of land and rock reaching out towards Scandinavia, and if this is so it was a highly appropriate birthplace for this fighting captain. At the age of seventeen, in 1739, he joined the Royal Navy. By 1760 he had reached the rank of captain. In the following year he captured a French frigate. His combat experience, combined with demonstrated skills in hydrography and combined operations, made him, when he was put on half-pay after the Seven Years War – the normal method adopted by the Admiralty when it had to reduce its manpower – a prime catch for the Russian navy when it launched a recruitment drive. Elphinstone received a commission as a rear-admiral in the Baltic in May 1769. Samuel Greig was born in 1735, the son of a shipowner in Inverkeithing. He went to sea in the merchant service before joining the Royal Navy, where he quickly reached the warrant rank of master's mate. He was still rated thus in 1762, although he had passed his examinations to be a lieutenant, and he also was attracted to transfer to the Russian navy, where swifter promotion beckoned.

Catherine II was crowned in the Cathedral of the Assumption in the Kremlin in September 1762. As a young Prussian woman, she had come to Russia to marry the heir to the throne, Peter, a grandson of Peter the Great and Catherine I. It was still a land of contrasts, in the view of a French diplomat, 'two different nations on the same soil . . . simultaneously in the fourteenth and the eighteenth centuries'.[9] Catherine II had great plans for her adopted country and, once she had disposed of her estranged husband (he was murdered in the summer of 1762 by officers loyal to her) she set about their implementation. In all she brought thirty British naval officers into her service. One of her ambitions was to continue the policy of Peter the Great to strengthen Russia and gain access to the Black Sea. The land war against Turkey was prosecuted successfully until Crimea was almost within Russia's grasp, and as part of a broader strategy against the Ottomans the decision was taken to send a Russian fleet from the Baltic to the Mediterranean.

Count Alexei Orlov, a scar-faced man of immense stature who was said to be able to down a bottle of champagne in one, was appointed to command this fleet, although he readily admitted he had little experience of the sea. Samuel Greig, who had already quietly made an impression as a competent and innovative officer and had risen in rank, was placed in command of a division of the fleet under Vice-Admiral Grigory Spiridov, and was taken on as adviser and flag-captain by Orlov. Whereas Greig exercised tact, Elphinstone made no secret of his opinion of the poorly equipped, poorly led fleet, and in essence he had good grounds for his complaints. The first fleet sailed from Kronstadt, while Elphinstone stayed behind to prepare a second of three 66-gun ships and two 32-gun frigates, 'the fitting out of which was likely to be attended with delay and many difficulties'.[10] Spiridov had gone away with most of the stores and the best officers, and Elphinstone also had to contend with the 'very tedious' Russian 'forms of office' until Catherine gave him the power to cut through the red tape. Once at sea, Elphinstone had other problems. One ship had to turn back, but she later caught up with the others at Copenhagen, and a frigate sank in the Gulf of Finland. Some officers enjoyed the delights of the Danish capital and neglected their duties to the extent that the fleet sailed on just before winter choked their passage with ice. Stormy weather in the North Sea scattered the ships and drove them into various English ports, and Christmas was upon them before they re-assembled at Portsmouth to effect repairs and recuperate from the rigours of the voyage.

At last, in the spring of 1770, the Russian ships assembled at Livorno. Elphinstone and Spiridov quarrelled vigorously until Greig dropped a word in Orlov's ear that it might be a good idea to let the fiery rear-admiral go off in command of an independent squadron to hunt on his own. After the capture of Navarino (now Pylos) Elphinstone, sailing in the 84-gunned *Syvatoslav*, along with the *Ne Tron Menya* and the *Saratov*, and the frigates *Nadezhda* and *Afrika*, found out that a fleet of Turkish ships was lurking off Nafplio on the east Peloponnese coast and engaged them on 27 May. 'We bore down upon them with all the sail we could croud, with colours flying, whilst the drums and trumpets animated us to battle.' The *Na Tron Menya* and the *Saratov* put three Turks out of action before a change of wind direction made them vulnerable to galley attack, but then Elphinstone attacked with explosive shells. The Turks withdrew into Nafplio. Although Elphinstone had had to fire on his own ships to encourage the reluctant commanders into the fray, he thought that the ordinary sailors 'fearless of danger . . . fought at their guns like lions'. On the following day, after another attack ending with a bombardment of the port, he sailed off to rejoin the main fleet.

On 3 July the Russians tracked down the main Turkish fleet to the bay of Çesme, opposite the hilly island of Chios, where some sixteen ships of the line with a large number of smaller vessels were anchored in three lines. At nine on the morning of the 5th Elphinstone went aboard Orlov's flagship to propose his plan of attack but found to his surprise that everything had been already decided: that the Russians would attack from the south, with Spiridov having the honour of leading the van, followed by Orlov and Greig in the centre, and with Elphinstone's squadron bringing up the rear. Elphinstone did not like this but Orlov was adamant, and the Orkneyman had grumpily to agree to obey orders, although he made it clear he thought the whole venture 'too uncertain for him to risque his reputation upon'.

At noon Orlov hoisted the red flag to signal the attack. The Russian ships ranged up and formed their battle line, gliding northwards alongside the enemy. Some of the Russian ships had difficulty in maintaining their position, and left and rejoined the line as the exchange of broadsides thundered across the sea. At one point the *Sv. Evstafii*, Spiridov's flagship, was fired on in error by Orlov's flagship, *Trech Ierarchov*, and then sailed into a fierce, close-range cannoning with the Turkish battleship *Real Mustafa*. The Turk's mainmast fell on the Russian's deck, and both ships blew up as fire took hold on them. Spiridov had already transferred to another ship before this happened. After over two hours of fighting, the Turkish fleet cut their cables and retreated into the bay to adopt a defensive battle line.

On the following day, the Russians subjected the ships and the shore to a bombardment but it must have been clear that something more effective would be needed to overcome them. Greig now masterminded a devastating blow to the Turks. Shortly after midnight on the 7th, he hoisted his broad pennant aboard the *Ratislav* to lead the *Netromena* and the *Europa* into the jaws of the bay, taking on the guns of the batteries and covering the advance of fireships. The *Authentic Narrative*, a near contemporary account of the event, says there were three of these, prepared from commandeered Greek boats, but the map in the same book plainly states there were four, two of which did not go in as the Russian officers were 'dead Drunk'. The largest of the fireships was commanded by Lieutenant Robert Dugdale. As it neared its target at the north end of the Turkish line, Dugdale's crew deserted him, either because they misunderstood their orders or because they panicked – they 'jumped into the boat and rowed away as fast as they could . . . whilst [the fireship] was going with all her sails set down the enemy'. Dugdale carried on alone until he was sure his doomed vessel would reach its target, 'fired a pistol into the train [the gunpowder], stayed to see it take fire, then boldly leaped into the sea and was fortunately taken up by a Greek boat (that was passing among the ships) just as he was sinking with fatigue.' In his understandable haste, he had fired too soon, and his fireship drifted ashore 'to little purpose'. In the second fireship, Lieutenant Thomas Mackenzie's crew stayed with him until the right moment. They abandoned the burning vessel to sail down on the southern end of the Turkish line, where it caused a 'conflagration, which soon raged with irresistible fury'. In the crowded anchorage the fire spread, provoking the author of the *Authentic Narrative* to write: 'A fleet consisting upwards of one hundred sail, almost in one general blaze, presented a picture of distress and horror, dreadfully sublime.' The damage to the Turkish navy was irrecoverable.

Catherine II heaped honours upon Orlov, although he was honest enough to admit privately that he owed everything to Greig, who was now promoted to rear-admiral. Elphinstone boiled with resentment at being overlooked – he had proposed a combined operation 'to pass the Dardanelles and burn Constantinople, and should now think myself morally certain of success', which had been rejected – and in 1771 he left the Russian service to return to the Royal Navy. The discreet Greig kept his thoughts to himself and prospered in Orlov's good books. In 1775 he became vice-admiral and was placed in command of the Kronstadt base; various honours and decorations also came his way and Catherine dined aboard his flagship after a fleet review. Greig oversaw many improvements to the main Baltic base and the fleet, but, predictably, his use of foreign experts provoked grumbling.

In 1788 other British officers in the Russian service persuaded him to support them in an effort to prevent John Paul Jones being promoted to rear-admiral. Jones had been born a Scot before emigrating to the Americas as a teenager and thereafter making a considerable name for himself in the American navy in the War of Independence, defeating the Royal Navy frigate HMS *Serapis* off Flamborough Head and at one point threatening to bombard Leith. In 1788 he joined the Russian navy. The ever-tactful Greig changed his mind over opposition to Jones's promotion, and Jones did become a rear-admiral and served in the Black Sea in June of the same year before he left the service.

War broke out in 1788 with Sweden again and in this conflict Greig played a leading part. His fleet blocked the Swedes in the Gulf of Finland and fought them off Högland on 17 July. The engagement was indecisive, with roughly equal losses on both sides, but the thwarting of the enemy's ambition to wipe out the Baltic fleet and to descend on St Petersburg determined the strategic outcome was in Russia's favour. For the rest of the summer and autumn Greig kept the Swedish ships bottled up in Sveaborg, at the entrance to Helsinki harbour, until in early October he fell ill aboard his flagship, the *Rotislav*, and died. Catherine wept for the loss and gave her rear-admiral a state funeral in Reval (now Tallinn). His son Alexis Samuilovich Greig became an admiral in the Russian navy.

EIGHTEEN

———◆•✖•◆———

'Oh woe unto these cruell wars in low Germanie'

T HE CASTLE OF Skokloster, built by Field Marshal Carl
Gustav Wrangel in the mid-seventeenth century to show off
his wealth and to house the booty and collections of objects he had
amassed during the wars in Europe, stands beside Lake Mälaren in the
rolling Swedish countryside some twenty miles north of Stockholm.
One of the first things to greet the visitor ascending the stone steps
from the courtyard to the first floor is an almost life-size figure of a
man painted on the inner face of a square pillar. Its colour and its
exuberance are a surprise. It is an image of David Drummond. Then
the visitor notices that there are figures limned on all the pillars – a
gallery of notables, among them two other Scots, Patrick Ruthven and
James King, according to the captions all as they were in 1623. The
figures comprise one of the tangible reminders of the presence of the
Scottish soldier of fortune in Europe.[1]

There are also many more concrete mementoes and traces of the
Scots' presence that survive in documents: in the words *Die Schotten*
inscribed beside phalanxes of pikemen and musketeers in an image
of the battle of Nördlingen; in the outlandish figures depicted in the
pamphlets or *Flugblätter* – literally flyleaves – that poured from
German presses during the Thirty Years War; in the clumsy signature
of Sir Alexander Leslie on a memo about the quartering of troops that
survives in the Stralsund archives; in the lists of soldiers in the
Krigsarkivet in Stockholm; in the entries in dictionaries of biography
in several countries; in place-names such as Keithstrasse in Berlin; and
in the tomb of Lord James Douglas in the Church of St Germain-des-
Prés in Paris.

According to one source, over thirty-five noble families in Sweden can trace ancestry back to Scottish mercenaries.[2] Several French noble families do likewise.[3] Descendants of one branch of the Spens family became ennobled as *Reichsfreiherr* in Bohemia and another married into a family in France.[4] The Polish Seym conferred nobility on thirteen Scots after the war with Russia in the 1660s.[5] More intriguingly, the town of Gurro in northern Italy is said to be home to descendants of the Scots survivors of the battle of Pavia in 1525, when the French army was defeated.[6] Some Italian families claim descent from Scottish troops under the command of Robertson of Strowan, who fought for Charles VIII of France in the late 1480s.[7] When he was researching for his book *Scottish Exodus* (Edinburgh, 2005), on the diaspora of Clan Macleod, Dr James Hunter met in Poland members of a Machlejd family, whose forebear was a Macleod who left Skye to fight for Gustavus Adolphus in the 1620s, survived, prospered and stayed in central Europe. Other Macleods went to France and the Netherlands. Their story must have been paralleled hundreds of times by people from other clans and kindreds whose descendants have become absorbed into the societies where they ended up. In the Low Countries during the period of the Thirty Years War 1,867 Scots soldiers appear in marriage contracts, one third to women with Scottish names and the rest to women with Dutch, English, German, French or Irish names.[8]

Memories of the mercenaries' experiences at home are now only patchy, although at the time of, for example, the Thirty Years War, the constant movement of people across the North Sea kept relatives quite well informed.[9] Apart from letters, printed news in the form of such publications as the *Swedish Intelligencer*, and books, there must have been in circulation a rich fund of anecdotes and stories from veterans, only a fraction of which found its way onto paper. There is one striking instance recorded by James Gordon, the minister of Rothiemay. In the winter of 1637–38, he noted, people heard drums being beaten on the hill of Dunecht, an omen of ill things to come: 'thes who had been trained up much of their lyves abroad in the German warres, affirmed that they could perfectly, by their hearing, discerne the marches upon the drumme, of severall forraine nationes of Europe, such as Frensh, Dutch, Danes, etc.' In regard to spectral noises heard near the Loch of Skene, Gordon went on: 'Some gentlemen of knowne integritye and truth, affirmed that . . . they heard as perfect shott of cannon goe off as ever they heard at the Battell of Nordlingen wher themselves, some yeares befor, had been present.'[10]

We might hope for some reflection of the mercenaries' experience to appear in folk songs and ballads. In these we can expect to hear the voices of the women, the wives, mothers, sisters and lovers left at home, who had to cope in a society deprived of many of its young, active males. Few songs seem to have survived four centuries with such traces, perhaps because, apart from a few masterpieces of the ballad tradition, words become changed through the ages better to suit the times. In the Greig–Duncan Collection (Aberdeen, 1981) of folksongs, the many versions of 'High Germany' suggest ideas, if not actual lines, that could date from the early 1600s. In *The Scots in Germany*, Th. Fischer quotes from two ballads without giving more detail about the sources; they seem also to belong to the 'High Germany' stable, and one goes:

> He's brave as brave can be;
> He wad rather fa' than flee;
> But his llife is dear to me,
> Send him hame, send him hame.
>
> Your love ne'er learnt to flee
> But he fell in Germanie;
> Fighting brave for loyaltie:
> Mournfu' dame, mournfu' dame!

A second song has the verse:

> Oh woe unto these cruell wars
> That ever they began!
> For they have reft my native isle
> Of many a pretty man.
>
> First they took my brothers twain
> Then wiled my love frae me:
> Oh woe unto these cruell wars
> In low Germanie.

The European experience, if one may summarise it in this phrase, left its mark on instrumental music. The 'Scots March', to whose stirring drum rhythms Robert Monro and his comrades often rallied, survives and can be found in John Purser's *Scotland's Music* (Edinburgh, 1992).[11] The pipe tune 'Dumbarton's Drums' is one of the oldest regimental marches and takes its name from the regimental commander Lord George Douglas, who was created Earl of Dumbarton in 1675.[12] In 1684 Dumbarton's Regiment, which had joined the British establishment fourteen years before, was redesignated His Majesty's Royal Regiment of Foot (the Royal Scots).

Some direct memories survived locally for quite some time. James Grant recalls in his book of 1851 how an octogenarian in Athelstaneford pointed out Sir John Hepburn's birthplace to him when he visited the village and said he had often heard his forebears speak of the man who had become a marshal of France. The description of Athelstaneford in the *Statistical Account of Scotland* (1794) devotes considerable space to Hepburn. The account of Inverkeithing in the same publication contains a few lines on Samuel Greig: 'the famous Admiral Greig was a native of this town, was educated under the present schoolmaster'. On the other hand, the clerical author of the description of the parish of Marnoch in Banffshire wrote gloomily that the place had produced no one of note except an Alexander Gordon who had become a major general in the army of Peter the Great; this is the Alexander Gordon who arrived in Moscow in 1696, and clearly Alexander Leslie of Auchintoul, who hailed from the same airt, had been forgotten or at least not considered worth the mention little more than a century after his death.

The German wars produced one remarkable home-grown novelist: Hans Jakob Christoph von Grimmelshausen. Born probably in 1621 into a baker's family in the small town of Gelnhausen, von Grimmelshausen was in Hanau during Sir James Ramsay's governorship in 1634 and later served as a musketeer. In his later life he took to writing fiction – fantastic, picaresque, madcap novels, the like of which had hardly been done before, as if this were the only way his art could handle the horrors he had seen – and in the most famous of these, entitled *Simplicius Simplicissimus*, usually translated as 'Adventures of a Simpleton', some of the action is set in Hanau and Ramsay appears as a character.[13] Friedrich Schiller takes a few liberties with historical fact in his drama on the death of Wallenstein, *Wallensteins Tod*, although he was well aware of the true course of the events of which he wrote; for example, he writes out Walter Leslie but keeps John Gordon and Walter Butler as the leading assassins, and he has 'Deveroux' and 'Macdonald' as two more plotters.

Sir Walter Scott turned on at least two occasions to the mercenary experience for material for his novels – in *Quentin Durward* and *A Legend of the Wars of Montrose*. In the former, set in the late fifteenth century in the reign of Louis XI, the eponymous hero travels to France to meet his uncle Ludovic Lesly, a member of the Garde Ecossais. In the second novel, Scott created such an enduring portrait of the seventeenth-century soldier of fortune in the character Dugald Dalgetty that Victorian popular historians used the fictional Dalgetty as a way of summing up the historical protagonists in their own accounts. Scott coins for Dalgetty a camp song from the wars:

> When cannons are roaring and colours are flying
> The lads that seek honour must never fear dying;
> Then, stout cavaliers, let us toil our brave trade in,
> And fight for the Gospel and bold king of Sweden.

Scott based the character on an old soldier he knew as a boy and successfully grafted onto him material about the Thirty Years War derived from Robert Monro's memoir.[14]

James Hogg also used a mercenary as a character in *Altrive Tales: The Adventures of Captain John Lochy, written by himself*, first published in 1832. The hero, Lochy, fights in Marlborough's army but quits British service to seek his fortune elsewhere, and ends up in the Swedish army of Karl XII in his wars against Russia in 1707–09. At one point, the Swedish king says to Lochy 'Ha, Lochy, glad to see you again . . . True Scots gentleman. Thought of making you governor of Smolensk.' Daniel Defoe drew on the experiences of soldiers in some of his fiction, for example in *The Memoirs of Major Alexander Ramkins*, published in 1719, which purports to have been written by 'a Highland officer now in prison at Avignon', and G.A. Henty (1832–1902) turned out in the late Victorian period a slew of historical adventure novels, some of which also are based on the activities of mercenaries in Europe. Some films have imaginatively tried to evoke the worlds covered in the book, although none makes reference to the Scots contribution; see, for example, the 1967 Czech film *Valley of the Bees*, about the Teutonic Knights, and the 1971 UK/US production *The Last Valley*, about the Thirty Years War.

While researching this book, I heard of a belief that the Scots always fought on the right wing of the armies in which they served so that they would not encounter each other in battle. Once, when the system broke down, according to this tale, the Scots who found themselves facing each other turned on their respective armies. This is clearly a myth but it carries in it perhaps an echo of a memory of service overseas, blended with the tradition that certain clans always claimed to fight on the right wing, the place of honour, in the battle line.[15] The memory of Gustavus Adolphus as the defender of the Protestant cause persisted in the Highlands into relatively recent times: a Cuthbert of Castlehill, Inverness, who fought at Lützen, had a descendant by marriage four generations later named Gustavus Aird (1752–1835) whose son was in turn called Gustavus and, as a Free Church minister in Creich, achieved some lasting fame for his defence of parishioners during the Clearances in Easter Ross in the 1850s.[16] A shoemaker buried in 1866 at Creich bore the name Gustavus Munro; during his lifetime he was always known as Havie and he played a key role in a struggle by the congregation to reject a minister they did not wish foisted upon them.

I began this book with an account of the 1612 incident in which a mercenary force bound for Sweden was ambushed and massacred in Norway. In contrast with much of the story of the mercenaries this episode is very well remembered in Norway and has been the inspiration behind several works of art and pieces of folklore. Two artists interested in traditional Norwegian life and landscapes, Adolf Tidemand (1814–76) and Marten Müller (1828–1911), collaborated on a dramatic depiction of the landing of the mercenaries in Romsdal-fjord. The picture has clansmen and a piper, and a fleet of ships with set sails, against the backdrop of mountains. Another painting, *Strømdal* by the artist Georg Fredrik (1856–1914), shows the Norwegian bonder at the moment of their assault. Cut logs tumble down on the line of Scots crowded along a narrow path, with the valley floor and the river far below. The mercenaries wear kilts and plaids and several have black bonnets with a red band, and they defend themselves with long muskets. Among them is a figure meant to be George Sinclair: he has a trimmed, red beard and a black hat with a white plume, and he fires a pistol. It is a fine, dramatic, narrative scene but it owes more to the romanticism of 1887 than to historical fact.

Sinclair was not of course the leader of the contingent but for obscure reasons he has become the tragic hero – in the Kringen area he outranks Peer Gynt as a tourist draw, and the roadside inn at Kvam is named after him. Sinclair's memorial stone, which has been moved at least twice in its existence, is matched with a monument by Kristen Holbø (1869–1953) depicting a woman blowing on a horn. Her name is Prillar Guri and she has become an essential part of the Sinclair legend, for sounding a warning of the mercenaries' approach on her goat horn. This part of the story could have a basis in fact, but this cannot be said of the mermaid that appears in the version told in the ballad composed by Edvard Storm (1742–94), a poem that became a standard item in the Norwegian school curriculum. 'Hr Sinklar drog over salten hav' has been translated into English three times; that in Calder's history of Caithness begins 'To Norway Sinclair steered his course/ Across the salt sea wave.' The mermaid rises from the sea to warn Sinclair to turn back, advice he of course spurns. Another memory of the incident is preserved in the fact that a sword with a certain type of basket hilt, claimed by tradition to have been introduced to Norway by the 1612 mercenaries, is called a *Sinclairsabler* or Sinclair sabre. The national dress of Norwegian women includes a type of decorated waistcoat – *bunader* – that varies from region to region; in Gudbrandsdalen there occurs a type of striped pattern that some claim owes itself partly at least to the tartan worn by the mercenaries. This is a charming notion but it begs the question of the extent of the use of tartan among the mercenaries. It must also be accepted that striped patterns akin to tartan can arise indigenously in any culture, although that does not rule out the possibility that some of the Scots who went to their deaths at the heels of Ramsay, Hay and Sinclair in 1612 were indeed wearing the designs so strongly associated now with their native land.

The gradual emergence of Britain's overseas empire in the second half of the eighteenth century and the growing need for soldiers to fight in colonial wars diverted Scottish eyes from Europe to territories further afield. With this trend came a gradual forgetting of what had gone before – that, in the seventeenth century, the Scots had a reputation in Europe as fighting men. It is not a reputation that is entirely enviable, although it has persisted in slightly different contexts to create a pride with a dark side. It is fine to be known as men to be relied on in a crisis but it also means the Scot became a man to be exploited when soldiers were needed and in the long run 'no great mischief if they fall', the words used of Highland soldiers by Major James Wolfe when clansmen were recruited to the British army after Culloden.[17] Fortunately, we also thrived in other walks of life – as merchants and scholars – and that aspect of our history also deserves to be remembered and celebrated. We have always crossed the North Sea to share in the common history of Europe, and by no means only as swordsmen for hire.

Notes and references

In writing this book I have drawn on information in a very wide range of sources. In the following notes only the main sources are listed, with some footnotes and suggestions for further reading. Information about many individuals is available on the website edited by Dr Steve Murdoch and Dr Alexia Grosjean at www. st-andrews. ac.uk/history/ ssne. Another invaluable source for brief biographies of many worthies is the *Dictionary of National Biography*.

The following abbreviations are used:
DNB – *Dictionary of National Biography*
RPCS – Register of the Privy Council of Scotland
SHS – Scottish History Society

O N E   *'God knoweth it greeved me much'*
1. The massacre of Scots mercenaries at Kringen in 1612 is mentioned briefly in Calder, 1887, and treated in full in Michell, 1886. The quotes from letters and documents are taken from Michell's book. A Norwegian translation of the latter was published by Jon Selfors in 1997.
2. RPCS, IX, 1610–13.

T W O   *'bandis of men of weare'*
1. Roberts, 1992.
2. Anderson, 2000.
3. Monro, 1637.
4. Ibid.
5. Ferguson, 1899.

6. *Letters and State Papers.*
7. I am grateful to Trevor Royle for this figure. For the background see his recent work *The Flowers of the Forest: Scotland and the Great War*, Edinburgh, 2006.
8. RPCS, II, 1569–78.
9. RPCS, IV, 1585–92.
10. Grant, 1851. There may be some truth in this claim as the Setons of Meldrum had acquired lands in the Garioch that had formerly been in the hands of the Kings; see Morison, 1905.
11. Monro, 1637.
12. Turner, 1829.
13. Skelton and Bulloch, 1912.
14. Forbes, 1864.
15. RPCS, XII, 1619–22.
16. RPCS, 2nd series, VII, 1638–43.
17. RPCS, 2nd series, II, 1627–28.
18. RPCS, 2nd series, VII, 1638–43.
19. RPCS, IX, 1610–13.
20. Quoted in Murdoch, 2001, from Spalding Club, *Selections . . . Kirk Session, Presbytery and Synod of Aberdeen*, Aberdeen, 1846.
21. Fraser, 1892.
22. Monro, 1637.
23. *Spalding Club Miscellany*, 1852. See also Glozier, 2000.
24. RPCS, 2nd series, I, 1625–27.
25. RPCS, 2nd series, VII, 1638–43.
26. RPCS, 2nd series, II, 1627–28.
27. Fraser, 1905.
28. Forbes, 1864.
29. Gordon, 1841.
30. Quoted in Fraser, 1873.
31. Quoted in Fallon, 1972.
32. RPCS, IV, 1585–92.
33. Ferguson, 1899.
34. Israel, 1995.
35. Fraser, 1889.
36. Grant, 1851.
37. Brzezinski, 1991, makes a good case for the tartan-clad soldiers being Irish members of Hamilton's levy, whereas most Scottish authors accept they are Highlanders. It is worth bearing in mind that in 1631 Mackay's Regiment was a long way from Stettin.
38. Fraser, 1873.
39. Brzezinski, 1991.

40. Fischer, 1902.
41. *Highland Papers*, Vol 1 (SHS).
42. RPCS, I, 1545–69.
43. There are many sources for information about weapons and armour in this period. I have drawn mainly on Caldwell 1979, 1981; Held 1959; Kellie 1627; Kelvin 1996; Wallace 1970; Whitelaw 1977. Barbour's *The Bruce*, Bk 17, lines 250–1.
45. Monro, 1637.
46. RPCS, IV, 1585–92.

THREE *'these proude Scottes'*

1. Worthington, 2004. The date for the first appearance of the surname Douglas is in GF Black, *The Surnames of Scotland*, New York, 1946 (reissued Edinburgh, 1993).
2. Skelton and Bulloch, 1912. None of the sources agree on the name of the archer who shot Richard and the evidence for it being a Gordon is extremely tenuous.
3. Ditchburn, 2000. See also *The Knights of St John of Jerusalem in Scotland*, I.B. Cowan, P.H.R. Mackay, A. Macquarrie (eds.), Edinburgh, 1983.
4. An excellent account of the Teutonic Knights is Eric Christiansen, *The Northern Crusades*, London, 1997. Scots who joined the Teutonic Knights are mentioned in Fischer, 1903 and Ditchburn, 2000.
5. Fischer, 1902, 1903.
6. Maxwell, 1902.
7. Macdonald, 1896.
8. Abercromby, 1715.
9. Monstrelet quoted in Hill Burton, 1864.
10. Quoted in Seward, 2003.
11. The text of a tablet commemorating the Douglases in Tours Cathedral is given in Wood, 1989.
12. There are many sources of information about the Garde Ecossais. See, for example, Wood, 1989.
13. *Inventaire Chronologique des Documents Relatifs à l'Histoire d'Ecosse conservés aux Archives du Royaume à Paris*, Edinburgh, 1839 (Abbotsford Club).
14. RPCS, II, 1569–78.
15. Skelton and Bulloch, 1912.
16. RPCS, I, 1545–69.

FOUR *'mony zoung and valzeand men'*

1. Fischer, 1907.
2. RPCS, XIV, 1545–1625.
3. RPCS, I, 1545–69.

4. RPCS, XIV, 1545–1625.
5. RPCS, II, 1569–78.
6. Fischer, 1907.
7. The main source for this account of Ruthven's experiences is Dow, 1965, with supplementary material from Fischer, 1907.
8. Dow states that Moncrieff was to survive his experience and return to Scotland to inherit his title and the family estates but he may be mistaken here, confusing Moncrieff with his son of the same name. According to *Burke's Landed Gentry*, William Moncrieff was the eldest son of the tenth laird, who had to flee from Scotland for joining the opposition to Mary, Queen of Scots, raised a regiment and was never heard of again after the plot to overthrow John III. The title passed to his eldest son, also William, on the death of tenth laird in 1579.
9. It is Dow's opinion that the Scots who fled to safety among the Russians were put to death.

F I V E   *'university of war'*

The main sources for this chapter are given below. Another source of information on the Scots presence in the Dutch wars is H. Dunthorne, 'Scots in the Wars of the Low Countries, 1572–1648' in *Scotland and the Low Countries 1124–1994*, ed. G. Simpson, Edinburgh, 1996. Dunthorne suggests Scots made up approximately 5 per cent of the Dutch army between 1572 and 1648. Ferguson's work focuses more on the Scots Brigade in the eighteenth century.

1. RPCS, II, 1569–78.
2. Balfour has an entry in the *Biographisch Woordenboek der Nederlanden*, Amsterdam, 1969, but is partly confused with his half-brother Barthold. Other information on the Balfour family background is provided by Ferguson, 1899.
3. Grimeston published his history of the Netherlands in 1627, and many of the quotes in this chapter are taken from his work. He based his account on two contemporary sources: Emanuel van Meteren's *Historia belgica*, 1598, and JF le Petit's *Grande chronique de Hollande*, 1601.
4. Ibid.
5. RPCS, II, 1569–78.
6. Ferguson, 1899.
7. Grimeston, 1627.
8. Ferguson, 1899.
9. RPCS, II, 1569–78.
10. Meteren, quoted in Ferguson, 1899.

11. Worthington, 2004 has more information on Semple's career in the context of a detailed consideration of Scots in Habsburg service.
12. Tayler, 1937.
13. Ferguson, 1899.
14. Ibid.
15. Grimeston, 1627.
16. A detailed account of the Battle of Niuewpoort can be found in van der Hoeven, 1998. The Scottish officers who fell in Ernest's desperate attempt to stop the Spanish advance were captains Arthur Stewart, John Kilpatrick, John Mitchell, Hugh Nisbet and John Strachan. Two others – Robert Barclay and Andrew Murray – were taken prisoner and murdered; both men and William Edmond have entries in the *Biographisch Woordenboek der Nederlanden*, 1969. Sergeant-Major Brogh and captains Caddel, Henderson and Ker escaped to Fort Albert with Edmond.
17. A contemporary account of the siege of Ostend exists in Special Collections, Glasgow University Library. Entitled *Belägerung der Statt Ostende*, it was published in 1604–05, probably in Cologne.
18. Grimeston, 1627.
19. RPCS, VI, 1599–1604.

SIX   *'a Company of pedeling knaves'*

1. There are many books dealing with the Scottish–Polish connection. See, for example, Borowy, 1941; Bulloch, 1932; Fischer, 1903; Frost, 2001; Seliga, 1969; Steuart, 1915.
2. Steuart, 1915.
3. Chamberlayne, quoted in Frost, 2001.
4. *Letters and State Papers*, 1838. The respectable Scots burgesses in Danzig were afraid that continued immigration from Scotland would lead to local magistrates classifying them 'with Jewes and Infidellis'.
5. Cieslak and Biernat, 1995.
6. The website www. jasinski.co.uk has much detail about Polish warfare in the sixteenth and seventeenth centuries. Brzezinski, 1988 provides detailed information about Polish forces in this period.
7. RPCS, II, 1569–78.
8. Fischer, 1903.
9. Frost, 2001.
10. *Sir Jerome Horsey His Travells*, in Bond, 1856.
11. Giles Fletcher, *Of the Russe Commonwealth*, in Bond, 1856.
12. This must have been the expedition led by Arthur Pett and Charles Jackman that sailed from England in July 1580. They penetrated the Arctic waters to the east of Novaya Zemblya.

13. Quoted in Steuart, 1915.
14. Fowler, 1656. Fowler includes in his history details of a plot hatched by Sigismund's advisers to assassinate Duke Karl. The plan was to have an actor with a sword kill the duke while he watched a play. It came to nothing when Karl did not attend the performance, but one wonders whether or not Shakespeare was aware of this when he wrote *Hamlet*.
15. Steuart, 1915.
16. RPCS, VII, 1604–07.
17. Steuart, 1913.

SEVEN   *'Your Majesty will need soldiers'*

1. Quoted in Frost, 2001.
2. Information on the Spens family can be found in *Burke's Landed Gentry of Scotland*. Several members became soldiers of fortune in Europe. For example, one Patrick de Spens who served in the Garde Ecossais married into French aristocracy who had a chateau in Gascony; and another Spens was ennobled in Silesia in the seventeenth century.
3. Fischer, 1907.
4. Macray, 1868.
5. Fallon, 1972.
6. In March 1610, the Privy Council dealt with the case of failure to reimburse recruitment for Sweden by Captains Johnne Borthuik and Andro Rentoun; the records mention 300 rex dollars (riksdaler) as the shipping cost and 4,000 merks as the approximate recruitment cost. In April 1627 the Earl of Nithsdale was granted £4,000 sterling to raise 3,000 men for Denmark (RPCS, 2nd series, I, 1625–27). Both of these instances suggest recruitment cost around £10 Scots per man, or a little under £1 sterling.
7. As well as Cockburn, the officers in the delegation were John Wauchop, Hugo Cochrane, George Douglas, Daniel Rogers, Robert Kinnaird, William Horne and Patrick Ruthven. They are listed in Latinised versions of their names in Fischer, 1907.
8. RPCS, VIII, 1607–10.
9. Napier, 1856.
10. The comment was made by the chaplain Robert Baillie and is quoted in Terry, 1899.
11. Fischer, 1907, gives a partial muster roll for this regiment.
12. Ibid.
13. Grosjean, 2003.
14. Quoted in Archibald Duncan, 'The Diplomatic Correspondence of Sir James Spence', Unpub MS, Uppsala University.

15. Brzezinski, 1991 and 1993, gives a detailed account of the Swedish army.
16. Monro, 1637.
17. Haythornthwaite, 1992.
18. RPCS, XIII, 1622–25.

EIGHT *'sure men hardy and resolute'*

1. For a history of the Habsburgs, see Wheatcroft, 1995.
2. The governors and the secretary landed in a midden and survived their plunge. There are many accounts of the incident and the war that followed. See Wedgwood, 1938, for one of the liveliest, and Bonney, 2002, for one of the most succinct.
3. William Crosse in Grimeston, 1627.
4. Ferguson, 1899.
5. Worthington, 2004; Polišensky in Murdoch, 2001.
6. Quoted in Worthington, 2004.
7. *Original Letters,* 1851.
8. Andrew Gray may have come from the North-East. In his biography of Sir John Hepburn, James Grant says Gray was a Catholic who had commanded Huntly's artillery at the battle at Glenlivet on 3 October 1594 and had been labelled a traitor by the General Assembly. If this was the same man, he had two good reasons to leave Scotland for Europe.
9. RPCS, XII, 1619–22.
10. Grant, 1851.
11. *A Most True Relation . . ., 1620.*
12. Crosse in Grimeston, 1627.
13. Wedgewood, 1938. Polišensky does not mention this but Pursell and Crosse say Mansfeld stayed loyal. He couldn't have done much anyway.
14. Benger, 1825.
15. See Anon, *Certaine Letters declaring in part the Passage of Affaires in the Palatinate from September of this present moneth of April,* Amsterdam, 1621. These letters were written by an unknown Englishman and note Gray's regiment 'did in three assaults repulse the enemie bravely'.
16. Crosse in Grimeston, 1627.
17. The translation is by Polišensky, who says the original is in bizarre Italian.
18. RPCS, XIII, 1622–25.
19. Crosse, who also lists nine regiments in the service of the Dutch in 1626 as being commanded by English officers: Vere, Viscount Wimbledon, Sir Charles Morgan, Sir Edward Harwood, the Earl of Essex, Sir John Burlacie, Sir James Leueston, Lord Willoughbie and Colonel Brague, as well as the Scottish regiment under Sir Francis Henderson.

20. Quoted in Ferguson, 1899.
21. Crosse in Grimeston, 1627.
22. Ibid.
23. Ibid.
24. The levy agreement between Sir James Spens and Alexander Hamilton is quoted in Fraser, 1889.
25. In his panegyric in praise of the Scots soldiers, Sir Thomas Urquhart of Cromarty mentions Sir Andrew Gray and Sir John Seatoun as being 'colonels under the pay of' Louis XIII of France. See Jack and Lyall, 1983.

N I N E   *'a rude and ignorant Souldier'*

1. RPCS, 2nd series, I, 1625–27.
2. Mackay, 1906.
3. Tayler, 1937.
4. RPCS, 2nd series, I, 1625–27.
5. Mackenzie, 1894.
6. Mackenzie, 1898.
7. Robert Monro uses the Old Style calendar for dates. Here they have been converted to New Style dates by adding ten days.
8. Monro probably means German rather than English miles, a considerably longer distance than the bare figure would suggest. A German mile was reckoned to equal 4.25 English miles.
9. Fraser, 1873.
10. Goodrick, 1908.
11. Crosse, in Grimeston, 1627, gives Serato as the site of Mansfeld's death; other authors claim the name of the place is unknown. Sydnam Poyntz stuck with Mansfeld until the remnants of the army reached Belgrade. Here Poyntz claims to have been enslaved by the Turks, but he later escaped.
12. Fraser, 1873.
13. RPCS, 2nd series, I, 1625–27; II, 1627–28.
14. Protestant Huguenots were besieged in the strongly fortified port of La Rochelle in 1628.
15. Mackay, 1906.
16. RPCS, 2nd series, II, 1627–28.
17. Watson, 1938, gives the story of the would-be saboteur.

T E N   *'new conditions from a new Master'*

1. RPCS, 2nd series, II, 1627–28.
2. RPCS, 2nd series, III, 1629–30.
3. Grosjean in Murdoch, 2001.

4. The surviving muster rolls for the Swedish forces are stored in Krigsakivet, Stockholm.
5. Fischer, 1907.
6. Brzezinski, 1991.
7. For the full background of the diplomatic and political situation the reader is referred to general histories of the Thirty Years War.
8. Some authors say that Monro and his comrades were wrecked on the island of Rügen, some 100 miles west of Rügenwalde, but it is clear from his narrative that this could not be the case and obviously the placenames have become confused.
9. According to Mackenzie, 1898, Robert Monro's first wife was the Irishwoman Jean Maver. He mentions her only once in his memoir.
10. *Swedish Intelligencer*, 1632.

ELEVEN   *'betwixt the Devill and the deepe Sea'*

1. Burnet, 1677.
2. RPCS, 2nd series, IV, 1630–32.
3. This brought to an end Reay's involvement in supplying soldiers to Europe. He was still being held in London when Gustavus Adolphus fell at the battle of Lützen and he was never able to recover the large sums he had spent on recruitment. To protect his estate he had to hand it on to his son in September 1637 (Mackay, 1906).
4. Much of the Marquis of Hamilton's correspondence at this time is given in Fraser, 1890.
5. *Swedish Intelligencer*, 1633.
6. Terry, 1899.
7. Burnet, 1677.
8. Goodrick, 1908.
9. Ferguson, 1899.
10. RPCS, III, 1578–85.
11. Monro, 1637.
12. Burnet, 1677.

TWELVE   *'nothing els but fire and smoke'*

1. Roeck, 1991.
2. Benger, 1825.
3. Fowler, 1656.
4. Grant gets the wording of Hepburn's remark from Schiller's history of the Thirty Years War. It sounds almost too theatrical to be literally accurate.
5. Turner, 1829.
6. Burnet, 1677. Subsequent quotes from King Charles are also from this source.

7. Monro, 1637.
8. For a recent, detailed account of the battle see Brzezinski, 2001.
9. Henderson survived the battle and at some point afterwards, probably in 1633, switched sides to Habsburg service. He was Catholic and this may have had something to do with his decision. For details of his varied and intriguing later career, see his entry on the Scotland Scandinavian and Northern Europe, 1580–1707 website (www.st-andrews.ac.uk/history) (SSNE ID Ref 53).

THIRTEEN   *'that bloodie monster of warre'*

1. Terry, 1899.
2. RPCS, 2nd series, V, 1633–35.
3. Fraser, 1892.
4. Terry, 1899.
5. At least according to Skelton and Bulloch. Other claims have been made for the details of Gordon's death.
6. Worthington, 2004.
7. RPCS, 2nd series, IV, 1630–32.
8. Turner, 1829.
9. Information from Nördlingen Stadtarchiv.
10. Goodrick, 1908.
11. Fraser, 1883.
12. Fraser, 1890.
13. *Hanauer Geschichtsblätter*, 3–4, 1919.
14. Goodrick, 1908.
15. Terry, 1899.

FOURTEEN   *'vertews and valorous atchievements abrod'*

1. Grant says he was knighted by Charles, the DNB is less certain
2. The Privy Council had reluctantly to try to meet Charles I's demand for 2,000 men to aid the Huguenots who had taken refuge in La Rochelle. In the event the expedition was a disaster. Among the recruits were 100 Highland bowmen who were at sea in a storm in the English Channel when La Rochelle fell. The enemy drove them to Falmouth. Their commander threatened to take his starving men to the Isle of Wight if nothing were done to alleviate their plight.
3. Spalding, 1850.
4. RPCS, 2nd series, V, 1633–35. Grant says that Richelieu mentions Hepburn with 'admiration, respect and frequently affection' in his correspondence.
5. Grant has the piper story. It sounds romantic but it is perfectly feasible.
6. The memoirs of the duc d'Espernon, London, 1670, quoted in Grant.

7. Letter from Richelieu to La Valette, 20 July 1636, quoted in Fischer, 1902.

8. The first monument to Sir John Hepburn was destroyed during the French Revolution but another was put up in 1921 in the form of a memorial tablet. Wood, 1989, provides much more detail on Hepburn and other Scots in French service.

9. RPCS, 2nd series, VI, 1635–37.

10. Fotheringham, 1899.

11. RPCS, 2nd series, VI, 1635–37.

12. RPCS, 2nd series, VII, 1638–43.

13. *Acts of the Scottish Parliament*, V, 656.

14. Ibid, 701. The English ambassador in Paris listed the following Scots regiments in France in January 1643: Col. Douglas (2,000 men); Earl of Irvine's New Regt of Guards (4,500); Lord Gray (1,000); Lord Lundy (1,000); Col. Fullerton (1,000); Earl of Lothian (100). The editor of the study in which this is quoted says the list is erroneous and overstates the position. Fullerton and Lundy never had command of regiments, and the Earl of Lothian's appointment was never confirmed. See Fotheringham, 1899.

15. The figures are from information in the Museum of the Thirty Years War, Wittstock, and from Wedgewood, 1938.

16. Terry, 1917.

17. Fraser, 1892.

18. *The Hamilton Papers*, quoted in Grosjean, 2003.

19. Swedish 'feathers' are mentioned in Terry, 1917, but Brzezinski, 1991, shows how they have a much older pedigree albeit under different names.

20. Worthington, 2004.

21. Maidment, 1845.

22. Tayler, 1937.

23. William Fraser visited his homeland briefly in 1670 to see his old mother and his boyhood friends. These included James Fraser, the author of the Wardlaw Manuscript (Mackay, 1905), who also noted that William and Hugh Fraser 'yong Clunvacky' were the only two now alive from the 'gallant crew who ventered overseas with their cheefes sone [James Fraser of Lovat]'.

FIFTEEN   *'keen and fiery genius'*

1. Mitchell, 1907.

2. Fedosov, 1996, gives a comprehensive listing of Scots in Russia.

3. Urquhart gives this anecdote in *The Jewel*.

4. RPCS, 2nd series, V, 1633–35.

5. Steuart, 1915.

6. Quoted by Dukes in Murdoch, 2001.
7. Ibid.
8. Baron, 1967.
9. Derry, 1979.
10. Kirkton, quoted in Steuart, 1915.
11. Mackay, 1905.
12. Robertson, 1859.
13. Skelton and Bulloch, 1912.

SIXTEEN   *'where I might again begin my fortune'*

1. Napier, 1859.
2. Leslie, 1869.
3. James Keith kept a journal, part of which at least was published in 1843.
4. Steuart, 1915.
5. This version of the encounter with the Kirkcaldy bellringer's son is taken from Grant, 1890, where it is credited to *Memoirs and Papers of Sir Andrew Mitchell.* The bellringer's name seems to have been James Miller!
6. The quote is given in Thomas Carlyle's biography of Frederick the Great, 1858–65.
7. One of the Austrian commanders was the Baron Loudon, a descendant of Sir Matthew Campbell of Loudon in Ayrshire. Fischer, 1902, gives details of other Scots in the service of European armies at this time.

SEVENTEEN   *'We bore down upon them with all the sail we could croud'*

1. Mackay, 1905.
2. The siege of Candia, a Venetian colony, began in 1647 and lasted for twenty-two years. Soldiers from various parts of Europe were attracted there to help the defence against the Ottoman assault. The siege ended in 1669 with a treaty between Venice and the Turks. Hugh Mackay of Scourie fought there as a volunteer and won a medal.
3. Grosjean, 2003.
4. RPCS, XIV, Addenda.
5. Michell, 1886.
6. Quoted in Grosjean, 2003. Additional information from the Vasa Museum, Stockholm.
7. Bridge, 1909.
8. Rodger, 2004.
9. These words are attributed to the French diplomat, Chevalier de Corberon, quoted in Troyat, 1979.
10. *Authentic Narrative*, 1772. This book was 'Compiled from several Authentic Journals by an Officer on board the Russian Fleet', a person widely believed to have been John Elphinstone himself.

EIGHTEEN   *'Oh woe unto these cruell wars in low Germanie'*

1. There are many more individual stories we could have included in this book if the space permitted. Everyone has heard of Thomas Cochrane, the tenth Earl of Dundonald (1775–1860), whose exploits as a frigate captain in the Napoleonic period became the model for many later fictional naval heroes; after leaving the Royal Navy in disgrace, he commanded the navies of Chile, Brazil and Greece before being pardoned for misdemeanours at home and returning to sail again under the White Ensign. A later soldier of fortune was Ranald MacDonell: he fought for Spain in the Peninsular War, and later in Portugal until he was killed at Vila Pouca in January 1847. Second generation immigrants of Scots descent also made their mark: Jacques Macdonald, a French-born son of Jacobite emigrants, became one of Napoleon's field marshals.

2. G. Elgenstierna, *Svenska Adelns Ättartavlor,* Stockholm, 1925–36. While writing this book, I heard from a lady in England who, in researching her family tree, found that her forebears include a Scot called BelFrage who emigrated to Sweden in the seventeenth century and eventually was elevated to the Swedish aristocracy.

3. Glozier, 2000.

4. Burke's *Landed Gentry of Scotland.*

5. Frost, R. 'Scottish soldiers, Poland-Lithuania and the Thirty Years War', in Murdoch, 2001.

6. The claim is made in *The Lost Clan* (Edinburgh, 1974) by Lt.-Col. Gayre of Gayre and Nigg.

7. Abercromby, 1715.

8. Glozier, M. 'Scots in the French and Dutch armies during the Thirty Years War' in Murdoch, 2001.

9. Some families retain memories of individual incidents. For example, while this book was nearing completion, I heard from a Danish lady, Mrs Nina Pidcock, how Scots garrisoning the fortified manor house of Beldringe, west of Praestø in Denmark, were ousted by Swedish forces sometime in the period 1619–23.

10. Gordon, 1841.

11. It appears in *Elizabeth Rogers' Virginal Book* from the 1650s.

12. Murray, D. *Music of the Scottish Regiments*, Edinburgh, 1994.

13. The novel is available in English, translated by Walter Wallich (New York, 2002).

14. In Lockhart's biography of Sir Walter Scott, the first section, written by Scott himself, describes how, as a boy, he spent time with 'an old military veteran, Dalgetty by name, who had pitched his tent in that little village [Prestonpans], after all his campaigns, subsisting upon an

ensign's half-pay, though called by courtesy a Captain.' The real
Dalgetty's German wars were those of the mid to late 1700s.

15. I am grateful to Sinclair Dunnett, Inverness, for this information.

16. This information is given in an anonymous book called *The Genealogy of the Families of Douglas of Mulderg and Robertsons of Kindeace with Their Descendants*, Dingwall, 1895. I am grateful to Alastair Macleod for bringing this to my attention, and for telling me about Gustavus 'Havie' Munro.

17. It must be stated the Wolfe admired the Highland soldiers' courage and endurance.

Bibliography

Abercromby, P. *The Martial Atchievements of the Scots Nation.* Edinburgh, 1715

Anderson, M.S. *Europe in the Eighteenth Century, 1713–1789.* London, 2000

An Authentic Narrative of the Russian Expedition Against the Turks by Sea and Land. London, 1772

Baron, S.H. (ed.) *The Travels of Olearius in Seventeenth-century Russia.* Stanford, California, 1967 (originally published in 1647)

Benger, Miss *Memoirs of Elizabeth Stuart Queen of Bohemia.* London, 1825

Bond, E.A. (ed.) *Russia at the Close of the Sixteenth Century.* London, 1856 (Hakluyt Society)

Bonney, R. *The Thirty Years' War 1618–1648.* Oxford, 2002

Borowy, W. *Scots in Old Poland.* Edinburgh, 1941

Bower, W. *Scotichronicon.* Aberdeen, 1987–91. (Watt, D.E.R. ed.)

Bridge, A.G. (ed.) *History of the Russian Fleet during the Reign of Peter the Great by a Contemporary Englishman.* London, 1909

Brown, K. 'Reformation to Union, 1560–1707' in R.A. Houston and W.W.J. Knox (eds.) *The New Penguin History of Scotland.* London, 2001

Brzezinski, R. *Polish Armies, 1569–1696.* Oxford, 1987, (2 vols)

Brzezinski, R. *The Army of Gustavus Adolphus 1: Infantry.* Oxford, 1991

Brzezinski, R. *The Army of Gustavus Adolphus 2: Cavalry.* Oxford, 1991.

Brzezinski, R. *Lützen 1632: The Climax of the Thirty Years War.* Oxford, 2001

Bulloch, J.M. *The Gordons in Poland.* Peterhead, 1932

Burke's Landed Gentry of Great Britain, Vol I: The Kingdom of Scotland. 19th edn. London, 2001

Burnet, Gilbert. *The Memoires of the Lives and Actions of James and William Dukes of Hamilton and Castleherald etc.* London, 1677

Calder, J.T. *Sketch of the Civil and Traditional History of Caithness from the Tenth Century.* Wick, 1887

Caldwell, D.H. *The Scottish Armoury.* Edinburgh, 1979

Caldwell, D.H. (ed.) *Scottish Weapons and Fortifications 1100–1800.* Edinburgh, 1981

Cieslak, E., Biernat, C. *History of Gdansk.* Gdansk, 1995. (trans. B. Blaim, G.M. Hyde)

Derry, T.K. *A History of Scandinavia.* London, 1979

Ditchburn, D. *Scotland and Europe: The Medieval Kingdom and Its Contacts with Christendom, 1214–1560.* East Linton, 2000

A Diurnal of remarkable occurrents that have passed within the country of Scotland . . . Edinburgh, 1833 (Bannatyne Club)

Dow, J. *Ruthven's Army in Sweden and Esthonia.* Stockholm, 1965

Dukes, P. 'New Perspectives: Alexander Leslie and the Smolensk War 1632–4' in Murdoch, 2001

Fallon, J.A. 'Scottish mercenaries in the service of Denmark and Sweden, 1626–1632'. Unpub PhD thesis, University of Glasgow, 1972

Fedosov, D. *The Caledonian Connection: Scotland–Russia Ties – Middle Ages to Early Twentieth Century: A Concise Biographical List.* Aberdeen, 1996

Ferguson, J. *The Scots Brigade in the Service of the United Netherlands 1572–1782.* Edinburgh, 1899

Fischer, Th. A. *The Scots in Germany.* Edinburgh, 1902

Fischer, Th. A. *The Scots in Eastern and Western Prussia.* Edinburgh, 1903

Fischer, Th. A. *The Scots in Sweden.* Edinburgh, 1907

Forbes, D. *Ane Account of the Familie of Innes.* Aberdeen, 1864

Fotheringham, J.G. (ed.) *The Diplomatic Correspondence of Jean de Montereul and the Brothers de Bellievre.* Edinburgh, 1899

Fowler, J. *The History of the Troubles of Suethland and Poland.* London, 1656

Fraser, W. *The Book of Carlaverock.* Edinburgh, 1873

Fraser, W. *The Chiefs of Grant.* Edinburgh, 1883

Fraser, W. *Memorials of the Earls of Haddington.* Edinburgh, 1889

Fraser, W. *The Melvilles, Earls of Melville, and the Leslies, Earls of Leven.* Edinburgh, 1890

Fraser, W. *The Sutherland Book.* Edinburgh, 1892

Frese A., Hepp F., Ludwig, R. (eds.) *Der Winterkönig: Heidelberg zwischen höfischer Pracht und Dreissigjährigem Krieg.* Remshalden, Germany, 2004

Frost, RI. 'Scottish soldiers, Poland-Lithuania and the Thirty Years War' in Murdoch, 2001

Glozier, M. 'Social status and the travelling Scot' in *The Double Tressure*, No. 23, 2000

Goodrick, A.T.S. (ed) *The Relation of Sydnam Poyntz 1624–1636.* London, 1908

Gordon, J. *History of Scots Affairs from 1637 to 1641.* Aberdeen, 1841

Grant, J. *Memoirs and Adventures of Sir John Hepburn.* Edinburgh, 1851

Grant, J. *The Scottish Soldiers of Fortune: Their Adventures and Achievements in the Armies of Europe.* London, 1890

Grimeston, E. *A Generall Historie of the Netherlands.* London, 1627

Grosjean, A. *An Unofficial Alliance: Scotland and Sweden 1569–1654.* Leiden, 2003

Haythornthwaite, P. *Frederick the Great's Army: Infantry.* Oxford, 1991

Haythornthwaite, P.J. *Invincible Generals.* Bloomington, Indiana, 1992

Held, R. *The Age of Firearms*. London, 1959

Hill Burton, J. *The Scot Abroad*. Edinburgh, 1864

Israel, J. *The Dutch Republic: Its Rise, Greatness and Fall 1477–1806*. Oxford, 1995

Keith, James. *A Fragment of a Memoir of Field-Marshal James Keith Written by Himself 1714–1734*. Edinburgh, 1843

Kellie, Sir Thomas. *Pallas Armata, or Militarie Instructions*. Edinburgh, 1627

Kelvin, M. *The Scottish Pistol*. London, 1996

Leslie, C. *Historical Records of the Family of Leslie*. Edinburgh, 1869

Letters and State Papers During the Reign of King James the Sixth: Chiefly from the Manuscript Collections of Sir James Balfour of Denmyln. Edinburgh, 1838

Letters to King James the Sixth from the Queen, Prince Henry, Prince Charles, the Princess Elizabeth and Her Husband Frederick King of Bohemia and from Their Son Prince Frederick Henry. Edinburgh, 1835

Macdonald A., Macdonald A. *The Clan Donald*. Inverness, 1896

Mackay, A. *The Book of Mackay*. Edinburgh, 1906

Mackenzie, A. *History of the Mackenzies*. Inverness, 1894.

Mackenzie, A. *History of the Munros of Fowlis*. Inverness, 1898

Macray, W.D. (ed.) *Letters and Papers of Patrick Ruthven, Earl of Forth and Brentford*. London, 1868

Maidment, J. (ed) *The Spottiswoode Miscellany*. Edinburgh, 1845

Maxwell, Sir H. *A History of the House of Douglas*. London, 1902

McLaughlin, M. *The Wild Geese: The Irish Brigades of France and Spain*. Oxford, 1980

Mitchell, A. (ed.) *Geographical Collections Relating to Scotland Made by Walter Macfarlane*. Edinburgh, 1907

Michell, T. *History of the Scottish Expedition to Norway, 1612*. Edinburgh, 1886

Monro, R. *Monro His Expedition with the Worthy Scots Regiment (Called Mac-Keyes Regiment) Levied in August 1626*. London, 1637.

Morison, A. *The Blackhalls of That Ilk and Barra*. Aberdeen, 1905

A Most True Relation of the late Proceedings in Bohemia, Germany, and Hungaria. Dated the 1. the 10. and 13 of July, the present yeere 1620. Held in British Library

Murdoch, S. (ed.) *Scotland and the Thirty Years' War 1618–1648*. Leiden, 2001

Napier, M. (ed.) *Memoirs of the Marquis of Montrose*. Edinburgh, 1856

Napier, M. *Memorials and Letters Illustrative of the Life and Times of John Graham of Claverhouse, Viscount Dundee*. Edinburgh, 1859

Original Letters Relating to the Ecclesiastical Affairs of Scotland, Vol. 2: 1614–1625. Edinburgh, 1851

Polišensky, J.V. *Tragic Triangle: The Netherlands, Spain and Bohemia 1617–1621*. Prague, 1991

Polišensky, J.V. 'A Note on Scottish Soldiers in the Bohemian War 1619–1622' in Murdoch, 2001

Pursell, B.C. *The Winter King: Frederick V of the Palatinate and the Coming of the Thirty Years' War*. Aldershot, 2003.

Rasch-Engh, R. *Herr Sinclair dro over salten hav: Skottetoget og kampene ved Kringen 1612*. Oslo, 1992

Roberts, M. *Gustavus Adolphus*, London, 1992

Robertson, J. (ed.) *Passages from the Diary of General Patrick Gordon of Auchleuchries 1635–1699*. Aberdeen, 1859

Rodger, N.A.M. *The Command of the Ocean: A Naval History of Britain, 1649–1815*. London, 2004

Roeck, B. *Als wollt die Welt schier brechen: Eine Stadt im Zeit alter des Dresiggjahrigen Krieges*. Munich, 1991

Royle, T. *Civil War: The Wars of the Three Kingdoms 1638–1660*. London, 2004

Sanderson, M.H.B. *Scottish Rural Society in the 16th Century*. Edinburgh, 1982

Seliga, S. in *Scotland and Poland: A Chapter of Forgotten History*. (S. Seliga and L. Koczy, eds.), Dundee, 1969

Seward, D. *The Hundred Years War*. London, 2003

Skelton, C.O. and Bulloch, J.M. *The Book of Gordon: Vol. III: Gordons under Arms*. Aberdeen, 1912

Skene, F.J.H. (ed.) *Liber Pluscardensis (The Book of Pluscarden)*. Edinburgh, 1877

Spalding, John. *History of the Troubles and Memorable Transactions in Scotland and England*. Edinburgh, 1829

Spalding, John. *Memorials of the Troubles in Scotland and England 1624–1645*. Aberdeen, 1850

Spalding Club Miscellany, Vol. 5. Aberdeen, 1852

Steuart, A.F. *Scottish Influences in Russian History*. Glasgow, 1913

Steuart, A.F. *Papers relating to the History of the Scots in Poland*. Edinburgh, 1915

Stewart, Sir David, of Garth. *Sketches of the Character, Manner and Present State of the Highlanders of Scotland*. Edinburgh, 1822

Tayler, A. & H. *The House of Forbes*. Aberdeen, 1937

Terry, C.S. *The Life and Campaigns of Alexander Leslie, First Earl of Leven*. London, 1899

Terry, C.S. (ed.) *Papers Relating to the Army of the Solemn League and Covenant 1643–1647*. Edinburgh, 1917.

Troyat, H. *Catherine the Great*. Henley-on-Thames, 1979

Tuchman, B.W. *A Distant Mirror: The Calamitous 14th Century*. London, 1979

Turner, Sir James. *Memoirs of his own life and times*. Edinburgh, 1829

Urquhart, Sir Thomas. *The Jewel*. (R.D.S. Jack and R.J Lyall, eds.). Edinburgh, 1983

Wallace, J. *Scottish Swords and Dirks*. London, 1970

Watson, F. *Wallenstein: Soldier under Saturn*. London, 1938

Wedgwood, C.V. *The Thirty Years War*. London, 1938

Wheatcroft, A. *The Habsburgs*. London, 1995

Whitelaw, C.E. *Scottish Arms Makers*. London, 1977

Wood, S. *The Auld Alliance*. Edinburgh, 1989

Worthington, D. *Scots in Habsburg Service 1618–1648*. Leiden, 2004

Index

25, 115, 118, 121–2, 125, 138, 143,
152–4, 215, 277
Mackay, Hugh, of Scourie 239–40
Mackay's Highlanders/ Regiment 15,
20, 24, 115–28, 132–7, 139, 144, 208
Mackenzie, Thomas 259
Magdeburg 150, 167
Mansfeld, Count Ernst von 99–101,
104–5, 107, 109–12, 120–1, 275
Mary, Queen of Scots 37–8, 58
Maurice of Nassau 66
Maximilian, Duke of Bavaria 104–5,
170–1, 173–5, 182, 188
Maxwell, Robert, Earl of Nithsdale 15,
18, 21, 116, 120, 123–4, 153
Mercenaries, Scots: common in
European armies 8–9, dress 24–25,
270, motives 12–18, mutinies 44, 79,
95, numbers of Scots 10, payment 21–
24, 60, recruitment 14–21, 83, 88, 274
reputation 9–10, 69, Scots
government attitude 11–12, weapons
25–27, 91, 271
Middleton, John 206, 224–5, 227
Moncrieff, William 41, 44, 272
Moncur, David 37
Monro, Robert 9, 13, 15–7, 116–9, 121–
8, 132–51, 156–66, 169, 171–5, 177–
80, 182, 186–90, 215, 218
Monro, Robert, the Black Baron of
Foulis 15, 117, 125, 137, 151, 156,
188–9
Mornay, Carolus de 43
Moscow 70–2
Muir, Alexander 254
Muir, James 253
Munich 173–4
Murray, James 254

Neff (Nevay), James (Jacob) 42, 74
Neubrandenburg 143–5
Nieuwpoort, battle 63–4, 273

Nördlingen, battle 195–6
Northern Seven Years' War 37
Nuremberg 175–81

Ochsenfurt 163
Ogilvie, George 238
Oldenburg, battle 121–3
Oliwa, sea battle 253
Orlov, Count Alexei 257–9
Ormiston, Andrew 52
Ossolinski, Jerzy 92
Ostend, siege 64–5, 273

Pappenheim, Count 150, 167–8, 170,
177, 183–5
Patton, Aristotle 59
Pavia, battle 34, 262
Peter I of Russia 233, 235–8, 242,
255
Poland, Scots immigration 66, 273
Polish Succession, War of 245
Poyntz, Sydnam 120, 156–7, 196,
276
Prague, defenestration 99, 275

Ramsay, Alexander 3–8, 167, 169
Ramsay, Andrew 2–3
Ramsay, David 152–4
Ramsay, Sir James, the Faire 182
Ramsay, Sir James, the Black 84–5, 89,
95, 156, 163, 176, 182, 200–1
Regiment de Douglas 210–1
Rhineland Palatinate 97–9
Richelieu, Cardinal de 169, 205–6, 210,
213
Riga, siege 94
Rocroi, battle 213
Romanov, Michael, tsar of Russia 80,
220–3
Rügenwalde 141, 277
Ruthven, Alexander 75
Ruthven, Archibald 39–45

BIRLINN LTD (incorporating John Donald and Polygon) is one of Scotland's leading publishers with over four hundred titles in print. Should you wish to be put on our catalogue mailing list **contact**:

Catalogue Request
Birlinn Ltd
West Newington House
10 Newington Road
Edinburgh EH9 1QS
Scotland, UK

Tel: + 44 (0) 131 668 4371
Fax: + 44 (0) 131 668 4466
e-mail: info@birlinn.co.uk

Postage and packing is free within the UK. For overseas orders, postage and packing (airmail) will be charged at 30% of the total order value.

For more information, or to order online, visit our website at **www.birlinn.co.uk**

Birlinn *Limited*
IMPRINTS: JOHN DONALD · POLYGON

NOVA TOTIUS GERMANIÆ DESCRIPTIO, Teutschland.